**Acknowledgments** My deepest gratitude to all who provided footage for this book as well as those who helped wrangle it: for the *Leverage* footage, Executive Producer, Dean Devlin of Electric Entertainment, editor Brian Gonosey, and composer Joseph LoDuca; for the *An Accidental Quest for Enlightenment* footage, Evergreen Films founders Pierre de Lespinois and Mike Devlin, as well as Patrick Devlin; the team members of SeaWorld Inc. and Busch Entertainment Corp. for their generous use of *The Making of Believe*; and for the inspiring *Playing For Change: Peace Through Music* footage, Timeless Media, LLC and Brent Miller, Raan Williams, Mark Johnson, Kevin Krupitzer, and Jonathan Walls. And thanks to artist, Tereza Djurkovic, for her video art renditions. It was a privilege to work with you all.

Special thanks to my Peachpit editorial and production teams for their tireless efforts: Serena Herr, Bob Lindstrom, Karen Seriguchi, Brendan Boykin, Chris Gillespie, Kim Wimpsett, Elissa Rabellino, and Eric Geoffroy. I see your hard work and dedication throughout these pages.

To the Apple Final Cut Studio team who cast an eye and offered direction: Patty Montesion, Steve Bayes, Dion Scoppettuolo, Kevin Magliulo, and Christopher Phrommayon. And to Kent Oberheu for his beautiful cover art.

Personal thanks to those who always seem to be ready with support when I need it: Lynne Weynand, for pointing me to Playing For Change and sharing her incomparable eye and ear, Susan Merzbach for her unique storytelling talent, Algie Abrams for his skillful ability to explain anything, Hubert Krzysztofik for his uncanny knowledge of everything, Diane Wright for her technical know-how and Steve Wright for his keen eyes. Although not a part of my writing team, you continue to support my own growth in this field.

Finally, to my business partner Shirley Craig and our Weynand Training team (www.weynand.com), my grateful thanks.

Apple Pro Training Series
# Final Cut Pro 7

Diana Weynand

Apple
Certified

Apple Pro Training Series: Final Cut Pro 7
Diana Weynand
Copyright © 2010 by Diana Weynand and Shirley Craig

Published by Peachpit Press. For information on Peachpit Press books, contact:

Peachpit Press
1249 Eighth Street
Berkeley, CA 94710
(510) 524-2178
Fax: (510) 524-2221
http://www.peachpit.com
To report errors, please send a note to errata@peachpit.com
Peachpit Press is a division of Pearson Education

**Apple Series Editor:** Serena Herr
**Editor:** Bob Lindstrom
**Project Director:** Shirley Craig
**Production Coordinator:** Kim Wimpsett, Happenstance Type-O-Rama
**Technical Editor:** Dion Scoppettuolo
**Technical Reviewer:** Brendan Boykin
**Copy Editor:** Karen Seriguchi
**Proofreaders:** Elissa Rabellino, Karen Seriguchi
**Compositor:** Chris Gillespie, Happenstance Type-O-Rama
**Indexer:** Jack Lewis
**Cover Illustration:** Kent Oberheu
**Cover Production:** Chris Gillespie, Happenstance Type-O-Rama
**Media Producer:** Eric Geoffroy

# Contents at a Glance

# Table of Contents

**Completing the Cut**

# Getting Started

Welcome to the official Apple Pro Training course for Final Cut Pro 7, Apple's dynamic nonlinear editing package!

This book is a comprehensive guide to editing with Final Cut Pro. It uses exciting real-world footage from the hit TNT series *Leverage*, the international music event *Playing For Change: Peace Through Music*, SeaWorld's "The Making of *Believe*" documentary, and *An Accidental Quest for Enlightenment* from Evergreen Films Inc. to demonstrate both the features of the application and the practical techniques you'll use daily in your editing projects.

Whether you're a seasoned veteran or just getting started in the editing field, Final Cut Pro 7 is flexible enough to meet all your editing needs. So let's get started!

## The Methodology

This is, first and foremost, a hands-on course. Every exercise is designed to enable you to do professional-quality editing in Final Cut Pro as quickly as possible. Each lesson builds on previous lessons to guide you through the program's functions and capabilities.

If you are new to Final Cut Pro, start at the beginning and progress through each lesson in order. If you are familiar with an earlier version of Final Cut Pro, you can go directly to a specific section and focus on that topic, because every lesson is self-contained.

### Course Structure

The book is designed to guide you through the editing process as it teaches Final Cut Pro.

You will begin by learning basic editing techniques and then refine your project by trimming and adjusting edit points and clip location. While exploring all of Final Cut Pro's editing tools, you'll learn to customize your interface, work with different types of edits, and even edit multicamera footage.

After working on several projects, you'll complete them by mixing the audio and adding transitions and titles. Finally, you'll add effects and finishing touches to your project and then prepare it for delivery, by exporting it as a file or outputting it to tape.

The lessons are grouped into the following categories:

- ▶  Lessons 1–3: Creating a Rough Cut
- ▶  Lessons 4–6: Refining the Rough Cut
- ▶  Lessons 7–8: Customizing and Capturing
- ▶  Lessons 9–11: Completing the Cut
- ▶  Lessons 12–14: Adding Effects and Finishing

In addition to the exercises, each lesson includes "Take 2" scenarios that present real-world challenges for you to practice what you've learned before moving on to new material.

At the end of every lesson, you will have an opportunity to hone your skills as you apply your own creative touches to an "Editor's Cut" project, which is designed to review everything you learned in the lesson.

## Using the DVD Book Files

The *Apple Pro Training Series: Final Cut Pro 7* DVD (included with the book) contains the project files you will use for each lesson, as well as media files that contain the video and audio content you will need for each exercise. After you transfer the files to your hard disk, each lesson will instruct you in the use of the project and media files.

### Installing the Final Cut Pro 7 Lesson Files

On the DVD, you'll find a folder titled FCP7 Book Files, which contains two subfolders: Lessons and Media. These folders contain the lessons and media files for this course. Make sure you keep these two folders together in the FCP7 Book Files folder on your hard disk. If you do so, Final Cut Pro should be able to maintain the original links between the lessons and media files.

1   Insert the *Apple Pro Training Series: Final Cut Pro 7* DVD into your DVD drive.

2   Drag the FCP7 Book Files folder from the DVD to your hard disk to copy it. The DVD contains about 7.8 GB of data.

Each lesson will explain which files to open for that lesson's exercises.

### Reconnecting Media

When copying files from the DVD to your hard disk, you may unintentionally break a link between a project file and its media files. If this happens, a dialog appears asking you to relink the project files. Relinking the project files is a simple process that's covered in more depth in the "Reconnecting Media" section in Lesson 7. But should the dialog appear when you are opening a lesson, follow these steps:

1   If an Offline Files dialog appears, click the Reconnect button.

   A Reconnect Files dialog opens. Under the Files To Connect portion of the dialog, the offline file is listed along with its possible location.

2   In the Reconnect Files dialog, click Search.

   Final Cut Pro will search for the missing file. If you already know where the file is located, you can click the Locate button and find the file manually.

3   After the correct file is found, click Choose in the Reconnect dialog.

4   When the file is displayed in the Files Located section of the Reconnect Files dialog, click Connect.

   When the link between the project file and the media file is reestablished, Final Cut Pro will be able to access the media within the project.

## Changing System Preferences

A few editing functions within Final Cut Pro use function keys also used by other programs, such as Exposé and the Dashboard. If you want to use the FCP editing shortcuts, you will need to reassign the function keys in these other programs.

**1**   From your desktop, open System Preferences.

**2**   In the Personal section, click Dashboard & Exposé.

**3**   Reassign the keyboard shortcuts for F9, F10, F11, and F12 to other keys.

Reassigning the shortcuts will allow Final Cut Pro to use these shortcut keys exclusively. At any time when using Final Cut Pro, you can return to System Preferences and change these key assignments.

## Using Final Cut Pro on a Portable

Some of the keystrokes identified in this book for desktop use work differently if you are using a MacBook Pro. Specifically, you'll need to hold down the Function key (fn) when pressing any of the F keys (F1 through F8). To avoid this, open the Keyboard & Mouse section of System Preferences, and in the Keyboard pane, select the "Use all F1, F2, etc. keys as standard function keys" checkbox. Even with this checkbox selected, however, you will still need to press the fn key when using the Home and End keys.

## About the Footage

Four sets of footage are used throughout this book. Together they represent different types of projects and media formats. The exercises instruct you to edit the footage in a particular way, but you can use any part of this footage to practice editing methods. Techniques you've learned using one set of footage in a lesson can be practiced with a different set of footage to create a new project. Due to copyright restrictions, however, you cannot use this footage for any purpose outside this book.

The footage, as it appears in the book, includes the following:

**SeaWorld Inc. and Busch Entertainment's "The Making of *Believe*"**—This documentary material was shot by SeaWorld Inc.'s San Antonio and Orlando media divisions while the theme park's training staff joined with Broadway directors, choreographers, and designers to create and rehearse the Shamu show *Believe*. The rehearsal and performance footage was shot on HDV at the San Antonio, Texas, SeaWorld facility, and the underwater material was shot on Betacam SP at the SeaWorld facility in Orlando, Florida.

*Leverage*—This footage is from the hit TNT television series starring Timothy Hutton, Christian Kane, Gina Bellman, Aldis Hodge, and Beth Riesgraf. The scene is from an episode titled "The Second David," which was the finale of the premiere season. The *Leverage* footage was shot using the RED ONE camera; the digital files were transcoded using Apple's ProRes 422 codec and then edited in Final Cut Pro.

*An Accidental Quest for Enlightenment*—Shot in Prince William Sound in Alaska, this footage was produced by Evergreen Films Inc. and used to create a promo for a television series and dramatic feature. It was shot in HD at 23.98 fps, and captured using the Apple ProRes 422 HQ codec. It was recompressed for the book using the new Apple ProRes 422 (Proxy) codec.

*Playing For Change: Peace Through Music*—This set of media is from the international documentary (of the same name) that recorded street musicians from around the world as they contributed their unique talent to create a universal mix of songs. Singer-songwriter Pierre Minetti wrote "Don't Worry," which is used in the second half of the book and highlights musicians from India, Africa, Netherlands, Israel, and elsewhere who added their own tracks. The footage was shot using DV, HDV, XDCAM, and 16 mm film at 29.97 frames per second (fps).

In the last section of the book, you will follow the lead of artist **Tereza Djurkovic** as you transform her footage into video art.

## System Requirements

Before using *Apple Pro Training Series: Final Cut Pro 7*, you should have a working knowledge of your Macintosh and the Mac OS X operating system. Make sure that you know how to use the mouse and standard menus and commands and also how to open, save, and close files. If you need to review these techniques, see the printed or online documentation included with your system.

For the basic system requirements for Final Cut Pro 7, refer to the Final Cut Pro 7 documentation or Apple's website, www.apple.com.

## About the Apple Pro Training Series

*Apple Pro Training Series: Final Cut Pro 7* is both a self-paced learning tool and the official curriculum of the Apple Pro Training and Certification Program.

Developed by experts in the field and certified by Apple, the series is used by Apple Authorized Training Centers worldwide and offers complete training in all Apple Pro products. The lessons are designed to let you learn at your own pace. Each lesson concludes with review questions and answers summarizing what you've learned, which can be used to help you prepare for the Apple Pro Certification Exam.

For a complete list of Apple Pro Training Series books, see the ad at the back of this book, or visit www.peachpit.com/apts.

## Apple Pro Certification Programs

The Apple Pro Training and Certification Programs are designed to keep you at the forefront of Apple's digital media technology while giving you a competitive edge in today's ever-changing job market. Whether you're an editor, graphic designer, sound designer, special effects artist, or teacher, these training tools are meant to help you expand your skills.

Upon completing the course material in this book, you can become an Apple Certified Pro by taking the certification exam at an Apple Authorized Training Center. Certification is offered in Final Cut Pro, Motion, Color, Soundtrack Pro, DVD Studio Pro, Shake, and Logic Pro. Certification as an Apple Pro gives you official recognition of your knowledge of Apple's professional applications while allowing you to market yourself to employers and clients as a skilled, pro-level user of Apple products.

For those who prefer to learn in an instructor-led setting, Apple offers training courses at Apple Authorized Training Centers worldwide. These courses, which use the Apple Pro Training Series books as their curriculum, are taught by Apple Certified Trainers and balance concepts and lectures with hands-on labs and exercises. Apple Authorized Training Centers have been carefully selected and have met Apple's highest standards in all areas, including facilities, instructors, course delivery, and infrastructure. The goal of the program is to offer Apple customers, from beginners to the most seasoned professionals, the highest-quality training experience.

For more information, please see the ad at the back of this book, or to find an Authorized Training Center near you, go to training.apple.com.

## Resources

*Apple Pro Training Series: Final Cut Pro 7* is not intended as a comprehensive reference manual, nor does it replace the documentation that comes with the application. For comprehensive information about program features, refer to these resources:

▶ The Reference Guide. Accessed through the Final Cut Pro Help menu, the Reference Guide contains a complete description of all features.

▶ Apple's website: www.apple.com.

# Creating a Rough Cut

# 1

# Editing in Final Cut Pro

You are about to take an exciting journey in film and video editing. As this book helps you explore Final Cut Pro, you'll travel from the first steps of project editing to the final stages of finishing and delivery.

For Final Cut Pro 7 newcomers, this book will be a step-by-step guide through the entire editing process. If you've already used the application, you will discover a wealth of new Final Cut Pro 7 features, and uncover many tips and tricks that you can apply to all your editing projects.

The first stage in editing is to take stock of what you've shot and to figure out what works and what doesn't. The next stage is to select portions of your footage and combine those to shape your story into a *rough cut*. Then you adjust and refine the cut, and finally you add music and sound or visual effects to dress it up. Simply put, editing is the most powerful stage of the production process because it's when the separate parts become a meaningful whole.

This section focuses on the first step: building the rough cut. In the next three lessons, you will be editing footage from a documentary about the making of SeaWorld's killer whale production, *Believe.* In this lesson, you will work with the Final Cut Pro interface, learn about the workflow of a project, play source footage, perform the basic steps of editing, and organize project elements. You will also learn about menus and shortcuts, as well as actions available with a two-button mouse.

## Opening Final Cut Pro

Before you get started, install the Final Cut Pro application, if necessary, and copy the lessons and media from the book's DVD to your hard disk. Instructions for doing this are in the Getting Started section of this book. After those two tasks are complete, you can move forward with this lesson.

You can open Final Cut Pro in one of three ways:

▶   In the Applications folder on the hard disk, double-click the Final Cut Pro application icon.

▶   In the Dock, click the Final Cut Pro icon.

▶   Double-click any Final Cut Pro project file.

Placing the Final Cut Pro icon in the Dock will make it easier to open the program in future lessons.

**1**   If the Final Cut Pro icon does not already appear in your Dock, find the icon in your hard disk's Applications folder and drag it to the Dock.

**2**   In the Dock, click the Final Cut Pro icon once to open the program.

If this is the first time you've opened Final Cut Pro, a Choose Setup dialog appears, where you choose the type of footage you are editing.

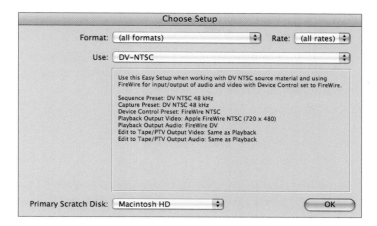

The default is DV-NTSC. For now, you can click OK to bypass this dialog because the settings you need are contained within these lessons. You will work with this dialog and these options in a later lesson. If the External A/V dialog appears with a message that it can't locate the external video device, click Continue. You do not need an external video device for these lessons.

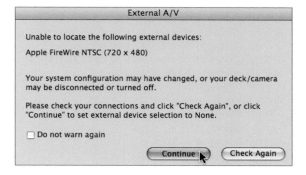

The program interface opens with the Browser window and a default project tab labeled Untitled Project 1. The Browser is located in the upper-left corner of the interface. If you have recently worked on other projects, those project tabs may appear here as well.

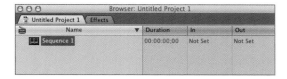

## Understanding the Final Cut Pro Interface

Four primary windows make up the Final Cut Pro interface: the Browser, Viewer, Canvas, and Timeline. The most basic functions of these windows can be divided into two activities: The Browser and Viewer windows are where you organize and view your *unedited* material, and the Canvas and Timeline are where you view your *edited* material.

There are two secondary windows: The Tool palette contains an assortment of editing tools, and the audio meters allow you to monitor audio levels.

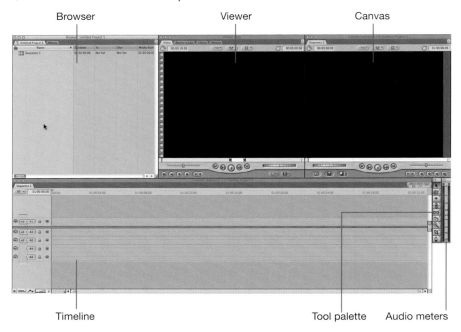

Each window fulfills a unique purpose in the editing process.

### Browser

The Browser is where you organize all of the project elements, or source material, you use when editing, such as video clips, music, narration, graphics, and so on. You can view the elements as a list or as icons.

### Viewer

The Viewer is where you view your source material and where you choose edit points. But you can also edit audio, modify transitions and effects, and build titles in this window.

### Timeline

The Timeline is a graphical representation of all the editing decisions you make. This is your workbench area, where you edit your material, trim it, move it, stack it, and adjust it. Here you can see all your edits at a glance.

### Canvas

The Canvas and Timeline windows are two sides of the same coin. Both display your edited project, but whereas the Timeline shows your editing choices graphically, the Canvas displays those edits visually like a movie.

### Tool Palette

The Tool palette is a collection of Final Cut Pro editing tools. Every tool has a shortcut key, so you can access each one directly from the keyboard.

### Audio Meters

The two audio meters reflect the volume level of whatever audio is playing. It could be a source clip in the Viewer that you screen before editing or the final edited piece that you view in the Canvas.

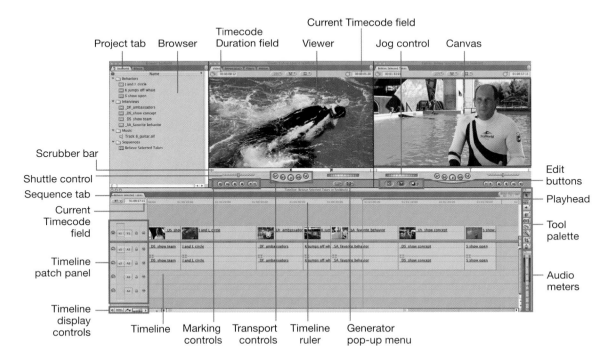

**Working with Final Cut Pro Windows**

The Final Cut Pro interface windows share similar properties with other Mac OS X windows. They can be opened, closed, minimized, and repositioned using the close, minimize, and zoom buttons in the upper-left corner of the window. Each window displays its name in the title bar.

**1**   Click the Browser to make it the active window.

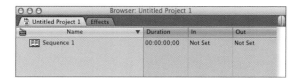

Browser window is active when selected.

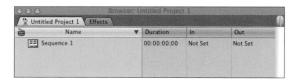

Browser window is inactive when another window is selected.

An active window has a lighter title bar, and you can easily read the window name. An inactive window has a dark gray, or *dimmed*, title bar that blends in with the name. Only one window can be active at a time. Making a window active in the interface is an important part of the editing process, because some editing functions will be available only if a specific window is active.

**2**   Click the Viewer window to make it active, and then click the close button in the upper-left corner.

In most Mac OS X windows, the close button is red. In Final Cut Pro, this set of buttons—close, minimize, and zoom—takes on the gray of the interface. But these buttons still perform the same functions that they do in other Mac OS X windows.

**3**   To restore the Viewer window, choose Window > Viewer, or press Command-1.

You can open and close each interface window by choosing the window name in the Window menu or by using a keyboard shortcut.

**NOTE ▶** Because of the small size of the Tool palette and audio meters, they each have just one button, which closes the window.

**4**   Drag the Browser window title bar to move this window away from its current position. Drag it again and allow it to snap back into its original position.

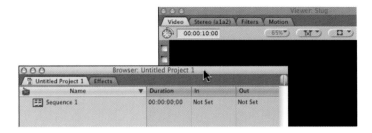

All Final Cut Pro interface windows snap into place, even though they are separate windows.

**5**   In the Browser window, click the Effects tab. Then click the Untitled Project 1 tab.

Tabs are used throughout Final Cut Pro to organize and display specific information and at the same time to maximize space in the interface. The Effects tab is where you select effects such as video and audio transitions and filters (these are covered in later lessons).

## Using Menus, Shortcuts, and the Mouse

In Final Cut Pro, some editors enjoy using keyboard shortcuts to choose editing functions. Others prefer choosing menu items, or clicking buttons or objects within the Final Cut Pro interface. Final Cut Pro also has a position-sensitive mouse pointer. When you move it over certain parts of the interface, the pointer automatically changes to allow you to perform a specific function in that location.

**1**   Move the pointer over the border between the Browser and Viewer. When the pointer changes to the vertical Resize pointer, drag right to dynamically increase the size of the Browser window and view more columns.

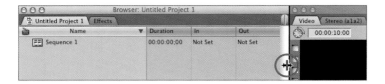

As you drag the Browser border, the Viewer and Canvas windows resize to accommodate the larger Browser.

**NOTE ▶** The Resize pointer may appear in several places throughout the Final Cut Pro interface. Whenever you see the pointer icon automatically change, you click or drag the mouse at that location.

**2**   In the Tool palette, move the pointer over the icon that looks like a magnifying glass.

A tooltip appears with the tool name and keyboard shortcut. Tooltips also appear when you place the pointer over buttons and other areas in the interface. If you wanted to use the keyboard shortcut to select this tool, you would press the Z key.

**NOTE ▶** You can turn tooltips off and on in the General tab of the User Preferences window (Option-Q).

**3**   Move the pointer over the first tool in the Tool palette, and click to choose it. The Selection tool is the default tool you use most frequently. Its shortcut is the A key.

**TIP** ▶ You will use various tools throughout the editing process, but it's a good habit to return to your Selection tool after you've used a different tool.

**4**   In the menu bar of the interface, choose File.

The Final Cut Pro menu bar organizes editing functions by category, such as View, Modify, Effects, and so on. Within each menu, specific functions are grouped together if they share a similar purpose. In the File menu, the New and Open functions are grouped together, as are the Save functions, Import, and so on. As in all Apple menus, black menu options can be chosen, but dimmed options cannot.

**NOTE ▶** In the book exercises, when you're directed to choose an item from a menu, such as Open from the File menu, it will appear as "Choose File > Open."

**5**   From the menu bar, choose Window > Arrange. A submenu appears.

**6**   Move the pointer over Standard in the submenu, but *don't release the mouse button*.

Keyboard shortcuts are displayed in menus and submenus to the right of the listed function. Similar functions often share the same shortcut letter.

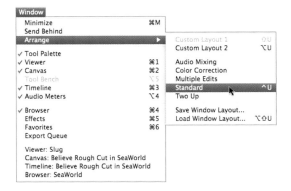

The shortcuts in this submenu all use the letter U with one or more modifier keys. There are four modifier keys: Shift, Control, Option, and Command (the Apple key).

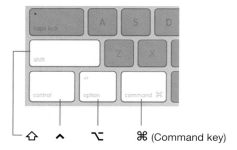

**7** Click Standard, or release the menu and press Control-U, to choose the default standard window layout. This command returns all windows to their default layout.

**8** Hold down the Control key and click (Control-click) in the gray area of the Name column in the Browser window.

**TIP** When using a two-button mouse, you can also access a shortcut menu by right-clicking in that area.

A shortcut menu appears with a list of options for that specific area. Control-clicking in different areas of the Final Cut Pro interface will produce different shortcut menus from which you can choose or change your editing options.

# Following a Workflow

Before you work with project elements, let's take a minute to review the nonlinear editing process and some of the terminology you'll need to know. You can divide the process into three primary activities: collecting the elements that will be edited into a project, editing those elements into a finished piece, and delivering the project.

### Collecting Project Elements

Final Cut Pro follows the usual conventions of a nonlinear editing process. That process usually begins with creating a new project. Projects can contain different kinds of elements, such as Apple QuickTime movies, music, sound effects, narration, and graphics. You combine these elements to form an edited version of the material. Project elements are displayed in the Browser window under a project tab.

Some of these elements, such as music, graphics, and photos, can be *imported* into the project, and some, such as source tape footage, have to be *captured*. Capturing material from the original source tape converts it to digital media files. The media files are actually QuickTime movies that play like any other QuickTime movie on your computer. One file is created for each portion of source footage you choose to capture. Each media file may be a different length, as measured in hours, minutes, seconds, and frames.

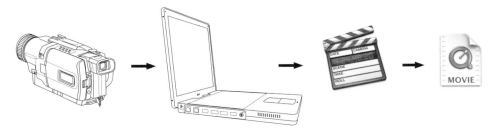

An alternative to capturing footage is transferring media files from digital sources such as cameras that record to CompactFlash (CF), Security Digital (SD), or other types of media cards, or that record directly to a hard drive. Footage ingested this way doesn't need converting as tape footage does. You simply use Final Cut Pro to transfer these footage files to your computer's hard disk or to an external hard disk. You will learn to capture or transfer your own source footage in Lesson 8.

### Editing a Project

Once the elements are collected into your project, the files are referred to as *clips*, and you use these clips to edit. A good portion of the editing process includes *screening* clips and *marking* edit points. Then you combine the marked clips to form a *sequence*. When you edit the sequence of shots together, you are not cutting the original media files. You are only specifying which portions of the original media you want to include and the order in which Final Cut Pro will show them.

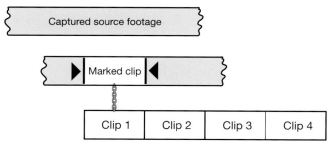

Edited sequence of clips

The Final Cut Pro editing process is nondestructive, which means that you can make a dozen changes to a clip in a project, but none will affect the original media file. For example, you can import a clip into a project, lower its audio level, make the image purple, and turn it upside down. The clip will play in that project with lower audio and upside-down purple people, but the media file on the hard disk remains unchanged. In fact, nothing you do in these lesson projects—including applying effects, transitions, and titles—changes the original media files. The project file is simply a container for all the editorial decisions you make.

Original media file

Changed clip in Final Cut Pro project

Original media file remains unchanged

### Delivering a Project

After you've finished editing a sequence, you will want to share it in some form with the world. That might mean making a videotape of your project so that a broadcast facility can play it in prime time or creating a file that you can post to a website or show on your iPod. With today's technologies, you can deliver your project to a broad audience in a variety of ways. Final Cut Pro provides you with several ways to deliver your project, from the simple to the complex, which you will learn about in a later lesson.

## Importing and Viewing Project Elements

When you opened Final Cut Pro earlier in this lesson, a new project was created for you automatically. The project file is a container—it holds the files or content you will use when editing your project. A new project contains no project elements except for a single sequence, which will contain your edited clips. As noted above, you must import, capture, or transfer the footage you want to edit. The footage for these lessons has already been captured for you and placed into media files in your FCP7 Book Files folder. When footage is already in the form of media files, you can simply import those files into a new project and begin editing.

You can import a single media file or a group of two or more files into your Final Cut Pro project. If you've already organized certain elements into their own folders on your computer, such as music tracks or sound effects, you can import those folders instead of the individual files. For this exercise, you will first import one media file and then repeat the steps to add several more. You will also change how you view project elements. Before you begin importing, let's practice good editing habits by naming and saving your project.

> **NOTE ▶** Make sure you've transferred the FCP7 Book Files folder from the book's DVD to your hard disk as described in "Using the DVD Book Files" in the Getting Started section of this book.

1   With the Browser window active, choose File > Save Project As, or press Command-Shift-S. In the Save As field, enter *SeaWorld*.

Once a project is saved to a target location, you can choose File > Save As, or press Command-S, to save your changes.

2   In the Save dialog sidebar, or first column, click the Macintosh hard disk icon; in the next column, click the FCP7 Book Files folder; in the third column, click the Lessons folder, and in the fourth column, click the My Projects folder.

The FCP7 Book Files/Lessons folder is where you will go to open the matching project in future lessons.

**TIP** If the Finder columns don't appear in the Save dialog, click the arrow next to the Save As field, and then navigate to the target location.

**3** In the lower-left corner of the Save dialog, make sure the "Hide extension" checkbox is deselected, and click Save.

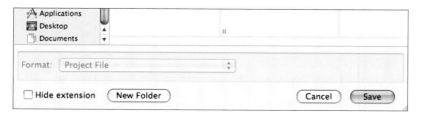

In the Browser window, the project name *Untitled Project 1* is changed to *SeaWorld* on the project tab and window title bar. The .fcp extension (for *Final Cut Pro*) does not appear here but is added to the name of a project in the Finder. The .fcp extension can make it easier for you or other team members to identify a project file when it's combined with other types of elements.

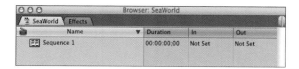

Notice the Timeline and Canvas windows. Anytime a sequence is open, its name appears on a tab in these windows. Remember, the Timeline and Canvas windows always display the same sequence but in a different way. Let's change the name of this sequence.

4   In the Browser window, single-click the sequence to select it, then click its name. When the name becomes highlighted, type *Believe Selected Takes*, and press Return.

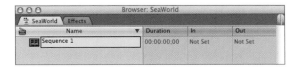

The name on the tab in the Timeline and Canvas windows changes to reflect the new sequence name. Currently, no audio or video clips have been edited into this sequence.

Sequence tab in Timeline window        Sequence tab in Canvas window

In this lesson, you will learn the basics of editing by building a selected-takes sequence in which you will edit different clips, but in no particular order. On projects that have a lot of footage, such as documentaries, it's a common practice to collect the best portions of the best clips into one location. This way, you can quickly sift through the more valuable footage when you start to shape your story.

Now that you've customized the name of the project and sequence, let's import some clips into the *SeaWorld* project.

5   Choose File > Import > Files, or press Command-I. In the Choose a File dialog, navigate this path: FCP7 Book Files > Media > SeaWorld > Believe.

**NOTE** ▶ If you copied the book files to a different location, such as a FireWire drive or your desktop, navigate to that location.

6    To import the **_DS_show concept** clip, single-click it, then click Choose. As with other files, you can also double-click the file to import it. In the Browser, click in the empty gray area to deselect the clip.

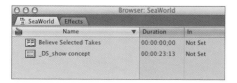

The clip now appears in the Browser window. The clip icon looks like a tiny piece of film complete with sprocket holes at the top and bottom. This clip represents a movie file on your hard disk, either video and audio or just video. To play the clip, you have to open it in the Viewer window.

**NOTE** ▶ If you see a thumbnail image of the clip instead of the filmlike clip icon, you are viewing the clips in icon mode. You'll learn about this mode later in this exercise.

7    In the Browser, double-click the **_DS_show concept** clip. The clip opens in the Viewer. Press the Spacebar to play the clip. Press the Spacebar again to stop playing it.

You will learn more about the Viewer in the next exercise. For now, it's clear that you need more clips to tell the *Believe* story. Rather than import one clip at a time, let's import several clips at once using the Command key.

▶ **About the *Believe* Footage**

Throughout this book, you will have the opportunity to work with four sets of footage, each representing a different genre—documentary, drama, music video, and television promo. The footage you'll work with throughout the first segment of this book is part of a human interest documentary shot at SeaWorld in San Antonio as the creative teams developed their killer whale show, *Believe*. Over the course of two years, the Busch Entertainment Company brought together killer whales and killer whale trainers, a Broadway producer, a Las Vegas director, a Los Angeles composer, set designers, and technicians who created a unique production for their premier show. *Believe* opened to the public in spring 2006 in all three U.S. SeaWorld locations. The footage was shot as HDV 1080i60.

As is the case with documentaries, news, reality television, and other projects where you don't have control over the surroundings, some of the audio is usable, and some is not. The trainers and whales rehearsed to a 20-minute music track that was used for the performance, and that music was recorded as part of the clips. For the book exercise, you will sometimes use just the video portion of the whale behavior clips, perhaps over a music track, narration, or dialogue clips.

**NOTE** ▶ The SeaWorld footage includes interview material, shots of whale behaviors, and underwater footage. To find the interview clips more easily, the clips were named with an underscore before the interviewee's initials, followed by a reference to what the person says. You will learn more about naming clips throughout this book.

8   Choose File > Import > Files, or press Command-I. The last import location appears in the Choose a File dialog. In the Believe folder, single-click the **_DF_ambassadors** clip. To add the following clips to the selection, hold down the Command key and single-click (Command-click) the following clips:

   ▶ **_DS_show team**

   ▶ **_SA_favorite behavior**

   ▶ **J and L circle**

   ▶ **K jumps off whale**

   ▶ **S show open**

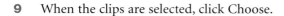 While holding down the Command key, you can click to add a clip to your selection (Command-click), or click a selected clip to remove it from your selection.

**9**    When the clips are selected, click Choose.

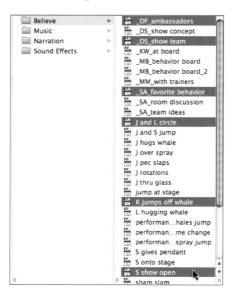

In the Browser, the imported clips appear under the Name column in alphabetical order. Notice that the interview clips appear together at the bottom of the list because those clip names begin with an underscore.

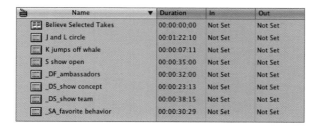

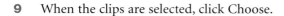 You can also use the drag-and-drop method to import clips or folders into a Final Cut Pro project. To do this, arrange your interface windows so you can see the Browser and a Finder window on your desktop. Navigate to the location of the desired clip or folder in the Finder window, and drag the clip to the Browser.

As you edit, you may not always be able to identify the content of the clip from its name. For example, can you tell whether the clip beginning with _SA is Sara's or Steve's interview? Sometimes it's helpful to view the clips as thumbnails, or *icons*.

**10** In the Browser window, Control-click in the empty gray area under the Name column. In the shortcut menu, choose View as Large Icons.

Now you can see the content of each clip. (It's Steve!) When a clip has sound attached to it, as these clips do, a small speaker icon appears in the lower right of the image. The sequence icon looks like two pieces of overlapping film, which reflects its purpose: containing a group of edited audio and video clips. To make the clip names easier to read, let's make the text size larger.

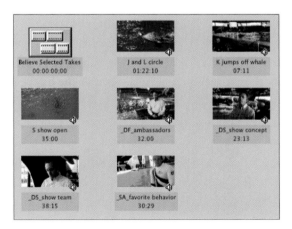

**TIP** If you're working with a smaller screen and can't see the other clips in the Browser, position your pointer over the clip area and scroll your mouse wheel up or down. You can also drag the vertical scroller down in the scroll bar. Or if you're using a Final Cut Pro-compatible portable or notebook computer with a Multi-Touch trackpad, you can scroll using two fingers on the trackpad.

**11** In any gray area of the Browser window, Control-click once again. From the shortcut menu, choose Text Size > Medium.

**12** To import a music track that was created for *Believe*, choose File > Import > Files. Navigate to the FCP7 Book Files > Media > SeaWorld > Music folder. Select **Track 8_guitar.aif**, and click Choose.

When a clip links to a media file that contains only audio—such as music, narration, or sound effects—a speaker icon represents the clip.

**TIP** ▶ Audio clips created in Apple's Audio Interchange File Format (AIFF) have an .aif file extension. Depending on how the clip was named, this extension may not be visible.

You can also import an entire folder of clips, if those clips have already been organized into a folder on your hard disk. This time, let's access the Import command from the shortcut menu in the Browser.

**13** In the Browser, Control-click in the gray area, and choose Import > Folder. Navigate to the FCP7 Book Files > Media > SeaWorld > Narration folder. Notice that the individual clips in the Narration folder are dimmed and cannot be selected. Make sure the Narration folder is selected, and click Choose.

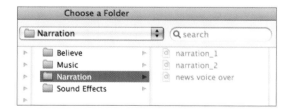

**NOTE** ▶ When you use the Import > Folder command, you can import only a folder of clips, not individual clips.

In the Browser, the Narration folder appears, containing any narration clips that were on the hard disk. In Final Cut Pro, folders are referred to as *bins*. This term comes from the days of film editing when pieces of cut film hung on hooks over large canvas containers called bins. These pieces of film, or film clips, would hang there until the film editor selected them for use in a sequence. Bins are used in the Browser to help organize clips and sequences in a project. You will work more with bins later in this lesson.

**NOTE ▶** In the FCP7 Book Files/Lessons folder, the Lesson 1 Project file contains all the clips that have been imported so far. If you need to catch up to this point, choose File > Open and navigate to this file to open it. If not, continue with your current *SeaWorld* project.

## Take 2

Although the role of an editor may vary from production to production, one thing never changes—the editor is always a popular person. Why? Because the editor brings the project together. Sometimes the edit bay—or cutting room—is the first place that documentary team members see what's been shot. And after shooting is completed, postproduction is where the director and producer focus their attention on the editorial possibilities. Exploring and shaping those possibilities is your job as an editor. And just as a director might shoot a "Take 2" to get a better performance from an actor, you can use these Take 2 scenarios to practice and improve your editorial skills in Final Cut Pro.

In the next exercise, you will learn a lot about the Viewer window as you screen the imported clips. But the director just walked in and would love to see a few of the clips—now! Take a minute to review the basic way to open a clip (double-click) and play it (press Spacebar) in the Viewer.

## Playing Clips in the Viewer

The Viewer window is quite versatile. You can perform numerous tasks here, including adding and adjusting effects, changing audio levels, and tweaking text titles. But you will spend most of your time in the Viewer window playing and marking source clips in preparation for editing.

The Viewer has multiple tabs across the top. The default is the first tab, Video, where you can view and mark your clips. When you first open Final Cut Pro, the Video tab displays a black *slug*, or placeholder. There is an audio tab (Stereo or Mono), where you'll work more closely with the audio of a clip. If no audio is present in the clip, no audio tab will appear. The Filters and Motion tabs will be used when you start to create effects in later lessons. In this exercise, you will learn different ways to open and play clips in the Viewer.

To view, or *screen*, a clip in the Viewer, you have to open it from the Browser window as you did in the previous exercise. There are several ways to open a clip into the Viewer. For this exercise, you will work with three methods:

▶   Double-click the clip in the Browser window.

▶   Drag the clip from the Browser to the Viewer window.

▶   Select the clip in the Browser and press Return.

**1**   In the Browser, double-click the **S show open** clip to open it in the Viewer. Press the Spacebar to play some of this clip.

In the Viewer title bar, the clip name and project appear. You can customize the Viewer window to see a larger image by dragging the border between the windows.

2    To make the Viewer window larger, move your pointer over the border between the Browser and Viewer. When the Resize pointer appears, drag left as far as you can. Drag the Viewer and Canvas border to the right. Drag the Timeline boundary line down until the image in the Viewer fills that window.

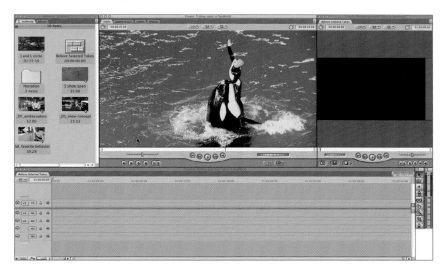

When you focus on one aspect of the editing process, such as screening your footage, it's helpful to arrange your interface for that purpose.

**TIP** You can dynamically resize more than one window at a time by dragging a border corner diagonally.

3    To save this window layout for future screening sessions, hold down Option and choose Window > Arrange > Set Custom Layout 1, then release the Option key. This custom window layout is now available for you to recall at any time.

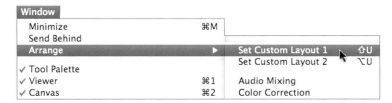

4    To play the **s show open** clip, click the Viewer's Play button in the transport controls area.

The next image shows Steve Aibel, the assistant curator of animal training at SeaWorld, San Antonio, Texas. He is rehearsing the killer whale show, *Believe*. Other whale trainers you will see in the source clips include Julie Sigman, Katie Wright, Leslie Popiel, and Bridgette Pirtle. The initials of their first names were used to identify the clips they are in.

**5**   When the clip stops playing, click the Play button again and this time watch the bar beneath the image area.

This is called the *scrubber bar*. The length of the scrubber bar represents the duration of the clip. The actual length of the clip appears in the Timecode Duration field in the upper left of the Viewer window.

**6**   In the Browser, find the **K jumps off whale** clip. To open this clip, drag it to the Viewer window. Look at the Timecode Duration field to determine the length of this clip.

**7**   Press the Spacebar to play this clip. When you see Katie jump off the whale, press the Spacebar to stop playing. Press it again to play. Notice the thin vertical line topped with a yellow triangle in the scrubber bar as the clip plays.

This is called the *playhead*. The location of the playhead corresponds to a specific frame in the clip.

In the upper-right corner of the Viewer window is the Current Timecode field. The number that appears is the *timecode* of the frame where the playhead is currently located. Timecode is a video labeling system that records a unique eight-digit number—representing hours, minutes, seconds, and frames—onto each frame of a clip or sequence. As the clip plays and the playhead moves, the timecode in this field changes to reflect the current playhead location.

8    In the Browser, single-click the **_SA_favorite behavior** clip to select it, and then press Return to open it in the Viewer. Whenever you open another clip in the Viewer, it replaces the previous clip in the Viewer window.

> **NOTE ▸** The Enter key is not used interchangeably with Return to open a clip. If you select a clip, bin, or sequence and press Enter, the name will be highlighted, allowing you to rename it.

9    As you play this clip, keep an eye on the Current Timecode field. Stop the clip just after you see the timecode number 01:03:10:00, after Steve says, "zoom to the bottom of the pool."

**TIP** ▶ If necessary, take a moment to make sure your audio monitors or computer sound levels are set to a good volume for screening and editing.

**10** In the Viewer, click the Stereo (a1a2) tab. Play the clip from this location and watch the visual display of the sound signal as the playhead moves through the clip.

When you open a clip that has audio attached, either a Stereo or Mono audio tab appears in the Viewer, depending on how the clip was captured. If you have two channels of audio, they may be shown together as a stereo pair, as in the current clip, or as two separate Mono tabs. In any one of these tabs, audio is displayed in the form of waves that represent the sound signal. This display is referred to as a *waveform*.

**11** To access the **S show open** clip again, click the Recent Clips pop-up menu button in the lower-right corner of the Viewer window. From the pop-up menu, choose the **S show open** clip.

The Recent Clips pop-up menu displays recently opened clips, with the most recent clip at the top of the list. The menu displays a default of 10 clips, but you can change that in the User Preferences window (Option-Q) to display up to 20 clips.

**TIP** ▶ You can use two additional methods to open a clip in the Viewer. You can select a clip and choose View > Clip, or you can Control-click the clip in the Browser and choose Open in Viewer from the shortcut menu.

## Navigating Clips

As you begin to edit, playing or screening clips will always be one of your first steps. But after you've played through a clip, you will soon want greater navigational control. For example, you may want to go back a few seconds to review an action, play faster through an area that is less important, move quickly to the head or tail of a clip, go backward or forward to find a specific frame, and so on. In the Viewer window, transport buttons as well as keyboard shortcuts give you this control. Visual clues also indicate when you are on the first or last frame of a clip.

In this exercise, you will open a clip that shows several actions of two whales and two trainers. By using buttons and shortcuts, you will move to and screen the different actions.

1    In the Browser, open a **J and L circle** clip. Press the End key to see the last frame of this clip. Then press the Home key to move the playhead back to the first frame.

**TIP** ▶ If you are using a portable computer, press the Fn (function) key and the Left Arrow key for Home, and the Fn key and Right Arrow key for End.

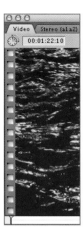

First frame of clip      Last frame of clip

In the Viewer, filmstrip sprocket holes appear on the left side of the image area when the playhead is on the first frame, or *head*, of the clip. They appear on the right when the playhead is on the last frame, or *tail*, of the clip.

**NOTE ▶** If the filmstrip overlays do not appear in your Viewer image area, choose View > Show Overlays. You can turn overlays off or on during the editing process.

**2**   Press End to move the playhead to the tail of the clip. Press the Left Arrow key several times and watch the trainer's right hand move up and down on the whale's pectoral flipper.

Pressing the Left Arrow and Right Arrow keys is a great way to navigate frame by frame to the beginning or end of a specific action. You can also hold down the Left Arrow or Right Arrow key to play backward or forward at a slow-motion speed.

**3**   Now press Shift–Left Arrow four times to move the playhead backward 4 seconds. Play from this position to the end of the clip.

Pressing the Shift key in combination with either the Left Arrow or Right Arrow key moves the playhead backward or forward, respectively, in 1-second increments. This is a helpful way to quickly move the playhead a specific amount of time—in this case, to play the last section of the clip.

**4**   To move back to the head of this clip in a different way, press the Up Arrow key to move the playhead to the beginning of the clip.

The Up Arrow and Down Arrow keys move the playhead backward to the head of the clip and forward to the tail of the clip, respectively.

**5**  In the Viewer scrubber bar, drag the playhead forward through the first section where the two trainers move in a circle. Then drag the playhead backward to about 00:14:03:20 and play this section.

Dragging through a clip this way is called *scrubbing*. You are viewing the clip, but not at the normal play speed. You can also drag the playhead to move quickly to the head or tail of a clip, or click in any part of the scrubber bar to bring the playhead to that location. As you scrub, you hear the digital audio of the clip.

**TIP**  To turn the clip audio off or on as you scrub, choose View > Audio Scrubbing, or press Shift-S.

The Viewer also has *shuttle* and *jog* controls that act like traditional VCR controls, scrubbing or scrolling through the frames of your clip.

**6**  Scrub the playhead forward to where the whale is pushing the trainer out of the water, around 00:14:32:00. Drag the jog control to the right, until you see the trainer's hands open up. Then drag the shuttle control to view the rest of this section. Stop at about 00:14:40:00.

Shuttle control                    Jog control

When you use the jog control, you hear the digital audio scrubbing sound. When you use the shuttle control, you hear an analog audio sound that can be useful when looking for a specific sound cue.

**TIP** ▶ A great use for the scroll button on a two-button mouse is to scrub frame by frame through an image as though you were using a jog control. Place the pointer over the image area in the Viewer and scroll up to scrub backward, and scroll down to scrub forward. The scroll ball on the Apple Mighty Mouse can move left and right as well.

7   The JKL keys provide additional ways to navigate a clip. Press L to play forward. Watch for the moment when the whale lifts the trainer out of the water and goes back under. Then press K to stop. Press the J key to play backward through this section.

These three keys—J, K, and L—provide a convenient way to screen a clip for specific actions. By pressing combinations of these keys, you can play a clip slow or fast, forward or backward, and frame by frame.

8   Move the playhead to the head of the clip. Hold three fingers over the J, K, and L keys, and try the following key combinations to reacquaint yourself with the whale's behaviors:

▶   Press L two or three times to play the clip faster. When you press L repeatedly, the clip speed is ramped up faster, then even faster.

▶   Press K to stop, then press J several times to play backward at faster speeds.

▶   Press and hold K and L together to play forward in slow motion.

▶   Press and hold K and J together to play backward in slow motion.

▶   Hold K and tap L to move forward one frame at a time.

▶   Hold K and tap J to move backward one frame at a time.

**TIP** You can also play backward by holding down the Shift key and then clicking the Viewer's Play button or pressing the Spacebar.

**9** To move the playhead to the head of the clip using a Viewer transport button, click the Go to Previous Edit button.

The Go to Next Edit button will move the playhead to the tail of the clip. Up Arrow and Down Arrow are the shortcut keys for these functions.

**10** To move to the exact location in this clip where the trainer opens her hands, click in the Current Timecode field and type *00143324*, then press Return.

**TIP** When entering a timecode, you don't need to click first in the Current Timecode field. Just make sure the Viewer window is active, then start typing the timecode. Final Cut Pro knows that you are typing a timecode and automatically places it in that field. Also, you never need to type preceding zeros or the colons or semicolons that separate numbers. However, the text of this book uses colons to make the timecode numbers easier to read.

The playhead moves to that specific timecode location. Often, in larger productions, an editor will receive a list of timecodes that represent specific edit points or important locations in a clip. Editors often begin their editing process by screening these "selected" takes.

**11** Move the playhead to the following timecode locations to review memorable frames from this clip:

00:15:16:27   Trainer lying on whale's chest

00:14:04:08   Two trainers in circle

00:14:45:13   Whale lifts trainer out of water

**NOTE** ▸ Additional features are available on portable Macs with a Multi-Touch track-pad. In addition to using the standard two-finger scroll, you can use three fingers and swipe up to move the playhead to the beginning of a clip, or swipe down to move the playhead to the end of the clip.

## Take 2

The director called and wants your input on the two other whale behavior clips in your project, **K jumps off whale** and **S show open**. Using different navigation techniques, take a moment to find a few trainer actions or whale behaviors you think the director might like to include in the rough cut. Also listen to the music track to determine how it might be used. Notice that when an audio-only clip is opened in the Viewer, the Video tab does not appear.

To review, you can navigate through a clip using any of the following steps:

▸ Use the navigation buttons and controls in the Viewer.

▸ Press the keyboard shortcuts, such as Up Arrow, Down Arrow, Left Arrow, and Right Arrow.

▸ Press the JKL keys to move forward or backward at different speeds.

▸ Enter a timecode in the Current Timecode field and press Return to go to a specific location.

## Marking and Editing Clips

As you screened the clips in the previous exercises, you probably saw some great whale actions and heard interesting comments you'd like to include in the *Believe Selected Takes* sequence. To edit just a portion of a clip into a sequence, you have to identify that portion by marking two *edit points* in the clip—a starting point (*In point*) and an ending point (*Out point*). You can use the navigation methods you learned in the previous exercise to move to the precise starting point and then set an In point, which lets Final Cut Pro know where to begin using the clip content. Next, you play the clip from the In point to see where you might want to stop using the footage, and here you set an Out point. And then you edit that portion of the clip into a sequence.

There are two ways you can set edit points in the Viewer:

▸ Click the Mark In and Mark Out buttons in the Viewer window.

▸ Press the keyboard shortcuts: I for In, and O for Out.

Mark In button ⌐ ⌐ Mark Out button

1   From the Browser, open the **_DS_show team** clip in the Viewer. (This clip features David Smith.) Play the clip and stop after David says, "all around the country." Note that the duration of this clip is 38:15 (38 seconds and 15 frames).

**TIP** ▶ Throughout this exercise, take an extra moment to create clean edit points. For example, press the Left Arrow and Right Arrow keys, or the JKL keys, to position the playhead where David's eyes are open and his mouth is closed before he speaks again.

Currently, the Timecode Duration field in the Viewer is reflecting the full length of the clip. When you mark this clip, this duration will change to reflect only the marked portion.

2   To set an In point at this location, click the Mark In button (beneath the shuttle control and Viewer transport keys).

An In point appears in the scrubber bar where the playhead is located. Notice the In point overlay in the upper-left corner of the image area, and the shorter duration that appears in the Timecode Duration field. This duration reflects the time from the new In point to the end of the clip.

3   Play the clip from this point and stop after David says, "what the overall content of the show would be." In the Viewer, click the Mark Out button to set an Out point at this location.

A new Out point appears in the scrubber bar where the playhead is located and in the upper-right corner of the image area. The Timecode Duration field reflects the length of the marked portion of the clip, and the scrubber bar becomes gray outside the marked area.

**TIP**  If you change your mind about an edit point, press Command-Z or choose Edit > Undo to remove the mark or return to a previous mark. The default number of undos is 10, but you can change that number in the General tab of the User Preferences window (Option-Q).

4   Click the Play In to Out button to see just the marked portion of your clip. This is the portion of the clip that will be edited into the sequence.

**TIP**  Even edit points can be saved as part of your project. To save the marks you create, choose File > Save, or press Command-S.

**5**   To edit this clip into the *Believe Selected Takes* sequence, click the red Overwrite button in the Canvas window.

Before the clip is edited into the Timeline, an alert message will probably appear to indicate that the settings of the sequence you've created don't match those of the clip you are editing.

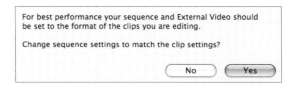

**6**   Click Yes to have Final Cut Pro automatically change the *Believe Selected Takes* sequence settings to match the SeaWorld footage.

**MORE INFO** ▸ You will learn more about changing sequence settings in Lesson 7.

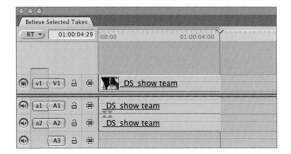

The marked clip is automatically placed on the Timeline tracks. The upper (blue) portion of the clip is the video, and the lower (green) tracks are the stereo audio. These tracks are a linear representation of time, proceeding horizontally from left to right. At the end of the clip is the playhead, which functions just as the Viewer playhead does. When you make an edit, the playhead repositions itself at the end of the clip, where you will most likely consider placing the next marked clip or edit.

**NOTE** ▸ In the next lesson, you will learn about the editing process in more depth. For now, these steps will serve as a basic introduction to how marked clips are edited from the Viewer to the Timeline.

**7**   Now open the **_SA_favorite behavior** clip from the Browser and play it. Position the playhead at the beginning of Steve's comment, "There's a behavior." This time, press I to mark an In point. Move the playhead to just after Steve says, "reason why we do this." Then press O to mark an Out point.

Using keyboard shortcuts produces the same results as the marking controls: They create In and Out marks in the scrubber bar and the clip image. You can also use a modifier key to go to or delete edit points:

▶   **Shift-I**       Move the playhead to the In point

▶   **Shift-O**      Move the playhead to the Out point

▶   **Option-I**     Remove the In point

▶   **Option-O**    Remove the Out point

▶   **Option-X**    Remove both the In point and the Out point

**8**   To edit this clip into the *Believe Selected Takes* sequence, click the red Overwrite button in the Canvas window.

Again, the playhead jumps to the end of the clip you just edited. Since this is a longer clip than the first one, it takes up more space in the Timeline.

When you've already screened a clip and can anticipate where you want to mark it, you can use an approach called *marking on the fly*.

**9**    From the Browser, open the **J and L circle** clip. Play the trainer-on-belly section at the end of the clip, and when you see Julie and the whale enter the frame (around 00:15:07:00), press I to mark an In point. If you need to redo your marks, replay the clip and mark again or drag the In point left or right in the scrubber bar.

Marking again after you've already marked an In or Out point simply replaces the old edit point with the new. You can also drag an edit point to a different location.

**TIP** ▶ When you mark an In point but no Out point, Final Cut Pro will edit the clip from the In point to the end of the clip. Likewise, if you've marked an Out point but no In point, FCP will edit the clip from the beginning of the clip to the Out point. With no marks, the entire clip is edited.

**10**    In the Canvas window, click the red Overwrite button to edit this clip into the sequence.

**TIP** ▶ If you can't see all the clips in your sequence, click in the Timeline window and press Shift-Z, the Fit to Window command. You can also use the scroll ball on your mouse to scroll through the clips in the sequence. You will learn more about managing Timeline tracks in the next lesson.

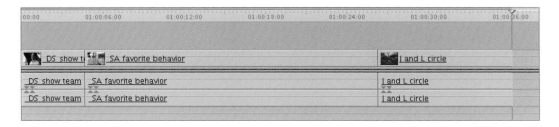

If you or someone on the production team has written down timecodes as references, you can enter a number and mark that location.

**11** From the Browser, open the **_DF_ambassadors** clip. In the Current Timecode field, enter *00:49:56:04*, and press Return. Press I to set an In point. Set an Out point at 00:50:14:26, and edit this clip into the sequence.

**NOTE ▶** In reality television programs, where there is a lot of footage to review, editors often receive a list of timecode edit points that have been selected by the writing team, which is responsible for building the story.

You can also set marks for a specific duration by entering that length of time in the Duration field.

**12** Open the **S show open** clip and mark an In point about 4 seconds in from the head of the clip, just as Steve is starting to emerge. In the Duration field, type *600* for 6 seconds, and press Return. An Out point is automatically set 6 seconds later. Edit this clip into the sequence.

**TIP** ▶ To move the playhead forward 4 seconds, position it at the head of the clip and press Shift–Right Arrow four times. You can also type *+400* in the Current Timecode field, and press Return. This repositions the playhead 4 seconds later.

**MORE INFO** ▶ There are numerous keyboard shortcuts using the Z key. In this lesson, you learned Shift-Z (Fit to Window), Command-Z (Undo), and just Z (Select the Zoom In tool). If you accidentally pressed other Z shortcuts, such as Option-Z (Show Timecode Overlays) or Control-Z (View Range Check), visual overlays will appear in your interface. If that happens, press those shortcuts again to turn them off.

## Playing and Navigating a Sequence

Now that you've started to build your rough cut, you will want to review what you've edited by playing the sequence. You can play and navigate a sequence in either the Canvas or the Timeline window. In fact, all of the play and navigation commands you used in the Viewer can be applied in the Canvas and the Timeline, sometimes with slightly different results. Like the Timeline, the Canvas has a playhead and a scrubber bar similar to the Viewer's.

1   To focus on the sequence image in the Canvas, resize the windows by dragging the border between the Viewer and Canvas as far left as possible. Then hold down the Option key and choose Window > Arrange > Set Custom Layout 2 to save this layout for future use.

2   In the Canvas, drag the playhead in the scrubber bar to the far left, or press the Home key.

What's the duration of the sequence you've been building? And where does the sequence start?

**NOTE** ▶ Depending on where you marked your edit points, your duration may be different from the one in the image below.

While the Viewer scrubber bar represents the length of one clip, the Canvas scrubber bar represents the length of the entire sequence. This length appears in the Timecode Duration field, positioned in the upper-left corner, just as in the Viewer. In the Current Timecode field on the right, you see that the playhead is at the first frame of the sequence, which is 1:00:00:00. This is the default starting timecode of all sequences.

**3**   To play this sequence, click the Canvas's Play button, or press the Spacebar. You can also press the L key as you did in the Viewer.

As you play the sequence, you see the playhead in the Timeline *ruler* move in tandem with the Canvas playhead. They are each playing the same sequence; the Canvas is displaying the image while the Timeline displays a graphical representation of the individual edits. Notice that the Timeline ruler displays the continuous timecode of the sequence, not of the individual clips.

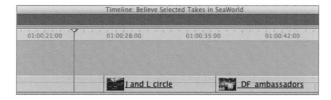

Entering a specific timecode in the Canvas or Timeline moves you to a specific place in the sequence.

**4**   To see which clip appears 30 seconds into the sequence, click in the Canvas's Current Timecode field and type *1:00:30:00*. Press Return. The playhead moves to the specific timecode location you entered. Or you can type this number in the Timeline's Current Timecode field instead.

**TIP** ▶ Just as in the Viewer, you don't have to click in the Current Timecode field before typing the timecode. With the Canvas or Timeline window active, just start typing the number and it automatically appears in this field.

You can also scrub through the Timeline to find interesting actions, just as you did in the Viewer and Canvas. You do this in the Timeline by dragging the playhead in the ruler.

5    In the Timeline, drag the yellow triangle of the playhead in the ruler into the **J and L circle** clip and find the point where the trainer's hand moves up and down on the whale's flipper. Then drag the playhead over the other clips.

When you drag the playhead within a clip, you don't feel it snap. As you drag the playhead across clips in the Timeline, it snaps like a magnet to the edit points between each clip.

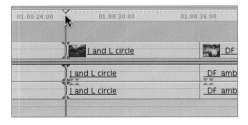

Playhead snapping to edit point

**NOTE ▸** The snapping function can be turned off or on in the Timeline button bar. Make sure it is on, or green, for this exercise.

6   To move to edit points earlier in the sequence, press the Up Arrow key several times. To move forward to later edit points, press the Down Arrow key several times.

In the Canvas and Timeline, pressing the Up Arrow or Down Arrow key moves the playhead to the first frame of the previous clip or to the next clip, respectively. The L-shaped symbol in the lower-left corner of the Canvas indicates that the playhead is positioned on the first frame of the edited clip.

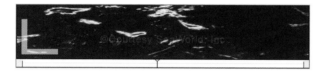

**TIP ▸** Another way to move backward or forward to a clip is to click the Go to Previous Edit or Go to Next Edit button in the Canvas. You can also press the ; (semi-colon) and ' (apostrophe) keys, which are conveniently located next to the J, K, and L keys.

7   Move the playhead to the first frame of the **J and L circle** clip. Now press the Left Arrow key to move one frame backward.

In the Canvas, the reverse L in the lower-right corner of the image area indicates that you are on the last frame of that clip. As in the Viewer, pressing the Left Arrow or Right Arrow key moves the playhead one frame at a time.

**8**    The J, K, and L keys work in the Canvas and Timeline just as they did in the Viewer. They can play the sequence forward or backward, step through it frame by frame, and play it in slow motion. Use the J, K, and L keys to move quickly through the longer clips in the sequence, and play slowly through the whale behavior.

**9**    To jump to the end of the sequence, press the End key.

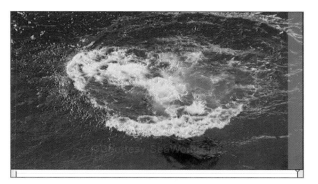

A vertical blue bar appears on the right side of the Canvas window, indicating that you are at the end of the sequence. There are no edits past this point.

**10**    Press Command-S to save your project.

When you save a Final Cut Pro project, everything about the project is saved, even the location of the playhead in a sequence.

**TIP**    You can use the Multi–Touch, three-finger gesture and swipe up to move the playhead to the head of the sequence, and swipe down to move it to the end of the sequence. A three-finger swipe left moves the playhead to the previous edit point, and right moves it to the next edit point. Rotating will scrub left or right in the Timeline.

## Organizing Project Elements

As you move deeper into the more creative aspects of editing, it's easy to bypass or ignore the organizational needs of your project. But any experienced editor knows that keeping a project well organized is essential to an efficient editing process. For example, in this lesson you imported four types of footage—narration, shots of whale behaviors, interviews, and a music track. The narration clips are already in their own folder. And while there aren't a lot of individual clips in your project, you might be adding more, and putting similar clips together will make them easier to find and access as you continue editing. Let's take a moment to organize those individual clips into folders, or bins, so they appear as neat as the Narration clips.

**1**   To see as many project elements as possible in the Browser window, Control-click in the empty gray area, and from the shortcut menu, choose View as List. To make the Browser window larger, press Control-U to return to the standard window layout.

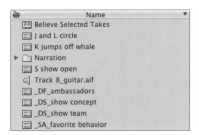

When a project contains more than just a few elements, viewing the items as an alphabetized list can be very helpful. Now it's easy to see the music, whale behavior, and interview clips you need to organize into their own bins.

**2**   There are three ways to create a bin. Create three bins in the Browser using any or all of the following methods:

▶   From the File menu, choose File > New > Bin.

▶   Press the keyboard shortcut, Command-B.

▶   In the Browser, Control-click in the gray area under the Name column, and from the shortcut menu, choose New Bin.

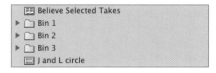

The new bins are placed in alphabetical order among the other project elements. Each bin is given a default sequential number, just like new sequences and projects.

3   To highlight the name, click the Bin 1 icon and press Enter (or Fn-Return if Enter shares the Return key on your keyboard). Type *Interviews*, and press Return. Name the other two bins *Music* and *Behaviors*.

> ▶ ☐ Behaviors
> ☰ Believe Selected Takes
> ▶ ☐ Interviews
> ▦ J and L circle
> ▦ K jumps off whale
> ▶ ☐ Music
> ▶ ☐ Narration
> ▦ S show open

Each time you change a bin's name and press Return, the newly named bin is placed in its appropriate alphabetical order.

**TIP** ▶ As with other files, you can also click the name of a selected item in the Browser to highlight it.

You've created three bins to organize the elements in this project. Now you will select the clips and drag them to their appropriate bins. You can drag a single clip or a group of clips at one time. The ways to select items in the Browser follow standard Mac OS X selection methods:

▶   Click an item to select it.

▶   Command-click to add an item to, or remove it from, the current selection.

▶   To select a contiguous list of items, click the first item and Shift-click the last item.

▶   Drag a selection rectangle around a group of items.

▶   Press Command-A to choose all items in the window.

The method you choose to select clips in the Browser depends entirely on where the clips are located: if they are side by side in a contiguous group, or spread out among other clips.

4   Drag the **Track 8_guitar.aif** audio clip (speaker icon) to the Music bin. (When the Music bin is highlighted, release the mouse button.)

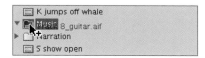

**TIP ▶** Whenever you drag an item in Final Cut Pro, make sure that the tip of the Selection tool pointer touches the specific destination, in this case the bin icon or name.

5    To place all the interview clips in the Interviews bin at one time, click the **_DF_ambassadors** clip, then hold down the Shift key and click the last interview clip, **_SA_favorite behavior**. Drag the selected clips to the Interviews bin.

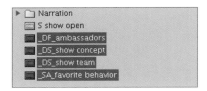

Pressing Shift when you select the last item will highlight all items between the first and last items.

**TIP ▶** You can also drag your pointer around a group of contiguous clips to select them. Be careful not to drag a clip by itself.

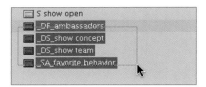

You can select any number of noncontiguous clips by Command-clicking a clip to select or deselect it.

6    To organize the whale behavior clips, click the **J and L circle** clip, then Command-click the **K jumps off whale** and **S show open** clips. Drag the selected clips to the Behaviors bin.

As you drag these clips together, only the name of the clip you clicked is displayed, along with the number of other items you're dragging.

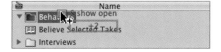

**TIP** ▶ When you create additional sequences in this project, you may want to create a Sequences bin. For now, consider adding a space in front of the sequence name to bump it up to the top of the list, or an underscore to push it to the bottom.

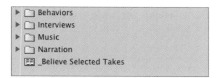

## Viewing Bin Contents

Now your clip arrangement looks neat and organized. However, as you begin to screen your clips for editing, you'll need to access the clips inside the bins quickly and easily. You can do this in several ways. Some methods work better if you're using a two-display editing setup, while others are best for portable computers or one-display setups. Let's look at different ways to display the contents of a bin so you can get to this material easily.

1    Next to the Behaviors bin, click the disclosure triangle to display its contents. Click it again to hide the contents of that bin.

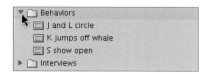

Clicking the disclosure triangle displays or hides the contents of the bin. This method works very well for portable computers that have limited interface space.

2    Double-click the Interviews bin. Then drag the Interviews in SeaWorld window by its title bar and position it away from the Browser.

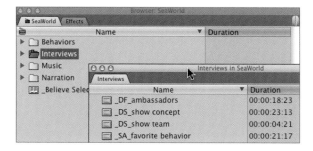

Double-clicking opens a bin as a separate window, which you can move anywhere in the interface. In the Browser, the Interviews bin icon changes to an open folder, indicating that the bin is open as a separate window or tab. If your editing setup includes two displays, a common practice is to move the entire Browser window to the left display, and to open the bins you are working with as separate windows in that display.

**3**   In the Interviews bin window, click the close button in the upper-left corner to close the window, or press Command-W. In the Browser, the Interviews bin icon changes back to a closed folder.

**4**   To view the contents of the Interviews bin a different way, hold down the Option key and double-click the Interviews bin.

The bin opens as a separate tab next to the *SeaWorld* project tab. In the Browser title bar, the bin is identified as being in the *SeaWorld* project.

**TIP**   If you are working with just one display, opening a bin as a separate tab is a helpful way to view and access clips without placing an additional window in the interface.

**5**   Click the *SeaWorld* project tab, then click the Interviews bin tab.

You can access an open bin tab or project simply by clicking its tab. Whichever tab is active appears brighter or highlighted, and its name appears in the Browser title bar. Notice that the slate icon on the *SeaWorld* project tab distinguishes it from any open bin tabs. You can also reorder the tabs so the project tab appears first.

**6**   Drag the *SeaWorld* project tab to the left over the Interviews tab, but *don't release the mouse button* until you see the tab order change. You can also reposition bin tabs in the same way.

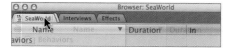

**7**  To return the Interviews bin to its closed bin configuration, Control-click the Interviews tab, or right-click it if you have a two-button mouse. From the shortcut menu, choose Close Tab.

> **NOTE** ▸ The Interviews tab does not have to be highlighted to close it.

You can also display and hide bin contents by pressing the arrow keys.

**8**  To navigate to a specific clip using shortcuts, follow these steps:

▶ Select the Interviews bin, then press the Right Arrow key to display the bin contents.

▶ Press the Left Arrow key to hide the bin contents.

▶ Press the Up Arrow or Down Arrow key to select a different bin at the same level. Select the Interviews bin again.

▶ Press the Right Arrow key once to open the bin and once again to move the highlight inside the bin to the first clip.

▶ Press the Down Arrow key several times until you highlight the **_SA_favorite behavior** clip.

▶ To close the Interviews bin, press the Left Arrow key twice.

> **NOTE** ▸ When viewing bin contents as a list, you have access to more than 60 columns of data in the Browser window. These columns may include information that Final Cut Pro registers about each item (number of audio tracks, frame size, frame rate, and so on) or descriptive information you enter for clarification, such as scene and take numbers. You will work more with these columns in later lessons. For now, if you need to make a column larger, perhaps to view a name, drag its column boundary to the right.

9 To save these organizational changes, press Command-S.

**TIP** ▶ How you organize your own project is a personal choice. If others are working on the same project, make sure the organizational structure is clearly defined.

## Editor's Cut

You've learned quite a bit in this lesson about screening and marking, basic editing, and project management. You've even practiced those skills while serving the needs of others when editing a Take 2. While those efforts might help produce the finished Director's Cut you see on the big screen, in the Editor's Cut you'll apply your newly-gained knowledge to realize your own unique creative vision.

For example, you could import the Believe folder with all the *Believe* clips, then mark and edit the ones listed below. The marked portion of these clips will be used in the next lessons. Remember, you're still adding the best takes to the *Believe Selected Takes* sequence. In the next lesson, you will put the clips in an order that tells the *Believe* story.

▶ From FCP7 Book Files > Media > SeaWorld, import the Believe folder.

▶ Screen and mark the following clips using the provided cues:

**_KW_at board** Mark from "Kayla's got the…" to "OK, great."

**_SA_team ideas** Mark "From the trainers'…" to "see in the *Believe* show."

**_MM_with trainers** Mark from the head of the clip to after the man raises his arm.

**S gives pendant** Mark the beginning and end of the camera zoom.

**performance_S spray jump** Mark the In point 1 second before whale appears; give this clip a 7-second duration.

**J and L circle** Select 3 seconds of the trainer sitting on the whale's nose, going up and down.

**uw_push two trainers** Select any 3 seconds.

**J and S jump** Mark the In point as they break the water's surface; no Out point.

**K jumps off whale** Mark the Out point after the director leaves the frame; set a 2:15 duration.

**uw_mom and calf jump** Mark any duration of 7:15.

## Saving, Hiding, and Closing Final Cut Pro

Make sure you save frequently throughout the editing process, whether you've made any edits or not. You may have made only minor organizational changes or marked a few clips, but you don't want to lose any of that work. Saving your project ensures that these decisions are reflected the next time you open that project. You can also hide the interface if you want to work on your desktop or in another program. You save, hide, and quit Final Cut Pro just as you would any other Apple application: from the menu or by using a keyboard shortcut.

1   Press Command-S to save changes in the current project.

2   To hide the interface, choose Final Cut Pro > Hide Final Cut Pro, or press Command-H.

The interface is hidden, and you see your desktop or any other programs you may have open.

3   Restore the Final Cut Pro interface by going to the Dock and clicking the application icon.

A small circle below or next to the Final Cut Pro icon in the Dock indicates the application is still open, even if it's not showing.

**TIP** Another way to move from one open application to another is to press Command-Tab repeatedly until the desired application is selected.

4   If you are finished working, quit the program by choosing Final Cut Pro > Quit Final Cut Pro, or by pressing Command-Q. If you are not finished working, leave the program open and continue with the next lesson.

When you close a project or quit Final Cut Pro, a prompt to save your work appears if you have made any changes since the last time you saved the project. If this window appears, click Yes to ensure that you are saving your most recent changes.

## Lesson Review

1.   Name three ways to open Final Cut Pro.

2.   What four modifier keys are often used in conjunction with keyboard shortcuts to initiate functions or commands?

3.  How do you access a shortcut menu?

4.  In what main menu can you find the Import command?

5.  Identify three ways to open a clip in the Viewer.

6.  Besides clicking the Play button, what keys on your keyboard can you press to play a clip or sequence forward?

7.  Which keys move the playhead forward or backward in one-frame increments in the Viewer, Canvas, and Timeline?

8.  How do you mark an In point or Out point on a clip?

9.  What button in the Canvas window do you click to edit a clip?

10. What visual indicator in the Viewer lets you know you are on the first or last frame of the entire clip?

11. What visual indicator in the Canvas window lets you know the playhead is on the first or last frame of an edited clip in the Timeline?

12. When viewing the audio portion of a clip, what do you see instead of a video image?

13. Identify three ways to create a bin.

14. What are the keyboard shortcuts to save, hide, and quit Final Cut Pro?

### *Answers*

1.  Double-click the application in the Applications folder, click the icon in the Dock, or double-click a Final Cut Pro project file.

2.  Shift, Control, Option, and Command

3.  Control-click (or right-click) an item.

4.  In the File menu.

5.  Double-click the clip in the Browser, drag it to the Viewer, or select it and press Return.

6.  The Spacebar and the L key.

7.  The Left Arrow and Right Arrow keys.

8.  Click the Mark In or Mark Out button in the Viewer, or press the keyboard shortcut, I or O.

9.  The red Overwrite button.

10. Filmstrip sprocket holes appear on the left side of the image in the Viewer to indicate the first available frame of media, and appear on the right side to indicate the last frame.

11. An *L* in the lower left means you're on the first frame of the edited clip, and a reverse *L* in the lower right means you're on the last frame.

12. A waveform display.

13. Choose File > New Bin, press Command-B, or Control-click in the gray area of the Browser and choose New Bin.

14. Press Command-S to save current changes, press Command-H to hide the application, and press Command-Q to quit the application.

**Keyboard Shortcuts**

**Organizing Project Elements**

| | |
|---|---|
| **Command-B** | Create a new bin |
| **Control-click (or right-click)** | Open shortcut menu |

**Moving the Playhead and Playing a Clip or Sequence**

| | |
|---|---|
| **End** | Take playhead to the end of the sequence or clip |
| **Home** | Take playhead to the head of the sequence or clip |
| **Down Arrow** | Move playhead forward in the Viewer to the end of the clip or the next edit point, and in Timeline to the first frame of the next edit |
| **Up Arrow** | Move playhead backward in the Viewer to the head of the clip or previous edit point, and in Timeline to the previous first frame |
| **Left Arrow** | Move playhead one frame to the left |
| **Shift–Left Arrow** | Move playhead 1 second to the left |
| **Right Arrow** | Move playhead one frame to the right |
| **Shift–Right Arrow** | Move playhead 1 second to the right |

### Keyboard Shortcuts

| | |
|---|---|
| **J** | Play clip or sequence backward in Viewer, Timeline, or Canvas |
| **K** | Stop playing clip or sequence in Viewer, Timeline, or Canvas |
| **K-J** | Play backward in slow motion |
| **K–tap J** | Move playhead one frame to the left |
| **K-L** | Play forward in slow motion |
| **K–tap L** | Move playhead one frame to the right |
| **L** | Play clip or sequence forward in Viewer, Timeline, or Canvas |
| **Shift-Spacebar** | Play a clip or sequence backward |

### Setting, Viewing, and Removing Marks

| | |
|---|---|
| **I** | Set an In point |
| **Shift-I** | Move the playhead to the In point |
| **Option-I** | Remove the In point |
| **O** | Set an Out point |
| **Shift-O** | Move the playhead to the Out point |
| **Option-O** | Remove the Out point |
| **Option-X** | Remove both In and Out points |

### Controlling the Application and Interface

| | |
|---|---|
| **A** | Select the default Selection tool |
| **Command-H** | Hide the Final Cut Pro interface |
| **Command-Q** | Quit Final Cut Pro |
| **Command-S** | Save changes in the project |
| **Command-Shift-S** | Save changes in an unnamed project |

## Keyboard Shortcuts

| | |
|---|---|
| **Shift-U** | Recall Custom Layout 1 |
| **Option-U** | Recall Custom Layout 2 |
| **Control-U** | Select the standard window layout |

# 2

# Building the Rough Cut

In the simplest terms, building a rough cut consists of marking clips and placing them into a sequence, as you did in the previous lesson. But the real work of building a rough cut is shaping a story. Rather than focus on a specific action within a single clip, you start to focus on how the clips fit together as a group. This is especially true for unscripted documentary footage such as the *SeaWorld* project's. Sometimes you have to edit a lot of clips before you find the story you want to tell.

In this lesson, you will learn several editing techniques that you can use to build and shape a rough cut of your story. For example, there are two ways to edit a marked clip into a sequence. The first is somewhat automatic and familiar from the previous lesson: You simply click a button to make an edit. The second approach is more hands-on. After determining a clip's proper location, you use the mouse to manually position it in the Timeline. This approach is referred to as *drag-and-drop editing*.

While you can make many types of edits in Final Cut Pro, the two types of edits you will work with in this lesson are *overwrites* and *inserts*. As you begin building a sequence, you will also learn to work with audio clips, create new versions of sequences, and open and change clips in the Timeline. Keep in mind that a rough-cut sequence will require trimming, adjusting, and finessing, but all of that is done in a later stage of the editing process.

## Working with Projects

In the previous lesson, you imported clips to use in editing a new Final Cut Pro project, a typical approach when you begin working with new footage. In this and all the following lessons, however, you will work with a project created specifically for each lesson. By using the book's projects, your sequences will match the exercises in each lesson.

**1**   If necessary, open Final Cut Pro by clicking its icon in the Dock.

   If a project was open when you last quit Final Cut Pro, such as the *SeaWorld* project, it will open automatically when you open the application.

   **TIP** ▶ Final Cut Pro opens with the most recent project as a default option that you can change in the General tab of User Preferences (Option-Q). In the future, if you want to open Final Cut Pro with an empty project, hold down the Shift key when you open the application.

**2**   Choose File > Open. In the Choose a File window, click the Column View button.

**3**   In the Choose a File window, navigate to FCP7 Book Files > Lessons.

   **NOTE** ▶ If you copied the FCP7 Book Files folder to a FireWire drive, select that drive in the first column.

4    Select the Lesson 2 Project file, and click Choose.

In the Browser window, *Lesson 2 Project* appears as a separate tab next to the Effects tab and all open projects. Notice that the window layout and text size don't change, as they are not project specific.

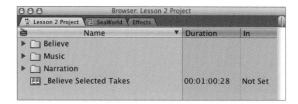

5    To close *SeaWorld* or any projects other than the *Lesson 2 Project*, click the project's tab to make it active and choose File > Close Project.

*Lesson 2 Project* contains some familiar project elements: a sequence and two bins, Music and Narration. It also contains one new bin, Believe, which contains all the interview and behavior clips that are available from the *SeaWorld* project.

> **TIP** ▶ If you want to create a backup of this project and change the backup without altering the original project file, choose File > Save Project As, and save the project in the FCP7 Book Files > Lessons > My Projects folder.

## Preparing a Project for Editing

Sometimes all you have to do to prepare a project for editing is import a few clips, then screen, mark, and edit them. In fact, those steps provide the basis for many projects. Mix in some music, titles, and effects, and you've got a finished sequence! On larger projects, such as documentaries and reality shows, there is often so much footage that additional preparation and organization is needed. For example, having one bin with 100 clips may not be as helpful as having 10 bins with 10 clips, each organized around a specific topic.

> **NOTE** ▶ In this lesson you are importing clips, but you can also ingest project elements by capturing or transferring files into your project.

To prepare for the editing exercises in this lesson, let's organize the project elements by placing bins within bins and creating two new sequences.

1   Click the disclosure triangle next to the Believe bin to view its contents. You may have to scroll up and down to see all the clips in this bin.

Three sets of SeaWorld clips are inside the Believe bin: interview footage, whale behaviors from the *Believe* show rehearsals and performances, and underwater footage. If you put each set of footage into a separate bin, it will be easier to locate specific clips when you're working on a particular section of the documentary. Let's organize this footage into separate bins *within* the Believe bin.

2   To create a bin inside another bin, in the Browser, Control-click the Believe bin. (You can also right-click if you have a two-button mouse.) From the shortcut menu, choose New Bin. Repeat this process two times to create three bins inside the Believe bin.

When you Control-click a specific bin to create a new bin, you are directing Final Cut Pro to place the new bin inside the bin you clicked.

**TIP** You can also use this method to import a clip directly into a specific bin. Control-click the target bin and, from the shortcut menu, choose Import > Files or Import > Folder.

3  Name the new bins *Interviews*, *Behaviors*, and *Underwater*. To rename each bin, you can select the bin and click the name to highlight it, or select the bin and press Enter. The bins are sorted alphabetically within the Believe bin.

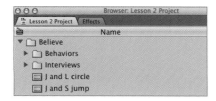

4  As you did in Lesson 1, drag the clips into their appropriate bins. Underwater clip names begin with *uw*, interview clip names begin with an underscore, such as *_SA*, and the remaining clips are behaviors from rehearsals and performances.

   When the clips are in their appropriate bins, it's easier to find a specific clip.

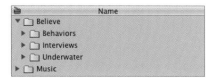

5  From the Believe > Interviews bin, open the **_SA_team ideas** clip. Click the Play In to Out button to see the marked portion of this clip.

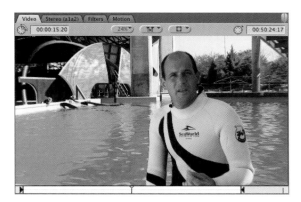

**NOTE** ► Some of the clips in this project have been marked in preparation for this lesson.

You will be editing two sequences in this project, so you will create two empty sequences for that purpose.

**6**    To create a sequence, choose File > New > Sequence, or press the keyboard shortcut, Command-N.

When you create a sequence, a sequence icon appears with *Sequence 2, 3*, or other sequential number in the Name field, depending on how many sequences are already in the project.

**7**    While the sequence name is still highlighted, type *Behaviors_v1*, and press Return. If necessary, click the name to highlight it, then rename it.

**TIP** ► It's not necessary to click in the Name field of a clip, bin, or sequence if the name is already highlighted. Simply start typing to replace the highlighted name with the new name.

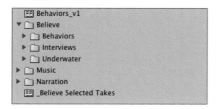

When renamed, the sequence is sorted alphabetically with the other project elements. Frankly, this ruins the look of your well-organized project. It could be time to create a separate bin for sequences.

**NOTE** ► In this lesson, an underscore was placed in front of the *_Believe Selected Takes* sequence name so it would appear beneath the bins at the bottom of the list.

**8**    Control-click the empty gray area under the Name column and, from the shortcut menu, choose New Bin. Name the new bin *Sequences*, then drag each sequence into the bin. Click the disclosure triangle to display its contents.

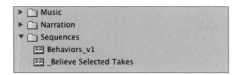

Your project looks organized once again. Now that you have a Sequences bin, you can create your next sequence directly in that bin.

**9**  Control-click the Sequences bin, and choose New Sequence. The new sequence is created *inside* the Sequences bin.

**10**  Name the new sequence *Inteviews_v1,* and press Return to accept the change. Press Return once again, or double-click the sequence, to open it in the Timeline.

Each open sequence is represented as a tab in the Timeline and Canvas windows. Although multiple sequences can be opened, only one sequence can be active or viewed at any given time. For now, let's close the *_Believe Selected Takes* sequence.

Sequence tabs in the Timeline window

Sequence tabs in the Canvas window

**TIP**  Adding version numbers to a sequence name is a common and helpful practice for tracking when major editorial changes have been made. In later exercises, when you work with this sequence, you will duplicate it, change the version number, and make changes to the new version.

**11**  In the Timeline, click the *_Believe Selected Takes* tab. The tab also becomes active in the Canvas. To close this sequence, Control-click the sequence tab in either the Canvas or Timeline window, and choose Close Tab.

## Editing a Rough Cut

In the previous lesson, you edited clips from the Viewer to the Timeline to combine selected takes from the SeaWorld footage. For simplicity's sake, all you did was click a  button, and the marked clip automatically appeared in the sequence. However, as you build a rough cut of your show, you will want to ask several questions about each edit. For example, do you want to edit audio and video from the same clip? Or will you take the video from one clip and audio from another? If you are editing audio, will you need to adjust the clip's audio level before editing it? You might also ask where you want to place a clip in the sequence— for example, before the whale jumps or after the underwater shot?

When deciding where to place a clip, you may also consider which Timeline track is the best to use. Often, a rough cut will use just one video track, though other video elements, such as titles, may be added later. However, you generally use several audio tracks in a rough cut. You may edit in the natural sound of a video action, a narration track, music, or sound effects. Even though this is a rough cut, it's important to follow a plan for the placement of these audio tracks and to be consistent throughout the editing process.

Organized use of audio tracks in the Timeline

**MORE INFO** ▶ You will learn more about mixing audio tracks in Lesson 10.

## Making Overwrite Edits

You can make several types of edits in Final Cut Pro, and each type places a clip in a sequence a little differently. An *overwrite edit*, which you used in Lesson 1, places a clip over whatever is currently on a Timeline track. The Timeline may be empty at that point, or another clip may be present. An *insert edit* positions a clip between other clips currently on a track. For this exercise, the audio and video will be edited to the V1, A1, and A2 tracks.

One clip overwriting another in a sequence

There are different ways to make overwrite edits. Later in this lesson you will drag an edit into the Timeline manually. For this exercise, you will use these more automatic methods:

▶ Click the red Overwrite button.

▶ Press the keyboard shortcut, F10.

▶ Choose the Overwrite option from the Canvas Edit Overlay.

> **TIP** Because you will be using the Viewer and Canvas windows equally in this exercise, press Control-U to make sure you have the standard window layout. Or you can resize your interface according to your own preferences.

**1**   To better see the playhead in the Timeline, drag it away from its current position to the middle of the sequence. Then drag it back to the head of the sequence, or press the Home key.

When you open a new sequence in the Timeline, the playhead is always positioned at the beginning of the sequence. When editing, you can use the playhead as a *target* that identifies the exact placement of the edit in the sequence. At the current target location, your first edit will appear at the head of this sequence.

**2**  To edit the **_SA_team ideas** clip at the playhead, or target, location in the Timeline, click the red Overwrite button in the Canvas window.

> **TIP** Whenever an alert message appears in these lessons asking whether you want to change the sequence settings to match the clip, always click Yes.

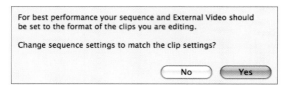

The video and two audio tracks between the In and Out points are placed at the playhead location. The playhead jumps to the end of the clip—or more specifically, the first frame of the space following the clip—awaiting the next edit. The blue end-of-sequence overlay in the Canvas indicates that you are at the end of the sequence.

**3**  Play the edited clip in the Timeline. When it's finished, the playhead remains at the end of the clip, which is a good target location for the next edit.

**4**  From the Interviews bin, open the **_MB_behavior board** clip. In the Viewer, click the Play In to Out button to see the portion you will edit.

All the clips you use in this exercise will be taken from the Interviews bin. The marked portions of these clips will give voice to the *Believe* story.

5   To edit this clip a different way, move your pointer over the red Overwrite button until you see the Overwrite shortcut, F10, appear in the tooltip. Press the F10 key to edit this clip into the sequence.

In the Timeline, the clip is edited at the playhead location, and the playhead automatically moves to the end of the clip, awaiting the next edit.

**NOTE ▶** To use the keyboard shortcut in step 5, make sure you have reassigned the Mac OS X functions in System Preferences. If you need help setting Preferences, see "Getting Started."

6   Open the **_SA_room discussion** clip and press Shift-\ (backslash) to play it from the In to the Out point. Press the F10 key to edit this clip into the sequence.

**TIP ▶** To find a shortcut for any button or function in the interface, simply move your pointer over that area. You can turn tooltips off or on in the General tab of User Preferences (Option-Q).

7   Open the **_KW_at board** clip and press Shift-\ (backslash) to see the marked portion of the clip. To edit this clip a different way, place your pointer in the image area of this clip, hold down the mouse button, and look for the clip thumbnail that attaches to the pointer.

**8**   Drag the thumbnail image to the Canvas window, but *don't release the mouse button.*

The Edit Overlay appears in the Canvas window with a palette of seven sections. These sections represent seven types of edits. Overwrite is the default edit option. To indicate this, the red Overwrite section has a brighter border around it, and the red Overwrite button is brighter.

Notice that the icon in the Overwrite section, like the Overwrite button, has a downward-facing triangle or arrow. This is a visual clue that you will be covering, or overwriting, anything in its place in the Timeline.

**9**   Drag the **_KW_at board** thumbnail image to the Overwrite section in the Edit Overlay. Play this group of clips from the beginning of the sequence.

**NOTE ▸** If the Overwrite section is highlighted in the overlay, you can drop the clip anywhere in the Canvas image area to make an overwrite edit.

Remember, this is a rough cut, and you will want to make many changes to it over the course of the editing process. One change might be to overwrite a portion of an edited clip. For example, the last clip in this sequence seems a little long. Let's shorten the end as you make the next edit.

**10**   In the Timeline, play the **_KW_at board** clip and stop after you hear Katie say, "OK, great."

**TIP ▸** To hear the audio as you drag the playhead through the clip, choose the View menu and make sure Audio Scrubbing is selected.

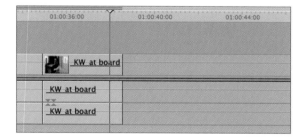

When you make the next edit, the new clip will overwrite the remaining portion of this clip.

**11** Open the **_DF_ambassadors** clip and view the marked portion. Drag the clip to the Overwrite section of the Canvas Edit Overlay.

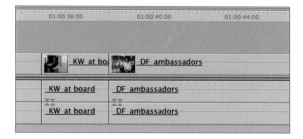

Now the **_KW_at board** clip is shorter in the Timeline than it was before. You can also overwrite an entire clip or a group of clips as you make an overwrite edit. Some editors consistently use this method of editing clips with extended lengths in the Timeline as a way to increase their flexibility in choosing where to place the next clip.

**12** Press Command-S to save the changes you've made to your project.

## Managing Timeline Tracks

After editing several clips to your rough cut, the earlier clips in the sequence will begin to move offscreen. Some Timeline management is required to shift the focus to a particular clip or area in the sequence, or to see all the clips in the Timeline window at the same time. Magnifying the tracks is one way to manage how you view your sequence. You can magnify or zoom in to your clips in two ways: horizontally, so the clips appear wider, or vertically, so the clips appear taller. Magnifying tracks does not in any way change the lengths of the clips in the sequence, only their appearance in the Timeline.

1 To zoom in to the **_KW_at board** clip to read its name, move the playhead to that clip and press Option-+ (plus sign). Press it again to zoom in further.

The more you zoom in, the wider the clip becomes. Only the visual representation of the clip is changing, not the clip length or duration.

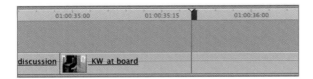

Two Timeline controls—the Zoom control and the Zoom slider—enable you to zoom in to a Timeline area or to slide the sequence left or right. Both are located at the very bottom of the Timeline, beneath the audio tracks.

Zoom control                Zoom slider

2 To see the clips at the beginning of the sequence in this zoomed-in view, drag the Zoom slider to the left. The Zoom slider changes the portion of the sequence that's visible in the Timeline.

**TIP** If you are using a mouse with a scroll ball, you can scroll through the sequence clips by dragging the scroll ball left or right. You can also drag two fingers across a Multi-Touch trackpad to scroll through a sequence.

3 To zoom out to see all the clips in your rough cut, drag the Zoom control to the right to shrink the visual representation of the clips in the sequence. You can also use the keyboard shortcut for zooming out, Option-– (minus sign).

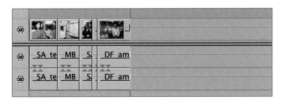

The Zoom control adjusts the horizontal scale of the tracks. Using the keyboard shortcut or Zoom control zooms the sequence in or out around the playhead location.

**TIP** ▶ When using a portable Mac with a Multi-Touch trackpad, you can also zoom using the pinch gestures. Pinch closed to zoom out of the Timeline, and pinch open to zoom in to the Timeline.

4   Move the playhead to the beginning of the second clip, **_MB_behavior board**, and press Option-+ (plus sign) two times to zoom in to that clip. Now drag the Zoom slider to the right to position the fifth clip, **_DF_ambassadors**, in the center of the Timeline. To jump back to the playhead location at the second clip, click the tiny purple line in the Zoom slider scroll bar.

This purple line represents the playhead in the sequence. Clicking it is a convenient way to bounce back to the current playhead location.

5   To see the entire sequence in the Timeline window, press Shift-Z.

In addition to magnifying tracks horizontally, you can also stretch tracks vertically, making them taller in the Timeline.

6   At the bottom of the Timeline, move the pointer over the Track Height control (to the left of the Zoom control). Click different columns to change the height of the tracks.

The taller the track, the larger the clip icon will be. When the track height is at its smallest, the clip icons will not be displayed.

7   Press Shift-T repeatedly to cycle through the height options. Choose the second- or third-tallest height to see a clear thumbnail image.

8   Click the Zoom In tool (the magnifying glass) in the Tool palette, or press the shortcut key, Z. In the Viewer, find the whale's dorsal fin in the **_DF_ambassadors** clip and click it a few times to zoom in to that area.

Sometimes you need to zoom in to the video of a clip to see or understand something in the background, or to add or create effects. And sometimes, perhaps when trying to press Command-Z or Shift-Z, you simply hit the Z key by itself and enlarge the image accidentally. If you see a blue scroller below or to the side of a clip in the Viewer or Canvas, you can resize the image as you did the sequence in the Timeline.

9   In the Viewer, press Shift-Z to see the entire image fit in the window. Notice that the blue scrollers no longer appear. Then press A to return to the default Selection tool.

> **TIP** ▶ You can click the Zoom In tool in the Timeline to zoom in to a clip, or drag a selection rectangle with the Zoom In tool to zoom in to a clip area.

## Making Insert Edits

Regardless of what type of project you're editing—a dramatic film, a documentary, commercials, a music video, or the local soccer game—the beauty of the nonlinear editing process is that you don't have to make all of your editorial decisions in a linear fashion as you did in the previous exercise. In a dramatic project, if you don't have all the footage captured for scene 1, you can start editing scene 2 and insert scene 1 at a later time. In the *Believe* documentary, you can edit together interview clips and later insert clips of whale behaviors.

When you insert a clip into a sequence, all the clips *in all the tracks* following the new clip are moved forward the length of the clip. Inserting a clip lengthens the sequence by the length of the clip.

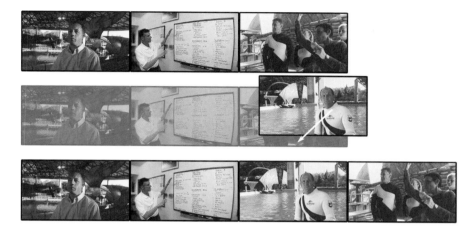

As with overwrite editing, you can use the location of the playhead to determine where a clip will be inserted. To make an insert edit, you use methods similar to those for overwrite editing:

▶  Click the yellow Insert button.

▶  Press the Insert keyboard shortcut, F9.

▶  Choose the Insert option from the Canvas Edit Overlay.

1  From the Interviews bin, open the **_DS_show concept** clip, and play the marked portion.

   This introduction of the *Believe* concept really belongs at the head of the sequence, before the trainers discuss their process.

2  In the Timeline, move the playhead to the beginning of the sequence, where you will insert the new edit.

**3** In the Canvas, click the yellow Insert button.

In the Timeline, the clip is inserted *before* the first clip in the sequence. All the other clips are moved forward to allow room for the new clip. Notice that the playhead is positioned at the first frame of the second clip. This is the correct position to continue inserting clips at that location.

**4** From the Behaviors bin, open the **J thru glass** clip, and play it from the In to the Out point.

Let's discuss where you want the audio of this clip to be placed in the sequence. You will edit the audio and video of this clip as marked at the current playhead location, after the first clip. However, in order to keep similar audio on the same tracks, you will edit the audio from this clip on Timeline tracks A3 and A4.

On the far left of the Timeline is the patch panel, where you control certain aspects of each individual track. All the tracks in the Timeline have a different number, such as V1 for the video track, and A1, A2, A3, and A4 for the audio tracks. These are referred to as *destination tracks*, and the controls with the track numbers are *Destination controls*.

To the left of the Destination controls are the *Source controls,* labeled v1, a1, and a2. The Source controls in the Timeline patch panel represent the video and audio tracks of the source clip in the Viewer. Looking at the Source controls, you know that the current clip in the Viewer has a video track and two audio tracks.

Although the order of the destination tracks is fixed, you can move and connect Source controls, or *patch* them, to any destination track. To edit the **J thru glass** audio tracks onto the A3 and A4 tracks, you have to connect the a1 and a2 Source controls to those tracks.

5   In the Timeline, drag the a1 Source control down to the A3 destination track. Then drag the a2 Source control down to the A4 destination track. Make sure that each Source control is connected to the Destination control, and that there is no break between them.

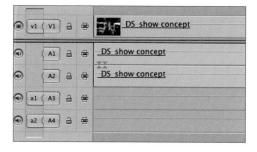

6   To insert the **J thru glass** clip into these tracks at this location, click the yellow Insert button in the Canvas.

The clip is inserted at the playhead location, and the remaining clips in the sequence are moved forward the length of the new clip. The new clip's audio tracks appear on A3 and A4, separating them from the interview clips on A1 and A2. The playhead is at the edit point, ready for the next clip.

7    To insert a whale clip at this location, open the **J hugs whale** clip and press Shift-\ (backslash) to play from the In to the Out. To edit this clip at the Timeline playhead location, press the keyboard shortcut, F9.

With the Source controls still patched to the A3 and A4 tracks, this clip's audio is placed on those tracks. Again, all the clips in the sequence are moved forward the length of the new clip to allow room for it.

8    Let's insert a whale clip after the **_SA_team ideas** clip. Drag the playhead and snap it to the edit point between the **_SA_team ideas** clip and the **_MB_behavior board** clip.

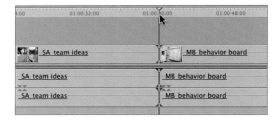

When the playhead snaps to an edit point in the Timeline, the playhead looks thicker, and brown snapping arrows appear around the clip's edit points. The snapping function is helpful when you're inserting clips, because you can be sure you are inserting a clip exactly at the edit point where the two clips meet.

9    From the Behaviors bin, open the **S show open** clip and play the marked portion. Drag the thumbnail of the clip from the Viewer to the Canvas Edit Overlay, but *don't release the mouse button*.

Like the Insert button, the Insert section is yellow, and its icon is an arrow pointing to the right, indicating that all the following clips in the sequence will be moved forward to allow room for the new clip you are editing.

**10** Drag the clip to the yellow Insert section, and when the section becomes highlighted, release the mouse button.

**11** From the Behaviors bin, open the **J pec slaps** clip and play the marked portion. Make sure the playhead is positioned after the **S show open** clip, and insert this clip at that location.

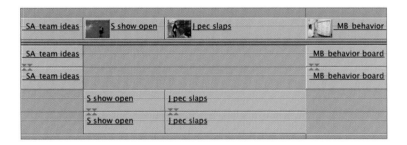

**12** If necessary, press Shift-Z to see the entire sequence. Press Home to go to the head of the sequence and play it. Then press Command-S to save your changes.

> **TIP** Some keyboard shortcuts are window specific. To apply a keyboard shortcut in a particular window, make sure that window is active.

Again, you are *prebuilding* a section of this documentary by placing in a logical order all the clips you want to use. In the following exercises, you will continue adding clips and adjusting their placement.

## Take 2

The producer thanks you for taking the time to play the current rough cut of the interviews. On her way out of the cutting room, she shares her hope of seeing a *montage* of
whale behaviors somewhere in the show. Since you want to please the producer, you
decide to start building that montage.

▶  Open the *Behaviors_v1* sequence and edit some of your favorite behaviors using
both overwrite and insert edits.

▶  When you're finished, click the *Interviews_v1* sequence tab to continue with the exercises.

## Editing Audio Clips

As you build your rough cut, you may find that adding audio—such as narration, music, or
sound effects—improves your sequence. For example, it might be nice to hear narration in
the current rough cut as you see the whale and trainer clips. In this exercise, you will edit
narration tracks, take a closer look at them in the Viewer, adjust their volume, and edit them
into the current sequence.

1   In the Browser, display the contents of the Narration bin. Double-click the **narration_1**
clip to open it in the Viewer. Click between the two Mono tabs.

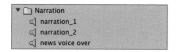

This narration was recorded with a single microphone input into channel 1 on a digital
video camera. Although both audio tracks were captured, only one track (Mono a1) has
sound on it. In the Timeline patch panel, there are two Source controls because there are
still two tracks of audio. You will want to edit just the mic track.

2   Click the Mono (a1) tab and play the clip. Mark an In point just before the narrator
begins speaking. Mark an Out point after the narrator says, "trainers have with the whales."

To navigate the waveform display in the Viewer, you use controls similar to the ones in the Timeline. Drag the Zoom control to zoom in or out, and drag the Zoom slider to move forward or backward in the waveform.

**3**   Move the playhead to the In point and zoom in by dragging the Zoom control to the left.

These controls magnify the waveform display in the Viewer just as they magnified the sequence in the Timeline. When you zoom in to a clip or a sequence as far as possible, the representation of time is expanded. The black bar next to the playhead indicates the width of a single frame.

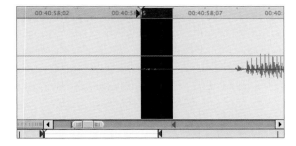

**4**   Press Shift-Z to display the entire audio track and see both edit points. Then play this clip again and look at the audio meters in your interface.

> **TIP**   Depending on the size of your computer screen, the audio meters may appear beneath the Tool palette or to the side. If you don't see the audio meters in your interface, choose Window > Audio Meters, or press Option-4 to open them.

The audio meters display two channels of audio with tiny numbers between them that represent *decibels*. That is the unit of measurement for audio volume. A good rule of thumb is to have the narration average around −12 dB on the audio meters. Depending on the level of the original media file, this may mean raising or lowering the audio level on the clip in the Viewer.

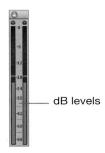

dB levels

Whether audio appears in the left or right audio meter, or both, depends on the number of tracks and how the audio is positioned, or *panned*, within the clip. Typically, stereo audio is distributed between both channels. With this clip, you see volume appear in both audio meters because the sound from track 1 is panned toward the middle between the two channels. Because there is only one recorded track of audio in this clip, let's direct it to one channel.

5   To pan the Mono (a1) audio track to the left, drag the Pan slider to the left, or enter *−1* in the Pan field. Now play the clip again. The volume level for this clip appears only in channel 1.

Above the waveform display is the Level slider and entry field. When you import a new clip, the volume reference is always 0, indicating zero change to the imported audio level. You raise or lower the clip volume according to how you want to use it in the sequence. You will want to hear some audio clips as primary audio, and other clips as background.

6   The goal is to keep the narration level at about −12 dB on the audio meters. Try each of the following options and preview the results until you reach that goal:

▶   Drag the Level slider to the left to lower the volume to −3 dB.

▶   Enter *6* in the Level field and press Return.

▶   Move the pointer over the pink audio level overlay in the waveform area. When it changes to the Resize pointer, drag down to 2 dB.

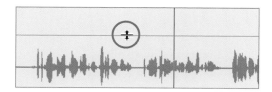

When you drag the Level slider, or enter a volume level, you see the pink audio level overlay move in the waveform display. Likewise, when you drag the audio level overlay, the Level slider moves and a new dB number appears in the Level field.

**NOTE** ▶ Remember, the dB number you see in the Level field represents a change of volume up or down relative to the original sound level of this clip, not to a specific dB on the audio meters.

Now for placement of the audio in the sequence. There are four tracks in the current sequence. A1 and A2 contain sync sound from the interview clips, and A3 and A4 contain sync sound from the whale clips. To keep the narration clips organized in the sequence, you need to create a new track.

7    In the Timeline, Control-click next to the A4 Destination control, and from the short-cut menu, choose Add Track. A new track, A5, is added to the sequence.

8    To patch the source audio in a different way, Control-click the A5 Destination control and choose a1 from the shortcut menu. Then click the a2 control to disconnect it from its Destination control.

> **TIP** ▶  You can either Control-click a Destination control and choose a source track, or Control-click a Source control and choose a destination track.

When a Source control is disconnected, that source track will not be part of the edit.

9    In the Timeline, position, or *snap*, the playhead at the head of the **J thru glass** clip.

Because there is no interview dialogue at this location, the narration can be the pri-mary audio over the whale clip sound.

To edit an audio clip, you can click the Overwrite button or press the keyboard short-cut. Or you can use a special icon to drag it into the Canvas Edit Overlay.

**10**  In the far right of the Viewer's Mono (a1) tab, move your pointer over the icon of a hand on top of a speaker. The pointer changes to a hand called the drag hand.

This is the drag hand. An audio clip has no image to drag, so you use the drag hand to drag the clip.

**11**  Drag the **narration_1** clip from the Viewer to the Overwrite section of the Canvas Edit Overlay.

Now the clip is placed at the playhead location on the targeted track without changing the placement of the edits that follow it.

**12**  Play this section of the sequence.

Although the narration may be a good idea, the whale clip's audio level overpowers it. Ultimately, you will want to lower the volume on all the whale clips to a background, or *mix*, level. For now, you can turn off the sound of the A3 and A4 audio tracks to focus on the narration.

**13**  In the Timeline patch panel, click the green Track Visibility control for the A3 track. Then click the A4 Track Visibility control and play the narration.

Each track has a green Track Visibility control in the Timeline patch panel. When the button is clicked to disable a track, that track turns dark and will not be seen or heard as you play the sequence.

## Take 2

After screening this section of the rough cut, and getting a call from his sister, who recorded the narration, the director asks you to add another narration track to the sequence. Here's your checklist to add the track:

▶   Mark edit points in the **narration_1** clip around the section where the narrator says, "More than anything … as well as to every performance."

▶   Edit the clip in the Timeline on the A5 track under the **S show open** clip. Notice that each narration clip has the same name to indicate that it was edited from the same source, or *master*, clip.

## Moving Clips in the Timeline

After you've edited a clip to the Timeline, you may want to move it within the sequence. For example, to better match the narration to the whale activity, you can move the narration clips earlier or later. You can select and move one clip's position in the sequence or select and move a group of clips on one or more tracks.

At other times, you may want to select a clip during the editing process to delete it, add an effect, view its properties, or make other changes to the clip. Selecting a clip in the Timeline follows the general Apple selection principles: Clicking a clip just once selects it, and clicking away from the clip deselects it.

**1**   In the Timeline, select the first **narration_1** clip by clicking in the middle of the clip. Then press Option-+ (plus sign) to zoom in to this area.

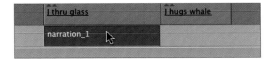

When you click the body, or the middle, of a clip, the clip turns brown to indicate that it is the selected clip; and the zooming occurs around the selected clip, *not* the playhead location.

**MORE INFO** ▶ Other Final Cut Pro functions zoom in to the playhead rather than a selected clip. They are Zoom In on Playhead, Zoom Out on Playhead, and Scroll to Playhead. Those functions have to be mapped to the interface. You will learn to do this in Lesson 7.

2   To deselect this clip, click in the empty Timeline area above or below the tracks. Don't click a track or you will select it.

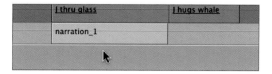

**TIP** ▶ Deselecting clips when you're not moving or changing them is always a good idea, so you don't accidentally change them.

3   Click the same clip again and move the pointer through the clip *without clicking or dragging it.*

The pointer changes to the Move tool. Like the Resize pointer that appears throughout the interface, the Move tool can't be selected from the Tool palette. It appears when a clip or group of clips is selected.

4   Drag the **narration_1** clip to the right, so it's underneath both the whale clips above it, but *don't release the clip.*

Two things happen. A small information box appears that displays a plus sign and a number. This is how far in time you have moved the clip forward from its most recent position. Also, the pointer changes to a down arrow.

**5**    Release the clip. This time drag the clip to the right until its Out point snaps to the Out point of the **J hugs whale** clip. Play this section of the sequence.

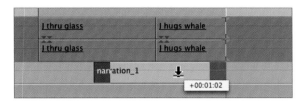

Just as the playhead snaps to edit points in the sequence, so do clip In and Out points snap to each other. When a clip snaps to another clip's In or Out point, brown snapping arrows appear, just as they do when you snap the playhead to the same location.

**TIP** ▶ If the clips are not snapping to each other in the Timeline, make sure the snapping function is turned on in the Timeline button bar.

You can also adjust clip placement by specifying an amount of time.

**6**    With the **narration_1** clip selected, type *−500*, to move the clip to the left 5 seconds and zero frames.

**NOTE** ▶ It may seem strange to just start typing a number without typing it in a specific location, but with the clip selected, Final Cut Pro anticipates what you want to do.

In the center of the Timeline, a Move field appears, displaying the number you typed. As when entering durations, you can skip the zeros and type *−5.* (minus 5 period) to represent 5 seconds earlier in the sequence. To move a clip forward, you simply type the number.

**7**    Press Return to enter this move amount and play the narration clip again.

The selected clip is moved backward 5 seconds. After you get the general placement of the clip, you can *nudge* the selected clip a little left or right to finesse its location. Let's bring the clip back to center without dragging it.

**8**   With the clip still selected, press the left or right angle bracket to center the clip beneath the two behavior clips on the V1 track. Play this section of the sequence to finesse the location. Pressing the angle brackets moves a clip in the following ways:

>   ▶   <   moves the selected clip backward one frame

>   ▶   >   moves the selected clip forward one frame

>   ▶   Shift-<   moves the selected clip backward five frames

>   ▶   Shift->   moves the selected clip forward five frames

> **TIP** ▶ The amount of adjustment when you use the Shift key in this situation can be changed in User Preferences > Editing > Multi-Frame Trim Size (Option-Q). The default is five frames.

**9**   To deselect the clip using the keyboard shortcut, press Command-Shift-A. Press Shift-Z to make the entire sequence fit in the Timeline window.

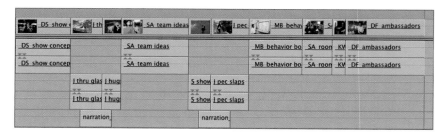

> **TIP** ▶ You can also apply these techniques to move a group of clips or even to move all the clips in the sequence to a location or by a specific amount. As in other Apple applications, you can select the entire contents of a sequence by pressing Command-A.

## Creating a New Rough-Cut Version

The editing process is all about making changes. You've just completed adding narration to the sequence. But you may not be sure that you'll like the narration and whale clips between the interview clips. Before you start deleting clips or making major changes, it's a good idea to duplicate the current version of the sequence and change the new version. This way, if you don't like the new changes, you can go back to the previous version and start again.

Sequence versions often add the version number, or topic, or both to the original name, such as *SeaWorld_v2_Inserts*, or *SeaWorld_v6_SFX*, to indicate if there's been a major change in the sequence from the previous version. Duplicating a sequence makes an exact copy of the edit information. It does not duplicate the source media.

**1**   In the Browser, Control-click the *Interviews_v1* sequence icon and choose Duplicate from the shortcut menu.

A duplicate sequence is created and placed under the original sequence in the Sequences bin in the Browser. The word *Copy* is added to the sequence name.

**2**   To rename this sequence, click in the name area, and type *Interviews_v2_ no narr*. Press Return to accept it. Press Return again to open that sequence in the Timeline.

**TIP** If you're not making a major change to your sequence but just want to back up the current version, you can add a date in the sequence name.

**3**   In the Timeline, click alternately the *Interviews_v1* and *Interviews_v2_no narr* sequence tabs.

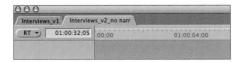

At this point, the two sequences should be identical. The A3 and A4 tracks are dark in each sequence and even the playheads are in the same location.

**4**   To close the *Interviews_v1* sequence, Control-click its tab in the Timeline or Canvas and choose Close Tab.

**NOTE ▶** In Final Cut Pro, you can have multiple projects and sequences open at the same time. Closing them in these lessons is a helpful way to focus on the current exercise steps.

You will continue working in the *Interviews_v2_no narr* sequence. In this sequence, you will delete the narration clips and a few of the whale clips.

5   In the Timeline, click the first **narration_1** clip to select it. To delete this clip, press the Delete key (next to the Plus key.) Delete the second narration clip the same way.

The clips are deleted, or *lifted*, from the sequence. Remember, deleting a clip removes it from the current sequence but does not delete the media file or the original master clip in the Browser.

**TIP ▶** You could select both clips, then delete them at the same time. Another way to delete selected clips is to choose Sequence > Lift.

6   Because there are no longer any narration tracks to compete with in this sequence, click the A3 and A4 Track Visibility controls to make those tracks audible again.

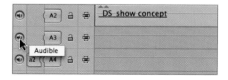

7   To remove the **J hugs whale** clip, click the clip on the V1 track to select it.

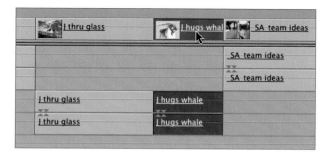

When a clip contains more than one track, such as a video and two audio tracks, selecting one track also selects or highlights the others.

**NOTE ▸** If clicking the V1 track of this clip did not select all the tracks, make sure the Linked Selection function is active (green) in the Timeline button bar. You will work more with linked selection in later lessons.

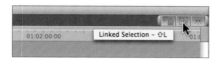

8   To remove all the tracks of this clip from the sequence, press Delete, or choose Sequence > Lift.

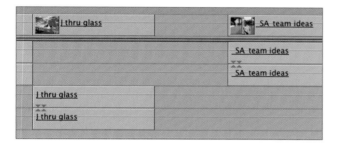

Deleting this clip leaves a gap in the sequence because it was between two other clips. But the gap itself can be deleted.

9   Click the gap between the **J thru glass** and **_SA_team ideas** clips. Press Delete.

Gap selected

Gap deleted

With this action, the remaining clips in the sequence are pulled up, or *rippled*, by the length of the gap. Rather than delete the clip and the gap in two steps, you can delete them at the same time using the *ripple delete* function.

**10** Press Command-Z two times to bring back the selected **J hugs whale** clip. Press Shift-Delete, or choose Sequence > Ripple Delete. Delete the **J thru glass** clip in the same way.

> **TIP** If you are using an extended keyboard, pressing the Forward Delete key will remove the clip and gap at the same time.

The clips are deleted, and the remaining clips in the sequence are pulled up in their place.

> **TIP** To delete a group of clips at one time, such as the whale behaviors, drag a selection rectangle around the clips and press Shift-Delete.

## Using Drag-and-Drop Editing

In the previous exercises, you've used the playhead to target an edit location and then clicked an edit button or dragged a clip to the Canvas Edit Overlay. But we are visual creatures. As you worked with clips in the Timeline, you may have identified a great spot for a new clip simply by eyeballing the target location. No need to go get the playhead, drag it back to where you're focused, and then click a button in a different window to edit the new clip. With drag-and-drop editing, you simply rely on your eyes to target the new location and manually drag a clip directly to where you want it.

As you drag a clip, you can rely on snapping to position the clip immediately adjacent to another one or to make a clean insert edit. Also, when you drag a clip to the Timeline, the position of your pointer in a track will determine the type of edit you make—overwrite or insert.

**1** At the end of the clips in the sequence, move the tip of your pointer up and down over the thin gray raised line of the V1 track.

This line appears as a reference in each Timeline track. Nothing happens now without a clip, but this is the line you will focus on when you drag a clip to the Timeline. Even when clips are on a track, you can see this raised line.

**TIP** ▶ Properly positioning your pointer is the key to drag-and-drop editing.

2   In the upper-right Timeline button bar, find the Snapping button. Click it several times, turning it on and off.

Snapping on          Snapping off

When snapping is turned on, or active, the icon is green and looks concave. When the function is off, the design is gray and appears flatter.

**MORE INFO** ▶ Every window has its own button bar that you can customize with a unique set of buttons representing functions, tools, or commands. You will customize button bars in Lesson 7.

3   Drag the playhead through the sequence and allow it to snap to the edit points. Then press N to turn off snapping, and drag again without snapping. Turn snapping back on for this exercise.

4   From the Believe > Interviews bin in the Browser, open the _SA_favorite behavior clip and play the marked portion. To target this clip's audio to the A1 and A2 tracks, Control-click in the Timeline patch panel and choose Reset Panel.

Even though drag-and-drop editing is a more manual approach to making an edit, you still need to target which tracks will be edited and where.

5   Click in the Viewer image area, and drag the _SA_favorite behavior clip thumbnail to the end of the empty V1 track in the Timeline, clear of any other clips, but *don't release the mouse button.*

Remember, this approach doesn't require that you position the playhead before making an edit.

**TIP** ▶ When dragging a clip from the Viewer, you can always return the clip to the Viewer to pause and rethink your edit before releasing a clip in the Timeline. You can also press Command-Z to undo that action and drag again.

**6** With clip thumbnail in hand, focus on the tip of your pointer, and drag it up and down over the thin gray line in the V1 track just as you did before.

When the tip of the pointer is positioned below the thin gray line, an overwrite edit is indicated with a down arrow and a solid dark box representing the clip's length.

When the tip of the pointer is positioned above the thin gray line, an insert edit is indicated with a right arrow and a hollow box representing the clip's length. In both situations, the thumbnail image remains the same.

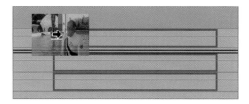

**7** Still holding the clip, position the tip of the pointer *below* the thin gray line so that the overwrite down arrow appears, and release the clip clear of the last clip in the sequence.

Because the pointer tip was below the thin gray line when you released the clip, the clip was edited as an overwrite edit positioned just where you dropped it. Even though the playhead was not used in making this edit, it has repositioned itself after the new clip.

**8**   To snap the **_SA_favorite behavior** clip to the last clip in the sequence, drag it left until you see the brown snapping arrows between the two clips.

The head of the shaded clip box beneath the thumbnail image snaps to the tail of the last clip in the sequence.

You can also add a clip to the sequence and position it in the same move.

**9**   From the Behaviors bin, open the **performance_S spray jump** clip, and play the marked portion. To edit just the video portion of this clip, click the a1 and a2 Source controls to disconnect both of them.

**10** Drag this clip to the Timeline but don't release it until you have followed these steps:

   ▶  Snap the clip to the end of the **_SA_favorite behavior** clip.

   ▶  Position the tip of the pointer below the thin gray line in the V1 track.

   ▶  Make sure you see the overwrite edit's visual clues—the downward-pointing arrow and the solid clip.

   ▶  Now release the clip as an overwrite edit.

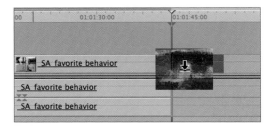

**TIP** ▶ When dragging a clip to the Timeline, always hold on to the clip with your pointer until you have positioned the clip exactly where you want it to go in the sequence and have chosen which type of edit you want to make—overwrite or insert.

You can drop a clip on top of another clip in the sequence, which will overwrite that clip or a portion of it. You can also insert a clip between two other clips.

**11** From the Interviews bin, open the **_DS_show team** clip and play it from the In to the Out.

To continue the explanation about the *Believe* show, let's insert this clip after the first clip in the sequence on the V1, A1, and A2 tracks. If you can't see the edit point between the first two clips, move the playhead to that area and use the Zoom control, the Zoom slider, or zoom shortcuts to zoom in to that edit point. In this situation, you are using the playhead not to place a clip, but to focus the zooming action.

**12** Reconnect or reset the a1 and a2 Source controls to the A1 and A2 destination tracks. Make sure snapping is on.

**13** Drag the **_DS_show team** clip from the Viewer to the Timeline and snap it to the edit point between the first two clips, but *don't release the mouse button*. Position the pointer above the thin gray line, which is indicated by a slight indentation in the clip thumbnail at that location. When you see the right arrow and the hollow clip box, release the clip.

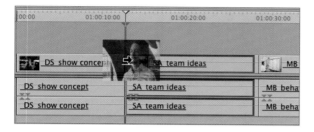

The clip is inserted, and the remaining clips are pushed forward the length of the clip.

**NOTE ▶** You can also insert a clip into the middle of another clip. For example, you might decide to break up the action of a long clip by inserting a different image for a few seconds. The long clip will be split into two parts, and after the new insert, the remaining portion of the original clip will continue to play.

**14**  From the Music bin, open the **Track 8_guitar.aif** clip and play it. To blend this music into the background, lower the volume to about –10 dB by dragging the audio level overlay or the Level slider or by entering *–10* in the Level field.

Let's say you want to keep an organized Timeline as it relates to your audio clips. If this is the first music clip you edit, you may want to consider the track destination for this and all other music clips and possibly add more audio tracks to accommodate the clips. By dragging an audio clip below the lowest existing track (and a video clip above the highest existing track), Final Cut Pro will automatically create the new tracks for you.

**15**  From the Viewer, drag the audio clip to the Timeline beneath the A5 track, but *don't release the clip*. Snap the head of this clip to the head of the sequence, and then release it in the gray nontrack area.

Two new audio tracks are automatically created for you to accommodate the stereo clip you just edited.

▶ Don't forget to save frequently (Command-S) throughout the editing session.

## Changing the Volume of the Edited Clips

After you edit a clip to the Timeline, it becomes part of the sequence and is referred to as a *sequence clip*. At times you will need to change certain aspects of a sequence clip after it's been edited. For example, in the *Interviews_v1* sequence, you had to click the Track Visibility controls for tracks A3 and A4 so that the whale clips' audio wouldn't compete with the interview or narration clips. But it would be nice to hear them all together. You just have to decide which one is the priority and lower the other clips' volume.

1   From the Browser, double-click the *Interviews_v1* sequence to open it in the Timeline. Click the A3 and A4 Track Visibility controls so you can hear those tracks.

    Because you created a new version of this sequence and made changes to that version, your original *Interviews_v1* sequence still has all the narration and whale clips you edited earlier.

2   Play the first few clips in this sequence. To adjust the volume of the **J thru glass** clip, double-click the clip in the Timeline.

    When you double-click a sequence clip in the Timeline, that clip opens in the Viewer so you can play or adjust it by itself. There are two indications that this is not the original source clip from the Browser but is the clip from the sequence. Look at the title bar of the Viewer.

When you open a source clip from the Browser, the name of the clip appears in the Viewer along with the project name. Here the clip name appears along with the name of the sequence it is in.

Now look at the scrubber bar. The two rows of dots, or sprocket holes, that appear throughout the scrubber bar are another indication that this is a sequence clip. It is not the original source clip from the Browser.

Whatever marks or settings you made to the clip prior to editing are exactly the same. In this case, the sound level is 0 dB, because you did not change it prior to editing.

3    In the Stereo tab, lower the volume of this clip to –15 dB. Click the Timeline to make it the active window, and play the area where the **J thru glass** and **narration_1** sequence clips overlap to see if you like the sound mix.

If the clip's audio tracks are a stereo pair, dragging one audio level overlay automatically drags the other to the same level.

4    If the clip is too loud, lower the volume even further. As long as you don't open another clip, the sequence clip in the Viewer can still be actively changed.

**TIP** ▶ If you are using a mouse with a scroll wheel, you can position your pointer over the Level slider and rotate the scroll wheel up or down to change the volume. You can even do this as the clip is playing.

5    In the Timeline, double-click the **J hugs whale** clip. Lower this volume to –15 dB. Play this clip in the Timeline to see if you like the new level.

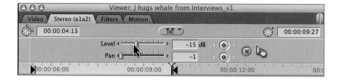

You can also change the audio level of a sequence clip directly in the Timeline.

**6**   In the lower-left corner of the Timeline, click the Clip Overlays control.

A pink audio level overlay appears over the raised line of each audio clip, representing the volume of that clip. This is the same overlay that you adjusted in the Viewer waveform area.

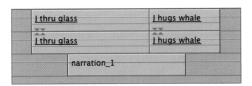

**NOTE** ▶ With clip overlays turned on, black overlay lines appear on the video clips. These lines represent the percentage of video opacity. You will work with these in a later lesson.

**7**   For greater control, let's make the tracks taller. In the lower-left corner of the Timeline, click the tallest column in the Track Height control, or press Shift-T to cycle through to the tallest option.

**8**   In the Timeline, find the **S show open** clip and move the pointer over the pink audio level overlay on the A3 track. When the pointer turns into an Resize pointer, drag down to –15 dB. Adjust the volume as necessary to create a good mix with the narration.

**NOTE** ▶ As you begin to drag the audio level overlay, the Resize pointer will change to the default pointer.

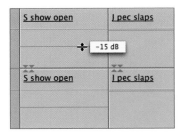

Because this clip has stereo audio, when you drag down one audio level overlay, both overlays of this clip's audio tracks are adjusted to the same level.

9   Adjust the level of the **J pec slaps** clip to a similar mix level and play these clips. Then press Command-S to save your project.

## Editor's Cut

Now that you have an arsenal of tools to edit a sequence, practice making over-write and insert edits using both the automatic and the manual drag-and-drop methods. Follow the steps below to continue adding to your montage of whale behaviors. Remember, you are still building a rough cut. You will learn to refine edit points in the next section.

▶   Open the *Behaviors_v1* sequence in the Timeline and edit clips into that sequence.

▶   To add a music track, import the **Track 12_believe short.aif** clip from the FCP7 Book Files > Media > SeaWorld > Music folder, and edit it at the head of the sequence on the A3 and A4 tracks.

▶   Turn off the Track Visibility controls for the A1 and A2 tracks.

**TIP** ▶ When you insert a clip, it will split all other clips in the Timeline at that location. To keep from splitting the music track, click the Lock Track controls for the A3 and A4 tracks. Diagonal lines appear over locked tracks to indicate that they are locked and cannot be changed.

**MORE INFO** ▶ Although Final Cut Pro editing functions work the same regardless of the footage in use, rehearsing them using different types of footage is a good way to hone your editing chops and gain greater control over the FCP tools, functions, and shortcuts. If you want to apply your new editing skills to other types of footage, open the Editor's Cut project file in the FCP7 Book Files > Lessons > My Projects folder. In that project, you will find the four sets of footage types—documentary, dramatic, music video, and television promo—used throughout this book

## Saving and Quitting

Always save frequently throughout your editing session, whether you've made any edits or not.

**1**   Press Command-S to save the current project.

**2**   Choose File > Close Project if you want to close this project.

If you want to keep working on this project the next time you open Final Cut Pro, you don't have to close the project prior to quitting the program. If you quit with a project open, it will open along with the program the next time you open Final Cut Pro.

**3**   Press Command-Q to quit Final Cut Pro, or continue to the next lesson.

## Lesson Review

1.   How do you create a bin inside another bin?

2.   What are the four methods you can use to create an overwrite or insert edit?

3.   What do you use to drag an audio clip from the Viewer's Audio tab to the Canvas Edit Overlay or to the Timeline?

4.   What are the keyboard shortcuts to zoom in to or out of an area of the Timeline?

5.   How do you change the track heights in the Timeline?

6.   How do you target a track in the Timeline?

7.   What controls in the Timeline patch panel turn off or on the video and sound of individual tracks?

8.   To select a clip in the Timeline, you click it once. Name two ways to deselect it.

9.   How do you change a clip's location in the Timeline?

10.   What are two ways to turn snapping off or on?

11.   When dragging clips from the Viewer to the Timeline, your pointer changes as you position the clip depending on the type of edit you're making. When you're making an overwrite edit, what type of arrow does your pointer change into? What is it for an insert edit?

12.   When you open a clip in the Viewer, what do you see in the Timeline patch panel?

*Answers*

1.   Control-click (or right-click) a bin and choose New Bin from the shortcut menu.

2.   Click an edit button; use a keyboard shortcut; drag a clip from the Viewer to the Canvas Edit Overlay; or drag the clip directly to a track in the Timeline.

3.  The drag hand.

4.  Press Option-+ (plus sign) to zoom in, and press Option-– (minus sign) to zoom out.

5.  In the Timeline display controls, click a track height in the Track Height control, or cycle through the options by pressing Shift-T.

6.  Drag a Source control to the target destination track.

7.  The Track Visibility controls.

8.  Click in the empty gray space above the track, or press Command-Shift-A.

9.  Drag the clip, or select it and enter a move amount.

10. Press N, or click the Snapping button in the Timeline.

11. The down arrow is for an overwrite edit; the right arrow is for an insert edit.

12. The representative source tracks from the clip appear as Source controls in the Timeline patch panel.

## Keyboard Shortcuts

| | |
|---|---|
| **Command-A** | Select all clips in the sequence |
| **Command-Shift-A** | Deselect all clips in the sequence |
| **N** | Turn snapping off and on |
| **Command-N** | Create a new sequence |
| **Command-O** | Open a project |
| **Shift-T** | Switch between track heights in the Timeline |
| **Z** | Select the Zoom In tool |
| **Shift-Z** | Fit the entire sequence in the Timeline window, or fit a clip image in the Viewer or Canvas window |
| **F9** | Make an insert edit |
| **F10** | Make an overwrite edit |
| **Control-click** | Open a shortcut menu |

# 3

| | |
|---|---|
| **Lesson Files** | FCP7 Book Files > Lessons > Lesson 3 Project |
| **Media** | FCP7 Book Files > Media > SeaWorld |
| **Time** | This lesson takes approximately 90 minutes to complete. |
| **Goals** | Set edit points in the Timeline |
| | Add cutaways |
| | Edit narration and music tracks |
| | Backtime clips |
| | Edit sound effects to video clips |
| | Copy and paste clips |
| | Edit using markers |
| | Play a sequence full screen and via iChat |

# Finishing the Rough Cut

With your clips edited into sequences, you're now ready to put the finishing touches on your rough cut. To finish a rough cut, you often edit new clips into a sequence that refer to, relate to, or synchronize with the clips that are already there. This is an important editing technique and one you will use frequently. In order not to disturb other clips already in the sequence, you mark In and Out points around just the portion of the Timeline you want to change or edit.

Marking in the Timeline is done, for example, when you cut video clips to a music track. First, you edit the music into the Timeline, mark where the beats occur, and then edit your video to those beats. Another example involves cutting to narration: You illustrate the narration by cutting to an appropriate image. And when editing an interview or a documentary, you'll frequently juxtapose different shots of the same person talking and then cover the awkwardness of successive talking-head shots by adding video *cutaways*.

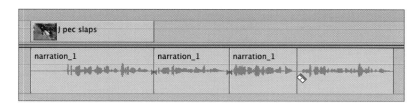

Razor Blade tool cutting narration track into separate clips

Marking in the Timeline follows the same procedures as marking in the Viewer, so you're already in the driver's seat in terms of knowing how it's done. But you will learn additional techniques for Timeline management and functionality in this lesson, such as copying, cutting, pasting, and deleting clips or sections of your sequence; creating new edit points; and adding markers. All these will help you finish your rough cut.

## Preparing the Project

For this lesson, you will open the Lesson 3 Project file, which contains the marked footage and sequences you need for this lesson. Then, you'll duplicate a sequence to create a new version for this project.

**1**   With Final Cut Pro open, choose File > Open, or press Command-O.

**2**   Open the Lesson 3 Project file from the FCP7 Book Files > Lessons folder on your hard disk.

**3**   Close any projects that may be open from a previous session by Control-clicking the project name tab in the Browser and choosing Close Tab from the shortcut menu.

In this project, the individual music and narration clips were combined into one bin named Audio. Notice that the sequence in the Timeline contains only clips that tell the *Believe* story.

**4**   In the Browser, display the contents of the Sequences bin. To create a new version of the *Interviews_v2_no narr* sequence, Control-click it and choose Duplicate from the shortcut menu.

**5**   Name the new sequence *Interviews_v3_cutaways*. Press Return once to accept the name, and once again to open the sequence in the Timeline.

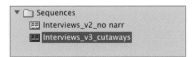

**6**   In the Timeline, close the *Interviews_v2_no narr* sequence.

Image from the *Interviews_v3_cutaways* sequence

## Adding Cutaways

To tell a story in the most concise way, you often have to edit together pieces of one or more *talking head* clips—individuals speaking to the camera—and put them in a logical order. Sometimes you have to edit different pieces from the same clip, or edit two clips of the same person next to each other. For example, in the previous lesson, you edited two clips of David Smith, first talking about the *Believe* concept and then about the *Believe* team. Both clips have *sync sound* of David talking on-camera. Although he tells a good story, it doesn't necessarily look good to cut from one on-camera clip of David to another, especially since he was wearing two different shirts in the clips.

Cutting from a person in one clip to the *same* person in the next clip is referred to as a *jump cut*. (Strictly speaking, jump cuts occur when you cut between slightly different angles of any single subject.) Jump cuts can be jarring to the viewer. The solution is to cover them up by editing a new shot of something else over the edit point. These replacement shots are referred to as *cutaways*. Cutaways can be selected from another area in the same clip or from completely different material. The cutaway source is often referred to as *B-roll* because it's not the primary footage, and no one is talking directly to the camera.

The first step in covering a jump cut is to place In and Out marks in the Timeline where you want the cutaway to cover the "guilty" edit point. Then you choose the source you want to use for the cutaway and set an In point. Using three marks to make an edit is often referred to as three-point editing (see sidebar below). The combination of any three marks will answer the three important questions in making an edit: Where is the clip's *location* in the sequence, what is the clip's *duration*, and what is the source's *content*?

▶ **Three-Point Editing**

*Three-point editing* is the term used to describe editing a clip to the Timeline with any combination of three edit points that determine the duration, location, and content of a clip. When you made edits to the Timeline in the previous lesson, you controlled the edit duration and content by setting In and Out points in the Viewer, and you located the edit by moving the playhead to a specific point in the Timeline. Those three points—Source In, Source Out, and playhead position—determined the duration, location, and content of the edit. That is one example of three-point editing. But you can also use Timeline In and Out points to determine the duration and location of a new edit.

1   In the Timeline, play the first two clips of the *Interviews_v3_cutaways* sequence. Press Option-+ (plus sign) to zoom in to those two clips to enlarge your view of the edit point.

This is the "guilty" edit point, the jump cut that needs covering. To make this edit point smoother, you can position a cutaway directly over the edit point, at the end of the first clip, or at the beginning of the second clip. Let's place a cutaway at the beginning of the second clip.

You follow the same general procedures for marking in the Timeline as you did when marking in the Viewer. You position the playhead where you want to set an edit point and press the shortcut keys, I and O, to set the In and Out points. You can also click the Mark In and Mark Out buttons in the Canvas window to set marks in the Timeline.

2   Snap the playhead to the beginning of the **_DS_show team** clip. In the lower left of the Canvas, you will see the first frame overlay. Press I to set an In point at this location.

An In point appears in the Timeline ruler, in the Canvas scrubber bar, and in the Canvas image area. In the Timeline, all the clips that follow the In point become lighter, or *highlighted*, to indicate they are part of the currently selected area.

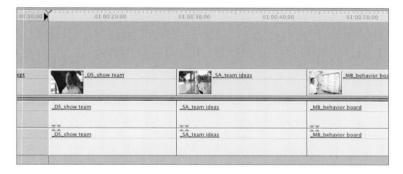

3   Position the playhead at the point where David finishes saying, "overall content of the show would be." In the Canvas, click the Mark Out button to set an Out point at this location. Then look at the Canvas's Timecode Duration field.

The Timecode Duration field shows the duration of the marked portion, not that of the entire sequence.

In the Timeline, only the material that falls within the marked portion appears highlighted. Since there are many things you could do with this marked portion of the sequence—delete it, copy it, replace it, and so on—this color shade difference helps you to see at a glance which portion of the sequence and which specific clips might be affected by your action. In the next step, you won't change the existing clips; you'll just add a new one.

4   From the Believe > Interviews bin, open the **_MM_with trainers** clip. Since you don't want the audio to compete with the interview clip, lower the volume to about *–18 dB* in the Level field, and mark an In point at the head of the clip.

The two marks in the Timeline identify the clip location and duration. All you need is an In point to identify where to begin using the source content. The In point of the source clip will be lined up with the In point in the Timeline, just as it did when you edited to the playhead in the previous lesson. The source content will continue until the Timeline's Out point.

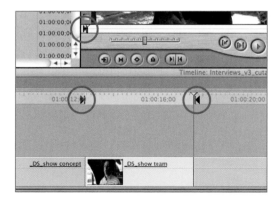

**NOTE ►** If you have In and Out points in both the Viewer source clip and the Timeline, and they represent different durations, the Timeline edit points will always take priority when making automatic edits, and the Out point in the Viewer will be ignored.

Before you edit a cutaway at this location, think about track placement. As you did in the previous lesson, you can target, or patch, the source audio for the natural sound, or *nat sound*, from the secondary clips to the A3 and A4 tracks. For the video, you can organize all the B-roll footage, or cutaways, on the V2 track. This will make the cutaways in the sequence easy to locate. But first you have to add a new video track.

**5**   In the Timeline patch panel, Control-click above the V1 track and choose Add Track from the shortcut menu.

**6**   Patch the v1 Source control to the V2 Destination control. Then patch the a1 and a2 Source controls to the A3 and A4 Destination controls, respectively.

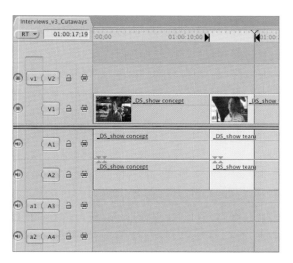

**7**   To edit this clip as an overwrite edit, click the Overwrite button.

> **NOTE** ▶ For this exercise, you must use the automatic methods of making overwrite edits—via the Overwrite button, keyboard shortcut (F10), and Canvas Edit Overlay—because Final Cut Pro ignores Timeline edit points when you drag a clip into a sequence.

The new clip's audio tracks are placed beneath the interview clips, and the video track is placed on the V2 track. The Timeline edit points have been removed, and the playhead is aligned to the first frame after this clip, where you will edit the next cutaway.

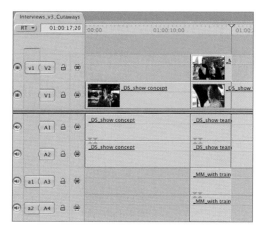

**8** Play the area around the new clip, and focus on the Canvas window to see how the edit looks.

The adjacent placement of the two David Smith clips is not distracting because you *cut away* to a different shot between them. (There is still the problem of the two different shirts, but you will cover the remainder of this clip in the next steps.)

**9** Now play the clip area and focus on the layout of the clips in the Timeline with an eye on what's happening in the Canvas.

When you stack clips on top of each other in a sequence, you get different results for audio and video. All of the audio clips combine into one mix of sound. Stacking video clips is different, however, in that whichever clip is on top wins.

In this sequence, you see the V1 video in the Canvas until the playhead reaches the V2 clip; then the V2 clip takes priority. When the playhead reaches the end of the cutaway on V2, you see the video on the V1 track again.

**TIP** ▸ Placing cutaways on separate tracks gives you the freedom to drag or reposition the clips after you've made the edits.

**10** Experiment with the placement of the **_MM_with trainers** clip by dragging it left over the center of the edit point. Play this clip, then reposition it to its original location at the head of the **_DS_show team** clip.

Remember, you can position a cutaway anywhere over an edit point, as long as it covers the jump cut between the two talking-head clips.

**11** In the Timeline, move the playhead to the first visible frame of the **_DS_show team** clip after the first cutaway and mark an In point for the next cutaway. Move the playhead to the last frame of this clip and mark an Out point.

**TIP** ▸ An easy way to find the Out point of a clip is to press the Up Arrow or Down Arrow key to move the playhead to the following clip's In point, then press the Left Arrow key to move back one frame.

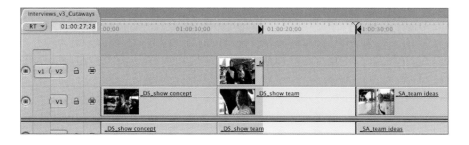

**12** Press Shift-I and then Shift-O to go to the In and Out points you set.

These shortcuts work just as they did in the Viewer. When you mark edit points in the Timeline, you don't need to reposition the playhead, because Timeline marks take priority over the playhead location.

**13** In the Believe > Behaviors bin, open the **S gives pendant** clip. Mark an In point at the beginning of the zoom-out, around 00:22:05:24. Be sure to lower the volume of the clip to allow David's clip in the Timeline to be heard. Try *–20 dB*.

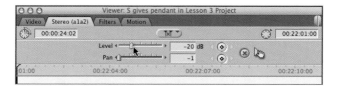

Again, since you have already defined the duration and location for this clip in the Timeline, you only need to indicate where you will begin using the source content.

**14** Edit this clip as an overwrite edit, using one of the automatic editing methods. Play the new clip.

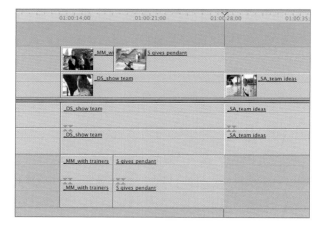

**TIP** In the Timeline, you can also set In and Out points on the fly as the sequence is playing, just as you did in the Viewer.

## Take 2

The director thinks the new cutaways create interest in the sequence and wants you to add a few over Steve's interview clip, **_SA_team ideas**. Editing some cutaways on top of this clip will show *and* tell Steve's story at the same time. Use the marking steps in the previous exercise to mark and edit the following two clips as cutaways over Steve's dialogue. Make sure to adjust the volume as needed.

**TIP** ▶ If a clip opens with marks, press Option-X to remove both the In and Out points at the same time.

▶ **_SA_room discussion** to cover:

"We took those ideas back to the parks, talked about it with the in-house staff."

▶ **_KW_at board** to cover:

"Then we put those sequences, and those ideas…"

**NOTE** ▶ Later in this lesson, you will delete the duplicate clips in the sequence as well as other sections you no longer want.

## Editing to Narration

Narration tracks are used in many film and video genres, including documentaries, news-based shows, reality television, and even dramas. In Lesson 2, you fit two short narration clips beneath the existing whale clips and positioned them to your liking. In many projects, the script or narration track comes first. Then you let it guide you in the selection of appropriate source material, based on what the narrator is saying.

In the next two exercises, you will edit a narration track in the Timeline, then mark portions of it to set the duration and location for each new video clip.

### Preparing the Narration Track

After editing the narration clip, there are a few things you can do to adjust the audio track in the Timeline and make it easier to edit. For example, in the Timeline audio tracks you can turn on audio waveforms, which are similar to those in the Viewer. You can also save a Timeline track layout, as you did a window layout, and recall it for use at a later time.

1    From the Audio bin in the Browser, open the **narration_2** clip and click the Mono (a1) tab in the Viewer to see the audio waveform. Mark an In point where the narrator begins to talk and an Out point where she stops talking at the end of the clip. Then play from the In to the Out.

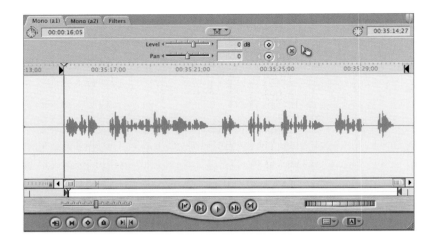

When you look at the audio waveform of this clip, it's easy to see where the narrator starts and stops talking. You could even mark an In and an Out based on the waveform display.

Since you will have just one narration clip in this sequence, you can place it on the A1 track along with the interview clips. If you were working in a sequence with a lot of narration clips, you might want to dedicate a separate track or tracks just for those clips.

**2**  To edit just the Mono (a1) track of this source clip, where the narration is actually recorded, patch the a1 Source control to the A1 Destination control in the Timeline patch panel. Then click the a2 Source control to disconnect it.

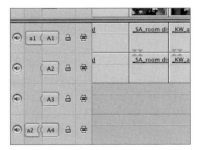

**3**  Drag the playhead to the end of the sequence, or press the End key, and edit the narration clip as an overwrite edit at this location.

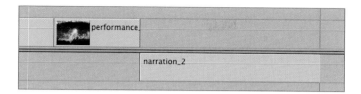

This is another example of a three-point edit. The two edit points in the Viewer identified content and duration, and the Timeline playhead determined location. As long
as you haven't set an In or Out mark in the Timeline, you can use the playhead to
target the edit location.

Since the audio waveforms were such a helpful reference in the Viewer, let's turn them
on in the Timeline audio tracks.

4   In the lower-left corner of the Timeline, click the Track Layout pop-up menu button.

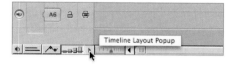

This pop-up menu provides several commands that change the display of your clips
in the Timeline tracks. You can also choose a different track height from the bottom of the menu.

5   From the pop-up menu, choose Show Audio Waveforms.

**TIP**  The keyboard shortcut to turn off and on audio waveforms is Command-
Option-W. The shortcut to turn off and on the pink audio level overlays is Option-W.

The same waveform display that you see in the Viewer appears on the audio tracks in the Timeline; it's just not as large. There are two ways you can enlarge the waveform and the narration clip: make the track height taller, and zoom in to the clip to expand it.

**6**   Position the playhead over the narration clip and press Option-+ (plus sign) a few times until this clip spreads across the Timeline window.

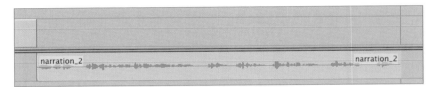

**7**   In the Timeline patch panel, position the pointer over the A1 track's lower boundary line. When you see the Resize pointer appear, drag down to make just the A1 track taller.

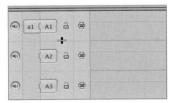      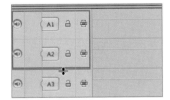

Pointer over A1 boundary line      Pointer dragging A1 boundary line down

Now you can clearly see where the narration stops and starts in this clip.

Each individual track in the Timeline can be adjusted for specific editing needs. You can save this track layout as you did the window layouts. But with the Timeline track layouts, you name the layout and recall it by name.

**8**   In the Timeline, click the Track Layout pop-up menu button again and choose Save Track Layout. In the Save dialog, name this track layout *A1 tall* and click Save.

Final Cut Pro automatically saves this layout in a folder named Track Layouts located in the following path: Users/[user name]/Library/Preferences/Final Cut Pro User Data. When you save other named layouts, such as window or keyboard layouts, they are saved to their respective folders within the Final Cut Pro User Data folder.

**MORE INFO ▶** In Lesson 7, you will learn how to load these layouts and transfer them to other computers.

**9** To recall this track layout at a later time, click the Track Layout pop-up menu button and you will see the saved layout in the middle of the menu.

### Dividing and Marking the Narration Track

To edit video clips to this narration track, you could quite easily play the narration clip and mark an In and an Out at the appropriate times. But you can use other Final Cut Pro tools and shortcuts as well. To continue editing to this narration clip, you will use a special tool to divide the clip after each sentence, making that part of the narration its own clip. Then you will use a different marking function to automatically set In and Out points around that segment of narration.

**NOTE ▶** Make sure snapping is on for this exercise.

**1** In the **narration_2** clip in the Timeline, mark an In at the first frame of this clip and an Out after the narrator says, "between man and killer whale."

Since the video you will edit in this location will be primary video, let's edit it to the V1 track. So as not to compete with the narration, you can edit just the video portion of the source clips for this section.

2   From the Believe > Behaviors bin, open the **J pec slaps** clip. Mark an In point where Julie starts to jump up and down, at around 00:06:45:15 (after the camera has panned past the other trainer).

3   Patch the v1 Source control to the V1 track and disconnect the a1 Source control. Edit just the video portion of this clip as an overwrite edit to the V1 track.

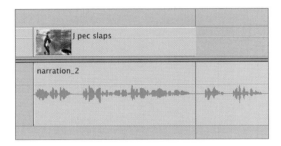

4   In the Tool palette, click the Razor Blade tool, or press B.

5   Move the Razor Blade tool to the A1 track, and snap it to the playhead location at the end of the **J pec slaps** clip. Click to create a new edit point in the audio track at this location.

*Through edit indicators* (red triangles) appear at the edit point. These tell you that, although there are two separate clips now, the source material continues *through* this edit point as it did in the original clip.

6   To create a new edit point at the end of the next sentence, play the clip and stop after the narrator says, "two different species." Drag the Razor Blade tool through the A1 track, snap it to the playhead at this location, and click.

Notice that every time you divide the clip, the name **narration_2** appears on the new clip.

With the clip divided around this sentence, you can delete this portion of the clip, copy it, move it, and also mark it.

7   Move the playhead over this segment of the **narration_2** clip, between the through edit indicators. In the Canvas window, click the Mark Clip button, or press X.

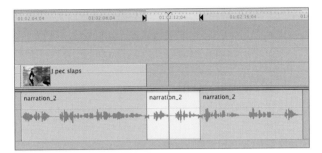

Pressing X at the playhead location places In and Out points at the first and last frames of the clip that the Timeline playhead is over. If you had not divided this clip, the entire length of the narration clip would have been marked.

**NOTE ▶** Even though the Razor Blade tool is selected, when you move the pointer into the Timeline ruler, the Selection tool reappears so that you can perform other functions such as playing or marking the clip.

8   From the Believe > Behaviors bin, open the **J hugs whale** clip and press Option-X to remove any marks. Then mark an In point 4 seconds in from the head of the clip, at 00:00:04:00. Edit this clip as an overwrite edit onto the V1 track and play the clip.

9   In the Timeline, use the Razor Blade tool to add one more edit point after the narrator says, "trying to bridge the gap between them." Move the playhead over this segment and press X to mark this clip. Press A to return to the default Selection tool.

**TIP** You can also create new edit points at the playhead location by choosing Sequence > Add Edit. Using this command's shortcut, Control-V, you can create edit points on the fly as a clip is playing.

To edit the next video clip, you will select the source content by where the clip ends instead of where it begins. To do this, you will set just an Out point on the source clip in the Viewer. Without an In point, the source's Out point will align to the Timeline's Out point. The source's In point will be determined by *backtiming* the clip, or filling in the distance back to the Timeline's In point. This is referred to as backtiming because Final Cut Pro starts from the end of the clip and measures the duration backward to determine where the clip begins.

**10**  Open the **L hugging whale** clip and find the point where Leslie is onstage with her arms around the whale. Mark an Out point just after she kisses the whale. Edit this clip and play it in the sequence.

Now the clip leads up to and stops just after Leslie kisses the whale, where you marked the Out point.

**11**  Use the Mark Clip function to mark the last segment of narration.

**12**  Open the **S show open** clip and press Option-X to remove any marks. To backtime this clip, mark an Out where Steve has his hand in the air, before he makes a fist. Edit this clip as an overwrite edit. Play this section of the Timeline to view your progress.

**TIP** ▶ When backtiming clips, make sure there is no In point in the Viewer. Otherwise, the clip's In point will line up with the Timeline's In point instead of lining up Out point to Out point. If you need to remove just the In point in the Viewer, press Option-I.

## Editing to Music

Marking a music track is a little different from marking a narration track. With narration, you refer to a script or wait for the end of a sentence or another verbal cue to set your marks. With music, you respond aurally to the rhythm of the beats and can usually anticipate when the next beat or musical phrase will occur. Final Cut Pro offers another way to mark a clip that is well suited to this situation, and that is to add *markers* as reference points in a clip or sequence. Instead of setting a single In or Out point, you create multiple markers in a clip or in an area of the Timeline.

Markers have a million great uses. You can think of them as sticky notes that remind you where you want to set an edit point, where the beats of music occur, where scene 3 begins, or simply where in the Timeline you stopped editing for the day. They can even be converted to edit points if you want to edit at that location, which is how you will use them in this exercise.

1   From the Audio bin, open the **Track 12_believe finale.aif** clip and play it in the Viewer. Using the audio meters as a reference, adjust the volume so that it averages around –12 dB. You may have to lower the music volume to about –10 to –12 dB. You will use this clip in its entirety.

This is the finale to the *Believe* performance. You will cut underwater shots of whales and trainers to this music. When you have more than one music clip in a sequence, you typically want to place them on their own tracks, say, A5 and A6. In this situation, because this is the only music clip in the sequence, you can place it on the A1 and A2 tracks to make it easier to view as you edit.

2   In the Timeline, use the Zoom slider, or a scroll ball on a two-button mouse, to scroll the sequence clips to the left. You want to see the end of the narration clips and plenty of empty Timeline space for your new edits. In the Timeline Track Height control, click the second height.

> **TIP** ▶ To reduce or enlarge all current customized track heights, press Shift-T to cycle through track height options. To conform all the tracks to a preset height, click one of the Track Height control options.

3   With the playhead at the end of the last narration clip, make sure the a1 and a2 Source controls are connected to the A1 and A2 Destination controls, and edit this music track as an overwrite edit.

> **NOTE** ▶ You will listen to the music to hear where you want to edit the video, so you won't need the audio waveforms turned on as a reference in the Timeline audio tracks. Press Command-Option-W to turn off the audio waveforms.

4   Position the playhead at the head of the music clip and press M.

Marker under playhead            Marker by itself in ruler area

In the Timeline ruler, a red marker appears at the playhead location. In the Canvas, a marker appears in the scrubber bar, and a default marker name appears as an overlay in the image area.

When editing music, setting markers on beats or phrases of music can be helpful and will allow you to apply other Final Cut Pro functions.

5  With the playhead on the marker, press M again to open the Edit Marker dialog. In the Name field, type *clip 1*, to indicate where the first clip will be edited over the music track. If you want to specify a particular color for the marker, click that color. Take a look at the other options, then click OK to close the dialog.

**TIP** ▸ You can also Command–double-click a marker to open the Edit Marker window.

In the Edit Marker dialog you can name the marker and include a comment, set a marker at a specific timecode location, create a duration for a marker, choose a marker color, and delete a marker. You can also add other types of markers here—

such as scoring markers for use with Apple's Soundtrack Pro application—and you can add compression and chapter markers if your Final Cut Pro sequence will be used in a DVD Studio Pro project. You will work with markers throughout this book.

**TIP** Using different marker colors, you can categorize your markers to see their purpose at a glance. You can use red markers for music cues, blue markers for audio changes, purple markers for special effects, yellow markers for director's notes, and so on.

6   To add a marker at the next strong musical downbeat, play the **Track 12_believe finale.aif** clip and stop when the singer sings "[be]–LIEVE" again. It's about 8 seconds from the first marker. Press M once to set a new marker. Then press M again and name this marker *clip 2*. Click OK.

**TIP** To delete a marker, move the playhead to the marker, and press Command-` (grave accent). If you want to reposition a marker you've already created, Command-drag the marker to a new location. Choose Mark > Markers to find other marker shortcuts.

With snapping on, you can snap the playhead to a marker. Make sure snapping is on for the following steps.

7   In the Timeline, drag the playhead over the second marker and notice the brown arrow that appears when the playhead snaps to the marker.

You can also add markers on the fly as you're playing a music track.

8   From the *clip 2* marker, play the music track and, as the music is playing, press M on the strong downbeat when you hear "[be]–LIEVE" again. Press M at the final "[be]–LIEVE" refrain, and once again at the end of the clip.

Now that markers are set for each music beat, you can use those markers to create In and Out points for new video clips.

**9**   Move the playhead between the first two markers, and choose Mark > Mark to Markers, or press Control-A.

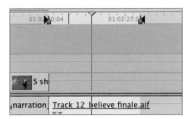

In the Timeline, an In point is placed on the first marker before the playhead, and an Out point is placed on the first marker after the playhead. Rather than marking an entire clip, you are marking the area between these two markers. With these two marks in the Timeline, you need only one mark in the Viewer to choose source content that will cover this portion of the music.

**10**   In the Browser, display the contents of the Believe > Underwater bin. Open the **uw_ push two trainers** clip. You will use this clip from the head, so you don't have to set an In point. Edit just the video from this clip as an overwrite edit to the V1 track, and play the clip.

> **NOTE ▶** Don't forget to disconnect the audio Source controls to edit just the video.

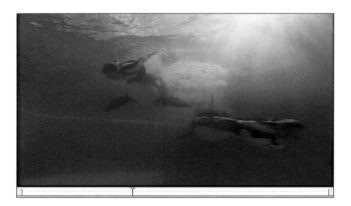

This clip is edited between the two markers, which represent one musical phrase or series of beats on the music clip. As in other edits, after you've edited the clip into the Timeline, the In and Out marks are removed.

**TIP** ▶ To undo an edit, perhaps to choose different source content, you can always press Command-Z, which returns you to the edit setup prior to the edit.

**11** Continue to use the Mark to Markers function outlined in step 9 to set edit points for one section of music at a time. Then edit the following three clips in this order:

▶ **uw_propel jump**—Mark when the dorsal fin is in view.

▶ **uw_rotations**—Set an In point at the head of the clip.

▶ **uw_mom and calf jump**—Set an Out point at the splash to backtime this clip.

**TIP** ▶ To go to a marker, you can Control-click in the Timeline ruler and choose a marker from the shortcut menu; press Shift-M to move forward to the next marker or Option-M to move backward to the previous marker; or press Shift with the Up Arrow or Down Arrow key to move backward or forward to a marker.

## Copying, Cutting, Pasting, and Positioning

When you edit a text document, you do a lot of copying, cutting, and pasting to get the order of words just right. In Final Cut Pro, you can copy, cut, and paste clips or portions of your sequence in the same way. To finish your rough cut, you may need to copy a sound effect to double its duration, or you may want to reuse a beauty shot of a whale jump in your opening. And just as Michelangelo carved his *David* out of a raw block of marble, you may decide to knuckle down and chisel the excess from your own masterpiece.

For some of these changes, you set In and Out points in the Timeline to mark and delete extraneous sections. There are other ways to condense a sequence, such as placing clips on top of others, similar to the cutaways you edited earlier in this lesson. There are also special Final Cut Pro shortcuts for cutting and pasting. Before you begin hacking away, you will create a new version of the current sequence.

**NOTE** ▶ If you are editing a broadcast program, the show's timing is critical. Longer-format programs, such as documentaries and films, tend to have more leeway, but you still need to keep an eye on moving the story forward.

**1** In the Sequences bin in the Browser, Control-click the *Interviews_v3_ cutaways* sequence and choose Duplicate from the shortcut menu. Name the sequence *Interviews_v4_cuts*. Open this sequence in the Timeline.

**2**   You will be cutting sections out of this sequence, so take note of the current sequence duration in the Canvas's Timecode Duration field.

Depending on how you marked your clips, your sequence duration may be shorter or longer than the duration in the image above.

**3**   Press Shift-Z to see the entire sequence. Then move the playhead to the head of the **_SA_favorite behavior** clip and play it along with the clip that follows it.

It would make more sense to see Steve jump over the sprayers as he's talking about the experience. But instead of going to the Browser and opening the source clip into the Viewer, then marking and reediting this clip, you can simply drag the jumping clip in the Timeline up to the V2 track and place it over Steve's clip on the V1 track.

**4**   Move the playhead in the **_SA_favorite behavior** clip to just after the point where Steve says, "zoom to the bottom of the pool." Drag the **performance_S spray jump** clip up to the V2 track, and then drag left to snap the head of the clip to the playhead. Play these clips to see how they work together.

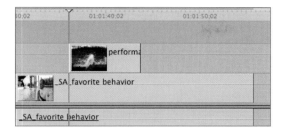

Now you see Steve jumping over the sprayers as you hear him talking about it. The **Applause FX 05.aif** clip was not linked to the clip of Steve jumping, so it did not move along with it.

**TIP** ▶ When locating a video action is the priority, you can drag one clip over another clip in the V1 track. This produces a two-up display in the Canvas window where, on the left, you see the frame preceding the clip you're dragging, and on the right, see the frame following the clip. Once you find the best location, drag the clip to that place in the V2 track.

5   Drag the **Applause FX 05.aif** clip left on its track and snap it to the head of the **performance_S spray jump** clip.

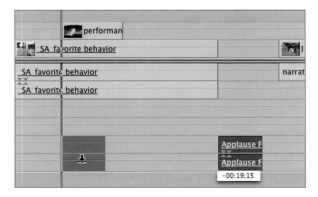

When you begin to mix these audio tracks together, this sound effect may be nice, but it doesn't cover the entire length of the performance clip. Let's copy the effect.

**6**   Select the **Applause FX 05.aif** clip and press Command-C to copy it. Position the playhead at the end of the first applause clip, and press Command-V to paste it at this location. Then deselect the second **Applause FX 05.aif** clip.

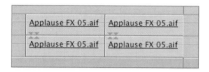

The same copy and paste shortcuts you've used in other applications—Command-C to copy, Command-X to cut, and Command-V to paste—also work in Final Cut Pro on the selected clip or group of clips.

**TIP**   You can also choose these options from the Edit menu, or by Control-clicking a selected clip and choosing Cut, Copy, or Paste from the shortcut menu.

However, even though dragging the clip of Steve jumping over the sprayers to the V2 track helped the story, it left a gap.

**7**   Play the second half of the **_SA_favorite behavior** clip. To delete this somewhat redundant section, and the empty space that follows this clip, mark an In point after Steve says, "That's just plain fun." Mark an Out point on the last frame of the gap before the **J pec slaps** clip. Choose Sequence > Ripple Delete, or press Shift-Delete.

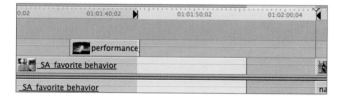

This removes the marked section of the sequence on all highlighted or selected tracks and pulls up the remaining clips in its place.

**TIP**   You can also press the Forward Delete key on an expanded keyboard to perform a ripple delete.

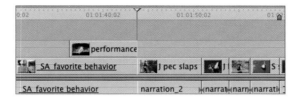

8   Play the **_SA_favorite behavior** clip again. Let's bring Steve back on-camera at the end of this clip saying, "That's just plain fun." Mark an In point just after he says, "come down with the whale," and an Out point on the last frame of this clip. If you haven't already done so, zoom in to this section of clips.

In the Timeline, all the tracks between the two edit points are lighter, indicating they will be involved in the next action.

9   Press Delete.

All the clips on all the highlighted or selected tracks between the two edit points are deleted. This isn't what you want. You actually want to delete only what's on the V2 track.

However, you can't use the Source controls to designate which tracks you want to delete or protect. The Source control is used only to edit a source clip from the Viewer *into* a specific Timeline track. Once a clip is already in the Timeline, you have to use a different track control, the Auto Select control, to make an internal change on a specific track.

10  Press Command-Z to undo the last action. In the Timeline patch panel, turn off the Auto Select controls for all the tracks you don't want to delete (V1, A1, A2, A5, and A6).

Now look at the area between the marks. Only the V2 clip is lighter, or selected, indicating it is the only track that will be affected by the next action.

**11** Press Delete, and turn on the Auto Select controls for all the tracks. Then play this section of clips. Now you see Steve on the V1 track say, "That's just plain fun."

You can use the Auto Select controls anytime you want to involve individual Timeline tracks in a specific internal action, such as deleting, copying, and pasting within the Timeline.

**TIP** Even though you turn off these controls for specific functions, it's a good idea to keep them turned on for all tracks until you need to use them again to control the track selection. To turn off or on all video or audio tracks but one, Option-click that track's Auto Select control.

In playing this section of clips, you may find that the first line of the narration, along with the video of Julie slapping the whale's flipper, could be a nice introduction if it were repositioned to the head of this sequence. To cut these clips and reposition them, you will use two variations on the cut and paste commands: ripple cut and paste insert.

**12** Press Shift-Z to see the entire sequence. Click the **J pec slaps** clip and Command-click the first **narration_2** clip to add it to the selection. To cut these clips and pull up the remaining clips, press Shift-X.

The ripple cut command (Shift-X), like the cut command (Command-X), doesn't delete the selected clips. It places them on the Mac Clipboard so that you can paste them in the next step. If you had used Command-X to cut the clips, it would have cut the clip but left a gap.

There are two options to pasting cut or copied material. One is to paste the clips at the playhead location using Command-V, which overwrites whatever material may be there. The other is to insert the clips using the paste insert command.

**13** Position the playhead at the head of the sequence. Choose Edit > Paste Insert, or press Shift-V, to insert this clip before the **_DS_show concept** clip.

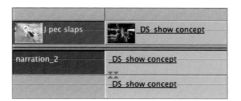

The paste insert command pastes copied or cut material as an insert type of edit. Command-V pastes clips as an overwrite edit.

## Take 2

The director is concerned about the length of the sequence and is hoping you can trim it down to 2:00:00. So get out your scissors and start cutting! Remember, to delete material, you can select a clip, or mark a portion of the sequence, and press Shift-Delete. Think of this as a rough form of trimming. You will learn other trimming techniques in the next lesson, but for now, hack away.

**TIP** ▶ If you have a clip selected in the Timeline and delete it, the selected clip will be deleted, not what's between the In and Out marks. Selected clips override In and Out marks.

## Screening and Sharing a Sequence

At this stage of the editing process, other members of the production team typically need to view and provide input on the rough cut. The question is, what's the best way to share the sequence with them? If they're down the hall, they can watch the sequence on your display screen. But what if they're across the country or around the world? Final Cut Pro makes sharing a sequence as easy as hooking up with a buddy on iChat! In Lesson 14, you will learn much more about sharing and exporting files. For now, let's begin with the folks down the hall.

1   In the Timeline, move the playhead to the head of the sequence. Then choose View >
    Video Playback > Digital Cinema Desktop Preview – Main. To initiate the preview,
    press Command-F12.

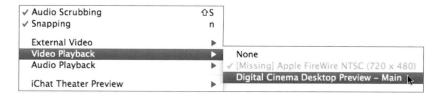

    Choosing this option allows you to use your entire display screen to preview a
    sequence in the Timeline or Canvas, or even a clip in the Viewer.

2   To play the sequence, press the spacebar or the JKL keys. You can also use your other
    navigation keys. To come out of the full-screen preview, press Esc.

    **NOTE ▸** When Digital Cinema Desktop Preview – Main is chosen in the View menu,
    you only need to press Command-F12 to reenter the full-screen preview.

    Once team members have screened the sequence, they may want to replay it and write
    down the timecode locations where changes need to be made. However, viewing the
    Current Timecode field when you're not sitting directly in front of the display can be
    difficult. The alternative is to open the Timecode Viewer.

3   Choose Tools > Timecode Viewer, or press Control-T.

    The opaque Timecode Viewer opens. You can size and position it anywhere on your
    screen. The Timecode Viewer always reflects the active source. For example, it will dis-
    play source timecode when the Viewer window is active, and sequence timecode when
    the Canvas or Timeline window is active.

    Now let's deal with the team members across the country or around the world. They
    want to see the sequence *now*. No time to create a digital file of the movie and post it
    to the web or the server. Instead, you can simply play it via iChat.

**NOTE** ▶ To share your sequence using iChat, you and your team members must have the iChat application on your computers and be logged in when you call.

**4** Open iChat, and invite a team member into a chat. Once the two of you are connected in the iChat window, return to Final Cut Pro.

**5** Arrange the windows so that you can see your video chat window and the Final Cut Pro Timeline.

**TIP** ▶ For these steps, you can click the close button in the Viewer window and position the iChat window in its place. This will allow you to see both iChat and Final Cut Pro at the same time.

**6** In Final Cut Pro, position the playhead at the head of the current sequence in the Timeline or a clip in the Viewer, and choose View > iChat Theater Preview > Start Sharing.

When you initiate iChat sharing, you will see the output of your Timeline in the small iChat inset window. Your buddy on the receiving end will see the sequence in the full window, and can expand that window to full screen.

**7** Play the sequence in the Timeline.

As you play and navigate the sequence, your colleague sees and hears the results. Your colleague can also hear you talk about the sequence as it plays. You can navigate the sequence using the same shortcuts as you did in the full-screen preview steps above.

8    When you are finished playing the sequence, and want to return to the default iChat configuration, in Final Cut Pro choose View > iChat Theater Preview > Stop Sharing. You will see your image return to the video chat window.

> **TIP** ▶ You can also choose View > iChat Theater Preview > Show Timecode to output a visual timecode of the sequence or clip you're playing.

### Editor's Cut

It's not your day off, but the director has left the building. All week long you've wanted to edit a *Believe* music video, with specific whale behaviors set to beats of music or narration. Now that you know how to mark music beats, split a narration track, convert markers to edit points, and backtime clips, you're ready to create your own masterpiece.

▶  Create a new sequence and name it *Believe Music Video*.

▶  Edit one video clip to V1 to change the sequence settings.

▶  Edit **Track 12_believe short.aif** to the A1 and A2 tracks.

▶  Edit video-only behavior clips to the V1 track.

**MORE INFO** ▶ In the next section of the book, you will work with a different set of footage from TNT's hit dramatic show, *Leverage*. Since your focus will be on fine-tuning a sequence, the *Leverage* sequences will already be edited for you. If you want to familiarize yourself with this footage, or even try your hand at cutting this scene, you can open the Lesson 4 Project file, create a new sequence, and work with the set of clips in that project.

## Lesson Review

1.  What are the keyboard shortcuts for setting In and Out points in the Timeline?

2.  What are two ways for marking the duration of a clip in the Timeline?

3.  What does the Auto Select control in the Timeline patch panel determine?

4.  When you mark an area of the Timeline and press Delete, will you leave a gap?

5.  What happens to the marked area of the Timeline when you press Shift-Delete or the Forward Delete key?

6.  In what menu do the lift and ripple delete appear?

7.  What mark is necessary in the Viewer when backtiming a source clip into a marked area in the Timeline?

8.  How do you patch Source controls to Timeline tracks?

9.  Which video track will you see when there is more than one video clip at the same location in the Timeline?

10. What is a three-point edit?

11. What marks are left behind after cutting with the Razor Blade tool?

12. What key do you press to add a marker at the playhead location?

13. How do you create In and Out points from Timeline markers?

14. In what menu can you find the Digital Cinema Desktop Preview?

15. With what Apple application can you screen your sequence long-distance in real time?

### *Answers*

1.  Press I to set an In point; press O to set an Out point.

2.  Position the playhead over the clip in the Timeline and press X to mark the duration of that clip. You can also click the Mark Clip button in the Canvas.

3.  If the Auto Select control is turned on for a track, the clips between the edit points on that track will be highlighted and included in the next action.

4.  Yes, pressing Delete alone leaves a gap where the material was edited. This type of delete is referred to as a *lift*.

5.  Pressing Shift-Delete or Forward Delete removes both clip and gap within the marked area. This type of delete is referred to as a *ripple delete*.

6.  The lift and ripple delete appear in the Sequence menu.

7.  You should have no In point and only an Out point in the Viewer to backtime the clip into the Timeline edit points.

8.  Drag a Source control to the desired Destination control, or Control-click either the Source or the Destination control and choose the appropriate option from the short-cut menu.

9.  You see the clip in the uppermost video track.

10. Using just three edit points to determine location, duration, and content.

11. Red through edit indicators.

12. The M key. Press M again to open the Edit Marker dialog.

13. Choose Mark > Mark to Markers, or press the shortcut, Control-A.

14. In the View menu.

15. iChat.

## Keyboard Shortcuts

| | |
|---|---|
| **Control-A** | Set In and Out points at marker locations on either side of the playhead |
| **B** | Select the Razor Blade tool |
| **M** | Set a marker in the Timeline ruler |
| **M** | When on a marker, open the Edit Marker dialog |
| **Shift-M** | Move playhead to the next marker |
| **Option-M** | Move playhead to the previous marker |
| **Control-T** | Open the Timecode Viewer |
| **Shift-V** | Paste cut or copied material as an insert |
| **X** | Mark the full length of a clip |
| **Shift-X** | Cut a marked selection and remove the gap |
| **Option-W** | Toggle clip overlays |
| **Command-Option-W** | Toggle audio clip waveform displays in the Timeline |
| **Delete** | Lift an item or section from the Timeline and leave a gap |
| **Shift-Delete (or Forward Delete)** | Remove an item or section from the Timeline and ripple the following edits up the duration of the gap |
| **Shift–Down Arrow** | Move playhead to the next marker |
| **Shift–Up Arrow** | Move playhead to the previous marker |
| **Command-` (grave)** | Delete marker at current playhead location |
| **Shift-` (grave)** | Relocate the marker forward to the playhead location |
| **Command–double-click** | Open a marker's Edit Marker dialog |

# Refining the Rough Cut

# 4

| | |
|---|---|
| Lesson Files | FCP7 Book Files > Lessons > Lesson 4 Project |
| Media | FCP7 Book Files > Media > Leverage; SeaWorld |
| Time | This lesson takes approximately 60 minutes to complete. |
| Goals | Understand trimming |
| | Trim using the Ripple tool |
| | Trim clips in the Viewer |
| | Trim an edit point by dragging |
| | Trim clips in the V2 track |
| | Extend an edit point |
| | Trim one track of a linked clip |

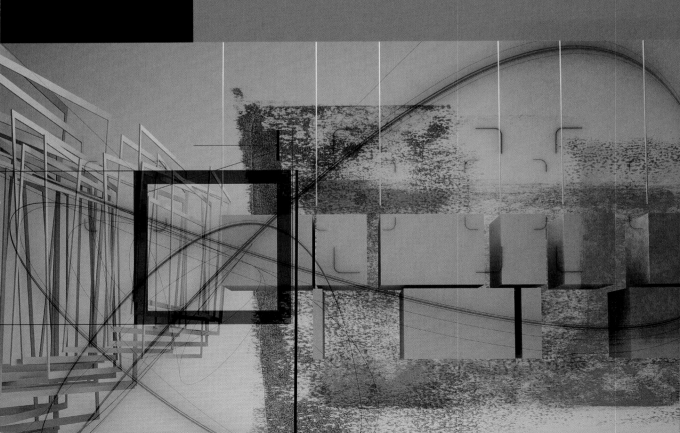

## Lesson 4
# Trimming Clip Duration

After you've built a rough cut, as you've done in the past few lessons, you will want to turn your attention to refining your sequences. In the next three lessons, you'll pursue three goals that will help you refine your rough cut and your Final Cut Pro editing skills. Your first goal, which you will tackle in this lesson, is to fine-tune the length of a single clip, to make it shorter or longer, bringing the sequence to an appropriate length. This is called *trimming*.

Ripple tool trimming a sequence clip in the Viewer's scrubber bar

The second goal is to trim clips based on how they work in conjunction with each other in a sequence. You can think of this as adjusting or refining the timing of your edit points—perhaps hitting a beat of music, changing the clip content, or refining a narration cue. For learning purposes, we will focus separately on trimming an individual clip and trimming two or more clips, although in an actual edit session, these techniques are often used in combination. You will learn additional trimming techniques and tools in Lesson 5.

Once you've mastered the basic trimming methods, you'll want to move on to the third goal: making your workflow more efficient. In Lesson 6, you'll learn when and how to use a new type of edit, and how to work with multiple-camera footage, as well as other Final Cut Pro features and techniques.

## Preparing a Project for Trimming

Since your focus in this lesson is on trimming clips already in a sequence, the exercises will involve sequences that have been cut together but that still have some rough edges, as any rough cut would. The footage you will work with is from the TNT television series *Leverage*. This is a scripted drama in which the actors follow a script, as opposed to a documentary or a news story of real people, places, or events. Since audio is such an important part of editing dramatic footage, you will change how you view the audio in the sequence.

1   Open Final Cut Pro, and choose File > Open, or press Command-O. Open the Lesson 4 Project file from the Lessons folder on your hard disk.

> **TIP** ▶ For the purposes of these lessons, always close any other projects that may be open from previous sessions by Control-clicking their name tabs in the Browser and choosing Close Tab from the shortcut menu. That way, your screen will more closely resemble the images in this book.

2   In the Browser, double-click the **Leverage_Sc33** clip to open it in the Viewer. To screen the clip on the Digital Cinema Desktop Preview display, press Command-F12.

This is a completed scene in the *Leverage* episode "The Second David." To practice trimming methods, you will work with an unfinished, or rougher, version of a portion of this scene.

▶ **About the *Leverage* Footage**

The TNT television series *Leverage* is a modern-day Robin Hood story about five high-tech thieves who leverage their skills in complex heists, helping average people fight those in power. Unfortunately, their previous job blew up their office building, so the team members split up for a three-month break. After realizing they work better together than apart, they reunite in "The Second David" episode to pull off the heist of their lives. The team includes actors Timothy Hutton (Nathan, or Nate), Gina Bellman (Sophie), Christian Kane (Eliot), Beth Riesgraf (Parker), and Aldis Hodge (Alec).

*Leverage* is shot with a RED ONE camera. The footage is ingested via Final CutPro's Log and Transfer function and the files are transcoded to Apple's ProRes 422 (Proxy) format. The sequences are edited in ProRes Proxy at a 1920 x 1080 resolution. The final locked sequence is reconnected to the native RED CODE files and color corrected using Final Cut Studio's Color application. The sequence is then rendered and returned to Final Cut Pro. A digital file is delivered directly to TNT which makes the production of this series a tapeless, all-digital workflow.

3   When you finish viewing the scene in full-screen mode, press Esc to return to the FCP interface. Now play the *Leverage_v1 rough* sequence in the Timeline. To view the larger Canvas layout, press Option-U.

> **TIP** ▶ If you no longer have the customized large Canvas window layout, you can resize the interface windows and refer to Lesson 1 for directions on how to save it.

All the clips in this rough cut are in the right order but need to be trimmed so that they're lengthened or shortened according to the scripted dialogue. For some clips, you may need to remove an unwanted or duplicated line. For others, you may need to extend the clip to allow a line to be completed.

Notice the blue and red markers that were placed for you in the Timeline ruler. The blue markers indicate where you need to trim a clip, and the red markers indicate where cutaways will be added later to cover jump cuts in the video.

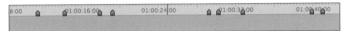

4   Drag the playhead to the first marker at the head of the sequence, and notice its name in the Canvas window. To move the playhead forward to the next marker, press Shift-M. To move to the previous marker, press Option-M. Use these keyboard short-cuts to find out how many edit points need to be trimmed in this sequence.

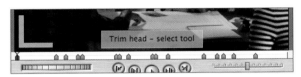

**NOTE ▸** You can also press Shift–Up Arrow to move the playhead forward to the next marker, and Shift–Down Arrow to move the playhead back to the previous marker.

Since dialogue is so important in dramatic material, let's change how you view the audio clips by turning on the audio waveforms in the Timeline, just as you did with narration clips in Lesson 3.

5   In the lower-left corner of the Timeline, click the Track Layout menu pop-up button and, from the menu, choose Show Audio Waveforms. You can also press the keyboard shortcut, Command-Option-W.

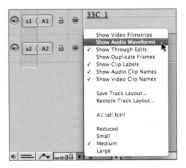

6   Zoom in to the first clip in the sequence. To make the audio waveforms taller, press Shift-T repeatedly to create a taller track height. Before you make changes to the clips

in this sequence, let's create a backup copy of it in the Browser. Having a backup sequence is helpful in case you don't like the changes you make and want to return to the original version.

**7**   In the Sequences bin in the Browser, Control-click the *Leverage_v1_rough* sequence and choose Duplicate.

A duplicate sequence is created in the same location as the original with the word *copy* added to its filename. This sequence contains the same settings and displays such as track height and audio waveforms as its parent sequence.

**8**   Click the video portion of the first clip, **33C_1**, then deselect it.

**NOTE ▶** The clip names in this footage indicate scene, take, and camera. For example, a clip named **33A_2 (B)** would indicate scene 33A, take 2, camera B.

The line beneath the clip name indicates that this clip's video and audio tracks are linked. With linked selection turned on in the Timeline button bar, selecting any video or audio track will automatically select all the tracks of the clip. Similarly, when you trim a linked clip, all the tracks of that clip are trimmed at the same time.

**9**   Play the first clip, **33C_1**, and watch the audio waveforms as you follow the dialogue. Then move the playhead to where you think this clip should begin.

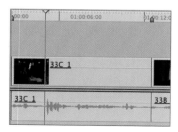

As part of the *Leverage* series workflow, eight tracks of audio are recorded and mixed down to one mono track for editing purposes. Listening to the clip, and even looking at the waveform, you can determine that the best place to start this sequence is when the character Nathan walks forward saying, "Grifter, hitter, hacker, thief." In the next exercise, you will trim the clip to this audio cue.

## Understanding Trimming

If you're new to the concept of trimming, it's quite simply a way to change your mind about where you want a clip's In or Out point *after* you've placed the clip in the Timeline. When you trim an edit point, you are lengthening or shortening the clip either at the head or the tail. In most situations, lengthening or shortening a clip in the Timeline affects the length of the entire sequence, because the clips that follow the trimmed clip are often pulled up or pushed forward to accommodate the new clip length.

You can trim a clip in four ways. Look at the graphical display below of these four options and compare the original clip length with the trimmed clips. First, consider the In point at the head of the clip:

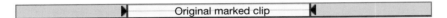
Original marked clip

Trim the In point to the left, and the clip will begin on an earlier frame. The clip will have a longer duration:

Earlier In point

Trim the In point to the right, and the clip will begin on a later frame, giving it a shorter duration:

Later In point

Consider the Out point at the tail of the clip.

Trim the Out point to the left, and the clip will end on an earlier frame and the clip will be shorter:

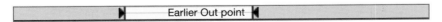
Earlier Out point

Trim the Out point to the right, and the clip will end on a later frame, making the clip longer:

Later Out point

When you play a sequence in the Timeline, you are seeing only the marked portions of the clips. However, you still have access to all the frames in the original media files. Remember that the maximum number of frames you can add to lengthen a clip in an outer direction (head or tail) depends on how much material is available in the original media file. The additional frames outside the marked portion of a clip are referred to as *handles*.

Let's continue this introduction to trimming by looking at some of the functions you will use during the trimming process. For these steps, you will trim two clips in the *Leverage_v1 rough* sequence using the default Selection tool.

> **TIP** For these exercises, make sure snapping is turned on in the Timeline.

1   With the playhead located in clip **33C_1**, press the Left Arrow and Right Arrow keys to finesse its position to where Nate starts speaking. If you can't hear the audio as you move frame by frame, choose View > Audio Scrubbing to turn on that function, and try pressing the arrow keys again.

The playhead gives you a *target* location for trimming the edit point. In this case, you will begin this sequence just before Nate speaks.

> **TIP** When finessing or trimming an edit point, keep an eye out for any distractions in the scene at the edit location. For example, in this clip, notice in the lower right of the frame that Sophie is turning her head. To make it a cleaner edit, you might consider trimming the clip a frame or two before she starts moving her head.

2   Move the pointer over the In point of the first clip in the sequence. When you see the Resize pointer, click the In point.

Just the edge of the clip is selected, not the body of the clip. If the entire clip were selected, you would end up moving the clip, not trimming it. The tracks are linked together and linked selection is on, so when you select the In point, both the audio and video In points are highlighted and can be trimmed together.

3   Move the In point to later in the clip by dragging the combined edit points right. Snap them to the playhead. Then play the clip.

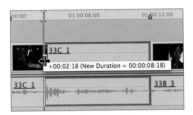

As you drag the In point to the right, the clip itself remains stationary and just the In point moves. The clip becomes shorter, and a brown boundary appears around it, indicating a new clip length. The new clip duration appears in the information box. Notice that the playhead becomes thicker and that snapping arrows appear at the top of the playhead when you snap the edit point to it.

**TIP** ▶ As you drag an edit point, make sure you always drag through the same track on which you selected the edit point. If you first clicked the V1 edit point, then drag through the V1 track.

Although this trimming method shortened the clip, it also left a gap at the head of the sequence. The gap can be deleted, but that requires an extra step. In the next exercise, you will use the Ripple tool, which removes the gap as you trim.

4   Click in the gap and press Delete.

5   Now play the second clip, **33B_3**, and focus on how it begins. To see a larger display of the audio waveforms, press Option-+ (plus sign) to zoom in to the Timeline at the playhead location.

In this clip, Nate repeats the word *crime*, which is redundant. It will have to be trimmed out to improve the sequence.

6   Play from the head of the clip and position the playhead just before Nate says, "There's a reason we work together." Don't forget to use the Left Arrow and Right Arrow keys to finesse the playhead location.

**7**   To trim this clip, drag the In point right and snap it to the playhead.

> **TIP ▶** When dragging an edit point that shares a location with another clip, it's helpful to click just off of the edit point. So, to drag an In point, you would click just to the right of the edit point, and to drag an Out point, click slightly to the left of it.

**8**   Click in the gap and press Delete.

Using the Selection tool to trim can be very useful when you shorten a clip or have empty space on either side of the clip you want to trim. But when clips are side by side in a sequence, the best approach is to use the Ripple tool.

## Rippling Edit Points

Final Cut Pro has a group of four tools that provide trimming solutions for any editing situation. In this exercise, you will use the Ripple tool.

The Ripple tool can trim the head or tail of a clip and, like the ripple delete function you used in the previous lesson, it will ripple the rest of the sequence's clips so that no gaps remain in the sequence. The Ripple tool is accessed via the Roll tool, the fourth button from the top in the Tool palette.

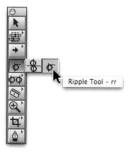

When you use the Ripple tool to trim an edit point, you drag an In or Out point left or right just as you did with the Selection tool. But when you drag with the Ripple tool, all the clips that follow are automatically pushed forward or pulled up for the length of the trim. In this sequence, there are 12 opportunities to apply the Ripple tool. You can think of these edit points as the "dirty dozen."

1   In the Timeline, play the second and third clips, **33B_3** and **33A_2 (B)**, and listen for the line "work together guys" in both clips. You can use the Ripple 1 marker as a reference.

**TIP** ▶ As always, zoom in to an area if necessary to see the waveform displays more clearly.

As in the previous trims, you can use the playhead to target where you want the dialogue to begin in this clip.

2   In the third clip, position the playhead just after the redundant line and before Alec says, "Yeah." Press the Left Arrow or Right Arrow key, or the JKL keys, to finesse the playhead location.

**NOTE** ▶ You may have noticed the frown on Alec's face at the head of the third clip. You will return his frown to the scene later in this lesson.

3   In the Tool palette, click the Roll tool and hold down the mouse button. When the Ripple tool icon appears (it looks like a single roller), click it. You can also press RR to select this tool.

**4** Without clicking or dragging, move your pointer over the third clip, **33A_2 (B)**.

The Ripple tool has an *X* on it, indicating that the tool cannot be applied to this area. You can use the Ripple tool only on a clip's In or Out edit point.

**5** Move the Ripple tool toward the clip's In point. Then move it just to the left of the edit point, over the previous clip's Out point. Notice that the tail of the Ripple tool changes direction.

Ripple tool over clip In point          Ripple tool over previous clip's Out point

When the Ripple tool gets close to the In point, the *X* disappears, and the tail of the Ripple icon points in to the right, toward the body of the clip you are trimming. When the Ripple tool moves over the previous clip's Out point, the tail points toward that clip. This is a visual clue to let you know which clip you are trimming.

**6** Return the Ripple tool to the third clip's In point. Drag the inside edge of the In point and snap it to the playhead location.

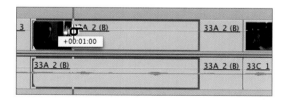

Like the Selection tool, the Ripple tool drags both the audio and video of the linked clip. As you drag the edit point, an information box appears with just the trim amount. There is no gap left, and all the clips in the sequence are pulled up by the amount of the trim.

**7** Play the fourth clip, **33C_1a**, at the Ripple 2 marker. Park the playhead after the redundant line, "was," and before Nate says, "OK."

Although the Ripple tool is selected, you can still play clips and navigate the sequence. The Ripple tool is active only when it's in the Timeline track area.

**8** Drag this clip's In point to the right, but don't release the mouse button.

Notice that when you use the Ripple tool to drag a clip's edit point to make the clip shorter, the clip boundary shortens to display a representative length.

Also, when you ripple an edit point, a two-up display appears in the Canvas to help you review or match the action from the Out point of one clip to the In point of the next. The Out point of the previous clip is displayed on the left, and the In point of the following clip appears on the right. As you drag an edit point, that edit point will update in the Canvas two-up display. The clip names and source timecodes appear over the clips as a reference.

**9** Snap the In point to the playhead. Play the new edit point.

**TIP** ▶ Sometimes you may want to use the waveform as a target and bypass the playhead altogether. With snapping turned on, it may be difficult to place the edit point precisely. When this occurs, press N to temporarily turn off snapping. You can also zoom in to the clip for greater trimming control.

Although this trim fixes the head of the clip, a redundant line at the end of the clip needs to be removed. In fact, the line "What about Maggie?" is heard in three adjacent clips at the Ripple 3, 4, and 5 markers.

**10**  Play the end of the fourth clip and continue playing through the Ripple 3, 4, and 5 markers. You will trim the Out point of this clip to the Ripple 3 marker after Alec says, "They know our faces."

You can use a marker as a target and snap to it in the same way you snap to the playhead.

**11**  Using the Ripple tool, drag the fourth clip's Out point to the left and snap it to the Ripple 3 marker. The same snapping triangles appear as when you snap to the playhead.

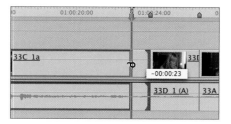

In the Canvas window, notice that two marker names appear at the same location. When you trim this clip, it ripples not only the clips that follow but also the marker locations. When you ripple markers, they maintain their relative relationships to the clips beneath them.

**12**  In the Sequence menu, make sure that the Ripple Sequence Markers command is selected.

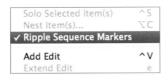

With the command selected, the markers will continue to ripple throughout the sequence as you trim your clips. If you don't want the markers to ripple when a trim is made, then deselect this function. You can also turn it off in the Timeline button bar.

## Rippling in the Viewer and by the Numbers

The Ripple tool, like other tools in Final Cut Pro, can be used in more than one window. Just as you can set marks in the Viewer and the Timeline, you can also *trim* marks in the Viewer and the Timeline. This is quite helpful, because when you open a sequence clip in the Viewer, you can see the area outside the range of the In and Out points, allowing you to find a target you can't see in the Timeline. In this exercise, you will trim an edit point in the Viewer and also trim a selected edit point in the Timeline "by the numbers," specifying a duration. You will also learn some shortcuts for selecting an edit point.

1   Play the area around the Ripple 6 and 7 markers.

Minor trimming adjustments are necessary in this area. Rather than dragging the Ripple tool to a target playhead or marker location, you will select the edit point and finesse it by pressing the [ or ] (left bracket or right bracket) key.

**2**   Move the playhead to the Ripple 6 marker over the **33A_2 (A)** clip. Then press V.

Pressing V selects the nearest edit point and moves the playhead to that location. Because you are using the Ripple tool, only an In point or an Out point will be selected, depending on which is closest to the playhead.

**3**   Press [ (left bracket) to move the Out point to the left one frame. Press it again to trim another frame off this clip.

> **TIP** ▶ You can also press < and > (left angle bracket and right angle bracket) to adjust selected edit points frame by frame. To trim five frames at a time, press Shift in combination with a bracket or an angle bracket to apply the multi-frame trim. You can change this default number of frames (from 1 to 99 frames) in the Editing tab of the User Preferences window.

Repeatedly pressing this key ripples the Out point one frame at a time. When you need to nudge more than a few frames (for instance, a full second or more), you can select the edit point and type the length of time, just as you type a duration in the Timeline to move a clip. Let's trim 1 second off the end of this clip.

**4**   With the Out point selected, enter –1. (period). Then press Return to enter this amount.

The Ripple trim amount appears in the Timeline beneath the ruler. After you enter the amount, the edit point moves to the left by 1 second. In the Canvas, the markers ripple as well, so you may see the Ripple 6 and Ripple 7 markers together on the same frame, depending on how much you trimmed the clip.

5    Press the U key repeatedly to highlight different sides of the edit point. Then make sure the In point of the next clip, **33D_1 (B)**, is selected.

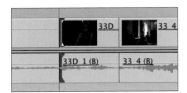

Pressing U when an edit point is selected cycles the highlight through three options: the Out point, both the In and Out points, and the In point. You can use the V key to select an edit point, and then press the U key to choose a particular side of that edit. Then trim the edit point by using the bracket keys, or by entering a specific duration.

**TIP** ▶ You can also press the V and U keys in combination with the default Selection tool to choose and trim an edit point.

6    Press ] (right bracket) to trim frames off this clip until Parker's line, "No, what about Maggie?" cleanly starts the clip.

Sometimes the clip's In or Out point stops short of a word or line. When you can't hear the line in the clip, you can't target the trim area in the Timeline. If you open the clip in the Viewer, you can see the area before the In point and watch an even larger waveform display.

7    Play the clip under the Ripple 8 marker, **33_4 (B)**, and listen to Alec's line "said that." It sounds cut off at the head of the clip. Double-click the body or the middle of the clip to open it in the Viewer.

With the Ripple tool selected, you can still double-click a sequence clip to open and edit it in the Viewer. With the clip visible in the Viewer, you can see the In and Out points and play beyond them.

**8** In the Viewer, click the Mono tab and move the playhead before the current In point to where Alec begins his sentence, "You just said that."

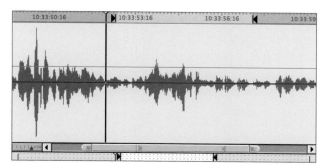

**9** To see this area in more detail, press Command-+ (plus sign) a few times to zoom in to the waveform at the playhead location. Finesse the playhead to the correct location using the Left Arrow and Right Arrow keys.

**NOTE ▶** Pressing Command-+ (plus sign) or Command-– (minus sign), respectively, will zoom in or out of a display in any active window. But pressing Option-+ and Option-– will affect only the Timeline.

As you zoom in to the playhead location, the playhead itself gets wider, representing the width of one frame.

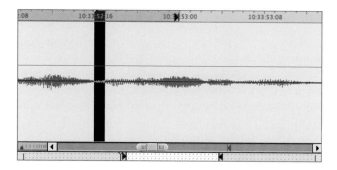

**NOTE ▶** Depending on the size of your screen and the window layout, your Viewer may appear different from the image shown here.

**10** Press I to set a new In point in the Viewer.

Because you still have the Ripple tool selected, pressing I resets the In point to the playhead location just as though you dragged the edit point there. The clip in the Timeline is now longer, and it starts with Alec saying, "You just said that."

**NOTE ▶** You can also drag the edit point in the Viewer's scrubber bar using the Ripple tool. However, you may not have as much control when dragging to a target edit location.

## Take 2

The director wants to screen this scene with a few of the actors and wants you to clean it up as much as possible. Take a minute to finesse the areas around the Ripple 4 and 5 markers. You will want to keep Parker's line, "What about Maggie?" in the **33D_1 (A)** clip and trim any redundant lines before or after it in the adjacent clips. Then tackle the four remaining edit points under the Ripple 9–12 markers. As a reminder, here are the ways you can ripple an edit point with the Ripple tool:

- ▶ Drag an edit point.
- ▶ Select an edit point, enter a precise trim amount, and press Return.
- ▶ Select an edit point and press a bracket key to trim one frame.
- ▶ Press Shift in combination with a bracket key to move the multi-frame trim amount.
- ▶ Open a clip in the Viewer and mark a new In or Out point.
- ▶ Press V to select the nearest edit point, press U to toggle the selection, and then apply any of the methods above.

**TIP ▶** Remember that when you zoom in and out in the Timeline, if an edit point is selected, you will zoom in to that edit point not to the playhead location. Press Command-Shift-A to deselect any selection; then you can zoom in to the playhead location.

## Trimming on the V2 Track

Using the Ripple tool is not the only way to trim an edit. As you saw earlier in this lesson, you can also drag an edit point using the default Selection tool. The problem with using the default Selection tool is that you cannot ripple the clips that follow, and you cannot drag an edit point into a neighboring clip.

The solution to this problem, and it's a handy one that many editors use, is to place cutaways on the V2 track, as you did in the "Believe" *Interviews* sequence in the previous lesson. When you edit some of your clips to the V2 track, you have elbow room to trim edit points by dragging them into empty track territory without having to ripple the clips around them.

**1**    In the Sequences bin in the Browser, open the *Leverage_v2* sequence and play it in the Timeline.

This is the trimmed sequence you've been working with, but it has cutaways added to the V2 track to match the originally aired sequence. The placement of the cutaways on the V2 track gives you the ability to reposition the clips earlier or later in the sequence. It also gives you more freedom to trim an In or Out using the default Selection tool.

> **TIP**    If a cutaway was originally edited to the V1 track, and you want to bump it up to the V2 track for greater flexibility, hold down the Shift key as you drag it up to keep the clip from moving left or right. You can also select the clip and press Option–Up Arrow.

**2**    Press A to choose the default Selection tool and zoom in to the first cutaway on the V2 track. Make sure snapping is turned on for these steps.

**3** At the Cutaway 1 marker in the Timeline, play the **33A_1 (A)** clip and the clips around it. To position this clip earlier, click in the middle of the clip and drag it to the left. Snap its Out point to the Out point of the first clip, **33C_1**, and play it.

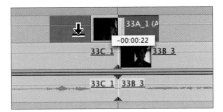

With the cutaway on a separate track, you can move the clip to reposition it, trim it by dragging its edit points, or even turn off track visibility to see what the sequence looks like without it.

**4** Control-click the **33A_1 (A)** clip in the sequence. From the shortcut menu, choose Clip Enable to deselect it.

This shortcut menu provides a long list of functions and changes you can apply to this clip. When you deselect Clip Enable, it's as though you turn off the Track Visibility control for that one clip. This can be a helpful feature if you want to preview an area of the sequence without a particular clip.

When the clip is disabled, it appears dark in the Timeline, just as it does when you turn off the Track Visibility control in the Timeline patch panel.

5    Play the first two clips in the sequence to see them without the cutaway. Then Control-click the **33A_1 (A)** clip again and choose Clip Enable to toggle the clip back on. You could also select the clip and press Control-B.

The cutaway in this location provides good dramatic tension. But it might be more dramatic if the cutaway were longer.

6    Click the **33A_1 (A)** clip's In point. To add an additional second to the head of this clip, type *−1.* (period). Press Return and play the clip.

Just as with the Ripple tool, you can trim a specific amount using the Selection tool as long as the edit point you're trimming has room to move on the track. You can also trim by pressing the bracket, or "nudge," keys. In this cutaway, Sophie blinks at the head of the clip. Let's trim away that blink.

7    With the In point of the **33A_1 (A)** clip still selected, press the ] (right bracket) key a few times (or try Shift-]) until the new In point has moved past the blink. Play the clip.

In addition to dragging with the Selection tool to trim an edit point, entering an amount, or nudging with the bracket keys, there's another way to trim.

8    Play the **33A_2 (B)** clip before the Cutaway 2 marker and the cutaway above it. Now move the playhead to just after Alec says, "was."

Dramatically, it would be nice if Sophie's cutaway hit right after Alec's line.

9    Click the In point of the **33A_1 (A)** clip, but don't drag it.

This time, you won't drag an edit point to the playhead; instead, you will *extend* the edit point to that location. Although it's a different technique, it produces the same result.

**10** With the playhead positioned where you want this edit point to be and with the edit point selected, press E, or choose Sequence > Extend Edit. Play these clips.

The In point is trimmed, or extended, to the playhead location. To review, extending an edit point requires that you do three things:

▶ Position the playhead at the target location.

▶ Select the edit point you want to move using the default Selection tool.

▶ Press E, or choose Sequence > Extend Edit.

Like the other trim options you've worked with in this lesson, extending an edit can make a clip longer or shorter.

**NOTE** ▶ You can extend an edit only if you have enough clip material to support the move. If you've placed the playhead out of the clip's range of material, you can't extend the clip to the new location, and no change will be made to that clip. Extend can also be used with multiple edit points. Command-click an edit point to add it to the selection.

## Take 2

The director's back with more actors who want to see the finished scene. Take a moment to trim or adjust the remaining V2 cutaways in this sequence. Don't forget, you can drag with the Selection tool, press the bracket keys, trim by an amount, and also extend an edit point, as long as elbow room is available on either side of the cutaway.

## Trimming One Track of a Linked Clip

Throughout this lesson, you have worked with clips that have linked tracks. You click one track and all tracks become selected when you're in the default linked selection mode. As you've seen, this mode also affects trimming. When you click one edit point, such as the video Out point, all Out points on all tracks of that clip become selected. This can be very helpful when you want to change the Out point of the clip the same amount on all the tracks. But sometimes you may want to trim just the video track of a clip to be shorter or longer than the audio, and vice versa.

The reason for this is that when the audio and video change at the same time in a sequence, the edit appears "harder" and more abrupt to the viewer. If one of the tracks cuts first and the other one follows, it softens the effect of the edit. Offsetting the edit points this way is a technique that's used frequently in the refining process.

**1**   In the Timeline, play the second and third V1 clips, and zoom in to that area.

Alec's response, "Yeah," may come a little too quickly after Nate's line, "There's a reason we work together." Let's add another second, or "beat," to the head of Alec's clip. Adding a beat will require you to open up the sequence. Since the clips on the V1 track are all side by side, you will have to use the Ripple tool.

**2**   Press RR to choose the Ripple tool. Then click the In point of Alec's clip, **33A_2 (B)**.

Because linked selection is still turned on, both the audio and video In points are highlighted and will be trimmed together.

**3**   Type *–20*, and press Return. Play the new edit point between the two clips.

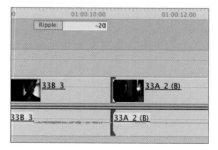

This trim created an extra beat and restored a nicely dramatic frown to Alec's face that wasn't included in the previous clip length. But it also reintroduced some redundant audio into the sequence. Rather than undo the trim you just made, you can trim the audio track to remove only the redundant audio.

This time, you don't want to ripple the change you make, so you will trim with the Selection tool.

**4**   Press A to select the default Selection tool.

**5**   Play Alec's clip, **33A_2 (B)**, and position the playhead just before he says, "Yeah." This is where you want the audio portion of this clip to begin.

Because you want to work with just one track of this linked clip, you have to turn off linked selection.

**6**   In the Timeline button bar, click the Linked Selection button (or press Shift-L) to turn it off.

Like snapping, linked selection is on, or active, when the button is green, and off when the button is dimmed.

**7**   On the A1 audio track, click the audio In point of the **33A_2 (B)** clip and drag it right to snap to the playhead. Play the clip.

When linked selection is turned off, you can select and trim a clip's audio or video tracks individually, even if the tracks are linked.

**NOTE** ▶ Before a show would air with this gap in the audio, an editor or sound mixer would edit in ambient room noise to fill in the blank spaces in the audio.

8    In the Timeline, click the Linked Selection button to turn that function back on.

You can choose to edit with linked selection on or off. For now, and for the purpose of this lesson, keep linked selection on, in its default state.

**TIP** ▶ To temporarily override linked selection in order to trim a single track of one clip, Option-drag the edit point. You will drag just the audio or video edit point you select.

## Take 2

On the studio lot, you bump into an old friend who is cutting a film the old-fashioned way. She asks you to show her how to trim in nonlinear editing. You're happy to oblige because it gives you a chance to review the trim options in Final Cut Pro. You open the *Leverage_v1_rough Copy* sequence in the Browser and turn off the markers (see the tip below). Rather than demonstrate the Ripple tool, you decide to start with something more familiar to her: the Razor Blade tool (B). You apply the Razor Blade tool to an edit point and delete the excess. Then you move on to the other trimming options to fine-tune the sequence.

**TIP** ▶ Although markers are a helpful training aid when following exercise steps, to turn them off in the *Leverage_v1 copy* sequence, choose Edit > Project Properties. Under Marker Visibility, deselect the blue and red marker checkboxes.

## Editor's Cut

While Final Cut Pro's editing functions work the same regardless of the footage you use, practicing on different types of footage is a good way to hone your editing chops and to gain greater control over the tools, functions, and shortcuts. Since you've been working with dramatic footage throughout this lesson, you may want to create your own editor's cut of the SeaWorld documentary footage you worked with in the previous three lessons. In the Browser > Sequences bin, open the *SeaWorld_v3_rough* sequence and trim the clips to the length of the music track.

## Lesson Review

1.  What does turning off linked selection in the Timeline do?
2.  What does the Ripple tool do when you use it for trimming?
3.  What is the keyboard shortcut to select the Ripple tool?
4.  What keys can you use as shortcuts to ripple a clip's edit point by a few frames?
5.  What is one advantage of trimming a clip in the Viewer?
6.  How can you disable a single clip in the sequence?
7.  What tools can you use to drag an edit point in the Timeline?
8.  What is the keyboard shortcut for extending an edit?
9.  How do you reposition a clip to an upper Timeline track without moving it horizontally?
10. What is the advantage of editing on the V2 track?

### Answers

1.  It allows you to select and trim one track of a linked clip.
2.  It ripples the trim amount through the unlocked tracks in the sequence.
3.  Pressing RR selects the Ripple tool.
4.   Press [ and ] (bracket keys) or < and > (angle bracket keys).
5.  You can view material outside the marked area.
6.  Control-click the clip in the sequence and deselect Clip Enable in the shortcut menu.
7.  Use the default Selection tool and the Ripple tool.
8.  The E key extends an edit.
9.  Hold down the Shift key as you drag, or select the clip and press Option–Up Arrow. To move a clip down, you press Option–Down Arrow.
10. It allows you to lengthen a clip without bumping into a bordering clip on either side.

**Keyboard Shortcuts**

| | |
|---|---|
| **B** | Select the Razor Blade tool |
| **Control-B** | Enable or disable a clip |
| **E** | Extend an edit |
| **Shift-L** | Turn linked selection off and on |
| **N** | Turn snapping off and on |
| **RR** | Select the Ripple tool |
| **U** | Cycle the selection of the Timeline edit point among In, Out, and both In and Out points |
| **V** | Select the edit point closest to the Timeline playhead |

# 5

**Lesson Files**  FCP7 Book Files > Lessons > Lesson 5 Project

**Media**  FCP7 Book Files > Media > Leverage > Promo

**Time**  This lesson takes approximately 60 minutes to complete.

**Goals**  Trim two edit points at the same time

Slip In and Out points

Roll edit points

Extend edit points

Slide a clip

Reposition a clip

Keep clips in sync

# Refining Edit Points

In the previous lesson, you used the Ripple tool to trim a clip longer or shorter, adding or removing a line of dialogue to refine the story. Ripple edits brought you very close to the intended length of your sequence. Now you're ready to polish the clip's content, edit points, and location without changing the overall length of the sequence. To do this, you will use three Final Cut Pro trimming tools: Slip, Roll, and Slide. Unlike the Ripple tool, these trimming tools can trim two edit points at once, which will save you time in editing. You will also use the Selection tool to reposition and copy clips within a sequence.

A clip's In and Out points being slipped in the Viewer and Canvas windows

## Preparing Your Sequence

As you continue to refine your rough cut, you may want to set up your sequence a little differently and use markers to identify areas that need adjusting. The footage you will be working with in this lesson is from *Leverage*, but rather than refine a scene, you will refine a promo for the show.

**1**   Choose File > Open, or press Command-O, and then open Lessons > Lesson 5 Project. Close any other open projects.

**2**   In the Timeline, play the *Promo_v2 Polished* sequence.

This sequence is cut together from several clips used in "The Second David" episode. The purpose of the *Leverage* promo, like any other promotional material, is to create interest in the show and perhaps evoke a sense of intrigue. Joseph LoDuca's music and the editor's quick cuts help to achieve this effect. To practice using the trimming tools, you will work on a rougher sequence; it's the right length, but it needs polishing to capture the best portions of the actors' movements.

**NOTE** ▶ In the first half of this promo, you'll see the Leverage characters scheming individually and bumping into each other in the process. In the second half, you will see the results of Nathan's organizational efforts as the individuals work as an efficient, synchronized unit.

**3**   Click the *Promo_v1 Rough* sequence tab and play this sequence.

Although both sequences are the same length, the placement or content of some of these clips could be more polished or better timed for a stronger effect.

Notice the three colors of markers in the Timeline ruler. During the rough-cutting process, you might use markers to remind yourself where you want to return to refine an edit point. The markers in this sequence have been added for that purpose. The three colors represent the three trimming tools and approaches you will learn in this lesson.

**4**   Control-click the Timeline ruler. From the list of marker names on the bottom of the shortcut menu, choose "use static image."

The playhead moves directly to that marker.

**5**   In the Canvas transport controls, click the Play Around Current Frame button, or press the \ (backslash) key.

The playhead moves back a specific number of seconds (called the *pre-roll* time), then plays the sequence through the playhead's original location, continues to play a few more seconds (*post-roll*), and returns the playhead to the original location. Rather than having to position your playhead manually before the edit point, you can see "around" the edit point.

Using this control throughout the lesson will be a helpful way to preview edit points, so let's take a moment to change the pre-roll and post-roll settings to suit your preferences.

**6** Press Option-Q to open the User Preferences window, and click the Editing tab. In the Preview Pre-roll field, enter *2.* (2 period) and press Return. Leave the Preview Post-roll at its default setting (2 seconds). Click OK to save this change.

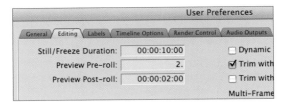

**7** Press the \ (backslash) key to preview this edit point with the new pre-roll settings.

In this lesson, you will be working with tools that outline or in some other way mark the clips or edit points you're adjusting. To see those markings more clearly, you can turn off the thumbnail images for the clips in this sequence.

**NOTE** ▶ Viewing Timeline clips without thumbnail images is often the preferred practice of editors who cut dramatic material. Without the thumbnails, you can more easily read clip scene numbers.

**8** Choose Sequence > Settings, or press Command-0, and click the Timeline Options tab. From the Thumbnail Display pop-up menu, choose Name. Click OK.

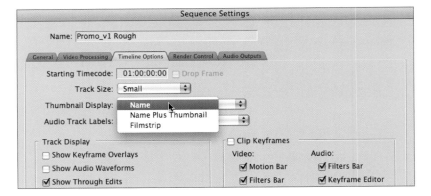

In the Timeline Options tab of the Sequence Settings window, you can change how the active or current sequence appears in the Timeline. For example, you can change the track size, turn off or turn on the audio waveforms display and through edit indicators, and even change the starting timecode of the sequence. In this situation, when you choose Name for the display, the thumbnail images no longer appear on the clips in the sequence. Instead, you see just the name of the clip, which in this project denotes the scene, take, and camera.

| 5–3 (F) | 16C–1 (A) | 16D–2 (A) | 13C–2 (B) | 13–2 (F) |
| 5–3 (F) | 16C–1 (A) | 16D–2 (A) | 13C–2 (B) | 13–2 (F) |

**TIP** ▶ To display the clip names larger in the Timeline, Control-click in the Browser's empty gray space and, from the shortcut menu, choose Text Size > Medium. This also enlarges the text in the Browser.

It might be helpful to create a backup of the original *Promo_v1 Rough* sequence in case you want to return to the original version and refine the edits in different ways.

9   In the Sequences bin in the Browser, Control-click the *Promo_v1 Rough* sequence and, from the shortcut menu, choose Duplicate. Leave the copy unopened in the Sequences bin.

## Trimming Two Edit Points

Three trimming tools in Final Cut Pro have one thing in common: They always preserve the current sequence length. The three tools—Slip, Roll, and Slide—never change the length of a sequence because they simultaneously change two edit points by equal amounts. You could use the Ripple tool to first trim one edit point and then the other. But these tools save you time by applying identical trim amounts to two edit points at once. One way to think about these three tools is to consider the number of clips that each tool affects.

**NOTE** ▶ The term *edit point* can refer to a single clip's In or Out point, but it can also refer to the juncture between adjoining clips.

### Slip Tool

The Slip tool trims both the In and Out points of a *single* clip at the same time. As you adjust the In and Out points together, you *slip* the contents of a clip to the left or right of its original edit points. The clip and sequence durations remain the same, but you are showing different clip content.

Starting clip content

Content after slipping

## Roll Tool

The Roll tool affects the edit point between two adjacent clips. It trims the Out point of one clip and the In point of the following clip simultaneously. If you roll left, the first clip will be shorter and the second clip will be longer. When you roll right, the first clip becomes longer and the adjacent clip becomes shorter. Rolling an edit point to the left or right does not change the overall sequence duration because, as the edit point of one clip changes, the neighboring clip compensates for the change.

Two adjacent clips

Rolling the edit point left

Rolling the edit point right

## Slide Tool

The Slide tool trims two edit points but involves *three contiguous clips*. You can shift, or *slide*, the middle clip into the one on the left, making the first clip shorter; the In point of the third clip adjusts to compensate, and the third clip becomes longer. Sliding to the right lengthens the first clip and shortens the third. In either operation, the middle clip remains unchanged, though its position shifts slightly left or right in the Timeline. Taken together, the length of the three clips remains the same.

Three contiguous clips

Sliding the center clip left

Sliding the center clip right

**NOTE** ▶ Just as you chose not to display thumbnail images in the current sequence, you can also choose to display *only* thumbnail images, as in the clip images above. To do this, in the Timeline Options tab of the Sequence Settings window, choose Thumbnail Display > Filmstrip.

## Slipping One Clip

As you edit, you may find yourself wanting to trim a clip so that it begins earlier or later, but you don't want to change the clip's duration. You can now use the Slip tool to slip the clip. Should you use the portion of the clip where a person is walking out of a room? Or earlier, when he's walking into it? Slipping allows you to select slightly different content without changing the clip length. However, you must have additional material—handles—on either side of the clip, or you will have no additional frames to slip.

### Using the Slip Tool

When you apply the Slip tool to a clip in the Timeline, think of the clip as what you see through your car windshield. The additional material to the left or right, outside your windshield view, is the handles of the adjacent clips. If an action occurs earlier or later in the clip, you can make it appear in the windshield by dragging the clip left or right using the Slip tool. You drag *right* to see earlier clip material (before the In point), or *left* to see later material (after the Out point).

**NOTE** ► For now, turn snapping off in the Timeline so it doesn't constrict you as you slip.

1   In the Tool palette, click the Slip tool (the fifth tool from the top), or press S.

Slip tool in Tool palette     Slip tool button

When you look closely at the Slip tool, you see what appear to be two Ripple tools facing each other. The two thin vertical lines represent the clip In and Out points. You could think of the Slip tool icon as two edit points on wheels, moving the edit points in tandem, left or right.

2   In the *Promo_v1 Rough* sequence, Control-click the Timeline ruler and choose the "show walk to rail" marker, or drag the playhead to the **5-3 (F)** clip. Press \ (backslash) to play around and through this clip.

show walk to rail

The energetic music begs for motion. It might be nice to see Parker move into her position at the rail instead of cutting to a static shot.

**3**  Click and hold down the **5-3 (F)** clip. You may have to zoom in to or out of the clip to see the complete outline. The Slip tool, although selected in a previous step, appears only when you position it over a sequence clip.

When you click the Slip tool, an outline of the entire range of the clip appears over the other sequence clips. The outline indicates the amount of media, or handles, to the left and right of the current clip content that is available for you to draw from while making a slip adjustment.

Since Parker is already in position, her walk to the rail would occur earlier in the clip. If you think about the windshield metaphor, you would drag right to slip the earlier material into the windshield view.

**4**  Using the Slip tool, drag right as far as possible, but don't release the mouse button. Look at the Canvas two-up display.

In the Canvas, the clip's new In and Out points appear along with the clip name and source timecode. The head-of-clip filmstrip overlay appears in the left frame to indicate that you are currently on the first frame of the clip. You cannot slip the clip any farther to the right. If you drag all the way to the left, you will see the end-of-clip overlay on the right frame.

In the Timeline, an information box appears showing the amount forward or backward that you have slipped the clip.

5   Release the mouse button and play the new clip content. If the playhead is still over the clip, you can press \ (backslash) to preview the clip content in that area.

After slipping this clip to the very beginning, you now see Parker approach the rail, but you abruptly cut away from the notebook action. Slipping is all about refining, so let's refine the content to include the walk *and* a beat after she flips open her notebook.

6   To reveal a later action, slip the clip left a few frames and focus on the right frame, or Out point, of the Canvas two-up display. After Parker's notebook drops down in the frame, release the clip, and play it.

As you look at the Canvas two-up display, you can focus on either the In or Out point, or both. But however much you trim or slip an edit point in one direction, the opposite edit point is changed by the same amount in the same direction. In the Timeline, the clip is still the same length but contains different content.

7   Play the **83-1 MOS** clip at the "use static image" marker.

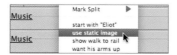

Because this is a short clip, keeping the shot on just one computer article would allow the viewer to read the title.

**NOTE ▶** *MOS is a film term that means the take was recorded without sound.*

8   Slip the clip to the far left and check the Canvas two-up display. If the same article appears in both the In and Out displays, release the clip and play it.

**TIP** ▶ To increase your precision when slipping or trimming a clip, hold down the Command key as you drag. This also applies to adjusting audio level overlays in the Timeline audio tracks.

### Slipping in the Viewer and by the Numbers

There are other ways to slip a clip. For example, you can enter the number of frames, or even the number of seconds, you want to slip, just as you did when using the Ripple or Move tool in previous lessons. In order to use numbers or other shortcuts to slip a clip, the clip must first be selected in the Timeline. Also, once a clip is in the sequence, you can double-click it and make slip adjustments in the Viewer. The Slip tool also provides a handy way to see a "blueprint" of your sequence clips.

1   In the Timeline, play the **13A-1 MOS** clip at the "try to slip me" marker. Then click it to see the brown outline of its media length. Try to slip this clip left or right, then release the clip.

    **TIP** ▶ When you want to adjust a particular clip or area in the sequence, it's always a good idea to zoom in to that area.

When you select a clip using the Slip tool, you see what handles you have, and in which direction, so you know what kind of slip adjustment, if any, you can make— little or big, earlier or later, or none. If you see no handles on either side of a clip, you know you can't slip this clip because the entire clip content is used in the sequence.

In the Canvas window, a filmstrip overlay appears on both frames of the two-up display to indicate that no additional media handles are available to slip this clip at its current length.

2   At the "arms up" marker in the sequence, play the **16C-1 (A)** clip. Then click the clip with the Slip tool to see the range of the clip's available media.

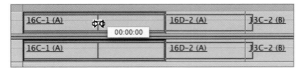

Since this is a promo full of action shots, you might want to see Alec doing something. From the brown outline, you can see that any action you choose will appear later in the clip.

3   Drag the **16C-1 (A)** clip to the left as far as possible and release the clip. Press \ (backslash) to play the clip in that area.

Another way to slip a clip is to open it in the Viewer. This option uses the Viewer to display the In point, and the Canvas to display the Out point. You may want to make those windows the same size before opening a clip.

4   If necessary, press Control-U to choose the default standard window layout. Double-click the **16D-2 (A)** clip at the "use the 'Shhhh!'" marker.

From the edit points in the scrubber bar, you can see that this clip has long media handles. Two rows of sprocket holes appear in the scrubber bar to indicate that this clip is already in the sequence.

5   Play past the current Out point to see what other material is available in the **16D-2 (A)** clip. Stop the playhead after Eliot says, "Shhhh!"

Sometimes clips have more than one action you can use in the sequence. Playing out-side the edit points in the Viewer is a good way to review your other options.

6    In the Viewer's scrubber bar, move your Slip tool over the In or Out point. Drag right and watch the new Out point in the Canvas window. When Eliot starts to bring his finger down from his mouth, release the mouse button.

> **TIP** If you want to snap an In or Out point to the playhead location, make sure snapping is turned on. You can press N as you drag the clip to toggle snapping on or off.

As you drag, both edit points in the scrubber bar move simultaneously. The first frame of the new clip content appears in the Viewer, and the last frame appears in the Canvas. As you slip a sequence clip in the Viewer, you are making that change to the clip in the Timeline.

> **TIP** After marking In and Out points in any clip in the Viewer, you can slip those edit points using the default Selection tool by Shift-dragging the In or Out point left or right.

7    In the Viewer, press the Play In to Out button, or press Shift-\ (backslash), to see the new **16D-2 (A)** clip material. Slip the In and Out points again until Eliot's finger comes down.

In the refining process, it typically takes more than one adjustment to get a polished result. After selecting an entirely new action, you may want to finesse the adjustment by a specific amount or by just a few frames. You can slip a clip a few frames using the same adjusting keys—< and > (angle brackets) or [ and ] (brackets)—as you did when adjusting move and trim amounts.

**TIP** ▶ Having two sets of adjusting keys on the keyboard can be useful. Sometimes your hand is close to the I and O keys, and reaching to the [ and ] keys is convenient. Other times you may find that using JKL and the < and > keys is more convenient.

To nudge or slip this clip by a few frames, you first have to select the clip. Although you can double-click a clip to open it in the Viewer, you can't click a clip to select it without holding down a modifier key.

8    To select the **16D-2 (A)** clip, hold down Shift. When the pointer changes to the default Selection tool, select the clip, then release the Shift key to revert to the Slip tool.

9    Position the playhead on the last frame of this clip to see the updated frame in the Canvas. Press > (right angle bracket) to slip the clip one frame earlier. Press < (left angle bracket) to slip one frame later. Fine-tune your adjustment so that Eliot completes his Shhhh! action. Then deselect the clip in the Timeline.

**TIP** ▶ A good way to think about the use of the < and > keys is to remember the windshield of a car and how you would drag this clip to fine-tune it. If you would drag right, use the > key. If you would drag left, use the < key.

Sometimes you need to slip a clip by a full second or more to get closer to the action or dialogue you want to use. Then, once you're in the ballpark, you can finesse the selection by slipping one frame at a time.

**10** Play the **66-3** clip at the "start with 'Eliot'" marker. To start this clip where Alec says, "Eliot," Shift-click the clip, type *–1.* (minus 1 period), and press Return.

**NOTE ▶** When you slip a clip by entering a number, the direction may seem reversed when you use plus or minus. Adding a minus sign to a number is the same as dragging the clip left with the Slip tool, and therefore choosing later clip content. A plus sign is the equivalent of dragging the clip to the right, or slipping earlier content into the clip.

**11** Play the clip, and if it needs additional adjusting, press the < or > (left or right angle bracket) key to slip one frame forward or backward, respectively. You can press Shift-< or Shift-> to move five frames at a time. Press Command-S to save the project.

**TIP ▶** Pressing Shift-< or Shift-> slips the multi-frame trim amount. The default is five frames, but you can change the default number of frames in the Editing tab of User Preferences (Option-Q).

## Take 2

You've just screened the entire sequence using the Digital Cinema Desktop Preview – Main option in the View menu. The slip adjustments are really helping to finesse the promo. However, you see that two clips that are supposed to match action, but may not match as closely as they could. Play the **13-2 (F)** clip at the yellow "match head turn" marker and the wide-shot clip that follows. Slip the action in the medium shot so that the last frame matches the first frame of the wide shot.

## Rolling Two Edit Points

When you don't like the way one clip cuts to the next—perhaps because the action doesn't match or the edit point doesn't hit on a beat of music or the narrator's pause—you may want to consider using the Roll tool. The Roll tool will trim both sides of an edit point at the same time. It will trim the Out point of one clip by the same amount that it trims the In point of the following clip. This allows you to adjust the edit point earlier or later without changing the overall length of the sequence.

The Roll tool is the fourth tool from the top in the Tool palette, in the same position as the Ripple tool. For some projects, especially dramatic scenes and interviews, you may use the Ripple and Roll tools in tandem. You might first apply the Ripple tool to refine a single clip's edit point, and then follow up with the Roll tool to adjust the way that clip's edit point works in conjunction with the clip next to it.

1   In the Tool palette, click the Roll tool, or press R.

The Roll tool icon looks like two stacked Ripple tools bisected by a thin vertical line representing the edit point. The Roll tool adjusts two sides of an edit point.

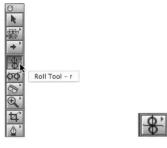

Roll tool in Tool palette     Roll tool button

The simplest reason to roll an edit point is that you want more of one clip and less of another but don't want to change the overall length of the two clips.

2   In the *Promo_v1 Rough* sequence, play the **11C-2** and **11B-1** clips around the green Roll 1 marker. Then click the edit point between these two clips.

**TIP ▶** In this sequence, the green roll markers are easily distinguishable from the yellow slip markers. You will learn how to add markers in Lesson 6.

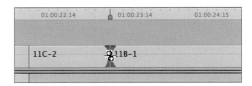

Both sides of the edit point are highlighted. Currently, the close-up of Alec's hands on the wires is a very short clip. Let's lengthen it by rolling the edit point into the following clip of Alec's face.

3   Drag the edit point to the right 19 frames and make note of the following conditions *before* you release the mouse button and then play the clips:

▶   In the Timeline, a brown outline surrounds both clips. This indicates that these two clips are involved in this adjustment. The outer edges of these boxes will not change; only the edit point in the middle will change.

▶   The duration of the roll appears in the information box.

▶   In the Canvas two-up display, the left frame displays the outgoing clip's new Out point along with an Out point overlay in the frame's upper-right corner. The right frame displays the incoming clip's new In point, along with an In point overlay in its upper-left corner. The clip names and source timecode locations also appear in the Canvas frames.

**NOTE** ▶   When the Caps Lock key is engaged, the two-up display is disabled in the Canvas.

Another use for the Roll tool is to adjust edit points that have a synchronous relationship. In other words, when the last frame of one clip matches the action in the first frame of the following clip, the clips are said to be *in sync*. Using the Roll tool on this type of edit point will maintain the matching action between the two clips.

4   Play the **13-2 (F)** and **5-3a (F)** clips around the green Roll 2 marker. Then press the Left Arrow and Right Arrow keys to compare the last frame of Sophie's medium shot with the first frame of the wide shot.

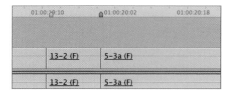

If you performed the previous Take 2 exercise, these two clips will appear in sync. If you trim or adjust just the Out point of the first clip or just the In point of the second, you will throw these clips out of sync.

5   Click the edit point between the **13-2 (F)** and **5-3a (F)** clips. Because these clips have sound, the video and audio tracks are included in the selection.

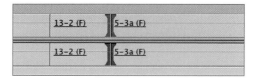

In the current clip, the wide shot begins with Sophie turned around almost entirely. To include more of her turning action in the wide shot, you have to roll back the edit point a few frames.

6   With the edit point selected, press the < (left angle bracket) key a few times, and play the edit point again.

In the Canvas, every time you adjust the edit point, you see an update of the first frame of the second clip, which is where the playhead is relocated. You have to press the Left Arrow key to see the new Out point of the first clip, or click the edit point using the Roll tool to see the two-up display in the Canvas. Because each roll adjustment trims both edit points together by the same amount, the clips remain in sync.

**TIP** To make the two-up display larger, press Option-U to use the saved large Canvas display; or manually resize the Canvas window.

In addition to maintaining synced relationships, rolling edit points is very helpful when you want an edit point to hit in a particular place in the sequence, such as on a music beat or at a narrator's cue.

**TIP** To snap to a marker in the following step, turn on snapping.

7  Find the green Roll 3 marker over the **13C_2 (B)** clip. Play that clip and the **13_2 (F)** clip that follows it. Drag the edit point between the two clips to the strong beat of music at the Roll 3 marker, and look for the snapping arrows around the marker before you release the edit point. Play the new edit point.

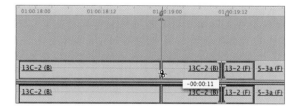

When you snap an edit point to a marker, brown snapping arrows appear beneath the marker in the Timeline ruler as they would if you snapped to the playhead.

**NOTE** ▶ Since rolling changes the length of each clip, you may need to go back and slip the content of the clips after you've rolled the edit point to its target location.

One technique that is used frequently in editing dramatic or interview footage is to roll just the video edit point between two clips. Offsetting the video edit from the audio edit helps to mimic the natural flow of dialogue and also lets you continue a character's action from one shot to the next, or to lead with it.

**TIP** ▶ Imagine observing a conversation between two people. First you listen to one person speak, and only after you hear the other person speak do you turn your head to look at him. This approach can be used anywhere two dialogue clips appear in the sequence.

8    Play the first two clips in the sequence, **8D-2** and **66-3**. Position the playhead in the second clip just after Alec says, "Eliot, what does."

In the first clip, Nate begins to raise his arm to drink from his glass. Rolling the edit point later will allow him to complete this action.

You can press a keyboard shortcut, the E key, to apply the next rolling adjustment. You used this shortcut in the previous lesson to extend an edit point. Rather than extend a single edit point, in this case you extend both sides of the edit point in tandem, exactly as if you used the Roll tool to roll it.

9    To select just the video edit point, hold down Option (to override linked selection) and click the edit point. Then press E to extend the edit point to the playhead location.

**TIP** ▶ You can extend an edit point after selecting it using either the Roll tool or the default Selection tool.

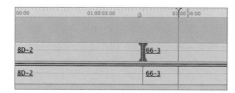

Video edit point selected

Video edit point extended to playhead

Since the playhead was parked where you wanted the new edit point to be, pressing E extends, or rolls, the selected edit point to that location.

**TIP** ► As with the Slip and Ripple tools, you can also enter a number to roll a specific amount of time.

**10**  Play the area again. If necessary, finesse the edit point by Option-clicking it and pressing the < or > (left or right angle bracket) key. Then press Command-S to save your work.

**MORE INFO** ► You can double-click an edit point to open the Trim Edit window. This window displays the two clips involved at the edit point. In this window, you can apply both the Ripple and Roll tools. To read more about the Trim Edit window, see the Final Cut Pro User Manual.

## Take 2

There's a screening of the current *Promo* rough cut in 10 minutes and you'd like to fine-tune the sequence as much as possible. As you're learning, when you finesse one edit point, it can affect the clips around it, requiring additional adjustments with a different trimming tool. So now that you're on a *roll*, take a moment to go through the current sequence to see if any clips *slipped* through the cracks that might need your attention.

## Sliding Clips to Refine Position

If you like a clip's length and content but want to adjust its position—maybe a little to the left or right between its neighbors—then you'll want to use the Slide tool. This third method of adjusting two edit points affects three clips. Sliding the middle clip maintains its content and duration but adjusts its placement between the bordering clips. This alters the duration of the two neighbors but not the overall sequence length.

Sliding is a fine-tuning adjustment that doesn't change the general location of a clip in the sequence but finesses its placement. The Slide tool shares the same location as the Slip tool in the Tool palette.

**1**  To access the Slide tool in the Tool palette, click and hold down the Slip tool until the Slide button appears, then choose it. You can also press SS to make the Slide tool active.

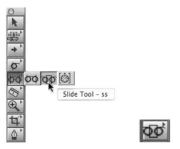

Slide tool in Tool palette    Slide tool button

**2**   In the *Promo_v1 Rough* sequence, play the area around the purple Slide marker.

Shots without sound, such as the computer screen shot, are flexible. In this case, you can slide the clip earlier to allow Parker more time to walk to the rail, or you can slide it a little later so that the Parker clip starts with the **Promo Music** clip.

**3**   Using the Slide tool, hold down the **83-1 MOS** clip. Notice the brown outlines in the Timeline, then release the clip.

| 8D-2 | 66-3 | | 83-1 MOS | ⬚⬚ | 5-3 (F) | | 16C- |
|---|---|---|---|---|---|---|---|
| | 66-3 | | | 113B-1 (A | 5-3 (F) | | 16C- |

This time brown outlines appear around all three clips involved with the adjustment. As you slide the middle clip, you will be making the clips on either side longer or shorter.

4   Slide the **83-1 MOS** clip to the left about 4 frames, but *don't release the mouse button.* Look at the clip in the sequence and then at the two-up display in the Canvas image area.

As you slide the middle clip, the outside edges of the adjacent two clips do not move; only the inner edges bordering the middle clip move to show how the clips are compensating for the adjustment.

In the Canvas two-up display, the two frames show the new Out point of the first clip and the new In point of the third clip. You can watch these frames as you drag to determine the best position for the clip you are sliding.

5   Continue dragging the **83-1 MOS** clip to the left until you no longer see any part of the rail. Release the mouse button, and play around this clip area.

By sliding the middle clip to the left, the outgoing **66-3** clip of the three men is shortened at the tail, and the incoming **5-3 (F)** clip of Parker is lengthened at the head. But the **83-1 MOS** clip is unchanged except for its position between the two clips in the sequence.

In the clip's new position, its timing seems off in relation to both Parker's clip and the music. To fix that, let's slide the middle clip to the right and snap its Out point to the **Promo Music** clip in the A2 and A3 tracks. This will position Parker's clip at the head of the music track.

> **TIP** When snapping is turned on, you can slide a clip and snap it to the playhead, markers, and edit points, just as with the other trim tools.

6  Using the Slide tool, drag the **83-1 MOS** clip to the right and snap its Out point to the **Promo Music** clip's In point. If necessary, you can Option-click the 5-3 (F) audio edit point and roll it to the head of the music track as well. Then, play these clips.

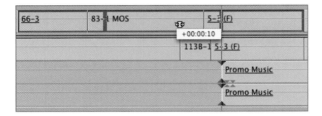

7  To finesse the position of the **83-1 MOS** clip, Shift-click the clip to select it. Press the < and > (angle bracket) keys to finesse its position frame by frame.

> **TIP** You can also press Shift to select the clip and enter an amount for a slide, or press Shift-[ and Shift-] or Shift-< and Shift-> to make multi-frame slide adjustments, just as you did with the Slip tool.

## Dragging Clips to New Locations

Sometimes, sliding a clip a little to the left or right just isn't going to solve a problem. You may need to reposition a clip to an entirely different location in the sequence. Since no new clips are added to the sequence, and you only make a location change, the overall sequence length remains the same. Repositioning, or *shuffling*, a clip to a new location in your sequence does not require any editing tool other than the default Selection tool and a modifier key.

1  In the Sequences bin, open the *Promo_v3 Repo* sequence, and play from the orange "repo starts here" marker.

This sequence was duplicated from the *Promo_v2 Polished* sequence, and a marker was added to identify the target area. Also, because each sequence can be set to a different type of Timeline display, the thumbnail images were turned off to make it easier to view clip names.

While the current order of the clips in this part of the sequence works, you could rearrange the order to create an alternative version. For example, you could position all the clips together of the characters answering their phones.

2   Press A to choose the default Selection tool, and make sure snapping is on.

**NOTE ▶** To reposition a clip successfully, you must use precise key combinations at specific times. Follow steps 3 through 5 carefully, and release the mouse only when instructed to do so.

3   Drag the **101_6** clip of Sophie left and snap its In point to the head of the **100A-2** clip, but don't release the mouse. Press and hold down the Option key.

When you press Option, the pointer changes to the Shuffle Edit pointer, a hooked downward arrow with a smaller arrow pointing to the right, indicating that you will be inserting the clip at this point and that the following clips will be rippled.

In the Canvas, look at the names of the clips in the two-up display. These are the frames that will appear on either side of this clip when you release the clip as an insert edit. Notice that the **100A-2** clip will be bumped to the right of the clip you're repositioning.

**NOTE ▶** If black appears in one of the Canvas two-up frames as you drag a clip through the sequence, either you are at the head or tail of the sequence, or you're over a gap that will be created when you move the clip.

The next step is important for positioning this clip successfully.

4    First release the mouse button, and then release the Option key. Play the area to see how the new clip placement works.

> **TIP** ▶ When you start to implement a major change in a sequence, such as shuffling clips for an alternative look, it's always a good idea to duplicate the original sequence and work with the duplicate, as you've done here. If you decide you don't like the alternative direction, you haven't lost your original work.

Sophie's phone clip (**101-6**) now follows Nathan's phone clip. As in other insert edits, the remaining clips in the sequence are pushed forward to allow room for the repositioned clip. Let's reposition Parker's phone clip to follow Sophie's.

5    Drag Parker's **102_3** clip left and snap its In point to the In point of the **100A-2** clip. Hold down the Option key. Release the mouse button, and then release the Option key. Play the clips in this configuration.

> **TIP** ▶ Look for the snapping arrows around the edit point to ensure that you are at the correct location.

There's another way to drag and reposition a clip, and that's to drag a copy of the original clip. This leaves the original in its current location but allows you to drag a copy to a different location and drop it as an overwrite or insert edit. Since you are really performing two steps in one—copying *and* pasting, it's important to think about which step you're performing and which modifier key you need.

Let's say, for example, you want to copy the **100A-2** cell phone clip and use it to kick off the cell phone segment. Rather than copy and paste the clip, you can simply drag a copy and insert it at a different location. But before you insert a copied clip, let's lock the music tracks so they won't be split when you insert the clip.

6   In the Timeline patch panel, click the Lock Track controls for the A2 and A3 tracks.

Locking tracks protects them from being changed accidentally or, as in this case, from being split at the insert edit point.

7   Adjust the Timeline so that you can see the target clip, **100A-2**, and the target clip location, the beginning of Nathan's **100-2** clip.

8   First click the **100A-2** phone clip and release the mouse button. When you see the Move tool, press the Option key. Move the pointer a little, and when you see the tiny plus sign next to the Move tool, start dragging left, but don't release the mouse button or the Option key.

The small plus sign indicates you are now dragging a copy of this clip, not the original.

The second part of this process is determining whether you want to release this clip as an insert edit or an overwrite edit. Holding down the Option key allows you to insert the clip. Releasing the Option key creates an overwrite edit.

9   To continue, snap the **100A-2** clip into position at the head of the **100-2** clip. Release the Option key, and you see a downward overwrite arrow. Press the Option key again, and the forward insert arrow returns. Release the mouse button to insert this clip at this location.

Hold down the Option key to make an insert edit.

Release the Option key to make an overwrite edit.

**10** Unlock the A2 and A3 tracks, and preview the area to see if you like where this new version is going.

## Take 2
You could order the clips in this sequence in several ways. The problem is that the director knows that too. Shuffle a few clips into different positions to see if you can find some interesting options to show the director.

## Keeping Linked Clips in Sync
As you continue to trim and adjust your sequence clips during the refining process, you may slip or trim one track of a clip only to realize that you have thrown the remaining tracks or other clips out of sync. This can easily happen when you lock some tracks and make changes to the unlocked tracks. Pressing Command-Z will undo any step in Final Cut Pro. But you can use other options to correct out-of-sync clips.

**1** Lock the A1 audio track.

In this example, let's say you previously locked this track as you were making insert edits, and simply left it locked.

**2** Press S to choose the Slip tool, and slip the first clip in the sequence, **8D-2**, to the left about 1 second. Release the clip and play it.

**NOTE** ▶ You will have to slip the clip on the V1 track because you can't slip or change a locked track.

When you play this clip, you can clearly see and hear that the video is out of sync with the audio tracks. However, if it is out of sync for only a few frames, you might not notice it as you watch the clip play in the Canvas. To warn you of a sync problem, big or small, red out-of-sync indicators appear on each linked track in the Timeline, indicating where you are out of sync.

If slipping just the video track was an oversight, you could press Command-Z to undo the move, unlock the A1 track, and slip both tracks of the clip together at one time. However, you also have other choices:

▶ Leave the audio where it is, out of sync.

▶ Slip the audio so the portion beneath the video returns to its original location.

▶ Slip the video back to its original location to match the audio.

3 In the V1 track, Control-click the red out-of-sync indicator and choose Slip into Sync. Make sure you click the red out-of-sync indicator and not the clip itself. Play the clip again.

Now the video track has been slipped so that it matches the audio, and the red out-of-sync indicators are gone.

**TIP** ▶ If linked selection is turned off, and you make editing changes such as moving or slipping a linked clip, out-of-sync indicators will also appear, and you have the same options to move or reposition the tracks back into sync. Don't forget, you can always press Command-Z to undo the previous actions.

**TIP** ▸ Sometimes you may want to purposefully slip a clip's audio out of sync. Rather than stare at the red out-of-sync indicators, you can select the tracks and choose Modify > Mark in Sync. The sync flags will be removed.

## Editor's Cut

The art of editing lies in an ability to refine and finesse sequences. Obviously, the more you practice those skills, the more quickly you will know which trimming tool is right in what situation. In the Editor's Cut bin in the Browser, you'll find a combination of *Leverage* and *SeaWorld* sequences from previous lessons. Use them to practice honing your slipping, rolling, sliding, and shuffling skills.

## Lesson Review

1. How can you display a list of markers that are in a sequence?
2. Where can you change the Timeline settings of the active sequence?
3. Which two edit points does the Slip tool adjust?
4. Which two sets of shortcut keys allow you to adjust edit points one frame at a time?
5. Which two edit points does the Roll tool adjust?
6. How do you adjust one track of a linked clip?
7. How many clips are affected when you apply the Slide tool?
8. Is extending two edit points most similar to rolling, slipping, or sliding edit points?
9. What modifier key is essential to reposition a clip in a sequence without overwriting any other material?
10. What does Option-dragging a clip do?
11. If one track of a clip has gotten out of sync with the other tracks, by being either slipped or moved, how do you resync those tracks?

### Answers

1. Control-click in the Timeline ruler. The markers appear at the bottom of the shortcut menu.
2. In the Sequence Settings window (Sequence > Settings).
3. The Slip tool adjusts the In and Out points of one clip.

4.  The < and > (angle bracket) keys, and the [ and ] (bracket) keys.

5.  The Roll tool adjusts one clip's Out point and the adjacent clip's In point.

6.  Turn off linked selection, or hold down Option before clicking the track.

7.  The Slide tool affects three clips: the position of the middle clip, and the durations of the adjacent clips.

8.  Extending changes an edit point in the same way rolling does.

9.  The Option key is used to shuffle a clip and ripple all other clips in the sequence.

10. Option-dragging creates a copy of a sequence clip and repositions the copy in a different location, leaving the original sequence clip in place.

11. Press Command-Z, or Control-click the red out-of-sync indicators on the tracks you want to adjust and choose "Slip into Sync" or "Move into Sync."

**Keyboard Shortcuts**

| | |
|---|---|
| **E** | Extend selected edit points to the playhead location |
| **R** | Select the Roll tool |
| **S** | Select the Slip tool |
| **SS** | Select the Slide tool |
| **\ (backslash)** | Play around the current playhead location |
| **[ (left bracket) or < (left angle bracket)** | Move the selected edit point or points left in single-frame increments |
| **] (right bracket) or > (right angle bracket)** | Move the selected edit point or points right in single-frame increments |
| **Shift-[ or < (left angle bracket)** | Move the selected edit point or points backward the length of the multi-frame duration |
| **Shift-] or > (right angle bracket)** | Move the selected edit point or points forward the length of the multi-frame duration |
| **Option-Q** | Open the User Preferences window |
| **Drag then press Option** | Insert a clip in a new location |
| **Option-drag** | Drag a copy of a clip to a new sequence location |

# 6

**Lesson Files**   FCP7 Book Files > Lessons > Lesson 6 Project

**Media**        FCP7 Book Files > Media > Leverage; SeaWorld

**Time**         This lesson takes approximately 90 minutes to complete.

**Goals**        Label and rename project elements

Create subclips using In and Out points

Create subclips using markers

Use markers to sync clips

Change poster frames

Create a storyboard

Work with replace edits

Edit multicam footage

## Lesson 6

# Refining the Editing Process

The tools you learned in the previous two lessons helped you trim and refine the individual clips and edit points in your sequence. In this lesson, you will learn new ways to organize and refine your overall workflow. A workflow is simply a process that develops from the kind of editing you typically do. Workflows are influenced by a particular format, by the genre you're editing, and by your hardware configuration. As you continue to develop your skills in Final Cut Pro, your workflow will evolve as you integrate different editing options into your own process.

In the upcoming exercises, you will take one clip and make mini-clips, or *subclips*, from it; color-code clips and use markers to synchronize action; use clips to create storyboards; organize and edit material shot with multiple cameras; and work with a third type of edit, the replace edit. As you begin to incorporate these strategies and procedures into your workflow, you will add tremendous power to your editing sessions.

## Labeling Project Elements

Sometimes you can refine your editing workflow by organizing clips into bins. Other times, you may find it helpful to rename a clip so that you can more easily identify it, or give it a color label to represent its category or type. When you apply these simple organizational strategies to your workflow, you step into a highly efficient and professional use of Final Cut Pro. Because this lesson is about different approaches to the editing process, you will begin by opening the project in a different way: by double-clicking a Final Cut Pro project file.

**1**   On your desktop, open a Finder window and navigate to the Lessons folder. To open the Lesson 6 Project file and open Final Cut Pro at the same time, double-click this project file.

The *Leverage* clips you need for this lesson are in bins labeled by category. The Marked Clips bin will be used for storyboard editing. You will use the Multicam Clips to learn how to edit a scene shot using multiple cameras. Notice that each bin is labeled with a different color. Adding color to your project elements is a great way to organize your material because your eye immediately recognizes it.

**2**   In the Browser, display the contents of the Multicam Clips bin.

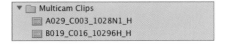

You can give any project item—bin, sequence, or clip—a color label to further organize your workflow.

**3**   In the Multicam Clips bin, double-click the **A029_C003_1028N1_H** clip to open it in the Viewer. Play a little of this clip from the beginning.

When a clip has a color label, the same color appears on the clip's tab in the Viewer. This can remind you of what type of clip it is (possibly B-roll or multicam), what scene it's in, or how you might want to use it in the project.

**NOTE ▶** In a later lesson, you will work with an excerpt from a musical documentary shot in different countries. Clips of performers singing or playing the same song were given the same colored labels.

You may recognize this clip as Nate's medium shot from scene 33 in Lesson 4. But you surely wouldn't recognize the clip by looking at its name. This is the media file name created by the RED ONE camera: It represents camera (A), reel (029), clip (C003), date (1028), unique ID (N1), and the type of RED file (H for half resolution). As part of the *Leverage* workflow, the assistant editors changed the name of these clips in the project to reflect the scene, take, and camera. Let's do the same.

4    In the Multicam Clips bin, select the **A029_C003_1028N1_H** clip and click its name to highlight it. Then type *33B-3 (A)*, and press Return. Change the name of the second multicam clip to *33B-3 (B)*.

When you change the name of the master clip in the Browser, the name also changes in the Viewer window's title bar. (If this clip had been edited into a sequence, the sequence clip name would also have changed.) The media file name does not change, however.

5    In the Browser, select the **33B-3 (A)** clip, and choose View > Reveal in Finder. When you reveal the original media file for this clip, you see that the original name has not been changed, only the name of the clip in this project.

**TIP ▶** To locate the media file of any clip in the Browser or Timeline, select the clip and choose View > Reveal in Finder. You can also use this command for a clip in the Viewer.

**6**   Close the Finder window. In the Sequences bin, Control-click the *Multicam* sequence and choose Label > B Roll from the shortcut menu.

In both the Timeline and Canvas windows, the *Multicam* sequence tab is now color-coded green to match the multicam clips.

**TIP**▶ While you can't change the label colors, you can change the label names in the Labels tab of the User Preferences window. To remove a label, Control-click the clip or a group of selected items and choose Label > None from the shortcut menu.

The *Multicam* sequence tab is currently in the first position in the Timeline and Canvas, but you can easily change the order of tabs to support your editing process. For example, you might want scene or act numbers to appear in order. Since you won't use the *Multicam* sequence until the end of this lesson, let's place it last in the series of tabs.

**7**   Drag the *Multicam* sequence tab to the right, after the *Sync with Markers* sequence tab. Do the same thing in the Canvas window.

**TIP**▶ Make sure you drag the tab horizontally across the tab area. If you accidentally drag the *Multicam* sequence tab out of the tab area, a new Timeline window is created. To correct this, drag the stranded sequence tab back into the main Timeline window tab area.

**8**    Click the *Promo_v4* sequence tab and play the sequence.

The *Leverage* promo sequence is similar to the one you worked with in the previous lesson, except that in this sequence, the clips are named for the characters' actions and are cut to a series of beats in the music track. Notice that each clip appears to be the same length in the Timeline. This sequence was created using the storyboard editing process. You will use that process later in the lesson to create a similar sequence.

In the previous lesson, you turned off the thumbnail images for these clips to make it easier to read the clip names. If the thumbnail images were larger, however, they might be useful in identifying the characters in each clip.

**9**    In the Timeline patch panel, position the pointer over the upper boundary of the V1 track. When the Resize pointer appears, drag up.

    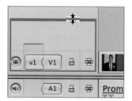

With the larger thumbnail images, the sequence looks almost like a storyboard of the action.

## Take 2

The director is complaining of having too many projects going on simultaneously. To make life easier and to create a smoother workflow, you suggest color-coding some of the sections of this project and placing the sequence tabs in the order you will review them. The director loves the suggestion and offers to take you to lunch! So you do the following:

▶ Color-code the *Promo_v4* sequence to match the color of the Promo Clips bin.

▶ Color-code the *Storyboard* sequence to match the color of the Marked Clips bin.

▶ Change the sequence tab order in both the Timeline and Canvas windows to *Promo_v4, Sync with Markers, Storyboard, Replace, Multicam.*

Finished sequence tab order

## Creating Subclips

In the previous exercise, you saw how helpful it can be to rename a clip. Another simple way to refine your editing process is to divide one long clip, or a clip that contains several actions, into mini-clips, or *subclips*. For example, let's say you're looking for the particular action of Parker pointing her laser to the right of the frame. In the 1-minute clip of Parker, she points and looks over a half dozen directions. Every time you want to view or edit a shot of her pointing to the right, you have to find it among all the other actions in the clip. Instead, you could create a shorter subclip of that specific action.

You may ask, Why not re-mark a different action in the clip and edit that action? That's certainly an option. But when you reedit the **Parker** clip over and over, each clip name in the sequence will reflect the master clip name, *Parker*, and won't contain a reference to the specific action. When you make a subclip, you create a new clip that stands on its own and has its own unique name, such as *Parker points rt*. And it can be accessed directly, as though you originally captured that action as a shorter, separate clip.

MORE INFO ▶ When you create a subclip, it becomes its own master clip. In the next lesson, you will learn more about working and editing with master clips.

**1**   In the Browser, find the Promo Clips bin and double-click the **Parker** clip to open it in the Viewer. Note its duration, then drag the playhead through this clip to review it.

The duration of this clip is 56:10. During that time, you see Parker point her laser and look in several directions within the frame: up, down, left, and right. By creating sub-clips from this clip, you can directly access each action.

To create a subclip, you mark In and Out points identifying the portion of the clip you want to stand on its own. Keep in mind that you're using these marks to create a new clip; you're not setting marks to edit tight around an action. You have to mark a bigger, or *fatter,* portion to create the clip in order to allow for trimming and refining during the editing process.

**2**   Play from the beginning of the **Parker** clip and set an Out point at about 12:17:43:16, just after Parker points the laser to *your* left. Set an In point at the head of the clip. Note the duration of the marked portion.

Even though you could have edited this clip without an In point, you can't create a subclip without setting both an In and an Out point in the clip.

**3**   Choose Modify > Make Subclip, or press Command-U.

The Browser window becomes active, and a new icon appears under the original clip in the Promo Clips bin. The subclip icon has jagged edges, as if it had been torn from the original clip. It also shares the original clip's name for the moment, but the text box is highlighted, awaiting a name change.

**NOTE** ▶ If the Make Subclip item is not available in the Modify menu, make sure the Viewer window is active and that you have marked both an In and an Out point in the clip.

4    Rename the subclip *Parker points left*, and press Return.

**TIP** ▶ Subclips are sorted alphabetically among the other clips in the bin. Giving a subclip a name that begins with the master clip name keeps it closer to the master clip and makes it easier to find.

5    Double-click the new **Parker points left** clip to open it in the Viewer. Press the End key, then press the Home key to see where this clip stops and starts. Play the clip.

The head-of-clip and end-of-clip filmstrips indicate where the media limits are for this subclip, and the Viewer's Timecode Duration field displays the distance between the In and Out points you used to create the subclip. With additional material outside the primary action, you can mark a subclip and edit it just like any other clip.

Let's create another subclip in which Parker reacts to seeing Sophie.

6    From the Browser, open the **Parker** master clip again, and set an In point at around 12:17:54:14. Set an Out point after Parker stops talking, at around 12:18:11:22, about a 17-second duration. Remember, you are not marking an edit, but a section of material.

**7**   Choose Modify > Make Subclip, or press Command-U. In the Browser, enter *Parker reacts* as the subclip name. The new subclip is sorted alphabetically with the other Parker clips.

> **TIP** ▶ After you edit a subclip into a sequence, you cannot lengthen the subclip. You can, however, remove the subclip restrictions you placed on it by selecting the sequence clip and choosing Modify > Remove Subclip Limits. This reverts the clip back to the original master clip length but retains the subclip name.

## Take 2

The director really likes the idea of having separate subclips for each of Parker's head turns because she can give each action its own clip and name. She reminds you that more head turns and reactions are in the **Parker** master clip. Find the following Parker actions, mark them, create subclips of them, and rename them as follows:

▶   12:17:42:08 Parker points right

▶   12:18:14:13 Parker says Hey

▶   12:18:25:06 Parker dashes off

When you're finished, open and screen each of the Parker subclips.

**NOTE** ▶ It's OK if one subclip overlaps another. Each subclip can be made of any portion of the original master clip.

## Adding Markers to Clips

When you're refining your workflow, it's always a good idea to look for ways to combine functions that complement each other. This can increase your efficiency and save time. For example, you've already added markers to a clip in the Timeline. In the next two exercises, you will add markers to clips in the Viewer, convert those markers to subclips, and use markers to align action in a subclip with action in another clip.

Adding a marker to a source clip in the Viewer is exactly like adding a marker in the Timeline ruler. But there's a difference in what you can do with a marker after you've created it in the Viewer. Once you add a marker to a source clip, the marker appears in the Browser, and you can use it to create a subclip *without* setting In and Out points.

> **MORE INFO** ▶ In Lesson 8, you'll learn how to add markers to clips during the capture process. When markers are added during content capture, they appear on the clip and can be converted to subclips using the steps in this exercise.

1   Open the **Parker** master clip in the Viewer. Press Option-X to remove any In or Out points.

Since you're familiar with the locations of Parker's actions in this clip, you will set markers at those actions. You create markers on a clip in the Viewer just as you did in the Timeline. You also name markers in the same way, and choose marker colors, by accessing the Edit Marker window.

2   Position the playhead before Parker points the laser to the left, around 12:17:38:04. Press M to create a marker, and press M again to open the Edit Marker window. Name this marker *Parker points left*, and click OK.

The default red marker is applied unless you choose a different marker color. You can choose any of the marker colors for clips just as you did in the Timeline.

**TIP** ▶ To choose a specific marker color as you create a marker, rather than press M, press Shift-1 through Shift-8 to add any one of the eight marker colors.

**3**  In the Browser, look at the marker beneath the **Parker** clip.

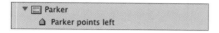

When you add a marker to a clip (or a subclip) in the Viewer, it is attached to the clip and appears as an entry in the Browser. You can rename or delete a marker in the Browser just as you do a clip or sequence. Let's continue adding markers to this clip.

**NOTE** ▶ When you want to delete clip markers in the Viewer, you can use the same keyboard shortcuts you used to delete sequence markers. Press Command-` (grave) to delete a marker at the playhead location, and press Control-` to delete all markers in a clip.

**4**  Add markers at the following locations in the **Parker** clip, and name each marker as follows:

▶  12:17:43:07  *Parker points right* (red marker)

▶  12:17:49:13  *Parker points down* (red marker)

▶  12:17:54:11  *Parker reacts* (blue marker)

**TIP** ▶ Practice using shortcuts to apply specific marker colors: Press Shift-1 to add a red marker, and press Shift-6 to add a blue marker.

**NOTE** ▶ These timecode numbers include pad, or handles, before the action you want to use in editing.

You should now have four markers in the Viewer's scrubber bar. Each marker represents a start point for a portion of this longer clip. The red markers indicate Parker pointing, and the blue marker indicates Parker reacting.

In the Browser, the four markers are attached to this clip.

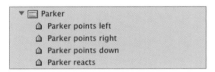

**5**    In the Browser, double-click the "Parker points left" marker and play it in the Viewer.

Unlike a subclip that has a specific Out point, this clip begins at the marker location and continues to the next marker in this clip. If the clip had no other markers, it would continue to the end of the clip.

**6**    In the Browser, select the "Parker points left" marker, then choose Modify > Make Subclip.

A new subclip is created with the marker name followed by *from* and the master clip name. Notice that Final Cut Pro is identifying this marker as a subclip.

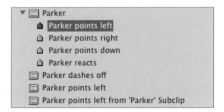

> **TIP**  If you can't see the full name of the new subclip, move the pointer between the Name and Duration column heads. When you see the Resize pointer, drag right.

**7**    Double-click the new subclip to open it in the Viewer, and play the clip. The subclip looks the same as the marker clip you opened and viewed.

**TIP** ▶ You can also use the Edit Marker window to enter a duration for a marker. When you convert a marker that contains a duration to a subclip, the subclip will be the length of the marker duration.

The real power and beauty of converting markers to subclips is that you can convert a group of markers to subclips in one simple step. But before you do, let's create a new bin to organize them.

**8**  Control-click the Promo Clips bin and, from the shortcut menu, choose New Bin. Name this bin *Parker's Markers*, and click its disclosure triangle.

**9**  Select all of the **Parker** clip markers, and drag them to the Parker's Markers bin. The selected markers are automatically converted to subclips.

**TIP** ▶ To convert markers to subclips, you can also select a group of markers, and choose Modify > Make Subclip.

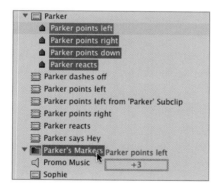

**TIP** ▶ Color-coding a master clip is a good way to find its subclip "children." You can also select the subclip in the Browser, and choose View > Reveal Subclip Parent Clip to find its parent or master.

## Using Markers to Align Actions

You can also use markers to sync action points between two clips in a sequence. When attached to a clip, a marker will always identify the same frame on that clip no matter where the clip is positioned in the sequence. To use a marker to sync action, you align a clip marker to a sequence marker or to another clip marker. In the following steps, you will align one of Parker's markers to a strong beat of music.

> **TIP** ▶ Think of incorporating markers into all of your sequences. You can mark strong beats of music, narration cues, or even potential edit points in the sequence. As you screen your source footage, you can mark shots you would like to accentuate by aligning them to the music or to the verbal cues in the sequence.

1   In the Timeline, click the *Sync with Markers* sequence tab and play the **Promo Music** clip.

    This is a practice sequence in which you will sync one clip to another using markers. In the middle of this music track is a strong downbeat where you can line up, or sync, a specific action from one of the promo clips.

2   Play the **Promo Music** clip from the beginning and find the beat at around 1:00:08:12. Position the playhead at this cue. Click the clip to select it, and press M to set a marker at this location.

    With a clip selected in the Timeline, the marker is placed at the playhead location on the selected clip, not in the Timeline ruler.

3   Drag this clip to the right, then back to the beginning of the sequence. Then deselect it.

    When you reposition this clip, the marker moves with it, continuing to reference the music beat no matter where the clip is positioned in the sequence. When the clip is deselected, you see the default red marker.

4   From the Promo Clips bin, open the **cell connects** clip. In the Viewer, create a purple marker (Shift-7) at 15:28:21:05, where a thumb touches the cell phone screen. Name this marker *connect*.

This would be a nice action to sync to a strong downbeat in the music track. Let's find a second action.

5   Create another purple marker at 15:28:27:06, where the 5:00 countdown begins. Name this marker *countdown*.

6   Drag this clip directly to the Timeline and release it anywhere on the V1 track.

> **TIP** ▶ Make sure snapping is on before you perform the next step.

7   To snap one of the **cell connects** markers to the **Promo Music** marker, drag the video clip over the Promo Music marker. Notice that the In point, Out point, and either marker will snap to the music clips' marker.

8   To snap a specific cell connects marker to the music clip's marker, hold your pointer directly above the first marker in the **cell connects** clip, and drag it over the music marker. When the markers snap to each other, release the clip and play the sync point.

With snapping turned on, the brown snapping arrows appear when you align the markers to each other. Let's see how the second marker aligns to the music beat.

**NOTE ▶** You can also snap a clip marker to a sequence marker in the Timeline ruler in the same way.

**9** Click above the second marker in the **cell connects** clip, and drag it over the music marker. When the markers snap together, release the clip and play the sync action.

Pointer positioned at the marker location before the clip is dragged

Snapping second marker to **Promo Music** marker

When you drag from a particular marker in a clip, you are indicating which marker you want to give snapping priority.

**NOTE ▶** You can also use other editing tools to snap markers to markers. For example, you can choose the Slip tool and position it over a clip marker, then slip the clip to snap one marker to another.

## Using Storyboard Editing

*Storyboards* explain the flow of a story with pictures or drawings. For example, to show how a scene will look when it's cut together, an artist sketches the intended camera shots and places them side by side as individual frames. This allows the director to imagine more clearly what the film will look like and to anticipate problems that may arise during the shoot.

The task of a video editor is no less demanding. To better visualize the clip placement in a sequence, you can create your own storyboard in Final Cut Pro using clips in icon view as the visual reference. Storyboard editing is a great tool for certain situations. For example, you may know what sound bites you want to use in an interview, but are not sure in what order you want them. Or you may be editing a montage of action shots, such as in the *Leverage* promo, but want to experiment with the arrangement of those shots.

Although storyboard editing is quite simple and requires only a few steps, you typically need to do a little preparation beforehand. For example, you need to arrange clips as icons in a bin, and you may need to change the representative frame for some clips to make them easier to identify.

**1**   In the Timeline, click the *Storyboard* sequence tab and play the music track.

In this exercise, some of the preparation has been done for you. For example, in order for one clip to be edited to every four beats of the *Leverage* promo music, clips were selected and marked with a 2:02 duration, the length of one measure of music at the current tempo.

**2**   In the Browser, close all open bins and double-click the Marked Clips bin to open it in a separate window. Look at the names and then the Duration column next to the Name column.

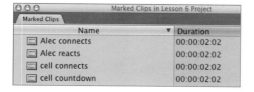

To make the clips easier to identify, their names were changed—just like the names earlier in this lesson—to reflect the character and the action. The clips have also been marked with the same 2:02 duration. To use these clips for storyboard editing, you will need to change the bin's list view to icon view.

**TIP ▶** If you're part of a postproduction team of editors and assistants, you should always discuss any naming conventions with the entire editorial group before making changes.

**3**    Control-click under the Name column and choose View as Large Icons.

If the bin window is small, you can't see all the clips. Let's make the window larger to accommodate the clip icons and rearrange the clips to fill the window.

**4**    Drag the lower-right corner of this bin down and to the right. (It's OK if the bin covers other interface windows.) Control-click in the gray bin area and choose Arrange by Name. Whenever you resize a bin window, you can arrange the clips to fit into that window size.

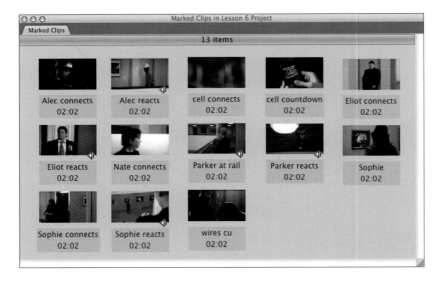

**NOTE ▶** You may recognize one of Parker's subclips as part of this group. When you create subclips, they stand alone in this type of layout and you can work with them individually.

Notice the clip icons associated with each clip. The frame you see representing the clip is called a *poster frame*, just as a movie poster is a visual representation of a film. The default poster frame is the first captured frame of a clip. In some cases, such as the **cell connects** clip, that frame doesn't represent the clip content as well as it might. Let's choose a different frame to use as its poster frame.

**5**   Double-click the **cell connects** clip to open it in the Viewer. In the Viewer, position the playhead when you see the thumb touch the cell phone screen. Choose Mark > Set Poster Frame, or press Control-P. In the Marked Clips bin, the new poster frame for this clip makes it easier to identify in this view.

**6**   In the Marked Clips bin, double-click the **Eliot reacts** clip. Use the same steps above to change this clip's poster frame to where Eliot has his finger to his mouth.

To use this group of clips to create a storyboard, you must first arrange them in the order you want them to appear in the sequence. Where you position the images in the bin determines how they eventually line up in the Timeline sequence. Final Cut Pro starts with the first clip at the upper-left corner of the bin and reads across the row. It then drops down to the next row, and so on, like reading a book.

For this exercise, to achieve a specific result, you will arrange the clips according to the following lists. To arrange the clips, you simply drag a clip into position, and when necessary, drag other clips out of the area.

**7**   Place these clips in the first row of the bin in this order:

▶   **Eliot reacts**
▶   **Alec reacts**
▶   **Parker at rail**
▶   **Sophie**
▶   **Sophie reacts**
▶   **Parker reacts**
▶   **wires cu**

**TIP** ▶ When arranging clips in icon view, you can drag clips off to the side or to a corner. You can even put them in a "dog pile" as you're building your storyboard layout.

8   Place these clips in the second row of the bin:

▶ **Alec connects**

▶ **Nate connects**

▶ **cell connects**

▶ **Sophie connects**

▶ **Eliot connects**

▶ **cell countdown**

Placing the clips in rows is part of what determines their order in the sequence. The other factor is how high they are placed within the row.

9   Place each clip a bit lower than the previous one so that the rows slant slightly down from left to right, as in the following image.

Higher clips, even though they are in the same row, will always go first when you edit the group to the Timeline. Higher-to-lower order overrides left-to-right order.

10  In the Timeline, disconnect the a1 Source control. In the Marked Clips bin, press Command-A to select all the video clips.

**NOTE** ▶ For the next step, you may need to position the Marked Clips bin so that you can also see the Timeline window.

**11** Drag the selected clip icons down to the Timeline and snap them to the head of the sequence. When you see the downward overwrite arrow, release the mouse button. Then play the sequence.

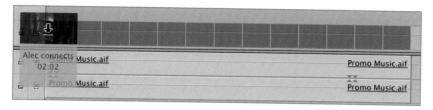

**NOTE ▶** Depending on the size of your Timeline, you may not see all of the clips in the window. If you don't, continue with the edit and then press Shift-Z to bring the sequence into full view.

All the clips are positioned in the Timeline just as they were in the Storyboard bin. Only the marked portions are edited.

With the storyboard edit complete, you can refine these clips with your editing tools. For example, if you want a slightly different selection of content in a clip, you can slip it, which will refine the content but maintain the original clip length. If you want to shuffle a clip to a different location, you can drag the clip to the new location, hold down Option, then release the clip.

**TIP ▶** As you did earlier in this lesson, you can drag up the V1 track boundary to see the V1 thumbnail images more clearly as you work.

## Take 2

The director likes the current *Leverage* promo of music and action clips. But the producer wants to see the clips in a different order. "No problem," you say. You know you're just a few short steps away from creating a second version—*without* disturbing the first.

▶   Add a new V2 track and target that track.

▶   In the Marked Clips bin, reorder the clips per the producer's vision.

▶   Drag the clips to the V2 track and release them as an overwrite edit. Tweak as necessary.

▶   To review the director's version on V1, turn off the V2 Track Visibility control.

Close the Marked Clips bin when you've completed this Take 2 exercise.

## Performing Replace Edits

After you've arranged clips in a sequence—by editing them either individually or as a group using the storyboard process—you can replace individual clips using a replace edit. This function is very helpful when you're at the stage of your editing process where you like the length and position of each clip in your sequence but want to swap out one clip for another using the original clip's length and location as a reference.

Unlike the overwrite and insert edits, the replace edit does not rely on In and Out points, either in the new clip or in the sequence. It relies solely on the location of the playhead in the Viewer and the Timeline.

1   In the Timeline, click the *Replace* sequence tab.

This is the completed storyboard sequence you created in the previous exercise. Notice that in this sequence the thumbnails have been turned off to make it easier to read the clip names.

2   Move the playhead to the first frame of the third clip, **Parker at rail**. Zoom in to this clip.

Unlike other types of edits where you mark In and Out points in the sequence, here you don't have to identify clip duration. In fact, edit points are ignored in a replace edit. Instead, the playhead identifies the clip and saves you from having to mark its duration. Since the clip has a specific length, only that portion of the sequence will be replaced.

3   From the Promo Clips bin, open the **Parker points left** subclip and scrub through it. Position the playhead just before Parker points the laser down, at around 12:17:39:03.

You will begin using this clip from the playhead location. Remember, with replace edits, you use just the playhead; you don't use In or Out points.

**TIP** ▶ If In or Out points appear in this clip and you find them distracting, press Option-X to remove them.

4    Since you want to edit only video, make sure the a1 Source control is disconnected. Drag the source clip from the Viewer to the blue Replace section in the Canvas Edit Overlay. Play the edit.

**TIP** ▶ You could also click the blue Replace button in the Canvas window.

The entire video portion of the Timeline sequence clip is replaced by source content, starting at the Viewer playhead position. In this case, the frame at the Viewer playhead is lined up and edited at the Timeline playhead position.

Notice that the clip name in the Timeline is the subclip name, not the master clip name. By creating, naming, and editing a subclip, you know exactly what content this clip contains.

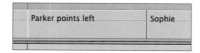

**NOTE** ▶ If the playhead is positioned in the middle of a sequence clip, the source clip playhead in the Viewer aligns with the sequence playhead, and source content fills the sequence clip before and after the playhead position.

Replace is a very simple type of edit, yet it can be used in many situations. You can synchronize actions by positioning the playhead on an action in the Viewer, positioning the Timeline playhead at a sync point in the sequence, and choosing Replace. You can mark an area of the Timeline and replace the content in the marked area. You can also use a replace edit to backtime a clip by placing the playhead at the desired Out point in both the Viewer and Timeline. The more you work with the replace edit, the more you will develop creative ways to use it.

**NOTE ▸** If you try to replace the sequence clip with a shorter source clip, or position the playhead in the Viewer too close to the head or tail of the clip, a message will appear saying, "Insufficient content for edit."

## Take 2

Unfortunately, the director has seen how easy it is to replace an edit in the sequence. Since she was having trouble deciding which action in the **Parker** master clip to use as the third shot in the *Replace* sequence, she wants you to show her the following options:

- ▸ Parker reacting to seeing Sophie
- ▸ Parker pointing down
- ▸ Parker looking up left
- ▸ Parker leaving frame

**TIP ▸** For this last edit, position the playhead in the Viewer where you want the source content to stop, when Parker has just left the frame. In the Timeline, position the playhead on the last frame of the third clip, and click the Replace button. This is another way to backtime a clip.

## Editing Multicam Footage

If your production uses multiple cameras to shoot the same event, you can take advantage of Final Cut Pro's *multiclip* feature. Whether you shoot with 2 cameras or 20, this feature allows you to group or sync together all the individual sources that recorded an event.

Then you can edit a sequence in real time, as if you were cutting it live in a sports production truck or television control room. Several types of productions use this function, including sitcoms, soap operas, reality shows, music concerts, and sporting events. Even dramatic television shows such as *Leverage* shoot some scenes rolling A and B cameras at the same time. With a little creative planning, anyone with a few cameras shooting an event can use this feature as well.

> **NOTE** ▶ With Final Cut Pro's multiclip approach to grouping clips, you can sync and play any set of clips at one time. The material does not have to share the same time-code, be in the same format, or even be shot at the same time or location.

### Organizing a Multicamera Editing Workflow

There are really just three stages to working with multicam footage in Final Cut Pro: creating the multiclip, organizing or modifying it, and then editing it. Before you begin shooting and capturing a multicam project, however, take a few steps to make the editing process smoother:

▶ If the production budget allows, add a timecode generator to send the same timecode to each camera or recording device. You can use the timecode as a reference to organize the sources.

▶ If a timecode generator is not an option, record a visual or sound cue, such as a clapboard, an audio pop, or a camera flash before the action begins, or after it ends, to help synchronize the sources.

▶ Assign each camera a number or letter that identifies that camera angle, such as A, B, C, or 1, 2, 3.

▶ Enter the camera angle number or letter during the log-and-capture process. While this is not a critical step, it can save you time organizing the clips during editing.

> **NOTE** ▶ In the *Leverage* footage, the camera information is included at the end of the clip name. The clips in the image above both captured the same scene and take, 33B-3, but from different camera angles, (A) and (B).

### Creating a Multiclip

When creating a multiclip, you group together a set of clips for the purpose of seeing them play at the same time. Before you actually group the individual clips into a single multiclip, you have to know how you will synchronize the sources. If you recorded the same timecode to all the sources, you can skip a few steps and proceed to making the multiclip. If you recorded an audio pop, clapboard, flash, or other audiovisual cue, you first have to set an In or Out point at that precise sync reference. If no reference was intentionally recorded, you can still create a multiclip by finding and marking the same cue, dialogue line, or visual reference in all the clips.

You can group up to 128 sources or angles into one multiclip and view up to 16 cameras at one time. For this exercise, you will create a multiclip using two clips from the *Leverage* scene you worked with in Lesson 4. These clips do not share the same timecode, so you will have to find the same dialogue line and set an In point in each clip.

**1**   In the Browser, close all open bins, and display the contents of the Multicam Clips bin. Double-click the **33B-3 (A)** clip and play the beginning of the clip.

This take of scene 33 was shot with two cameras: a medium shot of Nate and a wide shot of the entire group. Because there is no slate at the head of the clip, you will have to mark a dialogue line as a reference.

**NOTE ▸** Dramatic films and television shows always have a slate recorded at the head of takes. For the book's DVD, however, some of the clips had to be shortened to conserve space.

**2**    At the beginning of the clip, find the point where Nate says, "Grifter, hitter, hacker, thief." Position the playhead on the first sound of the *G* in "Grifter." Mark an In point at this location, or one frame before. You can also click the Mono tab to see or refine your mark.

> **TIP** ▶ To hear each frame as you scrub (or as you use the JKL or arrow keys), make sure in the View menu that Audio Scrubbing is selected.

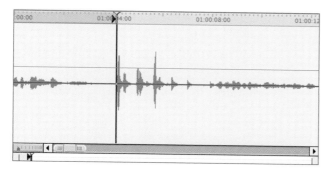

Keep in mind that this In point will be used for synchronizing the two clips, not for editing the clip. You will later set a different In point to edit the clip.

> **TIP** ▶ Marking a dialogue line as a sync point can work very well as long as you use the same reference for all the clips.

**3**    Open the **33B-3 (B)** clip. Play the beginning of this clip and listen for Nate's same line, "Grifter, hitter, hacker, thief." Mark an In point using the same reference you used for the previous clip.

While the A camera was shooting Nate throughout the scene, the B camera was shooting the wide shot of Nate and the group at the same time.

With the two clips marked, Final Cut Pro knows where to start playing them to be in sync.

4  To group the two clips as a multiclip, select them and choose Modify > Make Multi-clip. You can also Control-click one of the selected clips and choose Make Multiclip from the shortcut menu.

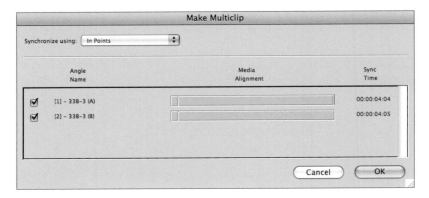

The Make Multiclip dialog appears, displaying the two clips. If no angle number was entered in the Angle column in the Browser, the clips are placed in alphabetical order, as they are here. The solid blue bars represent the clip content. The gray portion of the bar indicates areas where there is no clip content.

**TIP** ▶ If you need to group a lot of clips into a multiclip, take the extra step of giving each clip an angle number based on its position in the original shoot. You can enter angle numbers or letters for each clip in the Angle column in the Browser.

5  Click the "Synchronize using" pop-up menu to view the options. You can synchronize clips by In points, Out points, or Timecode. Choose In Points, which is the default option.

The clips are aligned according to the In point you set on each clip. If the clips all had the same timecode, you could skip the step of marking In points. In that case, you would choose Timecode as the sync option in this dialog.

**TIP** ▶ To deselect one of the multiclip angles from the multiclip selection, click the angle checkbox next to that clip.

**6**  Click OK.

A multiclip icon appears in the Browser. This icon always represents a group of clips. Notice that the name is italicized and begins with the angle 1 clip's name, **33B-3 (A)**.

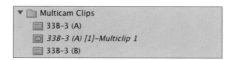

**NOTE** ▶ The number following a new Multiclip, Sequence, or Bin indicates the number of those items created in the project as you've been working, not necessarily the number of those items currently in the project.

**7**  Click the name portion of the multiclip. When it becomes highlighted, rename it *Sc 33B*, then press Return.

Because the angle and clip name are assigned automatically, only the name of the multiclip is changed.

**NOTE** ▶ A multiclip can contain any type of clip in the Browser, such as a graphic file or still image. You can also choose a bin and make a multiclip of all the clips in that bin.

### Playing and Organizing a Multiclip

Now that you've created a multiclip in the Browser, you're ready for step 2: to view it, organize it, and arrange your interface to better utilize this process. No matter how many—or how few—cameras you have in the multiclip group, it's important to organize or modify the multiclip in a way that best represents the original scene or event. That generally means positioning the images in the Viewer to make them appear as though you are watching the scene live. Let's start by playing the multiclip in the Viewer.

**1**   In the Browser, double-click the **Sc 33** multiclip to open it in the Viewer.

In the Viewer, both clips are displayed simultaneously according to angle number. Notice that the In point that you set to synchronize the clips appears in the scrubber bar. You can use all of the functions and shortcuts to play a multiclip that you use to play other clips.

**2**   Play the multiclip from the In point and watch to see if both clips are in sync.

**3**   To create a larger Viewer image area, choose Window > Arrange > Two Up.

**TIP** ▶ To make the Timeline window larger in this layout, drag the Browser and Timeline boundary to the far left.

**4**   Click between the two clips in the Viewer.

By clicking a clip in the Viewer, you are *switching* angles. The selected, or active, angle is highlighted with a blue-green outline.

In the Browser, the angle name and number on the multiclip change to reflect the active angle, while the name of the multiclip itself, *Sc 33*, remains constant. The multi-clip will reposition itself within the Multicam Clips bin according to the current sort order.

**TIP** ▶ If at any time you no longer see both multiclip angles in the Viewer, just double-click the multiclip in the Browser to reopen it.

5    In the Viewer, click the View pop-up menu and choose Show Multiclip Overlays.

The multiclip overlay displays each clip's angle number, name, and timecode. It works like other overlays in that you see it only when you scrub, not when you play the multiclip.

**6**    To see Nate's medium shot on the right, Command-drag the **33B-3 (A)** clip to
the right.

As soon as you begin to drag a clip to a new angle position, the clip in the original
angle position moves to allow for the new clip arrangement. When you have a lot of
camera angles to organize, you simply Command-drag each clip into whatever position makes the most sense for you.

**7**    Click the Playhead Sync pop-up menu in the Viewer. Make sure Video + Audio is
selected.

When Video + Audio is the active mode, you are switching to the video *and* audio of the clip you select. But when you change the mode to Video, you switch between just the video sources, and you can take the audio unaltered from one clip. This can reduce audio artifacts, such as pops at the edit points or uneven sound levels between the clips. Since the audio is the same on both of these clips, let's switch the audio to **33B-3 (A)** for the entire scene.

8    If it's not already selected, click the **33B-3 (A)** clip. Click the Playhead Sync pop-up menu again, and this time choose Video as the switching mode. Then click the **33B-3 (B)** clip.

The blue-green highlight separates when not in Video + Audio mode. The green highlight stays over the active audio source, and the blue highlight switches to the **33B-3 (B)** clip, indicating that it is the active video angle. By leaving the Playhead Sync option on Video, you can switch between just the video of these two clips, and take the audio from just one clip.

### Editing a Multiclip

Editing a multiclip into the Timeline is the same as editing a single clip. You mark your multiclip in the Viewer, position the playhead in the Timeline, and patch the Source control. You can even click the Overwrite or Insert button in the Canvas to make the edit.

Conceptually, however, editing multiclips is a little different from editing single clips. With multiclip editing, you edit the multiclip to the Timeline and *then* make editing choices about when you want to cut to a different angle.

**NOTE** ▶ In the Timeline, click the RT (Real-Time) pop-up menu and make sure Multiclip Playback is selected. You will learn more about the options in this menu in a later lesson.

**1**   In the Viewer, set a new In point about a second before the current In point, after the group stops talking and just before Nate starts to walk.

**2**   Make sure the **33B-3 (A)** clip is the active audio source (it will have a green highlight around it). Make sure the **33B-3 (B)** clip is the active video angle.

**3**   In the Timeline, click the *Multicam* sequence tab. Make sure the playhead is at the beginning of the sequence, and that the video and audio Source controls are patched to the V1 and A1 destination tracks.

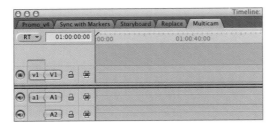

**4**   To edit the multiclip into the Timeline, click the red Overwrite button in the Canvas.

**TIP** ▶ Hold down the Option key to manually drag the multiclip into the Canvas Edit Overlay or directly to the Timeline.

In the Timeline, a mono audio track appears along with one video track. Multiclips are contained within one clip in the Timeline. You can see from the names on the tracks that the audio is from one clip and the video is from another. You also see the green label appear over the clip names and thumbnail image.

5   Play the beginning of the sequence.

When you play the sequence, you see only the active angle, or the top layer, play in the Canvas. To see the other angles play in the Viewer at the same time, you have to change the playhead sync.

**NOTE** ▸ Although you can double-click the multiclip in the sequence to open it in the Viewer, you still need to perform the following step to see all the angles play simultaneously.

6   In the Canvas, click the Playhead Sync pop-up menu and choose Open. (You can also choose View > Playhead Sync Open.) Play the multiclip again.

Final Cut Pro opens the multiclip into the Viewer and keeps it open as you continue editing, so you can see all the angles play at once. Notice in the Viewer's scrubber bar that the sprocket holes appear as they do when you open a single clip from the Timeline.

7   Without playing the multiclip, click each angle in the Viewer to see it appear in the Canvas.

In the Timeline V1 track, the thumbnail image changes whenever you switch to a different angle, as does the angle name on the clip. However, since the switching mode is set to Video in the Playhead Sync pop-up menu, the audio track doesn't change.

Switching from angle to angle is for screening purposes. To change the angle at a certain point in the sequence, you need to cut between angles in order to create edit points in the multiclip. The way you cut to a different camera, and make a new edit point in the multiclip, is to play the clip and select a different camera *as the multiclip is playing.*

8   In the Viewer, click the **33B-3 (B)** clip as your starting clip. In the Timeline, play the sequence and listen for cues where you might want to cut from one camera angle to the other.

Just as a director rehearses when to switch between cameras on a production shoot, you may find it helpful to review and rehearse certain edit possibilities, or *cut points,* before actually cutting the scene. For example, the first cut might be after Nate says, "Grifter, hitter, hacker, thief."

**NOTE** ▶ How frequently you cut, or how long you stay with each camera, is a personal choice. Feel free to experiment with your choices in this exercise.

In the next step, you can put on your director's hat and let the footage roll as you cut between the two camera angles in real time. This is often called *cutting on the fly.* To do this, you watch the individual images in the Viewer and click the one you want *when* you want to cut to it. Remember, once you've cut the new edit points, you can also fine-tune them with the Roll tool, as you did in the previous lesson.

9   With the Timeline window active, play from the beginning of the multiclip. After you hear Nate say, "Grifter, hitter, hacker, thief," click the medium shot of Nate in the Viewer. Then stop playing and view the edit.

In the Timeline, a new clip appears on the V1 track where you cut to the different angle. These clips are still part of the **Sc 33B** multiclip.

When zoomed in to the edit point, you can see the different clip names.

**TIP** ▶ To switch to a different angle at this location, place the playhead anywhere over the clip and click a different angle in the Viewer.

**10** Play the multiclip from this edit point, and click back and forth between Nate's medium shot and the wide shot.

When you click a new angle in the Viewer as the multiclip is playing, hollow markers appear in the Timeline ruler at your cut points.

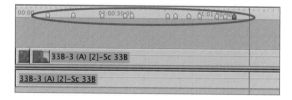

When you stop playing the sequence, edit points are created in the multiclip at each marker location.

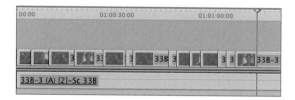

**11** Play the new multiclip to see how it looks. If you want to redo the entire take, press Command-Z to remove all the edit points that were created in the most recent take. If you want to adjust one or two of the current edit points, use the Roll tool so that the clips will remain in sync.

**TIP** ▶ If you need to collapse a multiclip into a single clip for output, you can select the clips in the Timeline and choose Modify > Collapse Multiclip(s).

## Take 2

Everyone has left for the day. Now's your chance to live your dream of becoming a director. Create a new sequence, edit the *Leverage* multiclip into it, put on *your* director's hat, and start cutting.

**MORE INFO** ▶ There are additional ways to switch and cut multiclips that use customized keyboards and button bars. You can find these described, along with other methods of editing multiclips, in the Final Cut Pro User Manual.

## Editor's Cut

You've learned a lot of great ways to refine your workflow in this lesson. But to really absorb these tools, you might consider applying them to different types of footage. For example, there is a long whale behavior clip you can subclip, and another you can match to a music track. And you can build a quick sequence by storyboarding the marked SeaWorld behavior clips to music.

All the elements you need are in the Editor's Cut bin in the Browser.

▶ **J and L circle** clip (SeaWorld Behaviors bin)—Create three subclips from this clip.

▶ *News Story* sequence—Add a marker at a narration cue, then sync a whale behavior clip to that marker.

▶ *SeaWorld Storyboard* sequence—Use the SeaWorld Marked Clips bin to practice storyboard editing.

## Lesson Review

1. How do you add a color label to a clip, bin, or sequence?

2. How do you create a subclip from another clip?

3. Where can you place markers?

4. Does snapping affect markers?

5. What modifier key is used to create a new poster frame?

6. What does the replace edit do?

7. How should clips be organized in a bin before making a storyboard-type edit?

8. What does it mean when a production is shot multicam?

9. How do you create a multiclip?

10. When creating a multiclip, what are the three ways you can sync clips or angles?

11. What modifier key do you use to modify the arrangement of multiclip angles in the Viewer?

12. What's the difference between switching angles and cutting angles?

13. Can a multiclip in a sequence be collapsed for output as a single clip? If so, how?

### *Answers*

1. In the Browser, Control-click the item and choose Label, then select a color.

2 Set In and Out points in the clip, then choose Modify > Make Subclip.

3. Place markers in the Timeline ruler or on a selected clip in the Timeline. You can also add markers to a clip in the Viewer.

4. Yes. When snapping is on, you can snap the playhead to markers and snap a clip marker to a sequence marker or to another clip marker.

5. The Control key is used to create a new poster frame (Control-P).

6. It replaces a sequence clip with a source clip, aligning the Viewer and Timeline playhead positions.

7. Clips should be placed in rows, with each clip in a row appearing slightly lower than the previous clip.

8. Multiple cameras were used to shoot the same action at the same time but from different angles.

9. In the Browser, select the clips you want to include in the multiclip and choose Modify > Make Multiclip, or Control-click a selected clip or bin and choose Make Multiclip from the shortcut menu.

10. You can sync clips or angles by In points, Out points, or timecode.

11. The Command key.

12. Switching changes the angle you see at the playhead location; cutting makes a new edit point at that location.

13. Yes, you collapse a multiclip by choosing Modify > Collapse Multiclip(s).

**Keyboard Shortcuts**

| | |
|---|---|
| **M** | Add a marker |
| **Option-M** | Move playhead back to the previous marker |
| **Shift-M** | Move playhead forward to the next marker |
| **Control-P** | Reset the poster frame in a clip |
| **Command-U** | Make a subclip |
| **Command-` (grave)** | When the playhead is over the marker, delete the marker in the sequence or selected clip |
| **Control-` (grave)** | Delete all markers in the sequence or selected clip |
| **Shift-` (grave)** | Move a marker forward to the playhead position |
| **Shift-1–Shift-8** | Choose a specific marker color |

# Customizing
# and Capturing

# 7

| | |
|---|---|
| Lesson Files | FCP7 Book Files > Lessons > Lesson 7 Project |
| Media | FCP7 Book Files > Media > Leverage; Quest; SeaWorld |
| Time | This lesson takes approximately 90 minutes to complete. |
| Goals | Reconnect unlinked media files |
| | Play sequences with multiple formats |
| | Work with master clips and match frames |
| | Log notes in Browser columns |
| | Find project items |
| | Customize shortcut keys and button bars |
| | Save and reload customized layouts |
| | Optimize user preferences |

# Customizing Final Cut Pro

As you develop your workflow and editing strategies, Final Cut Pro silently supports you in many ways. Even though much of this support goes on under the hood without your being aware of it, tapping into the way Final Cut Pro "thinks" can benefit all of your editing projects.

For example, one primary way that Final Cut Pro supports you is by collecting media file information, or *metadata*, while capturing your footage. This initially helps you identify and maintain the links between media files and project clips; but FCP also provides ways to customize, change, or add to that metadata throughout the editing process. In the next lesson, you will learn to capture media in various formats and to enter clip information.

In this lesson, you will add information, or *metadata,* to a clip that has already been captured, find and organize information in the project, play mixed formats within one sequence, and work with master clips and match frames. You'll also explore ways to reconnect offline media to clips, recall customized layouts and move them to other computer stations, customize the keyboard and button bars, and optimize your user preferences. While these aids don't always affect the look of your finished sequence, they do help you work more effectively.

## Reconnecting Media

To start this lesson, you will open the Lesson 7 Project file and find that some of the clips in the project are not linked to their media files. Final Cut Pro will always look for a media file in the same location that the file was in when you first captured or imported the clip into a project.

If a media file has been removed, renamed, or relocated, for example to a different drive, the link to the clip in the project may be broken; in that case, the clip goes *offline,* meaning it won't play in the project until it's reconnected. When that occurs, Final Cut Pro will ask for your advice on how to proceed.

1   In Final Cut Pro, open FCP7 Book Files > Lessons > Lesson 7 Project. An Offline Files dialog will appear, *but wait* to perform step 2 before moving forward.

> **TIP** ▶ As you work through this lesson, make note of any functions you might like to access via an onscreen button. Later in this lesson, you can add those functions to a button bar.

At some point, a few of the media files for this project were moved to a FireWire drive so that editing could continue at a different computer. They were then moved back to the Media/Quest folder. Now Final Cut Pro needs to relink the clips in this project to the media files in their current location.

When Final Cut Pro cannot find the media files that connect to your project clips, three things happen:

▶   An Offline Files dialog appears, indicating that some files have gone offline. You have the option of reconnecting the files or continuing with them offline. If you select Media Files in the Forget Files section and then click Continue, Final Cut Pro will assume that you don't want to connect the files, and it won't remind you about them in the future.

**NOTE ▶** A good time to select the Forget Files option is when you have slimmed down a project by removing some of the unused media files from your hard disk but haven't yet removed those clips from your project.

▶ In the Browser, the offline clips that do not link back to media files have a red slash over their icons.

▶ In the Timeline, offline clips appear white with a red-and-black thumbnail image.

**NOTE ▶** When the playhead moves over an offline clip in the Timeline, a "Media Offline" frame appears in the image area of the Canvas along with the media file name.

To view these media files in this lesson, you need to reconnect the clips to the original media files in their current location.

**2**    In the Offline Files dialog, click the Reconnect button.

A Reconnect Files dialog appears and lists the offline clips. The first clip (narration) is underlined to indicate that it is the next clip you link. If Final Cut Pro knows where it last found the files, it will list that location.

If you know where the files are located now, you can select Search Single Location and then navigate to the appropriate location. This will speed up the search, since Final Cut Pro won't have to check all the available hard drives and directories. Leave Search Single Location unselected for now.

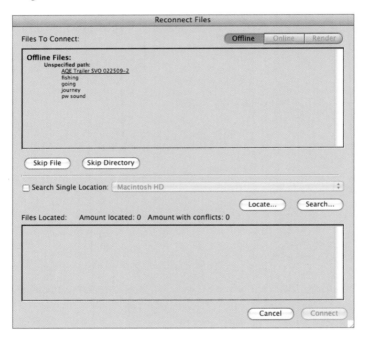

You have two options for finding a missing media file: Locate or Search.

Click the Locate button to look for the missing file manually. (Choose this option when the name of the media file has changed, or when you have more than one version of the media file, perhaps in different formats.)

Click the Search button to initiate an automatic search for the file. In this case, since you know exactly where the file is located, you will locate it yourself.

**3**    Click Locate. A Reconnect dialog appears.

4    Navigate to the FCP7 Book Files > Media > Quest > Quest Clips folder. Click the
     **AQE Trailer SVO 022509-2** file and then click Open.

     The default file search option is Matched Name and Reel Only. When this option is
     selected in the Reconnect dialog, only clips that match the original name are high-
     lighted and selectable.

     If the file you want to relink is dimmed and can't be selected, click the Show pop-up
     menu in the lower left of the Reconnect dialog and choose All Files. This will enable
     you to click any file. Also, you can deselect Matched Name and Reel Only if the file-
     name has changed and you'd like to relink to the clip with the new name.

     Once found, the clips are listed in the Files Located section of the dialog along with
     the file paths to their new locations.

     **NOTE ▶** If you changed something about your clip—such as reel number, timecode,
     or number of tracks—an alert will appear. If you are aware of the conflict and know
     this is the right clip, go ahead and connect to it. When a mismatch does occur, the num-
     ber of conflicts appears in the lower left of the dialog, and the clip name is italicized.

5    Click Connect, then press Command-S to save your project.

     In the Browser, the red slashes on the offline clips are removed because Final Cut Pro
     has reconnected these clips to their media files and can play them in the project.

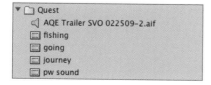

**NOTE ▶** If additional clips remain unlinked in the Reconnect Files dialog after you reconnect your own files, click Locate again and navigate to those files.

In the Timeline, the clip thumbnails are restored, and the Canvas window again displays a frame of the video clip.

At any point, if you change the name of the clip in the Browser, it will still be able to link back to the media file. However, if you rename the media file on the hard disk, you will have to reconnect the project clip.

**TIP ▶** To reconnect a clip that is offline, you can also Control-click the clip in the Browser or Timeline and choose Reconnect Media from the shortcut menu.

## Working with Mixed-Format Sequences

During production, many projects are shot in just one video format, such as HDV, DV, HD, and so on. Other shows may need to incorporate several formats in one project.

For example, sports or reality television productions may shoot some of the program in HD and then use DV for smaller *lipstick* cameras, which shoot hard-to-get angles such as the view from a skier's helmet. Then, they might add older SD (standard definition) material from previous shows that were shot on DigiBeta or Betacam.

In this exercise, you will play multiple formats in the same sequence and use two windows to view details about a clip or sequence.

**1**    In the Timeline, click the *Show Reel* sequence tab and play this sequence.

The *Show Reel* sequence is a rough cut that contains excerpts from three sequences. The yellow and blue audio clip labels identify the excerpts you've worked with in previous lessons (from *Leverage* and *Believe*, respectively); the unlabeled excerpt is from an upcoming lesson.

As you played the sequence, you may not have noticed any difference between the clips. But footage in this sequence is in three formats—HDV and two new formats, Apple ProRes 422 (LT) and Apple ProRes 422 (Proxy)—and has two frame rates—23.98 and 29.97 fps. Let's take a closer look at the format settings for these clips.

**2**    In the Timeline, Control-click the **sham slam** clip and from the shortcut menu, choose Item Properties > Format.

**TIP**    You can also Control-click a clip in the Browser to access the Item Properties window for that clip, or choose Edit > Item Properties.

The Item Properties window opens, displaying format information for this clip, including its compressor type, frame or video rate, and frame size (pixel dimensions). From this window, you see this clip was compressed using the HDV 1080i60 format, its video rate is 29.97 frames per second (fps), and its frame size is 1440 x 1080 (pixel and line count, respectively).

**NOTE ▶** In the Item Properties window, the Timing tab displays clip timecode, In and Out locations, and marked duration; the Logging tab contains information that was entered during the capture or editing process (in this tab you can also choose a color label for the clip); and the Film tab displays film information, if that was the originating format. The keyboard shortcut for opening the Item Properties window is Command-9.

When you need information about a clip, the Item Properties window is a good place to find it. You can also look under the hood of a sequence in the same way you just looked at a clip's properties.

**3**   To close the Item Properties window, click Cancel. With the *Show Reel* sequence tab active in the Timeline window, choose Sequence > Settings, or press Command-0.

Looking at the QuickTime Video Settings in the lower left of the Sequence Settings window, you see that the compressor type is HDV 1080i60. Above that, you see that the Editing Timebase is 29.97 fps and that its frame size is 1440 x 1080. These settings match the clip settings you saw in the Item Properties window.

These settings represent the SeaWorld footage, but they don't necessarily represent the other footage in this sequence.

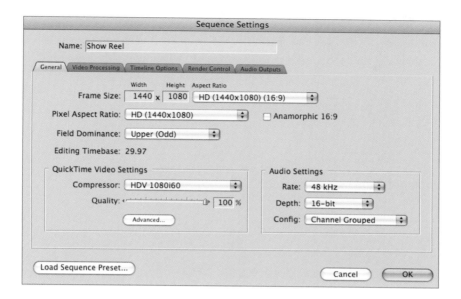

4    Click Cancel to close the Sequence Settings window. In the Timeline, Control-click the first *Leverage* video clip, **Eliot reacts-2**, and choose Item Properties > Format.

This clip is in the Apple ProRes 422 (LT) format; its video rate is 23.98 fps and the frame size is 960 x 720. Despite the different format, size, and frame rate of this footage, Final Cut Pro plays these clips without interruption and without the need to alter any settings.

**NOTE ▶** Changing the frame size of a clip is one way to reduce the media file size.

In the previous exercise, you reconnected project clips to media files on your hard disk. In the future, if you ever lose track of where a clip is located on your hard disk, or don't remember the media file name, just look at the Source row in the Item Properties window.

| Item Properties: Show Reel | |
|---|---|
| Format \ Timing \ Logging \ Film | |
| | V1 |
| Name | Eliot reacts–2 |
| Type | Clip |
| Creator | Final Cut Pro |
| Source | Macintosh HD:FCP7 Book Files:Media:Leverage:Promo:Eliot reacts–2.mov |
| Offline | |

**5**  Click Cancel to close this window.

### ▶ Apple's ProRes format

You may have worked with an Apple ProRes format in Final Cut Pro 6. This format provides a high-quality image and a small file size. Final Cut Pro 7 includes five versions of the ProRes format: Apple ProRes 4444, Apple ProRes 422 (HQ), Apple ProRes 422, Apple ProRes 422 (LT), and Apple ProRes 422 (Proxy).

Each format variant serves a different purpose in the postproduction process, from offline editing on a MacBook Pro using Apple ProRes 422 (Proxy), to advanced "digital negative" workflows for theatrical releases on film using Apple ProRes 4444. These options give you added flexibility when capturing, converting, or exporting your footage throughout the editing process. For more information about the Apple ProRes format, see the Final Cut Pro User Manual.

To change the settings of an existing sequence, you go to the Sequence Settings window. Let's change the current *Show Reel* sequence's starting timecode.

**6**  Choose Sequence > Settings, and click the Timeline Options tab. In the Starting Timecode field, enter *2:00:00:00*, for 2 hours. You can also enter the shortcut *2…* (2 period period period) and click OK.

> **TIP** ▶ Every period you add to a timecode or duration entry is read as two zeros.

In the Timeline ruler, notice that the sequence now starts at 2:00:00:00, rather than the default 1:00:00:00. If you had four active projects and each had its own *Show Reel* sequence, changing the starting timecode would be a good way to identify or code that sequence.

You can make other changes in this window, such as choosing to see thumbnails on the video tracks and waveforms on the audio clips. These changes affect the selected or active sequence only. They *will not* affect any new sequences you create. Those settings are controlled in the Timeline Options tab of the User Preferences window, which you will work with later in this lesson.

**TIP** ▶ You can also Control-click a sequence in the Browser and choose Settings from the shortcut menu to open the Sequence Settings window.

## Working with Master Clips

As you delve deeper into Final Cut Pro, you'll find that master clips are the foundation of any Final Cut Pro project, because they provide direct links to the media files on your hard disk.

In an effort to maintain this direct link, Final Cut Pro gives master clip status to a clip when it's the first use of that clip in the project. If you copy and paste that clip from one bin to another, or edit it into a sequence, the copied or edited clip will be an *affiliate* of the master clip, not the master clip itself.

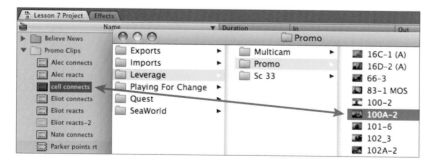

The main purpose of the master clip hierarchy is to *supervise* the naming of the clip. If you rename a master clip, all the affiliates (the other uses of that clip) will be renamed to follow the master clip name, making it easier to track the use of the clip throughout the project.

Likewise, if you rename an affiliate, the master clip is changed to give all instances of that clip the same name. This is why making subclips is so valuable. By creating a subclip, you can change the subclip name without duplicating the media or affecting the name of the original master clip or its affiliates.

1   In the *Show Reel* sequence in the Timeline, move the playhead to the **sham slam** clip and zoom in to this clip. Choose View > Reveal Master Clip, or press Shift-F.

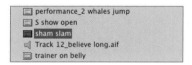

Even though the Believe News bin was closed in the Browser, the Reveal Master Clip command automatically opens the bin where the master clip is located and selects it. This is the clip that was originally used to edit the sequence clip. The sequence clip in the Timeline is an affiliate of this master clip.

2   In the Browser, click in the name area of the **sham slam** clip, and change the name to *whales tails*. In the Timeline, look at this clip in the *Show Reel* sequence, then click the *Believe News* sequence tab and look at the first clip in that sequence.

The clips that were originally named **sham slam** now appear as **whales tails** in both sequences. Whenever you change the name of a master clip, the names of all the affiliate clips throughout the project are also changed.

**NOTE** ▸ You often need to create different sequences for different uses. This *Believe News* sequence is simply the SeaWorld behaviors clips set to music. With the addition of an informative voiceover, it easily becomes a news story. This is often referred to as *repurposing* your material.

After you change a clip name in the project, you can easily change it back to its media file name, even if you don't remember what that was.

3   In the Browser, Control-click the **whales tails** clip, and choose Rename > Clip to Match File from the shortcut menu.

The name of the clip is restored, as is its alphabetical position in the bin. (In the same way, you can also change the name of the media file to follow the project clip name. You will learn more about this in Lesson 8.)

**NOTE ▶** When you create a subclip, it becomes a master clip because it is the first use of that new clip in the project. If you rename the master clip used to create the subclip, the subclip name will remain unchanged, yet the subclip will still link back to the original master clip media file.

In the previous exercise, you used the Item Properties window to see where a clip was located on your hard disk. Sometimes, it's helpful to go directly to that file location and to see what other files might exist for the project.

4   In the Browser, select the **jump at stage** clip. Choose View > Reveal in Finder.

A Finder window appears on top of the Final Cut Pro interface, with the master clip selected.

In addition to finding the master clip media file, you can use this function to scout for hidden jewels you haven't yet imported. You can also find the master clip of a subclip with this function.

5   Click in the Browser and select the **trainer on belly** subclip. Choose View > Reveal in Finder. Notice that the **J and L circle** clip is selected, then close the Finder window.

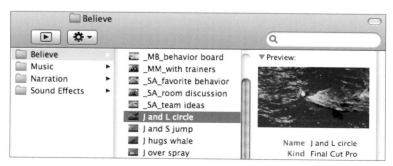

The clip revealed in the Finder window is the **J and L circle** master clip that was used to create this subclip.

**TIP** ▶ To find the master clip of a subclip in the Timeline, select the clip and choose View > Reveal Subclip Parent Clip.

**NOTE** ▶ When no master clip can be found in a project, Final Cut Pro can trace where the original media file is located and import it into your project.

Another time to use master clips is when you want to locate the original frame of a source clip that you used in a sequence clip, or vice versa. This is called finding a *match frame*. For example, you may want to know whether a clip in a sequence has matching audio in the master clip.

6   In the Timeline, position the playhead at the first frame of the **whale cu feeding** clip. Press F to search for the matching frame in the master clip.

In the Viewer, the matching master clip appears with In and Out points representing the exact length and content of the video clip. You could use these edit points to edit the matching length and content of this clip's audio into the sequence at the current playhead position.

**TIP** ▶ To find a match frame to an audio clip on the A1 track at the playhead location, deselect the V1 Auto Select control, and then press F.

## Take 2

An editor down the hall recently asked you how to bring in matching audio to support a video-only clip in the Timeline. At the time, you weren't able to give the right advice. Now you can. Try these steps in the *Believe News* sequence:

▶ Position the playhead at the first frame of the **K jumps off whale** clip.

▶ Press F to find the match frame in the master clip.

▶ Disconnect the V1 Source control in the Timeline.

▶ Patch the a1 and a2 Source controls to the A4 and A5 tracks.

▶ Click the Overwrite button.

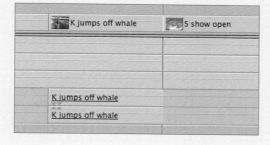

## Logging Information in Browser Columns

In the Item Properties window, you saw that clip information was organized onto different tabs according to topic. You can find this same information in the Browser columns. But unlike the Item Properties window, the Browser columns let you choose how to sort and display the clip information.

Not only can you reposition columns for easier access, but you can also hide some columns and show others that are more helpful to you. With more than 65 Browser columns to choose from in list view, you're sure to quickly and easily find a clip's reel number, scene number, log note, or other information you need to retrieve.

**1** In the Browser, close all open bins, and reveal the contents of the Believe News bin. To enlarge the window to see more columns, click the Browser's zoom button.

In the Browser, with the Name column selected, all the clips and sequences within a bin are arranged alphabetically, and all the bins are arranged alphabetically as well.

The downward arrow on the Name column heading indicates that the column is sorted in ascending order, from A to Z. Also, the Name column is lighter than the other columns, indicating that all the information in the Browser is sorted by name.

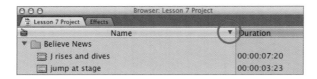

**2** To reverse the sort order, click the Name column heading. When reversed, the project elements of any column head are sorted in descending order, from Z to A. Click the heading again to return to the ascending sort order.

You can locate a clip based on a specific criterion—such as the type of tracks contained in a clip—simply by clicking a column heading in the Browser. For example, let's say you wanted to find just the audio clips in a bin.

**3** Click the Tracks column heading.

Now all the clips are organized according to the number and type of tracks contained in each clip.

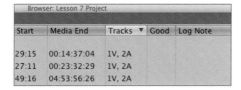

The audio clips are grouped together and are easy to spot. You could also, for example, click the Duration column to sort the clips by length and find a long clip to place behind the credit roll.

As you edit there may be times when you want to see a note you made about a clip, such as whether it was one of the better clips you captured. You can enter information into certain Browser columns for this purpose.

4    Click the **_SA_favorite behavior** clip in the Browser. Follow the row to the Good column and click in that column.

When you select a clip in the Browser, the information pertaining to this clip in the columns turns blue and the clip's row is highlighted with a darker bar. This helps you locate the correct line when entering clip information into a field.

You can log additional information about a clip, for example, by flagging all the clips with a certain subject during the capture process. If you don't enter information at that stage, you can add it at any time during editing. Let's flag all the clips where we see Steve.

5    On the **_SA_favorite behavior** clip line, click in the Log Note column. When the text field appears with a blinking cursor, type *steve*. Then click outside the field. (Pressing Return will open the clip in the Viewer.)

6    Click the **S show opens** clip and Control-click in the Log Note field for that clip. From the shortcut menu, choose *steve*.

Once you've entered a log note in an editing session, you don't have to enter it again. You can choose it from the shortcut menu.

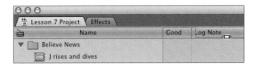 **TIP** ▶ You can also Control-click under the Label column to select a label color for a clip.

It's nice to have these references in the different columns, but not very helpful if you can't easily see the notes you've made. Although the Name column is a fixed column, all other columns can be repositioned simply by dragging the column heading left or right.

**7**   Drag the Good column to the left, next to the Name column. Then drag the Log Note column to follow the Good column.

When you drag a column heading, a rectangle appears representing that column. Adjacent columns shift their position to make room for the column you are moving.

You can also display additional columns that might be helpful at different stages of editing. For example, if you choose to view bin contents as a list, you don't have access to clip thumbnails, which are helpful when you first start working with new material. By adding another column to this view, you can maintain the list view and see the clip thumbnails at the same time.

**8**   Control-click the Good column heading. From the shortcut menu, choose Show Thumbnail.

**NOTE** ▶ There are two preset column layouts you can recall at any time: Standard Columns and Logging Columns.

A thumbnail appears next to each clip name. Not only are thumbnails a handy visual reference, but you can also scrub through them to preview the clip.

**NOTE ▶** When you add a new column to the Browser layout, it will always appear to the left of the column you Control-click.

9  To scrub through the **jump at stage** clip, drag across the thumbnail image to the right, and then to the left. To reset this clip's poster frame, drag across the thumbnail image to the right until you see the whale emerge, press Control, release the mouse button, and then release the Control key.

If there is a column that you don't feel is useful, you can always hide it to make room for other columns that are more valuable to you.

10  In the Browser columns, Control-click the Label 2 column. From the shortcut menu, choose Hide Column.

That column is removed from the current Browser layout, but it can be retrieved at any time by Control-clicking any column and choosing Show Label 2.

**NOTE ▶** Later in this lesson, you will learn to save this column layout.

## Finding Project Items

Final Cut Pro has a Find function that works similarly to the find function of many other applications. It even has the same keyboard shortcut, Command-F. Its purpose is to locate clips by names, notes, or other criteria.

The Find function allows you to locate a clip instantly when you want it or when someone else on the production team requests it. In fact, when you add information or metadata to a clip, as you did in the previous exercise, you can use that data to find the clip.

1  Press Control-U to return to the standard window layout. Then close each bin in the Browser to hide its contents.

Closing the bins isn't required for finding items, but it's helpful for demonstrating how the Find function works.

2  Click an empty space in the Browser to deselect everything, then choose Edit > Find, or press Command-F.

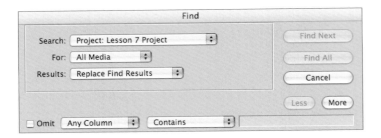

A Find window appears in which you can enter the name of the clip or item you want to locate, and the name of the project you want to search.

3 In the Search pop-up menu, choose Project: Lesson 7 Project if it's not already selected, and in the text field with the blinking cursor enter *sham slam*. Click Find Next, or press Return, to find this clip in this project.

The Believe News bin is automatically opened, and the **sham slam** clip is highlighted.

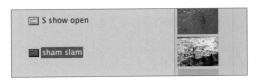

What if you don't know the clip name but remember entering a log note for it? Previously, you entered log notes for two clips that contained some action with Steve, the whale trainer.

4 Click in the Browser to deselect the **sham slam** clip. Press Command-F to open the Find window again, and type *steve* in the lower-right search field.

5 In the lower left, click the pop-up menu and choose Log Note. Click the Find All button to find all the clips that have *steve* entered as part of their log notes.

A Find Results window opens, listing the clips having the specified property, in this case, a log note that includes the word *steve*.

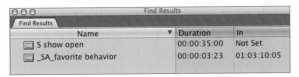

**6**    Reposition the Find Results window over the Timeline so you can see the other clips in the Browser. Now press Command-A to select all the clips in the Find Results window.

As soon as you select clips in this window, the same clips are also selected in the Browser window. You might use this approach to relocate a group of clips to a different bin in the project.

**7**    Close the Find Results window and, in the Browser, deselect the clips.

You can use a similar Find function to search for clips in the Timeline. To access it, the Timeline window must be active. If more than one sequence is open in the Timeline, you also need to choose the sequence you want to search.

You can search for one clip, or for a group of clips as long as their names share common text. For example, you might want to search for all of Sophie's clips in this promo.

**8**    In the Timeline window, click the *Leverage Promo* sequence tab and make sure the playhead is at the head of the sequence. Press Command-F. In the Find window, enter *sophie* in the Find field and click Find All to find all the clips that have *sophie* in their name.

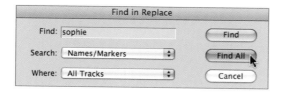

The playhead jumps to the first clip in the sequence that contains the word *sophie*, and highlights the other clips in the sequence that also contain *sophie*.

With these clips selected, you can move, copy, or modify them as a group. Let's say you want to build a separate promo around the Sophie character. You can Option-drag to copy them.

**9**    In the Timeline, with the Sophie clips still selected, press Option-– (minus) to zoom out. Option-drag the selected clips past the end of the last clip in the sequence. Release the clips in the empty gray area.

**NOTE ▶** In a later chapter, you will learn to stack clips on top of each other to build a composite image. Copying these clips could be used for that purpose as well.

## Customizing Shortcut Keys and Button Bars

Now that you're getting familiar with Final Cut Pro functions, buttons, and shortcuts, you might ask yourself whether you would redesign the system. Would you give a function another shortcut or use a different modifier key? Would you create additional buttons from commands you used earlier in the lesson?

Although you can't change the actual Final Cut Pro interface, you can change the keyboard shortcuts and add or group together buttons to facilitate your editing style.

**NOTE ▶** The changes in this exercise will not interfere with future lessons. But before customizing your keyboard layout beyond these steps, keep in mind that the exercises in this book use the default Final Cut Pro layout.

**1**  To open the Keyboard Layout window, choose Tools > Keyboard Layout > Customize.

In this window, you see a keyboard with icons on the keys that represent mapped Final Cut Pro functions. To the right of the keyboard is a list of functions and commands organized by menu set and function.

**NOTE ▶** The keyboard layout you see represents the computer you are using. A portable computer, for example, will not display a number pad.

You can access many Final Cut Pro functions by pressing a combination of keystrokes. Some keystrokes require one or more modifier keys. The tabs across the top of the keyboard area organize the keyboard shortcuts according to modifier keys—Command, Shift, Option, Control, or a combination of these.

Before you can make changes to this keyboard layout, however, you have to unlock it.

**2**  In the lower left of this window, click the Lock button to allow changes to the current keyboard layout.

**3**  In the command list area to the right of the keyboard area, drag the blue vertical scroller up and down to see the list of command sets.

The first nine sets contain all the commands in the Final Cut Pro menus. The items that follow are organized by editing function.

**4**  At the top of the list, click the File Menu disclosure triangle to display the commands in that menu.

If a command currently has a keyboard shortcut, it is listed to the right of the command. A few commands, such as Close Project and Import Folder, do not currently have keyboard shortcuts. Let's create a shortcut for Import Folder.

**5**  Click the Shift-Command modifier tab in the keyboard area.

Since Command-I is the shortcut for Import File, mapping the Import Folder function to the Shift-Command-I key will be easy to remember.

**6** Drag the Import Folder name or icon from the command list to the I key.

The new keyboard shortcut appears on the keyboard layout as well as to the right of the Import Folder command in the command list area. When you choose File from the main menu, you will see the new shortcut appear under File > Import > Folder.

**TIP** To reload the default U.S. keyboard layout, choose Tools > Keyboard Layout > Default Layout—U.S.

Although the interface buttons you see in the Viewer and Canvas can't be changed, you can add shortcut buttons to the button bar in the Browser, Viewer, Canvas, and Timeline windows. The Timeline default layout has three buttons; the other windows have only the button tabs with no buttons in between.

Viewer button bar with no buttons

If you edit extensively with your mouse, adding buttons for functions you use frequently can significantly speed up the editing process because you don't have to remember keyboard shortcuts or the menu you need in order to access a specific function.

**TIP** You can also open the Button List window by choosing Tools > Button List and add buttons from that list.

**7**  Click in the search field at the top of the command list to open an alphabetized list of commands. In the search field, type *audio*. Scroll through the audio commands. Then add *scrubbing* to narrow your search to "audio scrubbing."

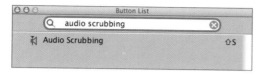

When you enter a general topic, such as audio, you see numerous commands from which you can choose. When you enter a more specific term, the options decrease.

**TIP**▶  After entering a word in the search field, don't press Return. Final Cut Pro will read it as a keystroke and try to search for items that use that keystroke. Also, if you want to return to the main function and command menu, click the X icon on the right of the search field.

**8**  Drag the Audio Scrubbing icon to the Viewer window and release it between the two button tabs to make it part of the Viewer button bar.

**9**  Hold the pointer over the new Audio Scrubbing button to view the tooltip that identifies it.

You can also customize a button by giving it a color or creating spaces around it to make it easier to find.

**10**  Control-click the Audio Scrubbing button. From the shortcut menu, choose red to color the button red. Control-click the button again, and choose Add Spacer.

Choosing button colors and adding spacers help organize and group buttons that belong to a similar category, such as audio.

To further customize your button bars, try taking these steps:

▶   Drag a button from one button bar to another.

▶   Option-drag a button to copy it from one button bar to another.

▶   Control-click a button and choose Remove > Button to remove it.

▶   To remove all the buttons in a button bar, Control-click a button and choose Remove > All.

## Take 2

The producer has just informed you that the budget has been cut on the current project and all the audio mixing will have to be done in-house on Final Cut Pro. After studying Lesson 10, "Mixing Audio Tracks," you'll be completely ready. For now, prepare for that session by adding the following audio buttons to the Timeline button bar and making them all the same color:

▶   **Clip Overlays**—turn on and off audio level overlays in the Timeline

▶   **Waveform Display**—turn on and off waveform displays in the Timeline

▶   **Audio Mixer**—open the Audio Mixer

## Saving and Loading Layouts

In earlier lessons, you changed window layouts and the layout of Timeline tracks. In this lesson, you've made changes to Browser columns, added buttons to button bars, added new shortcuts to the keyboard layout, and so on. It would be a real shame if you lost those layouts or moved your project to a different computer and had to customize them all over again.

With a few easy steps, you can save each and every one of the layout decisions you've made and even take your customized layouts with you wherever you edit. Final Cut Pro organizes saved layouts in individual folders in your Final Cut Pro User Data folder. Although they are organized in separate folders, the way you save each layout is the same.

**NOTE ▶** Changes you make to Browser or bin columns in a project remain until you change them again or load a previously saved layout. If you create a new project, it will have the default Standard Columns layout.

1   Press Command-H to hide Final Cut Pro. On the desktop, open a Finder window and navigate to Users > [user name] > Library > Preferences > Final Cut Pro User Data.

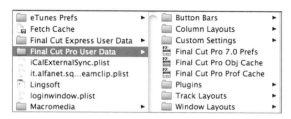

This is where all Final Cut Pro customized layouts, preferences, and even plug-ins for the current user are saved. Although you may not currently see individual folders for each layout category, when you initiate the Save Layout command, a folder for that category will be created in this location.

**NOTE ▶** If another user has been set up on the computer, that user's preferences and layouts will appear when he or she logs in and opens the application.

Let's save some of the layouts you've created in this lesson.

2   In the Dock, click the Final Cut Pro icon to restore the interface. To save the current Browser column layout with the Thumbnail column in view, Control-click any Browser column heading other than Name, and choose Save Column Layout from the shortcut menu.

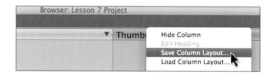

A Save dialog appears with a default layout name and a target save location. In this case, the target is Column Layouts. This folder is created for you automatically in the Final Cut Pro User Data folder specifically to organize Browser column layouts.

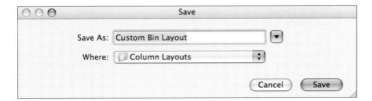

**3**   In the Save dialog, rename the layout *thumbnails*, and click Save.

You save window layouts the same way you save column layouts. In Lesson 1 you used the Custom Layout 1 and 2 options to save the "big Viewer" and "big Canvas" layouts. Those options work well when you're editing on one computer. But it doesn't create a backup for you or allow you to use those layouts on a different computer station.

**4**   Press Shift-U to recall the big Viewer window layout. Then choose Window > Arrange > Save Window Layout. In the Save dialog, name this layout *big Viewer*, and click Save to save it. Repeat the process to save the big Canvas layout.

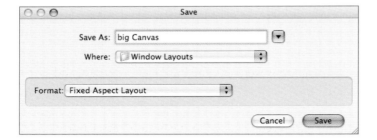

These layouts are saved in the Window Layouts folder.

The Timeline tracks can also be customized to your project's needs. For example, in the previous lesson, you enlarged the V1 track to create larger thumbnail images, which made it easier to identify the clips. Let's create a taller A1 track layout you can use for audio mixing.

**5**   In the Timeline, click the *Leverage Promo* sequence tab. Move your pointer over the A1 track boundary. When you see the Resize pointer, start to drag down. When you get a nice large height you like, release the mouse button.

> **TIP** Option-dragging will resize just the video or audio tracks, depending on which track you are dragging. Shift-dragging a track boundary will resize both audio and video tracks to the same customized height.

6   To save this track layout, click the Track Layout pop-up. From the pop-up menu, choose Save Track Layout. Name this layout *tall A1*, and click Save. This track layout is saved in the Track Layouts folder.

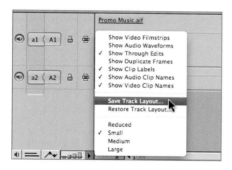

> **TIP** You can also turn on audio waveforms and audio level overlays and save that as an audio track layout.

7   To save the layout of buttons you recently added to the button bars, Control-click any button bar and choose Save All Button Bars. Enter *my buttons* as the layout name and click Save.

The combined button bar layouts are now saved in the Button Bars folder. As you continue to develop and add to the current layouts, you can rename the layouts for specific editing functions, such as screening clips, mixing sound, adding effects, and so on.

**TIP** ▶ To restore the default button bar layout, Control-click in the Timeline button bar and choose Remove > All / Restore Default from the shortcut menu.

**8**  To save the keyboard layout, choose Tools > Keyboard Layout > Save Keyboard Layout. Name this layout *my keyboard* and click Save. This layout is saved in the Keyboard Layouts folder.

Now all the layouts are saved in their appropriate folders in the Final Cut Pro User Data folder. If you change a layout during the course of editing, you can easily recall or load a saved layout.

**9**  In the Viewer, remove the new button you added by dragging it out of the button bar and releasing it.

As you remove and release a button, you see a puff of smoke, and the button no longer appears in the button bar. You cannot undo this step.

**10**  To reload the button bar you saved, Control-click any button bar and choose Load All Button Bars from the shortcut menu. In the Choose a File window, select the "my buttons" layout from the Button Bars folder and click Choose.

All the buttons you added are now returned to their saved layouts.

With all the layouts saved that can be saved, you're ready to take your editing on the road, or at least work on another system without having to re-create these same layouts.

If you choose to move your project to another computer, all you have to do is transfer the Final Cut Pro User Data folder to a flash drive, navigate to the new computer's Final Cut Pro User Data folder, and place the layouts you want to use in the appropriate folders.

If no folder exists, copy the entire folder from your flash drive to the new computer at that location. If you're "just visiting" a different computer, Final Cut Pro can load a saved layout directly from your flash drive without your having to actually copy it to the computer.

**TIP** ▶ You can save multiple layouts in each category. As you customize or adjust other customized layouts, save each layout as its own unique file. You can also save over an existing layout to update it with additional buttons, columns, or track options.

## Optimizing User Preferences

If you find yourself pressing Command-Z to undo several actions, only to find that the action you want to retrieve is the 11th undo, which is not available to you, then you will want to take a closer look at the user preferences in Final Cut Pro.

User preferences are a collection of options that determine how you personally work in your editing sessions. They cover editing choices such as the number of undos, the number of tracks you want to appear when you create a new sequence, how and when to back up your projects, and so on. User preferences apply to all open projects and are another way you can harness more power in Final Cut Pro.

**MORE INFO** ▶ You can find a precise definition of each preference or setting in the Final Cut Pro 7 User Manual.

**1** Choose Final Cut Pro > User Preferences, or press Option-Q.

The User Preferences window has six tabs. The General tab is where you choose assorted user preference settings. You will cover the capture preferences in the next lesson. Other options are covered throughout the book.

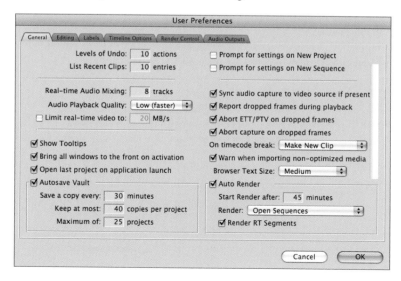

**2**   In the General tab, click the Levels of Undo field and enter *30*.

Now you can press Command-Z 30 times to return to a previous editing decision. If you want to see additional clips listed in the Recent Clips pop-up menu in the Viewer, you can change that here as well.

**3**   In the List Recent Clips field, enter *20*.

**NOTE** ▶ You can choose to open Final Cut Pro without opening the most recent project by deselecting "Open last project on application launch" in the General tab.

If you forget to save your project frequently throughout your editing sessions, Final Cut Pro will save it for you automatically. In the Autosave Vault section in the lower left of the General tab, you can set how often it saves.

**4**   In the "Save a copy every __ minutes" field of the Autosave Vault section, enter *15*.

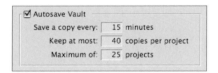

Now Final Cut Pro will automatically save a backup of your project every 15 minutes as you work. You can choose how frequently a project will be saved, how many versions of the project will be saved, and the maximum number of versions saved.

When the maximum number of versions is reached, Final Cut Pro moves the oldest version to the Trash before saving the current version. These backup projects are saved at this location on your hard drive: [user name] > Documents > Final Cut Pro Documents > Autosave Vault.

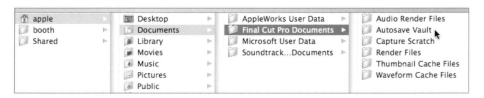

**TIP** As a backup, some editors set their Autosave to a different drive, just in case anything happens to the project files on their primary drive. You will learn to do this in the next lesson.

5   Click the Editing tab. In the upper right of this tab, click the Multi-Frame Trim Size field and type *10*.

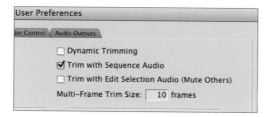

The Editing tab is where you set preferences for certain editing functions, such as previewing the pre-roll and post-roll and setting the multi-frame trim size.

The multi-frame trim size determines how much you nudge an edit point when you use the Shift-< or Shift-> key command. The default is 5 frames, but you can make it 10 frames or even 1 second. You can also choose a preferred duration for still images you import into your project.

When you applied labels to clips and sequences in the previous lesson, you chose a label color. But you can also reassign or rename a label color to better support your project.

6   Click the Labels tab. In the current green B Roll field, type *Multicam*.

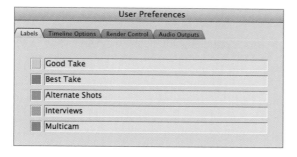

You can rename the label colors anything you want to reflect your project needs. The label colors cannot be changed, only the label names.

Earlier in this lesson, you made changes to existing sequences in the Timeline Options tab of the Sequence Settings window. If you want to make changes to a sequence *before* it's created—to add additional audio or video tracks automatically, or turn on the audio waveforms display, for example—you do that in the User Preferences Timeline Options tab.

**7** Click the Timeline Options tab. In the Default Number of Tracks area, enter *2* for Video and *6* for Audio. Select the Show Audio Waveform checkbox.

Here you choose settings for all *new* sequences. You can determine a default number of tracks so that each new sequence you create has that track configuration, and you can choose drop frame or non-drop frame timecode to ensure every new sequence displays that mode. Any changes made here will not affect any *existing* sequences, only new ones.

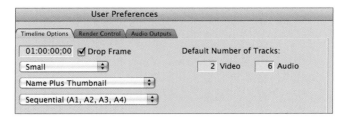

**8** Click the Render Control tab. This is where you enable or disable the most processor-intensive effects in Final Cut Pro.

**9** Click the Audio Outputs tab.

Here you can create custom Audio Output configurations. You can use these settings when outputting audio tracks to tape. For example, if your hardware supports it, you can create an Audio Output configuration that outputs up to 24 distinct tracks at one time.

**10** Click OK to accept the user preferences you changed.

**NOTE ▶** To revert to the default Final Cut Pro preferences, quit the application, and find the Final Cut Pro 7 Prefs file in the Final Cut Pro User Data folder. Drag this file to the Trash, and reopen FCP.

**11** Press Command-S to save your current project. With the Browser or Timeline window active, choose File > Restore Project.

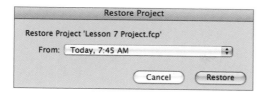

After a project has been saved in the Autosave Vault, you can restore an earlier project version. If you can recall the approximate time you were editing, you can simply restore the project with that time stamp. Restoring a project will automatically close the current project. So make sure to save the current project before initiating this command.

**NOTE** ▸ If the Autosave time has not elapsed, no choices will be available in the Restore Project dialog.

**12**  Click Cancel to close the Restore Project dialog. To create a simple change in this project, click the disclosure triangle on the Promo Clips bin. Choose File > Revert Project.

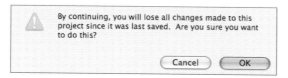

**13**  Click OK to revert to the previously saved project. Choosing this option reverts you to the most recently saved version of the project.

## Editor's Cut

Some editing activities are more creative than others. A clip log note that you created certainly won't change the clip's appearance in your Editor's Cut. But by customizing your project and interface—going "under the hood" of Final Cut Pro—you will be doing everything you can to keep your session running smoothly. So take  a few minutes to review the item and sequence settings in the project, add more buttons to a few button bars, and reconfigure your own personal Browser column layout. Then save any new button bars or layouts you've created.

## Lesson Review

1.  How do you sort by a column other than the Name column?
2.  How do you show a column that you don't currently see in the Browser?
3.  How do you search for a clip in the Browser using specific criteria?
4.  What determines whether a clip is a master clip in Final Cut Pro?
5.  What does it mean when a clip has a red slash through the clip icon?
6.  How can you look at the detailed information about a single clip or item?
7.  Where can you choose new interface buttons?
8.  Where are all customized layouts saved on your computer?
9.  In what menu can you choose User Preferences?
10. How do you make changes to an existing sequence?
11. How do you find a matching frame to a sequence clip?
12. What is saved in the Autosave Vault?

### *Answers*

1.  Click a column heading.
2.  Control-click a column heading and choose Show [column] from the shortcut menu.
3.  Select the Browser window and press Command-F to open the Find window, and choose specific search criteria.
4.  A clip is a master clip if it represents the first use of that clip in the project.
5.  The clip is offline and disconnected from its media file.
6.  Select the clip, and press Command-9 to open the Item Properties window. You can also Control-click the clip and choose Item Properties from the shortcut menu, or choose Edit > Item Properties.
7.  From the Button List window or the Keyboard Layout window.
8.  They are saved at Users/[user name]/Library/Preferences/Final Cut Pro User Data.
9.  From the Final Cut Pro menu.
10. Make the sequence active in the Timeline, or select it in the Browser, and press Command-0 to open the Sequence Settings window. You can also choose Sequence > Sequence Settings.

11. Position the playhead over the frame of the sequence clip, and press F.

12. Backup copies of your project file.

## Keyboard Shortcuts

| | |
|---|---|
| **F** | Find the frame in a sequence that matches the frame displayed in the Viewer, and vice versa |
| **Command-F** | Open the Find window |
| **Shift-F** | Select the master clip in the Browser |
| **Command-9** | Open the Item Properties window |
| **Command-0** | Open the Sequence Settings window |

# 8

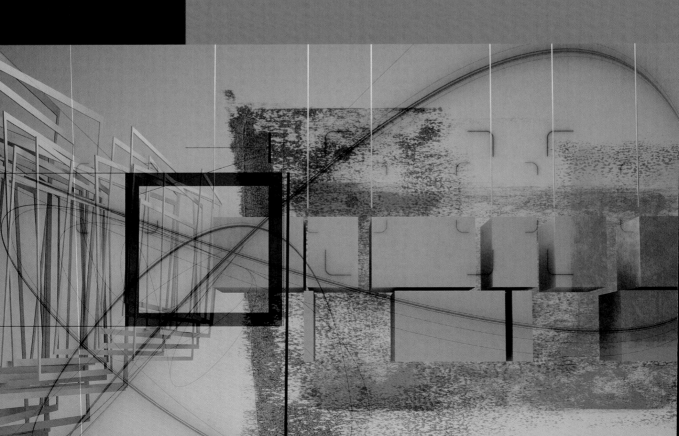

# Lesson 8
# Capturing and Transferring Footage

It may seem unusual for the first step of the editing process to appear in the middle of this book. The reason is simple. Now that you know how clip information is organized, how subclips are created, how markers are applied, and how you might want to shape your workflow, you can take better advantage of the many ways to capture and transfer your clips.

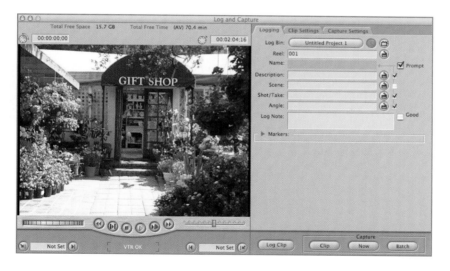

There are two primary ways to bring footage into your Final Cut Pro project. One is to capture footage from a videotape source. The capture process converts tape segments to digital media files that you use in editing. The first part of this lesson deals with capturing. With the advent of tapeless cameras, footage can now be recorded directly to a storage card or FireWire drive in the form of media files. Using this second technology, you can transfer the media files directly to FCP—without converting them—and begin editing immediately.

As video technology continues to evolve, editors have the opportunity to work with a variety of video formats. Whichever video format option you are using, capturing or transferring footage will play an important role in preparing for the editing process. While some decisions must follow the needs of your shooting format, other capturing decisions can follow personal preference.

## Connecting Sources for Tape Capture

The first step in capturing footage from a videotape source is to connect the capture device to your computer. Final Cut Pro can capture and control footage from certain camcorders and decks using just a FireWire cable. You can also capture in some video formats using a third-party capture card or an analog-to-digital converter with FireWire output.

Whatever your capture source, have that device running before you open Final Cut Pro. Otherwise, Final Cut Pro may not "see" the device, and you may have to reopen the application so that it can. When connecting a standard FireWire device, you might use these steps:

1   If Final Cut Pro is open, save your projects and quit the program.

2   Connect the FireWire cable from the camera to the computer.

4-pin FireWire          6-pin FireWire          9-pin FireWire

FireWire 400, also called IEEE 1394a, has two types of connectors. The smaller 4-pin connector usually attaches to a camera or deck. The larger 6-pin connector goes into your computer's FireWire port. FireWire 400 transfers data at 400 Mbps. FireWire 800, a higher-bandwidth version capable of transferring data at up to 800 Mbps, uses 9-pin-to-9-pin connectors.

You can also get 9-pin-to-4-pin and 9-pin-to-6-pin cables to work with other FireWire devices. Independent FireWire drives typically use 6-pin-to-6-pin or 9-pin-to-9-pin connectors.

**3**   Turn on the camera and switch it to the VTR (videotape recorder) mode. Load the source tape, and cue the footage.

Once you open Final Cut Pro, you can control the camera from within the application. For now, viewing the tape just confirms that you have loaded the right source or reel.

If you are using a third-party capture card, you can follow the manufacturer's instructions to connect the appropriate cables to your VTR and computer.

> **NOTE ▶** You can also connect your camera or deck to a separate video monitor or television set, or through a VCR, just as you would if you were screening a tape. However, this is not necessary, because you can use the Preview area in the Final Cut Pro Capture window to view your source footage.

## Choosing Preset Format Settings

Every new project contains a sequence that uses the default audio and video format settings. Final Cut Pro can automatically change the settings of an active sequence to match those of the first clip you edit.

But what if the *first* clip you edit doesn't represent the *majority* of the footage you will be editing? For example, you might need to edit a few DV clips at the head of a primarily HD sequence, or vice versa. In that case (and for this exercise), to maintain an efficient workflow, you would choose format settings that represent the majority of your footage.

Final Cut Pro makes it easy to choose accurate audio and video format settings by providing a list of default presets in the Easy Setup dialog. These presets include capture settings, sequence settings, device-control settings, and output settings. By choosing an Easy Setup preset, you simultaneously load all these settings at one time.

> **NOTE ▶** The Easy Setup presets are not attached to a specific project and can apply a group of settings to all new sequences. A single project can contain sequences created with several presets.

**1**   With a capture device connected to your Mac and turned on, open Final Cut Pro.

**2**   If other projects are opened in Final Cut Pro, press Control-W and follow the Save prompts to close them. Remember that the Canvas and Timeline windows will close when there are no open sequences to display.

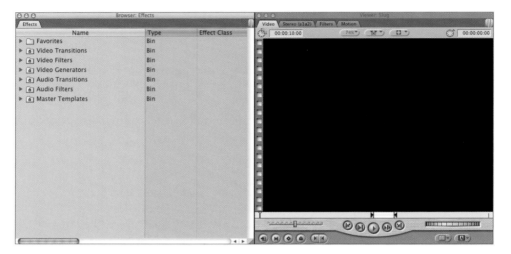

**3**   Choose File > New Project to create a new project. An Untitled Project tab appears in the Browser window.

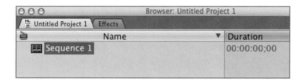

In Final Cut Pro, project files are containers. A project itself does not have any settings. The settings for your footage are attached to your sequences and, unless other settings are chosen, the default DV-NTSC audio and video format settings are applied to all new sequences.

If the majority of your footage is DV-NTSC, then you can use the existing sequence to edit. If it's not, you will need to delete this sequence, change the format settings, and create a new sequence.

**4**   In the Browser, select the *Sequence 1* sequence, and press Delete to remove it from this project.

5   To name and save this project, choose File > Save Project As, and type *Lesson 8 Project* as the new name. Save this project in the Lessons > My Projects folder.

You are saving only the project file to the Lessons folder, and not the media. You will set the media-files location later in this lesson.

**TIP** If you are using a server to store or share a project, it's a good idea to display the .fcp extension so that the file can be correctly identified. If you want the .fcp extension to be part of the name, make sure the browse columns are visible in the Save dialog, and deselect the "Hide extension" checkbox.

6   Choose Final Cut Pro > Easy Setup. In the Easy Setup dialog, click the Use pop-up menu. The Easy Setup dialog contains presets for several media formats with media settings that are appropriate for each format.

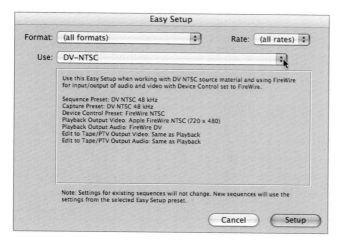

Rather than search through the myriad of options, you can limit, or filter, your search by choosing Format and Rate settings for your footage. The Use pop-up menu will then display only those presets that pertain to your footage format.

**NOTE** ▶ If you have loaded additional presets from a third-party company such as AJA or Blackmagic, those presets will also appear in the Use pop-up menu.

**7** From the Format pop-up menu, choose an appropriate format for your media.

This choice should reflect the actual format of your videotape source material.

**NOTE ►** For the purpose of this exercise, if you're not ready to capture your own video, choose PAL as the format and 25 as the rate. PAL is a video format used in Europe and around the world.

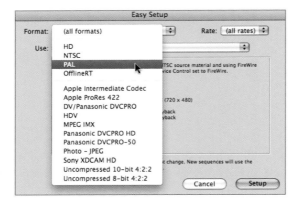

**8** From the Rate pop-up menu, choose the frame rate of your footage. Again, choose the actual frame rate used to shoot the footage.

**9** Click the Use pop-up menu again.

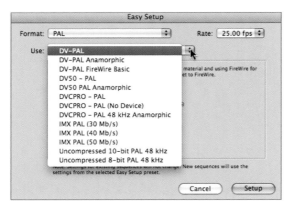

Depending on the format and rate you chose, the menu items may be greatly reduced, showing only those presets that fall under the chosen filter categories.

**10** Click the Setup button to accept the selected preset.

**11** In the Browser, press Command-N to create a new sequence. This new sequence contains the settings you just selected in the Easy Setup dialog.

> **TIP** ▶ If the first edit you make is in a different footage format than the sequence settings and the majority of your footage, click No in the prompt in order to preserve the correct sequence settings.

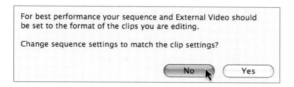

**NOTE** ▶ As you learned in the previous lesson, when you edit a clip of one format into a sequence with different format settings, Final Cut Pro conforms that clip to play within the sequence settings. For example, if you edit an HD clip into a DV-NTSC sequence, you will see black bars above and below the clip as a result of placing the entire widescreen HD clip inside the DV frame.

## Previewing and Marking Your Source

Once the video source is connected and the project is open and ready, you can control the camera or tape deck using controls in Final Cut Pro's Log and Capture window.

You can capture your tape footage in one of two ways. One method is to mark In and Out points to identify individual clips or sections that you want to capture. Marking source material for capture is very similar to marking clips for editing.

The other approach is to capture the entire tape at one time. The method you choose will depend on how much footage you need from the tape source.

In the this exercise, we'll mark In and Out points to capture selected footage from your tape. You will learn how to capture the entire tape later in this lesson.

**1** Choose File > Log and Capture, or press Command-8.

> **TIP** ▶ The size of the Log and Capture window always defaults to the size of the Canvas window. To make the Capture window larger, close it, resize the Canvas window, then reopen the Log and Capture window.

The Log and Capture window has two main areas: the Preview area on the left where you screen and mark your source tape, and the Logging area on the right. In the Logging tab, you log information about clips and select where and how you will capture footage.

Preview area         Logging tab

**NOTE** ▶ If you are capturing HDV footage and have selected the HDV Easy Setup, you will see a slightly different window. The log and capture options that appear function the same as those in the default window.

Notice that the Preview area is similar in layout to the Viewer and Canvas windows.

If your playback source device is not properly connected to your computer's FireWire port, you may see the following message:

When you click OK, the Log and Capture window will open, but you will only be able to log clips or use a noncontrollable device. If you want to capture from a FireWire device, close the Log and Capture window, turn on the capture device, then reopen the Log and Capture window.

**2**   Make sure you have a source tape in your camera or deck, and then click the Play button in the Preview area to play the tape.

Rewind        Stop    Play      Fast Forward

If your capture device is connected via FireWire or to a third-party capture card with a device-control cable, you will see "VTR OK" below the transport controls and you'll have direct control of the device in the Capture window. If not, you will have to control the device manually.

NOTE ▶ When you capture into Final Cut Pro using a FireWire device, you can preview the audio through Final Cut Pro, as you will learn later in this lesson; or you can monitor it through headphones or speakers plugged directly into the playback device.

**3**   Click the Stop button to pause the tape, then click it again to stop the tape.

When a tape in a camera or deck is stopped, the tape unwraps from the video heads, but the Preview area displays a freeze frame of the most recent frame played.

TIP ▶ Pausing your tape is more efficient than stopping it completely. But leaving the tape in pause mode too long can damage the tape or cause video dropouts.

**4**   Click the Rewind or Fast Forward buttons to quickly move backward or forward in the tape. Use the shuttle control, or press the JKL keys, to cue the tape to the action where you want to begin capturing.

When the tape is cued, you are ready to mark the section you want to capture. Marking a tape source is similar to marking a clip in the Viewer. In fact, you use the same marking controls or shortcut keys (I and O).

However, when you mark a clip in the Viewer, you place tight marks around the action you want to edit into the sequence. When you capture a clip, you need to capture a few seconds before and after the desired action. This creates the clip's pad, or *handles*, that you can use when adjusting edits in the Timeline.

There are two methods of creating handles in the footage. You can loosely mark the footage around the action you want to edit, creating handles as you mark. Or you can mark the action more precisely and add handles afterward.

Clip In Point Timecode field                Clip Out Point Timecode field

Go to In Point    Mark In                    Mark Out    Go to Out Point

Sometimes you don't know where the desired action begins until you see it, so for this example, let's mark the clip when the action first begins in your footage.

5    If necessary, refine the tape location to the point where the action begins. Then click the Mark In button, or press the I key, to set an In point at the current tape location.

The timecode for your mark appears in the Clip In Point Timecode field. Unlike the Viewer marks, this mark will not appear in the image area, and there is no scrubber bar to scrub to the marks.

**NOTE ▶** The specific timecode numbers you see in the images throughout this lesson will not match your own.

Since marking at this point doesn't give you the handles you need to adjust the clip during the editing process, you need to place the In point earlier.

6    To create a 3-second clip handle, click in the Clip In Point Timecode field, enter –3. (minus 3 period), and press Return.

When you enter this change, a new In point appears that is 3 seconds earlier than the previous mark, giving you a 3-second pad, or handle, before the desired action begins.

**NOTE ▶** Remember, you don't need to create extra pad if your original mark allowed for handles prior to the action you want to use.

As you play forward, look for an appropriate place to stop capturing this clip. You can mark a specific location and add a handle (for example, +3.) to the Out point at a later time.

But since you can more easily anticipate where an action ends than where it begins, you can mark this Out point on the fly as the tape is playing.

**7**   Press the Spacebar, or click the Play button, to move forward to where this portion of the action ends. Allow the tape to continue playing, and after about 3 seconds, press O to set an Out point.

**NOTE ▶** You can go to an In or Out point by clicking the Go to In Point or Go to Out Point button, or by pressing Shift-I or Shift-O. You can also preview the marked area by clicking the Play In to Out button. But remember, this is a tape source, so moving to the In and Out points on your tape will not happen as quickly as it does when you're working with a captured clip in the Viewer.

Marking on the fly is a quick and easy way to set your In and Out points. If you need to change a mark, you can mark again to set a new timecode location, or use the marks that you have as reference points and trim them backward or forward. Keep in mind that the marks you set while capturing usually don't have to be frame accurate.

**TIP ▶** If timecode was logged during the shoot, you can enter a timecode number and go to that specific location. You may still need to adjust that In point to include a handle.

## Logging Your Clips

Now that you have marked a source clip, you are ready to log information about that clip. If you look at the Logging tab of the Log and Capture window, you will recognize some of the fields—Name, Description, Scene, Shot/Take, Angle, and Log Note—because you previously saw them as Browser columns. Information you log at the capture stage also appears in the Browser columns for later reference.

Notice, too, that there is an area in which you can add markers during the logging process. Before logging a clip, however, it's a good idea to determine the best approach to organizing logged clips in the project.

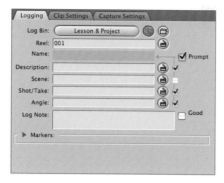

### Setting a Logging Bin

When you capture a clip, Final Cut Pro needs to know where to place the new clip icon in the project. The actual media file will be saved to your hard disk, but the clip icon linking to that media file will be saved to the current project in the Browser.

If you want to move quickly, you can capture all the clips into a project tab in the Browser and later organize them into bins. Or if you want to organize as you capture, you can create a new bin for each category, such as reel/tape number, scene, or exteriors.

In either case, Final Cut Pro needs to be told where to place the clip icons. This destination is called the *logging bin*. You can have only one logging bin active at any given time, no matter how many projects you have open.

1    If necessary, position the Capture window so that you can see both the Capture and Browser windows while doing these steps.

    In the Logging tab of the Log and Capture window, the project name, Lesson 8 Project, appears on the long oval Log Bin button.

    In the Browser window, a slate icon appears at the upper left of the Name column, indicating that this project is the current logging destination.

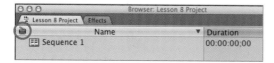

At this point, you can capture clips into your project and organize them into bins after capturing them. However, if you want to explore the option of capturing to a new bin, continue with the following steps.

**2**  In the Logging tab, to the far right of the Log Bin button, click the New Bin button.

A new bin is created in the current project with the default name Bin 1. The slate icon appears next to this bin in the Browser to identify it as the target location for new clips.

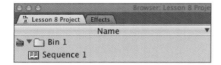

**3**  In the Logging tab, click the Log Bin button with the new bin name on it.

The new bin opens as a separate window, which allows you to view just the new clips you are capturing.

**4**  Close this window. In the Logging tab, click the Up button.

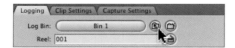

This takes the logging bin destination to a higher level, in this case back to the project level. In the Browser, the slate icon is attached once again to the project, not to the bin.

**5**  In the Browser, rename the new bin *Test Capture*, or any other name that's appropriate for the footage you're about to capture.

Let's use a different approach to assign this bin as the logging bin.

**6**  In the Browser, Control-click the Test Capture bin, and from the shortcut menu, choose Set Logging Bin.

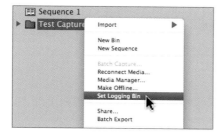

The slate icon now appears to the left of the Test Capture bin.

## Logging Clip Information

Before you begin entering information about a single clip, consider whether this clip is going to be part of a series of clips taken from this source. If so, you might want to create a clip-naming convention before you begin.

For example, dramatic footage, as in *Leverage*, uses scene, take, and camera numbers to identify a clip. In the SeaWorld *Believe* project, the interview clips had an underscore before the interview subject's initials, the behavior clips began with the trainer's initials, and the underwater footage began with *uw_*.

Unless you're working with a production group that requires a specific naming procedure, you're free to determine your own naming conventions. Just a word of advice: The more consistent you are in the naming stage, especially on a complex project, the easier it will be to find a clip during the editing stage.

Although you don't have to fill every blank, certain logging information is required—such as reel number and clip name—or Final Cut Pro will not capture the clip. You can also add additional logging information after you have captured the clip, as you learned in the preceding lesson.

1  Enter an appropriate reel number or name for your source tape. You can leave the default 001 reel number if you have just one tape.

   Ideally, you should use the same reel name or number that you used when labeling your tapes. That way you will always know from which source tape your clips were captured.

**2**  Try clicking in the Name field.

The Name field is not for entering information, just displaying it. The name is actually compiled from the four descriptive fields below it that have an active checkmark.

**3**  In the Description field, enter a description of the clip you want to capture, such as *gift shop ext, village ws,* or *dog cu.* Use a name that will help you distinguish between that clip and another while you are editing.

> **TIP**  When naming a clip, don't use a / (forward slash) as part of the name, as doing so may cause capturing errors.

Some clip names include a reference to camera framing, such as *ws* for wide shot, *cu* for close-up, or *ext* for exterior. If you lead with that information, all of the close-ups will be sorted together in the list view in the Browser.

That may be helpful, but if it's more helpful to find all the gift shop or dog shots quickly, you should add the camera-framing reference after the topic.

**4**  Make sure the Description checkbox next to the Slate button is selected, then press Tab or Return.

When selected, the information in the Description field automatically becomes part of the name.

**5**  If you're working with a script, enter the scene number and press Tab or Return. Some editors add the descriptive *Sc* before the number.

Not all footage is organized by scene, take, and angle. For many situations, you can leave those fields blank. For now, follow these steps so you can see how to deselect specific clip information in the Name field.

**6**  In the Shot/Take field, enter *tk 4,* and in the Angle field, enter *cam 2* (for camera 2).

Even though you've entered information in each field, you don't have to use it in the name that identifies the clip. The tiny checkboxes to the right of each field toggle each descriptive entry off or on.

**7**  Select and deselect the checkboxes next to each line to see how the name changes in the Name field. To use the scene and take numbers as the sole name, check those boxes and deselect the Description and Angle checkboxes.

Any one, or all four, of the descriptive entries can be included in the full clip name. Keep in mind that the longer a clip name is, the harder it may be to read when edited into a sequence in the Timeline.

You might find it more useful to enter the information but not to select the check-boxes to include the information in the name. The information remains attached to the clip, and you still have access to it in the Browser columns and through the Find function.

**8**  Next to the Shot/Take entry, click the Slate button.

Every time you click one of the slates, the next consecutive number is added to the descriptive entry. This is true even if no number was originally entered. To change to another number, click the number to highlight it, and enter a new number. Notice that the *tk* descriptive shortcut remains unchanged.

**9**  Deselect all the checkboxes except the Description checkbox. In many cases, this will be the primary source of your clip name.

**10**  Select and deselect the Prompt checkbox. Leave the box selected.

With the Prompt checkbox selected, Final Cut Pro will prompt you to verify the logged information before capturing or logging the clip. This allows you to check it, change it, or add to it before you capture.

**TIP** ▶ Keep in mind that Final Cut Pro links project clips to media files stored on your hard disk. Although you can rename clips and media files, it is always best to use an organized naming convention during the capture process.

**11** Enter a log note about the clip, such as *windy shot* or *great catch,* and select the Good checkbox.

After you capture this clip, the log note will appear in the Browser's Log Note column, and a checkmark will appear in the Good column. Again, you can enter anything in the Log Note field, but if you're going to take the time to enter something, make sure it's helpful information.

**TIP** ▶ If you would like to add markers as you log your clips, review the Take 2 exercise later in this lesson.

## Choosing Clip Settings

In the Clip Settings tab, you make selections about *how* you want to capture a clip. Do you want to capture just the video, just the audio, or both? How do you want to capture the audio—as mono tracks or as a stereo pair? How many audio tracks do you want to capture—two or eight?

Some of the options in the Clip Settings tab, such as the number of audio tracks you can capture, will depend on the type of deck or source you are using, and whether you are capturing via FireWire or a capture card.

**1** In the Log and Capture window, click the Clip Settings tab.

This tab is divided into Video and Audio sections. Each section has a checkbox to activate it. If you are capturing from a FireWire device, the video controls will be dimmed. If you are working with a capture card, you can use these controls to adjust the incoming video levels of your clip.

If you are capturing HDV, you will see a slightly different Clip Settings tab. In this tab, you have the option to create a new clip wherever you stopped and started your camera while shooting.

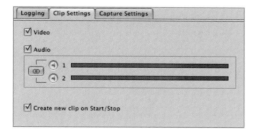

2    To capture the logged clip's audio and video, make sure the Video and Audio boxes are selected. To capture just one or the other, deselect the undesired element.

As you consider these options, keep in mind that audio files are not as large as video files. If you know you're going to use only the audio portion of a section of footage, perhaps for narration or ambient room noise, capture only the audio to reduce the file size and to conserve hard disk space. When you know you will use just the video portion of your source material, capture only video so that you won't have empty audio tracks attached to the clip.

**3**   In the Audio section, click the Stereo/Mono control connecting the two Capture Audio Channel controls (the speaker icons). Click it again to switch between capturing two audio channels as a stereo pair and capturing them as twin mono channels.

When this option is deselected, as it is in the image above, the audio tracks are *unpaired*, and the audio tracks are captured as separate channels.

Capturing audio as mono tracks is helpful when you use two mics during recording—perhaps a lavalier or lapel mic for the speaker and a boom mic for room ambience—as opposed to the stereo camera mic. Capturing the audio as twin mono channels gives you control over the individual tracks during editing.

Switching to the Stereo option will create a connecting bracket around the two audio controls, indicating that the tracks will be treated as a stereo pair. As you know, this can be helpful, because when you adjust the volume of one track or trim one track, the other track in the stereo pair is automatically adjusted the same way. The two audio tracks will also appear on just one audio tab in the Viewer.

> **NOTE ▶** After a clip has been edited into the Timeline, you can change two mono tracks into a stereo pair to adjust them simultaneously. Or, you can change a stereo pair into two mono tracks to adjust them separately.

**4**   Deselect the Stereo option, and click the Capture Audio Channel 2 control.

When the stereo option is deselected, you can choose whether you want to capture two mono channels or one individual channel of audio.

**NOTE ▶** If you are using a capture card that supports multiple-track capture, you can choose the number of tracks that you want to capture from the Input Channels pop-up menu. The tracks you select appear in the audio track area. Here you can toggle stereo or mono off or on for any set of tracks.

5 Select the Preview checkbox to listen to the source audio through Final Cut Pro as you screen and mark your clips, and also as you capture footage.

6 If you have color bars at the head of your source tape, click the Video Scopes button to view them.

The Live Waveform Monitor and Vectorscope window appears, displaying your incoming source levels. The Waveform Monitor on the left measures the brightness (luminance and black levels) of your incoming video; the Vectorscope on the right measures the color (saturation and hue).

**NOTE ▶** Keep in mind that you can view the color bars at the head of a DV tape, but you cannot change them at this point.

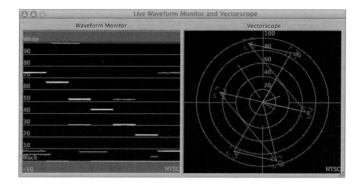

**7**   Close the Live Waveform Monitor and Vectorscope window.

## Choosing Capture Settings

Earlier in this lesson, you chose an Easy Setup suitable for the footage you were capturing. Those presets, along with other system and audio and video settings, ensure that your system is optimized for the most efficient workflow for that format.

The parameters of the Easy Setup trickle down into other areas of Final Cut Pro as well, including the Capture Settings tab in the Log and Capture window. In this tab, you determine three things: how you will control the playback device, what codec you will use to capture your footage, and where you will store it on your computer or FireWire drive. If you chose an Easy Setup for this capture session, some of those settings will already be selected in this tab.

> **NOTE ▶** As you move through the capture setup, it doesn't matter in which order you proceed. You can change your settings first and then move on to logging your clips, or you can log first and later choose your settings. But you must choose the appropriate settings before capturing clips.

**1**   In the Log and Capture window, click the Capture Settings tab.

Because you chose PAL as your format in the Easy Setup dialog earlier in this lesson, the Capture/Input is automatically set to that option here as well.

2  From the Device Control pop-up menu, choose FireWire NTSC, FireWire PAL, or another appropriate option.

If you are capturing from a device that cannot be controlled through FireWire, choose the appropriate preset, or choose Non-Controllable Device.

3  Click the Capture/Input pop-up menu.

Here is where you select the format in which your footage will be captured. You can capture a number of NTSC or PAL formats, including an assortment of options for DV, DVCPRO HD, and HDV. If the type of footage has changed, or if you want to capture using a format other than the Easy Setup preset, choose that codec here.

**NOTE ▸** If you are using a third-party capture card, such as the AJA Io or Kona card or the Blackmagic DeckLink card, those options will appear here as well.

If you shot a lot of footage, or have high-resolution footage, and don't have enough available hard disk space to store it all, you can also capture the footage at a lower-quality resolution, which will create smaller media files. You can edit your entire project using lower-resolution files. After the editing is complete, you can recapture just the footage in your final sequence at its full resolution.

**MORE INFO ▸** If your original media was HD, you might choose the Apple ProRes 422 (Proxy) codec to capture lower-resolution files at small file sizes, edit your sequence, and then recapture with a higher-quality Apple ProRes option. You can read more about this process in the Final Cut Pro User Manual.

**4**   To select the destination for your captured media, click the Scratch Disks button.

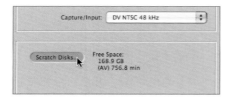

A dialog opens where you can reset the path to the targeted scratch disk or drive you will use to save your media files. The current scratch disk is listed along with the amount of currently available free space. You can choose different scratch disks for audio and video and for render files, which you will create in a later lesson. For now, capture them all to one destination.

> **TIP** ▸ If one scratch disk isn't large enough for your media-capturing needs, you can target up to 12 scratch disks. When the primary disk is full, the capturing continues on the disk with the most available space. This feature is very helpful when you're working with long-format projects or high-resolution footage.

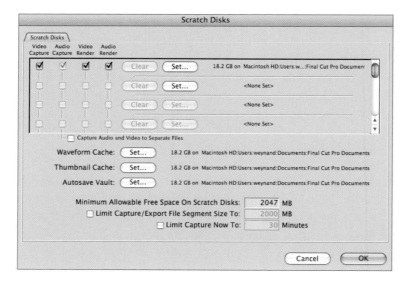

**MORE INFO** ▸ To learn how to determine the amount of disk space you may need for your project, refer to the "Calculating Hard Disk Space Requirements" section of the Final Cut Pro User Manual.

When you set the scratch disk, Final Cut Pro automatically creates folders in that location for each type of file. As those files are captured or created, it automatically places files in those folders. The default location for the scratch disk is Users/[user name]/Documents/Final Cut Pro Documents. Let's look at those capture folders.

**5**   Press Command-H to hide Final Cut Pro, and double-click the Macintosh hard disk icon, or press Command-Shift-N, to create a new Finder window. Navigate to Users > [user name] > Documents > Final Cut Pro Documents.

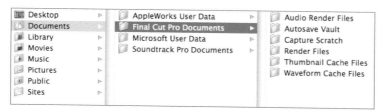

When you capture in a different project, a folder with that project name is created in the Capture Scratch folder, and the media files you capture are placed there. If you don't change the default scratch disk location, all the organizational work of correctly placing captured footage, render files, and backup project files saved in the Autosave Vault will be done for you, project by project.

**TIP** ▶ To save other types of files to separate locations—such as the backup files in the Autosave Vault—click the Set button and choose a destination.

**6**   Close the Finder window and return to Final Cut Pro. If you do want to change the currently selected scratch disk—to target a FireWire drive, for example—click Set.

A file browser appears in which you can select a different scratch disk.

**7**   Navigate to the location where you want to save your captured files, and click Choose. Then, in the Scratch Disks dialog, click OK.

When you set a new scratch disk, Final Cut Pro creates the same set of folders in that location as are in the default scratch disk location.

**TIP** ▶ Although the Final Cut Pro default is to capture media files to the internal hard disk where your operating system resides, digital media files make your hard disk work harder. For optimal performance of your software and operating system, capture media files to a separate hard disk drive.

There's another settings window where you can change the scratch disk, just as you do in the Capture Settings tab.

8    Choose Final Cut Pro > System Settings, or press Shift-Q.

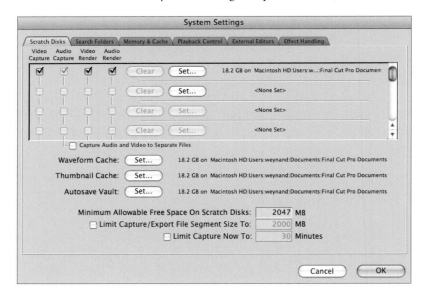

The first tab of this window shows the same scratch disk information that appears if you click the Scratch Disks button in the Capture Settings tab.

You can set the scratch disk in either location. If the desired scratch disk is set in the System Settings window, and you are not changing it, you do not have to select it in the Capture Settings tab. Notice that this window also follows the Easy Setup that you chose earlier in this lesson.

9    Click Cancel, then choose Final Cut Pro > Audio/Video Settings, or press Command-Option-Q.

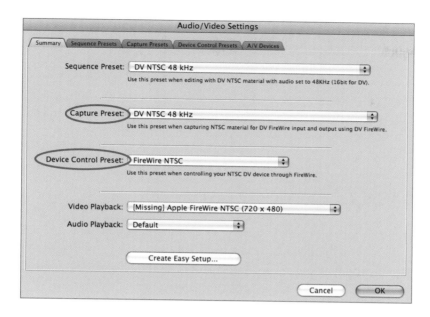

In this window, you can select the device-control and capture presets. If they are correctly selected, the same settings will appear in the Device Control and Capture/Input pop-up menus of the Capture Settings tab. Here, too, the settings reflect the Easy Setup you chose earlier.

**MORE INFO ▶** In Final Cut Pro 7, if your footage includes captioning in one of the supported formats, a QuickTime closed-captioning track is created in the resulting source media. Depending on the type of closed-captioning information that is present, this data may be viewable in QuickTime Player but not in FCP. For more information, see the Final Cut Pro User Manual.

## Choosing Capture Options

Now that you've chosen the right capture settings, targeted a scratch disk to contain the media files, and created a logging bin to organize the captured clips in the project, you're ready to choose which of the three capture options you want to use.

The lower portion of the Logging tab area has three Capture buttons—Clip, Now, and Batch—and a Log Clip button. These buttons appear regardless of which tab is selected in the Log and Capture window.

Each of the capture options converts footage from your tape source to computer media files. The Log Clip button builds a list to be captured later via batch capture. Although all the capture options create media clips, each performs the process differently.

> **MORE INFO** ▶ If you're capturing a project that originated on film, you may want to track the relationship between the keycode of the film frames and the timecode of the video you are capturing. You can refer to the Apple Cinema Tools User Manual for more information.

You can approach the capture process in several ways. In some situations, you may want to enter detailed information for a clip and then capture it before going on to the next clip. In other situations, you may want to log information about all of your clips, then capture them as a group.

Other times, when working with footage that doesn't have timecode, you won't be able to log any information. Sometimes you can choose to capture an entire tape and let Final Cut Pro automatically create the clips based on where the tape stopped and started.

**Capturing a Clip**

You began this lesson by marking a portion of the tape in the Preview area and identifying it in the Logging tab. Your next step is to capture the clip using the Capture Clip option. This creates a media file based on the In and Out points you set, complete with any log notes and markers.

Capturing clip by clip is a stop-and-start process. You mark a clip, log it, then capture it. Mark, log, and capture; mark, log, and capture. A good time to use this approach is when you have only a few clips to capture from your source or when you want to be precise about where a clip starts and stops.

1   Mark a new clip from your source footage, or use the clip you marked in previous exercise steps. Enter or amend the logging information.

2   In the Logging tab, click the Capture Clip button.

If you selected the Prompt checkbox next to the Name field, the Log Clip dialog appears. This is a good double-check to ensure all the logging information is correct before you actually capture the clip.

**TIP** If you do not want to be prompted for your log information each time you click the Capture Clip button, deselect the Prompt checkbox in the Logging tab.

**3**  If necessary, make changes to the clip log information, then click OK.

When capturing begins, a window displays the material you are capturing. Don't worry if the image seems jagged at this point. The display during capturing does not reflect the quality of the captured clip.

**NOTE ▶** If you are capturing HDV footage, the audio and video may appear to be out of sync. This is apparent only during the capture process. The final clip will capture in sync.

### Using Capture Now

If you did a great job shooting and want to capture every frame of your source tape, you can use the Capture Now option. With this option, you log information but you don't enter timecode In and Out points or markers. And because this process does not include a pre-roll to cue to a location, you can use it to capture the first few frames on a tape. You may also use this option when you don't have FireWire control over a source device, such as a nondigital camera, or when a source doesn't have timecode.

1   In the Logging tab, enter the next clip name and, if necessary, a new reel number.

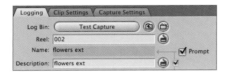

This is an important step. If you don't name the clip before you start the Capture Now process, Final Cut Pro will give the clip a default name.

**TIP ▶** If you do capture a clip with a name you don't want, you can change the clip name in the project, and then ripple that change back to the media file. Select the clip in the Browser, and choose Modify > Rename > File to Match Clip.

2   Cue the source tape about 10 seconds before the beginning of the action you want to capture.

This is a less exact method of capturing than the Capture Clip option, so make sure you give yourself an adequate pad before and after the action.

3   Play the tape from that point, and click the Capture Now button.

Make sure you give yourself a few extra seconds past the last action before continuing with the next step.

**4**   Press the Esc (Escape) key to stop capturing.

**5**   To limit the amount of time you automatically capture at one stretch, click the Capture Settings tab and then click the Scratch Disks button.

At the bottom of this tab is an option to limit the Capture Now process to a specified amount of time. The default is 30 minutes. To activate this option, select the Limit Capture Now To checkbox and enter an amount of capture time. If you want to capture only 40 minutes of your tape, enter *40*, and click OK.

**NOTE** ▶ When using Capture Now, you can easily capture long sections of material without realizing how large a file you are creating. Remember that 5 minutes of DV media will consume about 1 GB of hard disk storage space.

If you shot in a DV format (DV, DVCAM, DVCPRO, DVCPRO 50, or DVCPRO HD) and stopped and started the camera at different times, you can use the DV Start/Stop Detect function to streamline your workflow. It can be used to create subclips from long clips captured in either the Capture Clip or Capture Now mode.

**TIP** ▶ To practice DV Start/Stop Detect, you can import the **pond life** file from the Media/Imports folder, and then continue with step 6.

**6**   To apply DV Start/Stop Detect, follow these steps:

▶   Capture the long clip, and then open it in the Viewer.

▶   Choose Mark > DV Start/Stop Detect. Final Cut Pro will scan the clip looking for breaks in time when you stopped and started the camera.

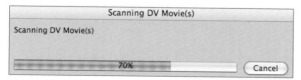

▶   Markers will appear on the clip wherever the original tape was stopped and started during recording.

▶ In the Browser, select a marker, and choose Modify > Make Subclip. A new subclip is created from the location of this marker to the next marker.

▶ To create subclips of all the individual markers, drag all the markers attached to this clip into a new bin. This creates individual subclips with durations from one marker, or shot, to the next.

### Logging Clips and Batch Capturing

The third capture option provides an efficient alternative to the "mark, log, capture" workflow. This approach separates the decision-making process (what to capture and what to name it) from the hardware process (cuing up the tape, playing it forward in real time, and converting the tape selection to a media file).

The first step is to mark and log the clips you want to capture; then you instruct Final Cut Pro to capture the entire list, or *batch*, of clips you've marked. You don't have to be present while the clips are being captured. As long as the mark points can be found on tape, FCP captures the clips automatically.

1   Mark a new section of footage, and enter the information in the Logging tab as you did before, but do not click a Capture button.

**2**  Click the Log Clip button, or press the keyboard shortcut, F2.

**NOTE ▶** To use the F2 shortcut to log a clip, make sure that key has not been assigned to an Exposé function in System Preferences.

If the Prompt checkbox was selected in the Logging tab, the Log Clip dialog will open, reminding you of your logging information. Click OK.

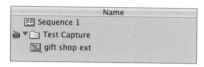

A new clip appears in the logging bin just as any other clip would, except this one has a red diagonal line over it to indicate the clip is *offline*. This means the clip information is there, but not the media content, because the media has not yet been captured. If a marker is attached, you will see a disclosure triangle next to the clip name.

**3**  Mark another portion of footage, and log the clip information in the Logging tab. Then click the Log Clip button again, or press F2.

Continuing this process creates a cumulative list of every clip you log, each with a red line through it indicating that it is offline media.

**NOTE ▶** The red offline media line can also indicate that a clip in the project has lost its connection to its media file because the file was moved, renamed, or deleted.

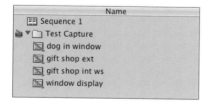

After you've logged several clips, you may realize that you made a mistake when entering logging information for one or more clips. For example, you may have had both audio and video selected when you wanted to capture only audio, or you really wanted to capture the clips as a stereo pair rather than mono tracks.

4   To change the track information of a logged clip before capturing it, select the clip in the Browser and choose Modify > Clip Settings. Make the changes, and click OK.

**TIP** ▶ You can also select a group of offline clips, choose Modify > Clip Settings, and make changes to the selected group at one time.

When you have completed logging all the clips you want to capture, and made any necessary changes to them, you can capture them all at once using batch capture. If you want to capture all of the clips in the current logging bin, you can skip the next step. If you want to capture only some of the offline clips, you must select them.

5   In the Test Capture bin, select the logged clips you want to capture.

6   In the Log and Capture window, click the Capture Batch button.

**TIP** ▶ To access the Batch Capture dialog when clips are selected, you can also Control-click a selected clip in the Browser and choose Batch Capture, or choose File > Batch Capture, or press Control-C.

The Batch Capture dialog opens. This is where you choose what you're going to capture and how.

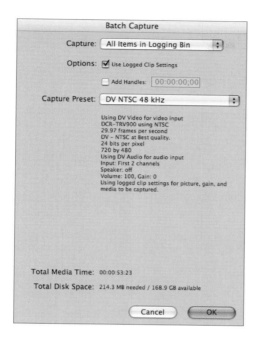

Four options are available in the Batch Capture dialog:

▶  **Capture**—Click the pop-up menu to choose which clips you want to capture (All Items in Logging Bin, Offline Items in Logging Bin, or Selected Items in Logging Bin).

▶  **Options: Use Logged Clip Settings**—Select this checkbox to capture the clips with all the settings that were present when you originally logged the clips.

▶  **Options: Add Handles**—Select this checkbox to add handles to the current logged clips only if you did not allow for handles while first previewing and marking the clips.

▶  **Capture Preset**—If you want to capture the selected clips using a preset different from the one the clips were logged with, choose that preset from this pop-up menu.

**NOTE** ▶ These options will change depending on which clips are selected in the Browser. Before making a selection, make sure you read the options carefully.

At the bottom of the Batch Capture dialog, calculations appear based on the capture settings you select.

**7**   Make the appropriate selections, and click OK.

The Insert Reel dialog appears, indicating that you are ready to capture. This dialog lists the source reel number, the total amount of clip time, and the number of clips.

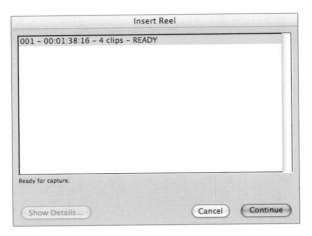

8   Click Continue.

Using all of your logged information, Final Cut Pro seeks out each clip on the specified reel and creates the QuickTime media file necessary for editing. You will see the material you are capturing in a capture screen.

When all clips on that reel have been captured, the Insert Reel dialog opens again, indicating the number of clips remaining to be captured. If all clips were successfully captured, there should be 0 clips and the status should be "DONE."

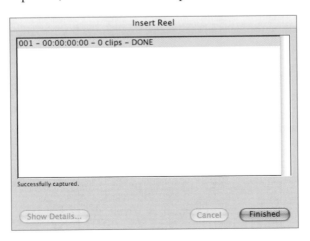

**9** When all of the clips are captured, click Finished. Then close the Log and Capture window.

If your list contains footage from another reel or tape, Final Cut Pro will prompt you to change reels and continue. When batch capture is completed, each of the selected clips in the logging bin will have footage connected to them, and the red lines will be gone.

## Setting Capture Preferences

The General tab of User Preferences contains options that relate to capturing. Certain user preferences will affect how you capture video. Some of these preferences help you troubleshoot or work around problematic video, while others smooth the capturing process. You can open the User Preferences window (press Option-Q) and look at four of these options.

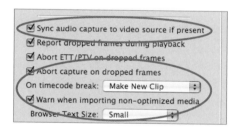

▶ **Sync audio capture to video source if present**—This option ensures sync for audio captured from a genlocked audio deck.

▶ **Abort capture on dropped frames**—If Final Cut Pro notices any frames of video being dropped or left out while capturing your source material, it will stop the capture process and report the dropped frames. You will lose all the media captured up to that point.

▶ **On timecode break**—If there is a break in the source-tape timecode, you have the option to make Final Cut Pro do one of three things: start a new clip at the timecode break, abort the capture process, or warn you that there was a timecode break after capturing is over.

▶ **Warn when importing non-optimized media**—Final Cut Pro will always optimize media files when capturing. On the rare occasion that it can't optimize a media file for multiple-stream real-time playback, it will warn you if this option is selected. Unless you are editing with multiple uncompressed video streams that demand maximum media file performance, you can usually leave the files as they are and continue editing normally. If you are working with standard definition DV captured in Final Cut Pro, your files are already optimized.

**TIP** ▶ Try capturing using the default User Preferences settings. If you have problems with dropped frames or timecode breaks, deselect one or more of the options and try again.

## Take 2

The producer has observed you adding markers to clips in your project but has just learned you can also add markers as you capture footage. (Once the clip is captured, the markers will appear with the clip in the Browser, where you can convert them to subclips as you did in Lesson 6.)

He wants to know whether incorporating markers during video capture of his Yellowstone HD documentary will improve the current workflow. You've seen one of the tapes: 60 minutes of a baby bear frolicking with its mother in the woods. What's your opinion?

Before you set markers, mark an In point where you want to begin capturing and an Out point where you want to stop. Then, in the Logging tab, click the Markers disclosure triangle to reveal the Marker controls. You use the Capture Clip option to capture the clip, or Log Clip to log the clip information.

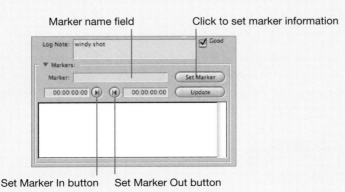

Marker name field          Click to set marker information

Set Marker In button     Set Marker Out button

## Transferring Files from Tapeless Sources

As new technologies develop, so do the possibilities for recording and capturing media. Instead of videotaping your footage, you may be recording it on an SD card using an AVCHD camera; via Panasonic's P2 solid-state acquisition; on Sony's XDCAM optical disc; or with a flash card or FireWire drive using the RED camera.

These options create digital files as you shoot. Instead of capturing the footage, you need only transfer, or *ingest*, the digital files into your project and begin editing immediately. You can even edit in the foreground while you ingest in the background. If you have footage in one of these formats, you can use it in this lesson. Otherwise, you can use the media provided in the Book Files.

> **NOTE ▶** When you insert a media card into your computer, or attach a card reader, it will appear as a drive icon.

**1** In Final Cut Pro, set either the project or a bin as the logging bin, as you did earlier in this lesson. Then choose File > Log and Transfer, or press Command-Shift-8. The Log and Transfer window opens.

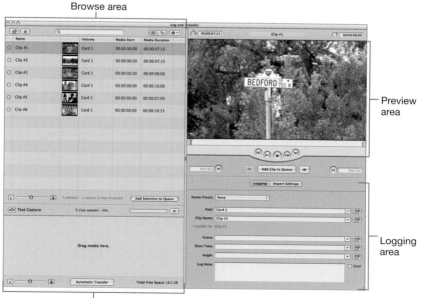

When a media card or drive is connected, Final Cut Pro will automatically display the media clips in the Browse area of the window. In the Preview area, you can screen a clip, mark the portion you want to transfer, and enter logging information similar to that in the Log and Capture window.

If you don't have a card with footage to transfer, but do have digital video files on your computer, you can point FCP to their locations.

**2**   In the Browse area, click the Add Volume button, and navigate to FCP7 Book Files > Media > Imports > AVCHD.

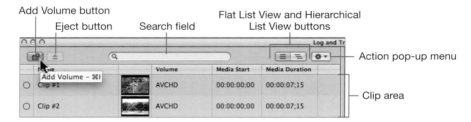

**3**   From the Action pop-up menu, choose Preferences. Notice that Final Cut Pro will automatically convert AVCHD footage to the Apple ProRes 422 format during transfer. Click Cancel.

**NOTE ▶** AVCHD is a densely compressed format created for efficient recording on small SDHC cards. It is not, however, an efficient editing format. This is why the default is to convert it to Apple ProRes 422, which is an extremely efficient editing format.

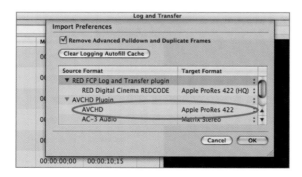

**NOTE ▶** Panasonic P2 footage can be transferred in its native AVC-Intra format.

4   If no image is present in the Preview area, click the first clip in the list, then click the Play button under the image to play the clip. Drag the playhead in the scrubber bar to scrub through the clip.

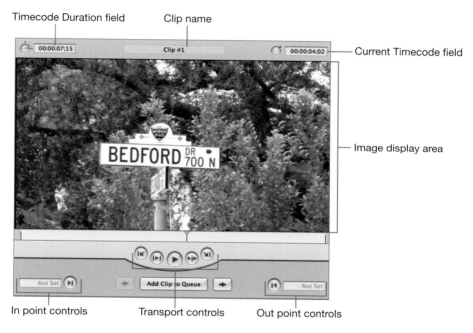

Timecode Duration field          Clip name          Current Timecode field

Image display area

In point controls          Transport controls          Out point controls

Because this is a digital file, you can scrub clips just as you would scrub a clip in the Viewer.

5   Mark In and Out points to identify the portion of the clip that you want to transfer. You can also mark a clip by pressing the I and O keys, or by clicking the Mark In and Mark Out buttons beneath the image. Note the clip's duration in the Duration field.

**MORE INFO ▸** You can drag a mark to adjust its location, just as you would a clip in the Viewer scrubber bar. But however you mark, you may find that the In or Out point does not stay exactly where you set it on AVCHD footage. AVCHD is encoded using MPEG compression, which does not record complete frame information for every frame. The playhead must align with a complete frame, called an I-frame, for you to set a mark. You can read more about MPEG compression in the Final Cut Pro User Manual.

**6**  To ingest the clip into your project, click the Add Clip to Queue button beneath the transport buttons.

The clip appears in the Transfer Queue. The progress indicator gear spins while the clip is transferred and the progress bar indicates the amount of media already transferred. When the transfer is complete, the clip is removed from the list.

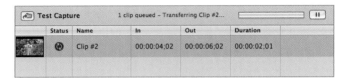

In the Browse area, the media map indicator in the clip's Status column is half filled to indicate that only a portion of this clip was transferred. You can also transfer the entire clip without screening it in the Preview area.

**7**  Drag Clip #2 down to the Transfer Queue.

> **TIP** ▶ You can transfer all of your clips at one time by selecting them all, or by pressing Command-A and dragging them as a group to the Transfer Queue, or by clicking the Add Selection to Queue button. If you want to change the name of a clip, click its name in the Clip list and enter a new name before transferring it.

When you drag a clip from the Browse or Preview areas to the Transfer Queue, Final Cut Pro will either begin transferring the clip immediately or put it in the queue to be transferred.

> **TIP** ▶ You can stop the transfer process by clicking the clip in the Transfer Queue and pressing Delete. Follow the prompts to remove the clip from the list.

**8**  When transferring is complete, close the Log and Transfer window. In the Browser, open the **Clip #1** clip and play it in the Viewer.

**9**   In the Browser, Control-click **Clip #1** and, from the shortcut menu, choose Item Properties > Format. Notice that the Compressor type is Apple ProRes 422.

## Take 2

The location manager shot some exterior locations in Beverly Hills, California, for an upcoming TV series about family life "in the hills." Will the director like any of these locations for the family's home? To find out, continue screening these clips in the Log and Transfer window, and mark just the portion you want to show the director.

## Lesson Review

1.  Before you can capture footage, what is the first thing you must do?

2.  Marking clips for capture is similar to marking clips while editing. True or false?

3.  You can enter a variety of clip information in the Logging tab. Give an example of logging information that appears in the Browser columns.

4.  When you choose a capture preset, what settings do you want it to match?

5.  What are the three capture modes you can use to capture footage?

6.  What is a scratch disk?

7.  How can you save time using the Batch Capture mode?

8.  You can choose only your computer hard drive as a scratch disk. True or false?

9.  What other settings window contains the scratch disk information like that on the Capture Settings tab?

10. What other settings window contains the device-control information like that on the Capture Settings tab?

11. What menu command do you choose to ingest from nontape sources?

*Answers*

1.  You must connect your source device via a FireWire cable or third-party capture card and turn it on.

2.  True.

3. Log note, good take, scene number, take number, angle number, clip name.

4. Your source footage settings. If you have a variety of footage, it should match whatever format represents the majority of clips or the highest quality, depending on the project and your hardware.

5. Capture Clip, Capture Now, and Batch Capture.

6. The target destination for your captured media files.

7. You can log individual clips and then capture them together at the same time.

8. False. You can set your computer hard drive or an external FireWire drive as your scratch disk.

9. The System Settings window.

10. The Audio/Video Settings window.

11. Choose File > Log and Transfer.

## Keyboard Shortcuts

| | |
|---|---|
| **Control-C** | Batch capture selected items |
| **Shift-Q** | Open System Settings window |
| **Command-Option-Q** | Open Audio/Video Settings window |
| **Command-8** | Open Log and Capture window |
| **F2** | Log a clip in the Browser without capturing media |
| **Esc** | Stop the capture process |

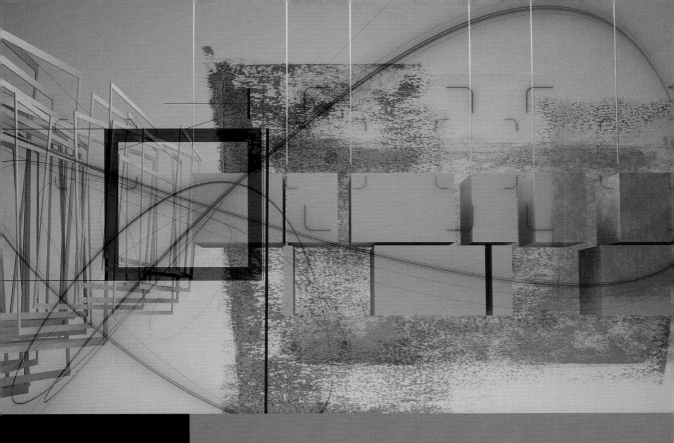

# Completing the Cut

# 9

**Lesson Files** FCP7 Book Files > Lessons > Lesson 9 Project

**Media** FCP7 Book Files > Media > Quest; SeaWorld

**Time** This lesson takes approximately 60 minutes to complete.

**Goals** Evaluate project needs

Understand transitions

Apply video and audio transitions

Apply global transitions

Copy and change transitions

Use the Transition Editor

Adjust edit points under a transition

Save favorite transitions

Change transition parameters

Preview and render transitions

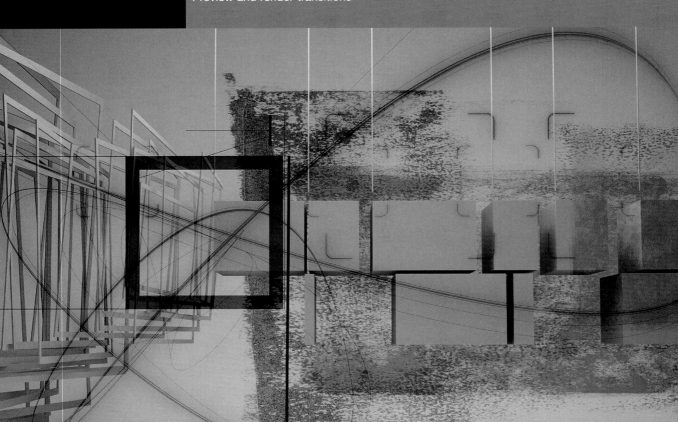

# Lesson **9**
# Applying Transitions

The next stage of the editing process is completing the sequence. Completing the sequence does not mean that you're ready to ship the final product; but it does mean that you're wrapping up the big things such as adding transitions to smooth edit points, mixing together audio tracks, and creating text for displaying the title or identifying the show's host, guest, or performer. Without completing these essential tasks, your sequence just won't be ready for prime-time viewing.

In the next three lessons, you will focus on each of these aspects: adding transitions, mixing sound, and creating titles. Add some special effects, and you are only a few short steps from your final output.

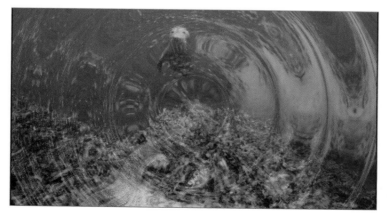

A ripple dissolve can be applied to an edit point between two clips.

This lesson covers transitions. Transitions add variety to your video by changing how it moves from one clip to the next. They can be used to smooth out an abrupt audio or video edit or to create a certain visual style for your sequence. In this lesson, you will explore how to apply transition effects to video and audio edit points, how to render effects, and how to choose the best settings to see the maximum number of effects in real time.

## Evaluating the Project

Not every project requires transitions. Some of the world's greatest films were created with nothing more than a fade-in at the head and a fade-out at the tail. Part of your job as an editor is to determine whether transitions will improve your sequence and, if they will, to choose the appropriate ones. This decision could be based on the style of the show or series. For example, dramatic material, such as in *Leverage*, typically cuts from one shot to the next, and transitions aren't required, whereas content cut to narration or music, such as the trailer for the program *Accidental Quest for Enlightenment*, might benefit from transitions to add to the serenity of the footage.

1   Choose File > Open or press Command-O, and open the Lessons > Lesson 9 Project file on your hard disk. Then close any other open projects.

> **TIP** Since you won't be screening source footage in this lesson, you can change your window layout to the larger Canvas view.

2   In the Canvas, notice the *Quest* sequence duration, and then play the sequence.

This is a 1-minute trailer for a program called *An Accidental Quest for Enlightenment*. The sequence has been edited to the correct length. Although it isn't complete, it already contains some necessary components: narration, music segments, several sound effects, and an end title that sits above the last V1 clip. Using a straight cut for each edit, however, does not enhance the video or help the rough edges in the music tracks.

**TIP** In editing, the emphasis is often placed on the video portion of a sequence. However, if the sound in your sequence is jarring as you cut from one audio clip to the next, viewers will notice it immediately. To smooth these edit points, you can apply an audio cross fade.

3    Play the sequence again and notice how the V1 clip names refer to the narration at each clip location.

Customizing a project means making it work efficiently for yourself and other team members. Because the narration clips were edited from three long master clips, changing their names would only give you three aural or text cues. By renaming the video clips, you create helpful references to the narration script throughout the sequence.

**TIP** Another opportunity to use this naming convention is with music videos. You can name the video clips after the lyrics to see where you are in the song.

▶ **About the *An Accidental Quest for Enlightenment* footage**

This footage was produced by Evergreen Films Inc., of Los Angeles. It was shot on location in Alaska's Prince William Sound using a Sony HD camera at 1920 x 1080 and 23.98 fps. The material was originally shot for a *National Geographic* special, but it will also be used in an upcoming dramatic feature. Evergreen Films Inc. was founded by Emmy Award–winning director Pierre de Lespinois and Silicon Valley entrepreneur Mike Devlin. Together they bring leading technology to all aspects of film and high-end television production.

In the Timeline, notice that the sequence is referred to as *Quest*, which makes it easier to identify. The shorter name also allows room to add version numbers. Let's duplicate this sequence and rename it.

**4**   In the Browser, Control-click the *Quest* sequence, and from the shortcut menu, choose Duplicate. Rename the new sequence *Quest_v2_transitions*. Open this sequence in the Timeline.

Now that you know how to go "under the hood" of a clip or a sequence, let's find out the format of the *Quest* footage.

**5**   In the Timeline, select the first clip and press Command-9.

Although this footage was shot at the highest possible HD quality, the captured media files were recompressed using the Apple ProRes 422 (Proxy) format, which reduced the file sizes for the book's DVD.

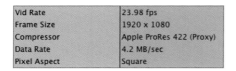

| Vid Rate | 23.98 fps |
| Frame Size | 1920 x 1080 |
| Compressor | Apple ProRes 422 (Proxy) |
| Data Rate | 4.2 MB/sec |
| Pixel Aspect | Square |

**6**   Click Cancel and press Command-0 to open the Sequence Settings window. Notice that the sequence settings match the clip settings.

**TIP** ▶ Since you'll often use these two functions in tandem, a helpful way to remember their shortcuts is that the number keys 9 and 0 appear next to each other on the keyboard.

**7**   Click the Timeline Options tab and notice that the Thumbnail Display is set to Name Plus Thumbnail. Click Cancel to close this window.

When tracks are very short, they will not display thumbnails even if that is the current display option. Until you become more familiar with this new footage, it might be helpful to make the Timeline V1 track taller to enlarge the thumbnails.

**8**   In the Timeline patch panel, drag the V1 boundary up. Because only one clip is on the V2 track, the show title, drag the V2 boundary down to reduce its height.

**TIP** ▶ To reduce the height of all the audio tracks, Option-drag an audio track boundary upward.

Changing the V1 track height allows you to view the sequence as though it were a storyboard. This, together with renaming the clips, makes it easier to work with footage edited by someone else.

**NOTE** ▶ You can also leave the video clips smaller to more easily read their names. Customizing your layout is about making decisions that improve your workflow.

**9**   Look at the Timeline ruler above the above the **AQE Title** clip at the end of the sequence.

This colored horizontal line is a *render bar* and indicates the render status of a clip. You will see these render bars appear when you add transitions. You'll learn more about rendering later in this lesson. For now, let's make sure you're seeing as many real-time effects as possible.

**10**  To make sure you see as many real-time effects as possible, click the RT pop-up menu in the Timeline, and from the shortcut menu, choose Unlimited RT. Click the RT pop-up menu again, and make sure you see a checkmark next to Dynamic in both of the places it appears.

## Understanding Transitions

Whether or not you've ever applied a transition to your own sequence, you've probably seen a million of them on television and in films and intuitively know what they are. A transition is an effect applied to the edit point between two clips in a sequence. Instead of cutting from one clip to the next and making an immediate change, a transition creates a change over time from the outgoing clip to the incoming clip.

Several types of transitions can be applied in Final Cut Pro. One frequently used transition is a *cross dissolve*, which mixes video from the outgoing clip and video from the incoming clip at the edit point. As one clip fades out, the other clip fades in.

This mixing process uses the handle of at least one of the two clips that make up the transition. In audio, this process is called a *cross fade*: The end of one audio clip fades out while the beginning of the next one fades in.

> **TIP** ▶ A good trick for determining the length of a clip's media handles is to click the clip with the Slip tool without dragging left or right. You will see the handles extending past the brown boundary box on either side of the clip. When there is no additional media on one end of a clip, as in the figure below, a boundary handle appears on only one side.

## Viewing Transition Options

Final Cut Pro organizes its effects into two categories: transitions and filters. (Filters are covered in Lesson 13.) You can choose a transition effect from one of two places: the Effects menu or the Effects tab in the Browser. Each place contains the same set of transition effects organized in separate Video Transitions and Audio Transitions bins.

1   In the Browser, select the Effects tab. If this tab is in icon view, Control-click in the gray area and choose View As List from the shortcut menu.

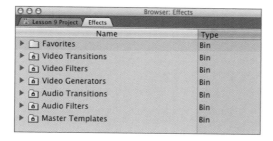

The Effects tab has seven bins. Three bins contain video effects, two contain audio effects, and two can be used to store and organize your favorite effects or to apply a Motion template. In this lesson, you will use just the Video Transitions and Audio Transitions bins.

2    Display the contents of the Audio Transitions bin.

This folder contains two audio cross fades: 0dB and +3dB. A 0 dB Cross Fade has a slight dip in the audio level at the midpoint of the transition. The +3 dB Cross Fade is designed to produce a fade without having this dip in the middle. The +3dB Cross Fade is underlined, meaning it is the default transition.

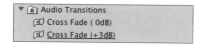

3    Click the disclosure triangle next to the Audio Transitions bin to hide its contents. Then display the contents of the Video Transitions bin.

There are nine bins of video transitions, each with its own set of transition styles and parameters.

4    Click the disclosure triangle next to the Dissolve bin to display its contents.

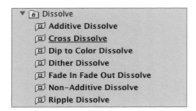

Various dissolve transitions appear here, including the underlined Cross Dissolve, which is the default video transition. Notice, too, that the Dissolve transition names are in boldface type, which means they can be played in real time (RT) at normal play speed after you apply them.

**5** Choose the Effects menu.

Six of the Effects bin titles appear here, including Favorites, Video Transitions, Video Filters, Audio Transitions, Audio Filters, and Master Templates.

**6** From the Effects menu, choose Video Transitions > Dissolve.

The same dissolve options appear here, although currently dimmed, that appear on the Effects tab in the Browser.

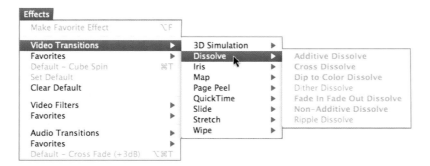

Although you can choose any transition from either location, the Effects tab includes additional information that might come in handy as you edit.

**7** Click in the Browser window and then click the zoom button to expand the window. Drag the Length column heading to the left to place it next to the Name column.

All audio and video transitions have a default 1-second duration. Changing the length in this column changes the default duration of a specific transition.

## Applying Transitions

The ways you apply a transition are a little like the automatic and manual approaches to editing you used in Lesson 2. The manual approach is to drag a transition from the Effects tab to an edit point in the Timeline. This approach relies on your own eye and judgment to place the effect correctly.

The automatic approach makes use of the Effects menu, but you must first target the edit point so that Final Cut Pro knows where to place the transition you select. You can also apply a transition to a group of clips—or the entire sequence—at one time. You apply audio and video transitions the same way.

While there are a variety of video transitions to explore, in this exercise you will focus on dissolves.

> **TIP** ▶ Make sure snapping is turned on throughout this lesson, and whenever necessary, zoom in to the Timeline so you can more easily identify clips and transitions.

1    In the Timeline, play the first two clips: **pw sound** and **going**. Then click the video edit point between them to select it.

By selecting the edit point between the two clips, you are giving Final Cut Pro a target location to place the transition you choose from the Effects menu.

> **NOTE** ▶ Your V1 video track may appear taller than those pictured in these images.

2    Choose Effects > Video Transitions > Dissolve > Cross Dissolve. Play the new dissolve transition.

> **NOTE** ▶ Depending on your computer's processing power, Final Cut Pro may not be able to play every frame of a transition, and some may stutter as they play. You will learn how to render these and eliminate stutter later in this lesson.

The **pw sound** clip fades out as the **going** clip fades in. Since the default length for all transitions is 1 second, this is a 1-second dissolve centered over the edit point.

Handles for each clip extend out to either side of the edit point. Notice that the transition name appears on the icon between the two clips. The dark upward and downward shading represents the handle portion of each clip fading in and out.

**NOTE ▶** Keep in mind that a 1-second dissolve in this footage consists of 24 frames, because it was shot at 24 frames per second. The dissolve is divided over the edit point as 12 frames on the outgoing clip side and 12 frames on the incoming clip side. When you're working with 29.97 fps NTSC footage, the dissolve is evenly split with 15 frames on either side of the edit point.

Another way to target an edit point is to position the playhead directly on it. For this edit point, let's apply a different type of dissolve transition.

3   Press the Up Arrow or Down Arrow key to move the playhead to the next edit point, between the **going** and **fishing** clips. This time, choose Video Transitions > Dissolve > Ripple Dissolve. Notice the render bar above the clip and then play the transition.

To apply a transition manually, you have to see both the target edit point in the Timeline and the transition you want to apply in the Effects tab. When you drag the transition icon to an edit point, it is colored dark brown to indicate how it will be placed. You have the option of releasing the transition centered on the edit point, or to the left or right of it.

4   In the Timeline, make sure you can see the next transition, between the **fishing** and **journey** clips. From the Effects tab, drag the Cross Dissolve icon to the Timeline over this edit point and position the pointer so the transition icon is even on both sides, then release the mouse button. Play this transition.

**TIP** ▶ Make sure you place the icon over the edit point. You could also place it over the body of the clip, but that would produce a different result: a transition on both ends of the edit.

Since Cross Dissolve is the default video transition, you can also apply it using a keyboard shortcut. Using a shortcut is an automatic approach and requires that you target the edit point, as you do when you choose a menu option.

5    Select the next edit point in the sequence, between the **journey** and **immersed** clips. Press Command-T to add the default video transition, and play the transition.

If you want to dissolve into and out of a clip, you need to apply one transition to the head of the clip and another to the tail. You can apply both in one step, using either the manual or the automatic method.

6    Select the **poets** clip, and press Command-T. The default transition is added to both ends of the selected clip. Play this clip.

**TIP** ▶ Dragging a transition to the body of a clip will also apply a transition to both ends of the clip at once.

This method, as well as the others in this exercise, works the same for audio. Now that you've added dissolves around the **poets** clip, let's place cross fades around the **bark** sound effect beneath it by using a similar keyboard shortcut.

**NOTE** ▶ The music segments and sound effects used in this sequence were exported from Soundtrack Pro. You can read more about this Final Cut Studio application in Lesson 10.

7    On the A2 track, select the **bark** clip. Press Command-Option-T and play the clip.

When a single audio clip includes a two-track stereo pair, a cross fade is placed on each end of the clip and on each track.

Notice that the cross fades are included *within* the content of the clip because there are no adjoining clips on either side of it.

NOTE ▶ Video and audio transition icons look alike except for the transition name that appears on it. When a track is very short, however, you won't see the transition name.

To apply transitions globally, you simply select the group of clips—or set In and Out points to identify the range—and apply the transition.

8  Play the section of three sound effects clips, **geese**, **water**, and **stream**. Notice that the music edit is a little abrupt. Then mark In and Out points around this section.

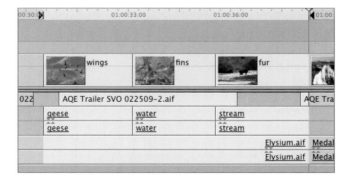

9  To apply transitions to the clips within this range:

  ▶  Press Command-T to apply the default video transition.

  ▶  Press Command-Option-T to apply the default audio cross fade.

  ▶  Press Option-X to remove the In and Out points.

> **TIP** ▶ You can also press Command-A to select all the clips in a sequence and use the keyboard shortcut to apply the default transition to all video or audio edit points at one time. Or you can drag any transition to a group of selected clips.

**10** Play the section again and notice how the cross fades smoothed the music edit.

When a clip is used in its entirety in a sequence, or from the first frame or last frame of the media file, there won't be any clip handles to extend past the clip to create a transition. To remedy this, you can position, or *align*, a transition to end or start on an edit point.

**11** Play the edit point between the **who wins** and **my fall** video clips toward the end of the sequence. Press S to select the Slip tool, then click and hold down the **my fall** clip.

In the Canvas, you see the head-of-clip overlay in the left frame. This means there is no additional media, or handle, at the head of this clip to mix with the outgoing clip before the edit point.

In this situation, you can start the transition to begin at the edit point instead of centering on the edit point. The outgoing clip extends past the edit point for the full length of the transition.

**12**  Press A to return to the default Selection tool. From the Effects tab, drag the Dip to Color Dissolve icon to the right side of the edit point between the **who wins** and **my fall** clips, but don't release the mouse button.

When a transition icon is aligned on the right side of the edit point, you see the full length of the dissolve appear over that clip.

**TIP** ▶ When choosing the Start On Edit alignment, make sure you position the icon for the longest possible transition without selecting the entire clip.

**13**  Release the transition on the right side of the edit point, and play it.

This transition starts at the edit point and dips to black as it transitions from one clip to the next. Since this is a different type of transition from the Cross Dissolve, you see a different name on the transition icon.

**NOTE** ▶ This type of transition can be modified to dip to any color. You will make those modifications later in this lesson.

Start On Edit is one of three transition alignments you can choose, along with End On Edit and Center On Edit. The End On Edit alignment is used when an outgoing clip has no extra media to extend past the edit point.

When you add a transition to a clip at the beginning of the sequence, the clip will transition from black instead of from another clip.

**NOTE** ▶ If you try to center a dissolve on an edit point that doesn't have any handles, you will end up with a one-frame transition.

**14**  In the Timeline, press Home to move the playhead to the head of the sequence. Choose Effects > Video Transitions > Dissolve > Cross Dissolve, and play the new transition.

The **pw sound** clip fades up from black. You can also use this approach to fade out a clip at the end of a sequence.

**TIP** You can add buttons to the Timeline button bar for Add Video Transition and Add Audio Transition. Using buttons follows the automatic approach and requires that you first target the edit point or identify the group of edit points.

## Take 2

You walk into the cutting room after a break and see a note from the director: "I want to preview this sequence with dissolves on every edit. Back in 5." Since you don't have much time, you think about the fastest approach to applying dissolves to every edit point in the *Quest* sequence. You'll probably come up with the following:

▶ Duplicate the *Quest* sequence and rename it *Quest_v3_all in*.

▶ Open the new sequence and press Command-A to select all the clips.

▶ Press Command-T to apply transitions to the video clips.

▶ Press Command-A again, then press Command-Option-T to apply transitions to the audio clips.

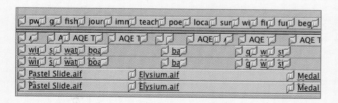

**TIP** If you don't have long enough handles to cover the length of a transition, a shorter transition will be applied.

## Modifying Transitions

When you find a transition that's just right in one location, you may decide to apply it to several other edit points. Rather than reapply a new transition each time, you can simply copy and paste the one that's already in the Timeline.

You can even copy a transition from one sequence in a project to another sequence in a different project. After it is applied, you can easily modify a transition to give it a longer or shorter duration. You can also reassign a different transition as the default.

**1**  In the Quest_v2_transitions sequence, Control-click the edit point between the **began** and **conquest** video clips (above the **Medal Ceremony.aif** music track). From the shortcut menu, choose Add Transition 'Cross Dissolve,' then play the two clips.

Like all other transitions, this has a default duration of 1 second. Let's lengthen this transition to create a more dramatic effect.

**2**  Move the pointer over either edge of the Cross Dissolve icon between the **began** and **conquest** clips. When the pointer changes to a Resize pointer, drag the edge away from the edit point as far as possible, but don't release the mouse button.

Drag the transition edge to lengthen or shorten a transition

As you drag outward from the edit point, an information box indicates how much the transition has been lengthened, along with the new duration. If you cannot drag any farther, you have either reached the limit of one or both of the clips' media, or you've reached the next edit point or transition in the Timeline, as in this example.

**3**   Drag the edge of the icon back toward the edit point until you've reached a new duration of 3 seconds. Release the mouse and play the transition.

> **TIP** ▶ When dragging a transition inward to reduce its duration, temporarily turn-
> ing off snapping will give you greater control, as will zooming in to that area of the
> Timeline.

The longer transition creates the effect of one clip superimposed over another.
Another way to change the length of a transition is to enter a specific duration
amount.

**4**   Control-click the Dip to Color Dissolve between the **who wins** and **my fall** clips, but
not on the actual edit point directly between the two clips.

A shortcut menu appears with options to adjust this transition. Here you can choose
a different transition alignment. You can also use the copy and paste commands to
copy and paste a transition. If you want a specific length for the transition, you can
simply enter it.

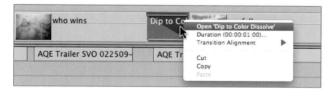

> **TIP** ▶ Always click to the side of the actual edit point to select the transition icon. If
> you click in the middle, the edit point itself will be selected, and a different shortcut
> menu will appear.

**5**   Choose Duration from the shortcut menu. When the small Duration dialog appears,
enter *12* for a new 12-frame duration. Press Return to enter the number, then press
Return again, or click OK, to close the dialog. Play the new transition.

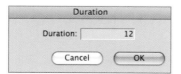

NOTE ▶ Since this tape's source frame rate is 24 frames per second, 12 frames represent a half second. If you are editing in NTSC 29.97, you enter 15 frames for a half second.

Notice that the width of each transition icon in the Timeline also represents its length.

Often, you'll choose a transition that you can use repeatedly throughout the sequence to create or maintain a certain style. If you know you want to apply a specific transition other than the Cross Dissolve, you can make that transition the default video transition. You can also change the default transition length. Let's make the Cube Spin the default transition.

6   In the Effects tab in the Browser, close the Dissolve bin and display the contents of the 3D Simulation bin. To make Cube Spin the default transition, Control-click the Cube Spin icon and choose Set Default Transition from the shortcut menu.

NOTE ▶ The 3D Simulation transitions apply preset 3D changes to clips at the edit point. These might include resizing, flipping, zooming, and/or distorting the image.

Once the default transition is set, a line appears under its name. Any transition can be the default transition, but there can be only one default video transition and one default audio transition at a time. Now let's change the default transition length.

7   If necessary, expand the Browser window to see the Length column, or make the Name column narrower. Click in the Length column for the Cube Spin transition and enter *2.* (2 period), to create a 2-second default transition.

When you apply this transition in the next step, its duration, or length, will be 2 seconds. Because the Cube Spin transition is the new default, you can use the keyboard shortcut to apply it to an edit point.

8   In the Timeline, select the edit point between the **locals** and **survival** clips. Press Command-T to apply the new default transition at this location, then play the transition.

**TIP** ▶ You can also apply a default transition by choosing Effects > Default – [Transition Name], or by Control-clicking the edit point and choosing the transition from the shortcut menu.

Some transitions have additional parameters that can be modified. In the Cube Spin transition, you can change the spin direction, add a border, and so on. You will learn to make parameter changes in the next exercise.

**TIP** ▶ Once a transition is placed into the Timeline, you can copy and paste, or Option-drag, that transition to a different edit point. You can always press Command-Z to undo a step and return to a previous transition, or return the edit point to a simple cut.

After you've applied transitions to your sequence, you will occasionally need to delete one, some, or all of them from your sequence. To delete transitions, follow these steps:

▶   To delete a single transition, select it and press Delete.

▶   To delete a few transitions, select one, Command-click the others, and then press Delete.

▶ To delete all transitions of the same type, press Command-F. In the Find window, type the transition name, such as *cross dissolve*, or just type *cross* to find both cross dissolves and cross fades. Then click Find All. When those transitions are selected, press Delete.

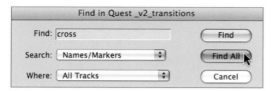

**TIP** ▶ When all of the named transitions are selected, you can also choose to replace them all at one time by choosing a new transition from the Effects menu.

## Take 2

After you've created a new sequence and added the default transition to every edit, the director says that the transitions are too long. They should all be a half second, not a full second. He's going down the hall for more coffee. Can he see the new version when he returns?

▶ Duplicate your previous effort—just in case he changes his mind again.

▶ Set a new default transition for video and audio with shorter lengths.

▶ Find and delete the current transitions.

▶ Select all the clips and apply the new video and audio default transitions by using the keyboard shortcuts.

## Using the Transition Editor

As with other Final Cut Pro functions, you typically have several ways to achieve the same result when adjusting transitions. Most of the time, if you need to adjust a transition's length quickly, you will make changes directly to the transition in the Timeline, as you did in the previous exercise.

An alternative way to change transitions is to work in the Transition Editor, which will appear as a tab over the Viewer window. The Transition Editor displays a graphical representation of the components and parameters of a single transition. In this window, you can make several changes to the transition without having to access a menu.

1   In the Timeline, move the playhead to the fourth clip in the sequence, **journey**, and zoom in to that area. Make sure no other clips or transition icons are selected or you will zoom in to those selected items.

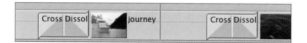

At the head and tail of this clip are cross dissolves. Let's take a closer look at a cross dissolve in the Transition Editor.

2   At the head of the **journey** clip, Control-click one side of the Cross Dissolve icon, and choose Open 'Cross Dissolve' from the shortcut menu. You can also double-click one side of the icon.

**NOTE ►** If you accidentally double-click the middle of the transition over the edit point, the Trim Edit window will open. To close it, click the close button or, in the Timeline, click in a gray area above a video track as though you were deselecting a clip.

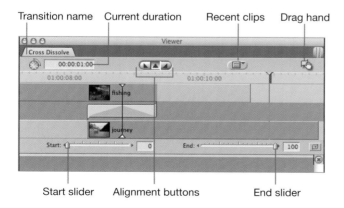

The Transition Editor opens in the Viewer with a graphic representation of the current transition. You have already adjusted or selected some of the options that appear here, such as duration and alignment.

**NOTE ▶** The Start and End percentages beneath the graphic display are typically used for wipes or other types of transitions in which you want the wipe pattern to begin at a midpoint from its original starting location.

3   In the Transition Editor, click the End On Edit alignment button (on the right) and then the Start On Edit alignment button (on the left). Then click the Center On Edit button (in the center).

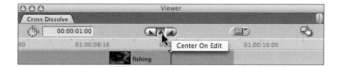

The graphic representation of the dissolve in the Transition Editor changes each time, as does the transition on the edit point in the Timeline.

**TIP ▶** If your window layout is still on the larger Canvas display, you may want to press Control-U to return to the standard window layout in order to see a larger Transition Editor.

4   Click in the Duration field and type *48*, then press Tab, Return, or Enter.

Since the video frame rate for this footage is 24 frames per second (23.98), entering *48* in the Duration field creates a 2-second transition.

5   In the Transition Editor, move the pointer over the transition icon.

The pointer turns into the Roll tool, allowing you to adjust, or roll, the edit point left or right to improve the timing of the edit without changing the transition. Notice the light blue area on the outer edge of each clip. These represent the clips' handles.

**6**   Drag the transition icon left and look at the Canvas two-up display. When you see a big fish tail on the left frame, release the mouse button and play the transition.

In the Timeline, the edit point and transition appear later in the sequence.

You can also drag a transition from the Transition Editor to a different edit point.

**7**   In the upper-right corner of the Transition Editor window, drag the drag hand icon to the previous edit point between the **going** and **fishing** clips.

Applying a transition from the Transition Editor replaces whichever transition was on an edit point with all the current transition parameters displayed in the Transition Editor. If there aren't enough handles to apply the current transition length, a transition is applied to the maximum extent of the handles.

Let's make changes to another type of dissolve: the Dip to Color Dissolve you added later in the sequence. To move directly to that transition, you can use the Find function.

**8**   Click in the Timeline and press Command-F to open the Find window. In the Find field, type *dip to color*, and click Find.

The playhead moves directly to the first Dip to Color Dissolve transition in the sequence and the clip is selected. In the Canvas, you see jellyfish in the first frame of the transition.

9    Control-click the Dip to Color Dissolve icon and choose Open 'Dip to Color Dissolve' from the shortcut menu. If it's still selected, you can press Return.

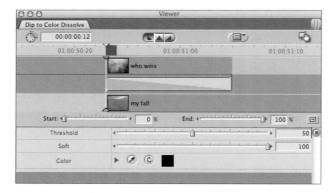

This dissolve has a few more parameters than the default Cross Dissolve transition, including color controls where you can choose the color that a clip dips to during the transition.

**10** In the Transition Editor, click the Select Color eyedropper in the color controls.

**11** Move the eyedropper into the Canvas window and click the upper jellyfish. Then play this transition.

In the color controls, the color picker changes from the default black to the color you clicked in the Canvas, and the transition dips to this color between the two clips.

**TIP** ▶ To search or preview different colors before selecting one, select the eyedropper and drag around the Canvas image. The color picker will reflect whatever color the eyedropper picks up. When you see the color you want, release the mouse button.

## Changing Transition Parameters

Dissolves are the simplest types of transitions. When you apply a transition with several parameters, such as a Page Peel or Cube Spin, you must modify the parameters in the Transition Editor. The more complex a transition is, the more parameters you can adjust.

After you've adjusted a transition to your liking, you can save it as a favorite transition and apply it to other edit points. As you work with complex transitions, you will find that most of them can play in real time; but some may have to be *rendered*, which you will do in the next exercise.

**NOTE** ▶ When you apply a new transition to a transition already placed at an edit point, the new transition replaces the existing one, and the new transition's duration is conformed to the existing duration.

1   Move the playhead to the edit point between the **immersed** and **teachers** clips. Choose Effects > Video Transitions > Iris > Star Iris. Play this transition, then reposition the playhead over the edit point.

Parking the playhead on the transition allows you to make adjustments in the Transition Editor while viewing them in the Canvas. Make sure you do this in the following steps before you make changes.

**NOTE** ▸ The term *iris* gets its name from film and video cameras. Like your eye, the iris mechanism opens or closes to change the amount of light coming through the lens. Each Iris transition, utilizing a specific shape, opens to reveal the next clip.

2   To open this transition, double-click one side of the transition icon (not the edit point itself).

Under the transition graphic display are parameters that can be adjusted via slider or numerical-entry box. Some parameters in other effects use pop-up menus. Most parameters are self-explanatory after you've changed the parameter values and looked at the effect in the Canvas.

**NOTE** ▸ Clicking the tiny triangle at the end of each slider will change the numerical value of that parameter by single increments.

**3**   Experiment with the different settings for this transition as you view the results in the Canvas window. When you are through making changes, click the Reset button (the red X) to return to the default settings for this effect, and make sure the playhead is once again positioned on the edit point.

Many transitions, including this Star Iris effect, have a border whose thickness you can adjust. When the border value is 0, you see a hard edge. When the value is greater than 0, a border color appears.

**4**   To create a thin border, type *10* in the Border number field, and press Tab.

Rather than use the default black border, let's select a border color from one of the Final Cut Pro color pickers.

**5**   Click the black color picker in the color controls. In the Colors window, if a color wheel appears and it's black, drag the control on the vertical slider all the way up to see the brightest colors.

**TIP**   You can resize the Colors window by dragging the lower-right corner.

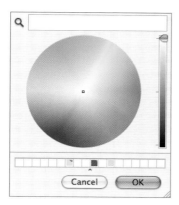

At the top of the Colors window are icons representing five color-picking layouts: Color Wheel, Color Sliders, Color Palettes, Image Palettes, and Crayons.

**6**   Click each icon to see how that color picker displays color choices. Then click the color wheel icon and drag your pointer around inside the color wheel.

As you move over a color, that color appears in the horizontal swatch above the color wheel.

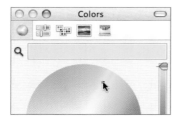

To the left of the color swatch is a magnifying glass. This tool is similar to the eye-dropper you used in the previous exercise except that it can select a color from anywhere on your display. It differs in that it magnifies the colors so you can see exactly what color you're picking before you click it.

**7**   Click the magnifying glass next to the color swatch. In the Canvas, position it over the yellow seaweed beneath the seal, and click.

In the Colors window, the color swatch changes to reflect your most recent selection.

Many television shows, networks, and companies repeatedly use a favorite color for borders, text, backgrounds, and other elements as part of a brand style. If you think you might use this particular color in a different transition elsewhere in your sequence, you can store it in the saved color swatches.

**NOTE ▶** This is the Mac OS X Colors window, so the saved color will be available for use in other projects or applications on the same computer.

8   Click in the large color swatch and drag down into the color palette area beneath the color wheel. Release the color in one of the squares. Then click OK.

**TIP ▶** By dragging down on the color palette area, you can expose additional squares that can be used to store favorite colors.

The border is now the same yellow you picked from the seaweed image.

**TIP ▶** To change an existing color in the Transition Editor, click the triangle next to the Select Color eyedropper. Drag the S (Saturation) and B (Brightness) sliders to adjust the amount and brightness of the color. Drag the H (Hue) slider to change the actual color you picked.

Another parameter commonly found in Iris transitions is Center. It allows you to reposition the center point of the iris movement to anywhere in the image. Let's position it over the seal's chest.

9   Select the point control (the crosshair button) for the Center parameter in the Transition Editor. Move the pointer into the Canvas window and click the seal's chest. Play the transition.

The Star Iris transition now begins over the seal.

**NOTE ▶** The red crosshair icon in the image represents the current center point.

Now that you've customized this transition, you may want to save it in the Favorites bin to use again. Before you save this transition, make sure you can see the Favorites bin in the Effects tab in the Browser.

**10** In the Effects tab, click the disclosure triangle next to the Favorites bin to display its contents. Unless you have added your own favorite effects to this bin, it will be empty.

**11** Click the Viewer window, and choose Effects > Make Favorite Effect, or press Option-F. You can also drag the drag hand icon to the Favorites bin and release the mouse button when the bin becomes highlighted.

In the Favorites folder, a new Star Iris transition with all of your changes appears. You can rename any favorite effect to reflect some parameter you changed, such as *star yellow border*.

**MORE INFO ▶** Some shows use a logo to wipe across the screen, transitioning from one scene to another. In Final Cut Pro 7, you can create this type of wipe—called an *alpha transition*—and once it's created, reuse and retime it. You can learn more about alpha transitions in the FCP User Manual.

## Previewing and Rendering Effects

Final Cut Pro can play multiple streams, or layers of effects, in real time. How the transitions are played back, however, depends on your computer hardware and video format, as well as some option settings that you can choose.

You sometimes have to give up either image quality or a consistent frame rate to see all the effects play together. Or you may have to preview, or *render*, the transition.

Rendering processes a selected item in the sequence—in this case the transition between two clips—and creates a separate clip. That clip is stored in the Render Files folder on the designated scratch disk and is played back in the sequence as a separate but invisible clip—meaning that it does not appear in the Browser or the Timeline.

A render bar in the Timeline displays a color for each effect that indicates whether it needs to be rendered. As you applied transitions throughout this lesson, you were probably aware of the changing colors on the render bar.

1    In the upper left of the Timeline under the sequence tabs, click the RT pop-up and notice that Unlimited RT is selected. Then release the mouse button.

You have been working in Unlimited RT. This setting tells Final Cut Pro to do what it must to play as many effects as possible in real time, even if it has to drop out some of the effect parameters, or not play every frame. The other mode is Safe RT. This option tells Final Cut Pro to play an effect only if it can do so without dropping frames.

NOTE ▶ It's acceptable to drop an occasional frame while previewing and playing effects. When you are ready to output your sequence in a later lesson, you will change these settings to achieve the highest quality without dropping frames.

2    In the Timeline, press Shift-Z and scan the ruler area for any yellow or orange bars. From the RT pop-up menu, choose Safe RT and release the mouse button.

Depending on your computer's configuration, you may see a red render bar above the Ripple Dissolve you added earlier in the sequence.

**3**   Click the RT pop-up again and look at the quality settings under Playback Video Quality and Playback Frame Rate.

The lower the quality and frame rate, the more effects Final Cut Pro will be able to play in real time. Choosing Dynamic ensures that at any given moment you will have the best possible quality at the best possible frame rate while maximizing the number of effects that will play in real time.

By choosing Safe RT, however, you are asking Final Cut Pro to play only those effects it can safely play in real time without reducing quality or dropping frames.

**4**   Scan the Timeline again and notice the change of color in the render bars.

The render bar actually contains two thin regions. The upper region represents video; the lower region represents audio. A render bar can appear in the Timeline ruler above a transition, or above the body of a clip when a speed or other type of effect has been applied.

When no effects have been applied, as is the case for the audio clips, a dark gray line appears, indicating that a clip with no effects applied appears in this location.

**NOTE ▶** If no clip is present at a specific place in the sequence, the render status bar will be blank at that location.

▶ **Render Bar Colors**

Different colored lines in the render bar indicate the status of an effect or the capability of Final Cut Pro to play the effect in real time given the current RT settings. The render status of an effect will depend on the speed of the computer you are using. The status of an effect is indicated by one of the following colors:

- ▶ **Red**—Must be rendered to play in real time.
- ▶ **Orange**—Exceeds the computer's real-time playback capabilities, but can still play if Unlimited RT is selected, although it may drop frames.
- ▶ **Yellow**—Can play in real time but may approximate certain attributes.
- ▶ **Green**—Will play in real time but not at full quality.
- ▶ **Dark green**—Can be played and output in real time with no rendering.
- ▶ **Blue-gray**—Already rendered.
- ▶ **Dark gray**—No rendering required.

**5**  Move the playhead before the Ripple Dissolve transition and play it.

The outgoing clip plays at normal play speed until it gets to the transition, when *Unrendered* appears in the Canvas image area for the duration of the transition. In Safe RT mode, Final Cut Pro doesn't even try to play this effect in real time. Yet there is a way to preview this effect.

**NOTE** ▶ Your playback results may vary depending on the processing power of your Mac.

**6**  Drag the playhead back before the transition once again. This time, press Option-P. You could also press Option-\ (backslash), or choose Mark > Play > Every Frame.

The clip plays at normal speed until the playhead reaches the transition. At that point, the clip slows down to process the transition, then picks up again when it has passed the transition area.

When Final Cut Pro can't play all the effects, even when set to the Unlimited RT mode, previewing is a good way to get a sense of the effect without rendering it.

> **TIP** ▶ If you use Option-P a lot, you might consider adding that function, Play Every Frame, to the Timeline or Canvas button bars.

**7** This time, drag the playhead manually through the transition area to see unrendered transition frames. Press the Left Arrow and Right Arrow keys to move through it frame by frame.

This is somewhat like scrubbing an effect. But to see this effect play in real time in Safe RT mode, you must render it. There are three render options:

▶ **Render Selection**—Select one or more effects and render the selected items.

▶ **Render All**—Render all items that need rendering.

▶ **Render Only**—Render only those items that are of a specific render status color.

**8** Click the Sequence menu and look at each of the three Render options.

**9** In the Timeline, click the Ripple Dissolve transition once. To render it, choose Sequence > Render Selection, but don't release the mouse button.

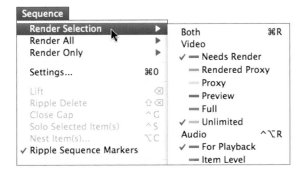

In the Render Selection submenu, the different render status colors appear. If the render color that is above the Ripple Dissolve in the Timeline is not checked in this menu, your effect will not be rendered.

**10** Make sure you see a checkmark next to the red render bar, or whatever color appears in your Timeline, and choose Sequence > Render Selection > Video, or press Command-R.

A progress indicator bar appears. When rendering is complete, a blue-gray render status bar appears above the transition, indicating that it has been rendered.

**NOTE ▶** If a transition has already been rendered, changing its duration or any other aspect will require it to be rendered again.

**11** In the Timeline, click the RT pop-up and choose Unlimited RT. This is the best mode for trying out different effects.

**TIP ▶** To change the scratch disk designation where render files are saved, press Shift-Q to open the System Settings window.

## Editor's Cut

Now that you know how to add and modify transitions, you can duplicate the original *Quest* sequence and apply a different transition to each edit point. If you want to go back a few additional steps, you can make additional revisions to the *Quest* sequence to create a true editor's cut.

For example, you might roll edit points to hit different narration cues, slip clips to choose different content, or ripple clips to lengthen or shorten the sequence. You can apply these trimming tools to clips and edit points that already have a transition. Don't forget to begin by customizing the sequence, which could include changing the track heights and giving the sequence a color label.

## Lesson Review

1. From what two places can you choose a transition effect?

2. When you use the automatic approach to applying a transition, what must you do first?

3. In what ways can you target a clip or clips when you want to apply multiple transitions?

4. What are three ways to change the duration of a transition in the Timeline?

5. What are the three ways a transition can be aligned to an edit point?

6. How can Command-C and Command-V be used on transitions?

7. How do you open the Transition Editor?

8. How are more complex transitions different from dissolves?

9. What RT setting should you choose when you want to preview as many effects in your sequence as possible?

10. In what three ways can you save a favorite transition?

11. How do you set a new default transition?

*Answers*

1. Choose transition effects from the Effects tab in the Browser and from the Effects menu.

2. Before applying a transition from the Effects menu, you must target the edit point.

3. Select a clip, select a group of clips, set In and Out points, or select all the clips in the sequence.

4. Drag the edge of the transition icon; Control-click the transition icon, choose Duration from the shortcut menu, and enter an amount in the Duration window; or open the Transition Editor and change it in the Duration field.

5. Use Center On Edit, Start On Edit, and End On Edit.

6. Selecting a transition and pressing Command-C copies the transition. Deselecting the transition, moving the playhead to the target edit point, and pressing Command-V pastes the copied transition.

7. Either Control-click one side of the transition icon and choose Open [transition] from the shortcut menu, or double-click one side of the icon in a sequence clip.

8. They have additional parameters, such as border width and color, that can be adjusted in the Transition Editor.

9.   Choose Unlimited RT and Dynamic.

10.   From the Transition Editor, drag the drag hand icon to the Effects tab and release it in the Favorites bin; choose Effects > Make Favorite; or press Option-F.

11.   Control-click the transition in the Effects tab and choose Set Default Transition from the shortcut menu.

## Keyboard Shortcuts

| | |
|---|---|
| **Command-C** | Copy a selected transition |
| **Option-F** | Save a favorite transition |
| **Option-P** | Preview a transition (Play Every Frame command) |
| **Shift-Q** | Open the System Settings window |
| **Command-R** | Render a selected transition |
| **Option-R** | Render all transitions in the Timeline |
| **Command-T** | Apply default video transition |
| **Command-Option-T** | Apply default audio transition |
| **Command-V** | Paste a copied transition |
| **Option-\ (backslash)** | Preview a transition (Play Every Frame command) |

# 10

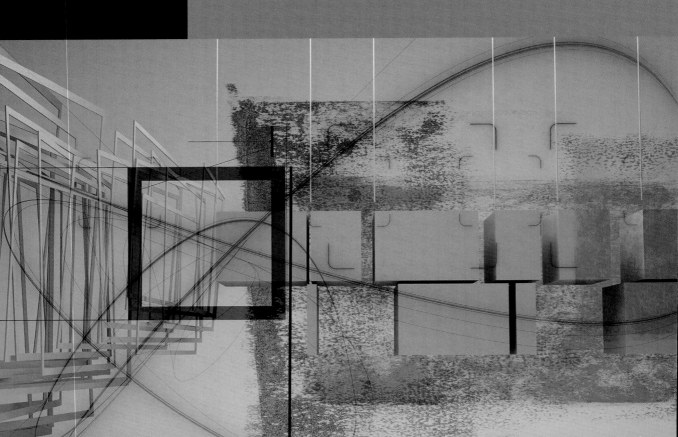

# Mixing Audio Tracks

Another aspect of completing your sequence is mixing multiple audio tracks into one balanced, overall sound. In Final Cut Pro, you can work with up to 99 tracks of audio in one sequence.

In this lesson, you will add additional tracks to the Timeline, edit music and sound effects, and blend these tracks together with interview clips to create a final mix. You'll also apply additional Timeline controls to help manage and preview audio clips, and work with two separate tools for mixing audio and recording your own voiceover.

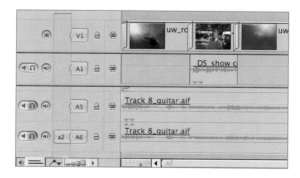

Audio controls and a static audio region in the Timeline

## Preparing the Project for Mixing

Before you dive into mixing audio tracks, you should take a moment to evaluate the current status of the audio in your sequence. Are there enough sound effects? Would a different music track improve the piece? Would the addition of audio transitions help smooth out any rough edges, as they did in the previous lesson? Once you determine what's needed, you can import additional audio clips to complete the sequence. You can also add tracks to the sequence in preparation for the new audio clips.

1   In the Lessons folder on your hard disk, open the Lesson 10 Project file. In the Timeline, play the *Believe Mix_v1* sequence.

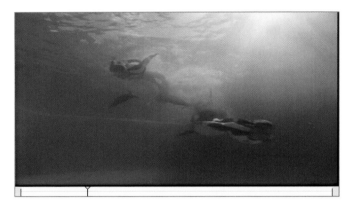

This promo was cut together using *Believe* interview and behavior clips. In many of the behavior clips, rehearsal music was mixed in with sounds of the whales in the water. Since a new music track is going to be added, these clips were edited as video-only clips, so the music tracks wouldn't compete. There was no audio attached to the original underwater whale clips. However, these video clips might benefit from some sound effects.

2   In the Browser, display the contents of the Sound Effects bin. Open the Scuba Breathing.aif clip and play a few breaths of it.

Sometimes, you edit a sound effect to match a specific action in your sequence, such as a door slam or a balloon pop. Other times, you just need an ambient sound to give an image some depth. This scuba sound effect might add some fullness to the underwater clips.

> ▶ **Working with Soundtrack Pro 3**
>
> The effects in the Sound Effects bin were all exported from Soundtrack Pro. In that program, you can search for additional music or sound effect files to use in this or other sequences, and export those sound effects as individual clips for use in Final Cut Pro. The royalty-free music loops and sound effect files in Soundtrack Pro provide an excellent way to complete the audio of a project.
>
> You can add scoring markers to a sequence in Final Cut Pro, identifying where you want certain sound effects to occur. You can then export that sequence from FCP, import it into Soundtrack Pro, and add music or sound effects clips at those scoring markers. You can also send a sequence to Soundtrack Pro to clean up audio pops and make other changes or corrections.

**3**   Open the **Water Lake 1.aif** clip and play a few seconds of it. Then lower the volume to −21 dB, and play it again.

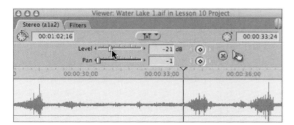

Some effects sound outrageously unrealistic at full volume. But when you lower the volume, they sound more believable. With this clip's volume lowered, it can double for a whale's splashing sound.

> **TIP** ▶ When you lower the volume of a master clip in the Browser, every time you edit that clip into a sequence it will already be at a rough mix level.

**4**   From the Music bin, open the **Track 8_guitar.aif** clip and play about 20 seconds of it.

This is the music track you will use to help dramatize the promo. Since you already have interview sound bites in the sequence, you will have to raise and lower the volume of this clip so you can hear the on-camera individuals when they speak. This is sometimes referred to as *animating* the volume levels. In this lesson, you will learn two ways to animate volume.

Before you edit these new clips, you need to add more audio tracks to the sequence. You need at least two tracks for sound effects and two tracks for the music score. Rather than add these tracks individually, you can add them all at one time.

**5**   Click the Timeline, and choose Sequence > Insert Tracks.

An Insert Tracks dialog opens in which you can select the types of tracks you want to insert as well as the number and location. You can insert tracks after the last track or before the base, or lowest, track number. Even though the Insert Video Tracks check-box is selected, the number of tracks is set to 0 by default, so no new video tracks will be inserted.

**TIP** ▸ You can open the Delete Tracks dialog by choosing Sequence > Delete Tracks. Here you can delete all unused video or audio tracks at the same time.

**6**   In the Insert Tracks dialog, enter *4* in the Insert Audio Tracks field. Leave the default After Last Track selected, and click OK.

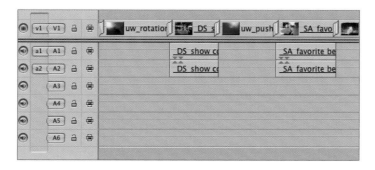

Whenever you work closely with audio in the Timeline, it's a good idea to display the audio level overlays to help you adjust the volume, and to view the audio waveforms as a visual reference to clip content. Let's turn on those functions using keyboard shortcuts.

**7**    Press Option-W to turn on the audio level overlays, and press Command-Option-W to turn on audio waveforms in the Timeline. To make the audio waveforms easier to read, press Shift-T to increase the Timeline track height.

> **TIP** ▶ If you added audio buttons in Lesson 7, you can click those to turn these functions on and off.

With audio waveforms turned on, you can take a closer look at the clips in the sequence. One thing to look for is whether there are any "dead" audio tracks. Sometimes an audio clip is captured as a stereo pair but the audio is recorded on only one track. Having an additional track of dead audio in the sequence can be misleading since it doesn't accurately represent the clip.

Look at the clips in the Timeline. The **narration_2** clip has no audio waveform on the A2 portion of this clip, yet a stereo pair indicator connects the two clips. You can unlink the stereo pair clip and remove the empty track of the clip.

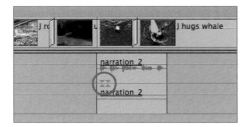

**8**    Select the **narration_2** clip. Choose Modify > Stereo Pair, or press Option-L. Deselect the clip.

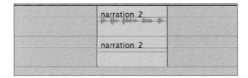

The stereo pair indicator no longer appears. You can turn off or on the stereo pair status of any clip. This allows you to remove the dead audio from the clip, or to change the volume on each track independently when, for instance, two separate microphones were used for recording.

**9** On the A2 track, select the **narration_2** clip, and press Delete.

**TIP** ▶ If you want to boost the audio for a single mono clip, you can copy and paste the clip beneath itself, select both audio clips, and make them a stereo pair.

**10** Play the **narration_2** clip and watch the audio meters.

This mono clip plays in the left audio channel only. Typically, you'll want the narration or voiceover to be heard in both channels. To direct this audio to both channels, you can pan it to the center by choosing that command from the Modify menu in the Viewer Audio tab, or by using a keyboard shortcut.

**11** In the Timeline, select the **narration_2** clip, and choose Modify > Audio > Pan Center, or press Control-. (period). Play the clip again.

Now the single mono track of audio is panned to the center and heard through both channels.

**NOTE** ▶ If you double-click this clip to open it in the Viewer, you will see a pan setting of 0, which represents center. To pan a mono audio track left, enter *–1* in the Pan field, and to pan it right, enter *1*. With a stereo clip, *–1* indicates that the left and right audio channels will be heard in the left and right speakers, respectively; *1* indicates that the left and right channels will be reversed.

## Editing and Organizing Audio Effects

The most important aspect of organizing audio tracks is to edit similar types of clips into the same or neighboring tracks. This will make them easier to modify. There are ways in which you can select, monitor, and modify all the clips on a single track. Placing all of the sound effects on one track, the dialogue on another track, music on still another, and so on, will make it much easier to modify them.

Some editors like to edit their sound effects beneath the video clips they support, and place the music clips on the lowest tracks. Others prefer placing the music tracks beneath the dialogue or interview clips to view them as a reference when mixing the volume levels. You can experiment to see what approach works best for you and your sequence. Just be consistent with the tracks you select when editing similar clips in any given sequence.

To edit and organize the sound effects in this exercise, you will use editing techniques different from those you learned in previous lessons.

1   With the `Track 8_guitar.aif` clip in the Viewer, drag the drag hand icon down into the Timeline to the A5 and A6 tracks, and release the clip at the head of the sequence as an overwrite edit. Play some of this music track in the sequence.

You might be able to complete some sequences by simply mixing a music clip into the existing audio sources. Other sequences might require several music sources. And others, such as this one, require sound effects to add some atmosphere to the whale behavior shots.

2   Return the playhead to the head of the sequence. Patch the audio Source controls to the A3 and A4 tracks.

Since the A3 and A4 tracks are empty, you don't have to worry about overwriting any other material.

**3** In the Viewer, click the Recent Clips pop-up menu and choose the **Scuba Breathing.aif** clip. Lower the volume to –10 dB. Mark an In point just before the sound begins, and edit this entire clip as an overwrite edit.

**NOTE ▶** As you edit sound effects, it's helpful to lower the volume to a background level, even though you may need to readjust that level when you mix it with other clips in the sequence.

Three underwater whale clips are in this sequence. The first two, toward the beginning of the sequence, are now supported by this scuba sound effect. Later in this lesson, you will animate the volume so you don't hear the scuba sound while the individuals are speaking. Let's split off a portion of this sound effect and reposition it under the third underwater clip.

**4** Position the playhead over the middle of the **_SA_favorite behavior** clip. Press B to select the Razor Blade tool, snap it to the playhead in the A3 or A4 track, and click to create a new edit point in the **Scuba Breathing.aif** clip.

When sound effects are more generic, such as this one, it's easy to work with them in the Timeline. You can copy and paste them, or razor blade and reposition them, and they will still sound pretty good.

**5** Press A to return to the default Selection tool, and drag the second **Scuba Breathing .aif** clip to the right beneath the **uw_propel jump** clip (before the **narration_2** clip). To allow room for effects on either side of this clip, drag the In and Out points to match the length of **uw_propel jump**.

An easy way to add a new sound effect is to mark the length of the corresponding video clip in the Timeline.

**6**    In the Timeline, move the playhead over the previous clip, **J rotations**, and press X
to mark the length of this clip. From the Viewer's Recent Clips pop-up menu, choose
**Water Lake 1.aif**, and edit this clip as an overwrite edit.

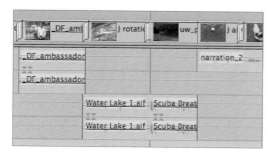

This clip does not appear to be long in the Timeline, but it has plenty of media
handles so that you can later add a transition at the beginning or end of the clip.
To add this sound effect to the remaining video clips, you can drag a copy of it and
trim it longer.

**7**    Select **Water Lake 1.aif**. Option-drag the clip right. Snap the new clip's In point to the
end of **Scuba Breathing.aif**. Release the Option key, then release the clip as an overwrite edit.

To trim this clip's Out point to the end of the sequence, you could drag the edit
point right and snap it to the other clips' Out points. Or you can extend it using an
extend edit.

**8**    Snap the playhead to the end of the sequence, select the **Water Lake 1.aif** clip's Out
point, and press E.

> **TIP**    For a more complex sound mix, you can insert new tracks and add additional
> sound effects beneath the current effects. To insert a new track between two existing
> tracks, in the Timeline patch panel Control-click the track that you want the new
> track to follow, and choose Add Track.

## Take 2

The sound mixer is out of town. But the producer wants to screen the sequence fully mixed to hear how the sound effects are working. So you have to make certain effects sound realistic.

For example, when you play the **performance_S spray jump** in the Timeline, you see that the peak moment is midway in the clip, when Steve jumps out of the water and over the spray. This is where a big crowd cheer should be. You will have to alter an applause clip to make this happen.

▶ From the Sound Effects bin in the Browser, open **Arena Crowd Cheer.aif**. Play until after the crowd roar settles down, then mark an In point and enter a 5-second duration for this clip. Lower the volume to –15 dB.

▶ In the Timeline, position the playhead at the head of the **performance_S spray jump** clip, and edit the **Arena Crowd Cheer.aif** clip as an overwrite edit.

▶ In the Timeline, position the playhead where Steve is out of the water and at the top of the spray.

▶ In the Viewer, mark an In point in the **Arena Crowd Cheer.aif** clip a few frames into the crowd roar, and create a 6-second duration. Edit this clip as an overwrite edit. If necessary, add a transition to smooth the edit point. Now it sounds as though the crowd is responding to Steve's jump.

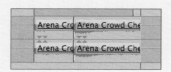

## Monitoring and Adjusting Audio Levels

After you've prepared your sequence, adding sound effects and music, you can set the relative audio level for each clip in the sequence. You begin by monitoring and setting the levels for the highest-priority tracks—those tracks that must be heard above all others. Often, those are the clips with sync sound, dialogue, or narration.

In this exercise, you will use another set of Timeline track controls, audio controls, to monitor individual tracks. You'll also select all the clips on one track and adjust the volume for a group of selected clips.

**TIP** Before you begin monitoring audio levels, set your computer to a comfortable sound level.

1   Move the playhead to the beginning of the sequence. In the lower left of the Timeline, click the Audio Controls button, which is represented by a speaker icon.

This expands the audio controls area of your Timeline window to reveal the Mute and Solo buttons. The Mute buttons are the speaker icons on the left, and the Solo buttons are the headphone icons on the right. When you solo a track, you hear just that track and no others. This is a good way to isolate a track when setting its volume. When you mute a track, you don't hear it at all.

### Setting Decibel Levels

In digital audio, no part of the *overall* audio signal of the *combined* tracks may exceed 0 dB (decibels), or the sound will be clipped and distorted. This differs from analog audio, which uses a different dB scale and often averages sounds at around 0 dB.

In order not to exceed the 0 dB level for all tracks, you set the primary audio tracks—such as dialogue and narration—well below that level, perhaps between –12 dB and –6 dB. You might set the music volume to –15 or –18.

These settings allow you to combine the sound clips with an overall level well below the 0 dB peaking level, at about –6 to –3 dB. If, however, adding audio tracks causes the volume to peak, you have to adjust your mix accordingly.

2   To hear how the music plays alone against the video, click the A5 and A6 Solo buttons, and play the sequence. As the sequence is playing, click the A1 and A2 Solo buttons to add the sync sound to the mix.

Clicking a Solo button isolates that track while simultaneously muting all the other tracks. When you click a Track Visibility control (the green button next to the Solo button) as the sequence is playing, it stops the sequence. When you click a Solo or Mute button, it adds or drops that track from the preview without interrupting the sequence playback.

**3**  Toggle off the Solo buttons for the A5 and A6 music tracks. Play the sequence again and look at the audio meters as you play just the A1 and A2 tracks.

The audio levels of these clips are fairly close. However, some of the sync sound and narration clips are a little below –12 dB, and other clips are a little above –12 dB. To give these clips a more uniform level, you can apply a function that normalizes the audio to a specific dB level.

Since you will want to modify all the clips on the A1 and A2 tracks, select them all using yet another selection tool.

**4**  To select all the clips on the A1 and A2 tracks, press T to select the Select Track Forward tool, the third tool in the Tool palette. On the A1 track, click the **_DS_show concept** clip.

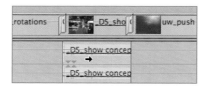

Five track selection tools are in the Tool palette, and each one either selects the clips located before or after the place you click, or it selects all the tracks. With the current clips selected, you can modify them as a group.

**5**  Choose Modify > Audio > Apply Normalization Gain. In the Apply Normalization Gain dialog, enter –6 in the "Normalize to" dBFS field, and click OK.

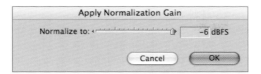

In this dialog, the dB level is referred to as dBFS, which stands for *decibels full scale.* This means that the current highest volume of each clip will be raised to the level you entered. When you play these clips again, they will peak at −6 dB in the audio meters.

**NOTE ▶** In this situation, Final Cut Pro applies an audio filter to the clip that boosts the volume level, or gain. If you double-click one of the filtered clips, and click the Filters tab in the Viewer, you can see the specific gain adjustment. You will work with filters in a later lesson.

6    Press A to return to the default Selection tool. Play the A1 and A2 clips again and notice the change in the audio meters. Now the sync sound and narration clips sound a little more robust.

Let's listen to the sound effects in conjunction with the music track.

7    Click the A1 and A2 Solo buttons to remove the sync sound from the mix, and toggle on the A3–A6 Solo buttons. Play the music and effects together.

The current volume level of the breathing effect is a little high and distracting.

**NOTE ▶** In many productions, music and effects are mixed together for final output, while the narration or dialogue remains on a separate track.

8    In the first **Scuba Breathing.aif** clip, drag the audio level overlay down to −16 dB. Play this clip again with the music.

**TIP** ▶ For greater control as you drag an audio level overlay, press the Command key. You can also double-click a clip to open it in the Viewer and enter a volume adjustment in the Level field.

If you use an effect several times in the same sequence, you may very likely want to play all uses of that effect at the same volume level. Rather than change the volume of each clip individually, you can copy and paste levels from one clip to another.

**9**   In the Timeline, select the first **Scuba Breathing.aif** clip. Press Command-C to copy the clip.

When you copy a clip, you copy everything about it, including the audio levels. Since you have another **Scuba Breathing.aif** clip later in the sequence, you can paste just the volume level from the first sound effect to the next.

**10**   Control-click the second **Scuba Breathing.aif** clip in the sequence. From the shortcut menu, choose Paste Attributes. In the Paste Attributes dialog, under the Audio Attributes column on the right, select the Levels checkbox. Watch the pink audio level overlay in the clip as you click OK.

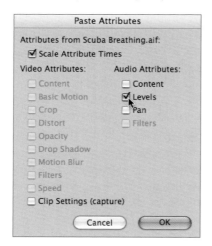

You can also modify the levels of more than one clip at a time. You do this by selecting the clips you want to change, and then modifying the overall gain or volume for those selected clips.

**11**   Play the first **Water Lake 1.aif** clip in the sequence.

With the music playing up full, it's a little hard to hear the sound effect at its current volume level. You will need to raise the volume on both of the **Water Lake 1.aif** clips in the sequence by the same amount, so let's adjust the clip levels at the same time.

**12** Select the first **Water Lake 1.aif** clip, and Command-click the second clip to add it to the selection. Choose Modify > Levels. In the Gain Adjust dialog, enter 6 as the dB level in the "Adjust gain by" field. Watch the audio level overlays in the Timeline as you click OK. Play the clips again.

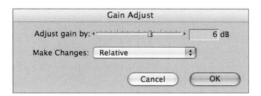

In the Gain Adjust dialog, you are not entering a specific or absolute dB value. This is a relative adjustment. By entering 6, you are raising the volume 6 dB from its current level. Because both clips were selected, you raised the volume on both clips at the same time by the same amount.

Now let's focus on how the music mixes with the sync sound. At full volume, the music overpowers the individuals talking, so you will adjust the music volume to create an optimum mix level. For music, that is typically around −15 dB or even −18 dB, depending on whether the music genre is a soft ballad or driving hard rock.

**NOTE ▶** In the next exercise, you will raise and lower the sound level within the music clip, allowing you to fade it up to a fuller level when the individuals aren't speaking.

**13** Solo the A1, A2, A5, and A6 audio tracks. Play the **_DS_show open** clip with the music track. Bring the music volume down to about −15 dB so it doesn't overpower the sync sound clips.

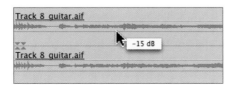

**TIP** ▶ You can modify the music volume on the fly as you play other sequence clips by using a mouse with a scrolling wheel or ball. Double-click a clip to open it in the Viewer, position the mouse pointer over the Level slider, and rotate the scroll wheel up and down as the sequence plays.

## Take 2

The producers for this project are sticklers for detail. You've got to polish the existing sound effects before you can play back the sequence for them. To complete adjusting levels in this sequence, listen to the crowd cheer sound effects under the **performance_S spray jump** video clip. Solo the sound effect with the music clip, and adjust the effect to an appropriate mix level. And don't forget to add cross fades to all the sound effects to smooth some of the more abrupt edit points. It's a good thing you know a handy tool (Select Track Forward) to select the sound effects, and a keyboard shortcut (Command-Option-T) to add cross fades to all of them at once!

## Applying Transitions to Fade Volume

You've finished the lion's share of audio mixing, which set the audio levels of individual clips at their appropriate mix levels. Sometimes that may be enough to complete the sound mix for a project. In this sequence, the music track was lowered so that the sync sound clips could be heard, but the music now sounds weak when no one is speaking. By changing the music volume to rise and fall around the sync sound clips, you can create a dynamic feeling to this soundtrack.

There are two ways you can change, or *animate,* the sound levels. One method involves adding an edit point and an audio cross fade where you want to change an audio level. The other method, which you will learn in the next exercise, uses keyframes. To ensure that you're working with all the volume changes made in the previous exercises, you will open a new sequence with those changes already applied.

1   In the Sequences bin in the Browser, open the *Believe Mix_v2_blade* sequence.

     **NOTE** ▶ If you made all of the changes in the previous exercises, you can continue working with that sequence.

For this exercise, you don't need to evaluate audio levels or clip content, so you can turn off the audio waveforms. Since you will be focusing on the music and sync sound clips, you can mute the A3 and A4 sound effects tracks.

**2**  In the *Believe Mix_v2_blade* sequence in the Timeline, press Command-Option-W to turn off the waveform displays. Make sure no Solo buttons are on and then click the Mute buttons for the A3 and A4 tracks. If you added the Display Waveform button in Lesson 7, you can click it to turn off the display.

**NOTE ▶** Another reason to turn off the audio waveforms when you don't need them is that they use additional RAM, just like video thumbnails.

One way to animate the music volume is to divide the music track into separate clips, then change the volume within each new music clip.

**3**  Move the playhead to snap to the In point of the **_DS_show concept** clip. Press B to select the Razor Blade tool, and click the A5 track at the playhead location. Press A to return to the default Selection tool.

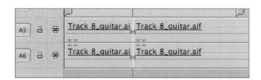

A new edit point is added to the music clip, creating two separate clips.

**4**  To change the volume of the first **Track 8_guitar.aif** clip, drag the audio level overlay up to 0 dB. Play through the edit point to hear the change in volume.

This successfully gives you two different levels, but cutting from one audio level to another makes for an abrupt transition. Applying a cross fade would help smooth the fade from one audio level to the next.

5   Select the edit point between the first two music clips, and press Command-Option-T to add the default audio cross fade between these two clips. Play the edit point again.

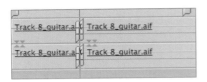

**NOTE** ▶ If you hear beeps as you play these clips, change the Real-time Audio Mixing to 10 or 12 tracks in the General tab of User Preferences.

To proceed with the razor blade and cross fade approach, you would repeat steps 3 through 5, adding edit points, changing the clip volume, and applying cross fades. But first, let's change the Timeline track display so the A1 and A5 tracks appear on top of each other. This will make it easier to see where you need to create the new edit points.

6   In the far right of the Timeline, at the audio/video divider, drag the lower thumb tab in the vertical scroll bar down until just the A1 track is in the static region. Now drag the blue scroller down to scroll through the remaining tracks until the A5 track is as close as possible to the static A1 track.

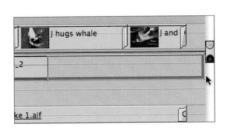

Creating a static track

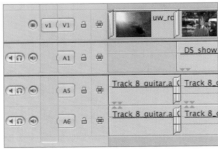

Scrolling tracks to display A5 against A1

**NOTE** ▶ Depending on the screen resolution and the size of your Timeline window, the blue scroller may not appear. To make the tracks taller, either resize the Timeline or press Shift-T.

**7** Press B to select the Razor Blade tool. In the A5 track, snap the razor blade to the **_DS_show concept** clip's Out point, and click to create a new edit point. Create edit points at the head and tail of each sync sound and narration clip in this sequence.

On the clips where the A1 sync sound is *not* present, you need to raise the volume to 0 dB. Rather than adjust the volume on each individual clip, you can set the volume as a group.

**8** To change the volume of all the clips that are *not* beneath a sync sound or narration clip, select those clips and choose Modify > Levels. With 0 dB in the "Adjust gain by" field, click the Make Changes pop-up menu and choose Absolute. Click OK.

This option changes clip volume to an absolute value.

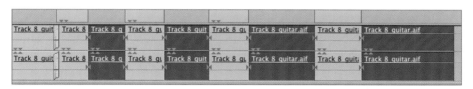

**NOTE ▶** Another way to accomplish this task is to use the Paste Attributes method you learned earlier in this lesson.

**9** To simultaneously apply a cross fade to each of these edit points, press T to select the Select Track Forward tool and click the second clip in the A5 track. Press Command-Option-T, and play the sequence. Press A to return to the Selection tool.

**TIP ▶** Don't forget, to finesse individual cross fades, you can roll the edit point left or right and change the cross fade length.

## Setting Keyframes to Change Volume

Another way to raise and lower the music volume is to set a *keyframe* where you want to change the audio level. A keyframe identifies the frame in a clip where you want to animate a change, any change. In this lesson, it's volume. By setting a keyframe directly on the audio level overlay, you are giving a precise command as to when and how the audio should change.

> **NOTE ▶** All keyframes in this exercise will be added to the **Track 8_ guitar.aif** music clip.

**1** From the Sequences bin in the Browser, open the *Believe Mix_v3_keyframes* sequence.

This sequence has a static A1 track so you can see the music next to the sync sound clips.

> **TIP ▶** If you want to return to the normal Timeline track display without a static region, drag up the lower thumb tab of the static region and release it.

To raise the volume before the first sync sound clip, you need to set two keyframes around that edit point on the music audio level overlay.

**2**    As a visual guide, move the playhead to the In point of the **_DS_show concept** clip, and press P to select the Pen tool. Move the pointer into the **Track 8_guitar.aif** clip and over the pink audio level overlay *before* the playhead.

The tool looks like a pen only when the pointer is over the clip's audio level overlay.

**3**    Click with the Pen tool before the playhead position. Make sure you click *on* the audio level overlay.

A pink diamond, or keyframe, appears on both tracks of the stereo music clip at the playhead position. This first keyframe establishes or secures the point where you want to begin fading the audio.

**TIP** ▶ To delete a keyframe, press PP to select the Pen Delete tool and click a key-frame, or Control-click a keyframe, and from the shortcut menu, choose Clear.

**4**    Move the Pen tool to the right of the playhead and click the audio level overlay of the **Track 8_guitar.aif** clip.

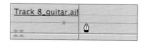

Although you haven't changed the volume yet, this is the location in the clip where you want the fade to stop and level off. With two keyframes in place, you can now adjust an audio level overlay to create an audio fade.

**5**    Press A to return to the default Selection tool. Move the pointer over the audio level overlay to the left of the keyframes. When you see the Resize pointer, drag up to 0 dB and release it. Play the audio fade.

The audio volume stays constant until the playhead reaches a keyframe. At that point, the audio volume begins to change in the direction of the next keyframe, in this case dropping to a lower volume level.

**NOTE ▶** You can think of keyframes as thumbtacks or pushpins that hold a rubber band in place, allowing you to drag the other side up or down.

After David stops talking, let's add two more keyframes to fade the audio from its "down under" volume to an "up full" volume. This time, you will use the default Selection tool and the Option key to access the Pen tool.

6   Position the pointer on the pink audio level overlay of the music clip just before the Out point of the **_DS_show concept** clip. Press the Option key, and when the Pen tool appears, click the audio level overlay. Set a second keyframe just past the Out point of the **_DS_show concept** clip using the same method.

**TIP ▶** When you press the Option key and move your pointer over an existing keyframe, the pointer changes to the Pen Delete tool.

Before adjusting the level, you can set another two keyframes to limit the fade to a specific area.

7   Set two keyframes around the In point of the **_SA_favorite behavior** clip. With four keyframes in place, drag the audio level overlay up between the middle two keyframes to 0 dB. Play this section of the sequence.

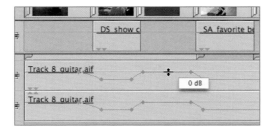

Once a keyframe has been placed on an audio level overlay, it can be raised or lowered to alter the volume at that location. It can also be repositioned left or right to change where the fade starts or stops.

**TIP** ▶ It may be helpful to turn off snapping for the next step.

8  Play the last portion of the music clip, then zoom in to it to make that area larger. To fade out the volume, Option-click the audio level overlay under the last video edit point. Option-click again about halfway to the music clip's Out point.

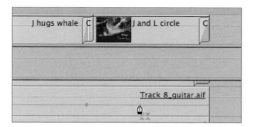

When you set a keyframe directly on the edge of a clip, it can be difficult to access. Setting it well inside the clip gives you greater control as you position the keyframe into place.

9  Move the pointer over the second keyframe. When the pointer changes to a crosshair, drag the keyframe down until you see "–inf dB" (infinity dB) in the information box. Then, drag the keyframe toward the right corner of the clip, staying inside the clip's edge. Play the clip.

**NOTE** ▶ The crosshair is not a selectable tool. It is a part of the Pen and Select tools and allows you to move a keyframe.

As you drag a keyframe up and down or left and right, an information box appears, displaying the distance and direction you've moved the keyframe from its original position, or the dB level change. You can also make these changes in the Viewer.

**10** Double-click the **Track 8_guitar.aif** clip, and drag the Zoom slider to the right to move to the end of this clip. Using the audio waveform as a guide, drag the second keyframe left or right to position it where the music ends.

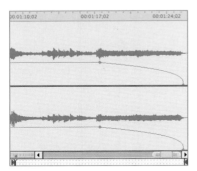

The Viewer's waveform display is much larger than that of a sequence clip, which can make it easier to fine-tune keyframe placement. You can also add new keyframes here.

**TIP** ▶ You can set keyframes in the Viewer's Audio tab before editing a clip to the Timeline.

## Take 2

Before your project is sent out of house for further sound work, the producer wants you to continue adding keyframes to animate the music volume around the sync sound clips.

You can also animate the **Scuba Breathing.aif** clip so you don't hear the scuba sound while someone is talking. To smooth the other sound effects' edit points, you can apply cross fades or add keyframes to fade them in and out.

## Using the Audio Mixer

Now that you understand how to set keyframes and manually mix audio in the Timeline, you're ready to mix tracks in real time using the Audio Mixer.

There are several ways to access the Audio Mixer. One is to select the Audio Mixing window layout, which incorporates the Audio Mixer into the interface. Another is to choose Tools > Audio Mixer. This opens the Audio Mixer as a separate window that you can place wherever you like. Before you create a new mix, let's explore the Audio Mixer.

**1**   Click the Timeline to make that window active, and choose Tools > Audio Mixer, or press Option-6. Drag this new window to the left over the Browser window area.

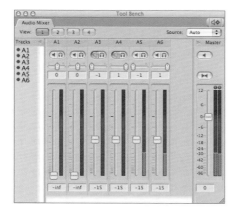

When you open the Audio Mixer, it appears within the Tool Bench window as a tab. There are six audio tracks currently represented in the Audio Mixer—the same number of tracks you have in your sequence. If the active sequence had 20 audio tracks, 20 tracks would appear in the Audio Mixer.

**TIP** ▶ If you are working with several tracks and don't want to see them all at one time, you can hide a track by clicking its Track Visibility control.

**2**   In the Audio Mixer, make sure the Record Audio Keyframes button in the upper-right button bar is deselected so that no keyframes will be created while you practice.

**3**   In the Audio Mixer, click the A3 and A4 Mute buttons to return these sound effects to the mix.

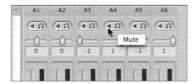

The Mute and Solo buttons in the Audio Mixer work interchangeably with those in the audio controls in the Timeline.

**4**  In the Timeline, play the sequence from the beginning, but watch the faders in the Audio Mixer.

The track faders move in response to the keyframes and sound levels you set in these clips. Instead of raising or lowering the audio level overlay in the Timeline, you can use these faders to adjust the audio levels.

**5**  Move the playhead over the **_SA_favorite behavior** clip and look at the position of the clip's audio level overlay. In the Audio Mixer, drag the A1 fader down to about −20 dB and release the fader. Look again at the clip's audio level overlay in the Timeline. Then press Command-Z to undo this change.

**NOTE ▶** When changing volume on a stereo pair, dragging one fader adjusts the volume on both tracks.

Changing the volume of a clip in the Audio Mixer changes the audio level overlay on the clip in the Timeline. In the Audio Mixer, the dB level in the field below the fader changes to reflect how much you have raised or lowered the sound from its original 0 dB level. You can also enter a value in a field and press Return, which will move the fader to that level.

Once the individual mix levels are set for each track, you can adjust the overall output level for your sequence by using the Master fader on the far right of the Audio Mixer. You can also mute all tracks at once using the Master mute button.

**6**  If the Master area is not open, click its disclosure triangle.

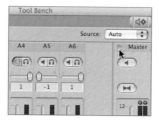

7   Play the sequence from the beginning, and as it plays, look at the Master audio meters. Drag the Master fader up to raise the overall volume level or drag it down to lower it.

While you never want to exceed 0 dB, you typically aim for a lower final output level, such as –6 or even –12 dB, to ensure that the sequence will play back within a safe range in any situation, on different systems, and on all equipment.

The levels in the Master fader reflect the output levels of the active sequence. When you change the level in a sequence using the Master fader, that output level will remain until you change it again.

**NOTE ▶** Any changes made to the Master fader will affect the level of the mix as it's played back or output to tape. For this lesson, you will focus on balancing or mixing the individual tracks, and not outputting them to tape.

In a moment, you will automatically add a new set of keyframes to the **Track 8_guitar .aif** clip. To do this, you need to start with a clean slate: a music track that is at 0 dB and has no keyframes.

8   Control-click the **Track 8_guitar.aif** clip and choose Remove Attributes from the shortcut menu. In the Remove Attributes dialog, make sure Levels is selected under the Audio Attributes column, and click OK.

All the keyframes are removed from this clip and the audio level overlay is returned to the 0 dB level of the original clip.

9   In the Audio Mixer button bar, click the Record Audio Keyframes button to toggle it on.

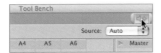

With this option turned on, any adjustments you make by dragging a track fader *while the sequence is playing* will automatically add keyframes to the clip in the Timeline.

Since the Audio Mixer works in real time, take a moment to think about the process. First, you will begin to play the sequence, then click and hold the A5 (or A6) fader control and watch the playhead move in the sequence.

As the playhead approaches the first sync sound clip, drag the A5 fader down (to about –15 dB) while David is speaking, then back up to its original 0 dB level after he finishes talking. You can release the fader button until you're ready to drag it down under the next sync sound clip.

**10** Follow these steps to create a live mix:

▶ Move the playhead to the head of the sequence, and press the Spacebar to begin playing. Position your pointer over the A5 fader.

▶ As the playhead approaches the first sync sound clip, drag the A5 fader down so you can clearly hear David but still hear the music in the background. If you want to, you can release the mouse button at that level.

▶ At the end of the first sync sound clip, drag the A5 fader back up to its original level, and release the mouse button.

▶ Keep watching the playhead, and as it approaches the second sync sound clip, drag the A5 fader down and under again, then up full.

▶ Continue dragging down and up around each sync sound clip until the sequence is finished playing.

When you stop playing, keyframes appear to identify peaks in the music clip where you raised and lowered the faders. To adjust your mix, you can raise or lower these keyframes, reposition them, delete them, or manually add new ones as you did in a previous exercise.

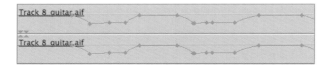

**NOTE ▶** In the Editing tab of User Preferences, you can choose a different level of automatic keyframing, either more or less sensitive to your fader movements. Start with the current default, which is the middle level.

The Audio Mixer is a powerful tool. Using it to set keyframes automatically may require practice before you achieve the desired results.

Keep in mind that setting keyframes automatically isn't right for every project. It's most helpful when you have one long audio source, such as music or a sound effect, that continues through a portion of your sequence. Sometimes, manually controlling the individual keyframes—with the Pen tool, for example—may give you the best result.

## Recording a Narration Track

As you move your project toward completion, you may find you're still missing a narration track. Perhaps you were given a written script for the narration, but the news reporter or narrator hasn't gotten into the studio to record it. The problem is that you now need the audio track for timing purposes or for seeing how the narration fits your video. The solution may be to record your own unofficial narration, which is sometimes referred to as a *scratch track*.

To record a voiceover in Final Cut Pro, you use the Voice Over tool. You can use a digital camera, a USB microphone, or an internal microphone on a laptop computer as your recording device. The Voice Over tool will create a new audio clip directly in the Timeline. To prepare for your new scratch track in the current sequence, let's first disable the current narration clip and set In and Out points in the Timeline for a new voiceover.

**NOTE ▶** If you are using an external microphone or camera mic, connect the device to your computer.

1   In the Timeline, Control-click the **narration_2** clip, and from the shortcut menu, choose Clip Enable to toggle off visibility for this one clip.

You will now record your own version of the narration script in this same location. To mark this area, you need to set In and Out points.

2   Move the playhead to the beginning of the **J and L circle** clip. Press I to create an In point. In the Canvas Timecode Duration field, enter *12.* (12 period) to create a 12-second duration, and press Return.

These In and Out points will create a clip somewhat longer than the original narration to give you some extra pad as you record.

**NOTE ▸** If no In and Out points are present, the voiceover track begins recording at the playhead location and continues until the end of the sequence.

**3**   To open the Voice Over tool, choose Tools > Voice Over.

If Final Cut Pro does not detect a recording device, an alert appears. If Final Cut Pro detects a microphone source, the Voice Over tool appears as a tab in the Tool Bench window. Notice that the Audio Mixer tab is still open in the Tool Bench window.

The Voice Over tool is divided into four areas: Status, Audio File, Input, and Headphones. The first step is to specify the track where you want the new narration. The target track appears in the Audio File area.

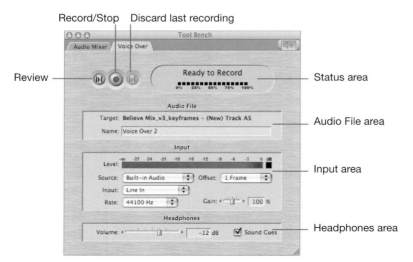

When you record a voiceover, Final Cut Pro places a new audio clip on the a2 track or the lowest-patched audio track at the marked location. If a clip is already in that location on that track, the new audio clip is placed on the track beneath it. If no track exists, Final Cut Pro will automatically create a new track for the clip.

**NOTE ▶** Audio recordings made using the Voice Over tool are saved as media files in your project's Capture Scratch folder.

4   In the Timeline, drag the a2 Source control to the A6 Destination control and note the new target information in the Audio File area.

The Voice Over tool will always target the track beneath the lowest patched track.

**TIP ▶** If you don't see an a2 Source control in the Timeline patch panel, Control-click in the track area and choose Reset Panel from the shortcut menu. You can also open a clip with two tracks of audio into the Viewer.

With the a2 Source control patched to the A6 destination track, the target for the new voiceover is A7. Although it doesn't currently exist, Final Cut Pro will automatically create this track after you record the voiceover. Since the Voice Over function records only one channel of audio, or mono audio, it needs only one track.

5   In the Audio File area, enter *scratch narration* as the name for this voiceover track.

6   In the Input area, choose the correct source from the Source pop-up menu. If it's DV, choose 48000 Hz from the Rate pop-up menu and 3 Frames from the Offset pop-up menu.

Final Cut Pro will display a default Input configuration based on the audio recording device it detects. A recording offset amount is included as one of the default settings. If your device does not support a 48000 Hz sampling rate, you won't see that option.

**NOTE** ► In digital audio, a *sampling rate* represents the number of times per second that a sample is taken from an audio source to represent that sound. The more samples taken, the more accurately the audio is represented in digital form. Audio sample rates are measured in Hertz and written as Hertz (Hz) or kilohertz (kHz), such as 48000 Hz or 48.0 kHz.

**7**   Start talking to set the Gain recording level in the Input area.

**TIP** ► If you use headphones for this process, you can listen to the other audio tracks in the sequence as you record the narration, without recording those audio tracks.

**8**   Deselect the Sound Cues checkbox.

When the checkbox is selected, you will hear sound beeps as a cue during the 5-second countdown before recording, and once again prior to the Out point.

If you're not using headphones, however, the beeps will be picked up and recorded as part of your clip. Instead, you can deselect Sound Cues and watch the Starting countdown in the status area to see when recording begins and ends.

Before you begin, look for the Ready to Record signal in the status area. Here's what will happen: You will click the Record button. The playhead will immediately jump backward for the pre-roll, while the Ready to Record status area will turn yellow and count down from five. It will then turn red and begin recording. When you are finished reading the narration lines, click the black Stop button.

**9**   Click the Record button, and record the following lines:

"Two worlds. Two different species—trying to bridge the gap between them. And how do you bridge that gap? You believe."

The recording ends at the Out point. In the Timeline, the new voiceover clip appears on the new A7 track between the previous In and Out marks.

**TIP** ▶ If you want to stop a recording in process, or if you don't have an Out point, click the Stop button. You can also click the Discard Last Recording button to discard an unwanted track. This step cannot be undone.

**10** Play back the clip by clicking the Review button or by playing the sequence in the Timeline. Close the Voice Over tool.

Each time you record a new version, or *take*, a new clip is placed in another track in the Timeline and labeled with the next highest take number. These different takes, or versions, are actually QuickTime movies that are stored in your project's Capture Scratch folder.

## Importing Audio Files

Importing audio into Final Cut Pro is a simple task, but not all audio file formats are created equal. For example, a CD track is recorded at a 44.1 kHz (kilohertz) sampling rate, while high-quality audio for video—including DV, XDCAM, HD, and so on—is recorded at 48.0 kHz. Yet Final Cut Pro will play a CD track in the Timeline without rendering it. Still, the best practice is to ensure that your audio files are QuickTime movies (.mov) or QuickTime-compatible files, such as AIFF (.aif) or WAVE (.wav). These audio file formats contain uncompressed audio data.

Using file formats that are not QuickTime compatible, such as MP3 and AAC, could require rendering in your sequence. You can avoid rendering by utilizing applications such as iTunes or QuickTime Player Pro to conform your audio files. You can also use Final Cut Pro's Batch Export option to convert a group of files to different settings.

You can read more about the Batch Export function in the Final Cut Pro User Manual and read about conforming files in iTunes and QuickTime in those applications' user manuals.

**TIP** ▶ As you begin editing a new sequence, make sure your first edit is a video clip that represents the desired video and audio format. If you edit a music or other audio track first, the video format will remain the current Easy Setup.

### Editor's Cut

From the Sequences > Editor's Cut bin, open the *Quest* sequence. You'll see narration on A1, some sound effects on A2 and A3, and music tracks on A4 and A5. To review audio mixing, copy and paste (or Option-drag) the existing sound effects and place them under the bare V1 clips. You may need to solo the A2 and A3 tracks while you preview and finesse those effects. To mix the tracks, start by setting the appropriate narration level, and add the other tracks into the mix. Don't forget to apply transitions to smooth the audio edit points.

## Lesson Review

1. What button do you click in the Timeline to display the Mute and Solo buttons?
2. What result do you get when you click the Solo button on a track?
3. How can you add several tracks to the Timeline at one time?
4. How do you make the audio level overlay appear on clips in the Timeline?
5. When would you turn on audio waveforms in the Timeline?
6. What tool do you use to set a keyframe on the audio level overlay?
7. How can the Pen tool be accessed without selecting it from the Tool palette?
8. How do you reposition a keyframe or change its volume level?
9. How can you paste just the audio level from one clip to another?
10. In what menu do you find the Audio Mixer?
11. To mix tracks in real time and automatically create keyframes on a clip, what must you do in the Audio Mixer?
12. What tool do you use to record your own voiceover, and where do you access it?
13. What two commands in the Modify menu help to change audio levels, and in what way?

### Answers

1. The Audio Controls button in the lower left of the Timeline.
2. That track becomes the only audible track as you play the sequence.
3. Choose Sequence > Insert Tracks.

4.  Press Option-W, or click the Clip Overlays control in the lower left of the Timeline, to the left of the Track Height control.

5.  When you want a visual representation of a clip's audio signals to evaluate or to edit audio clips.

6.  The Pen tool.

7.  Press Option and move the pointer over the audio level overlay on a Timeline clip. The Pen tool appears on the overlay line.

8.  Drag left and right to change its position and up and down to change its volume level.

9.  Copy the clip that has the desired audio level and paste just the audio levels using the Paste Attributes command.

10. The Tools menu.

11. In the Audio Mixer button bar, click the Record Audio Keyframes button to turn it on. Then play the sequence and adjust the clip volume by dragging its track fader.

12. The Voice Over tool, found in the Tools menu.

13. Modify > Levels brings up the Gain Adjust dialog, where you can raise or lower volume for all selected clips. Modify > Audio > Apply Normalization Gain resets the peak decibel level of the clip.

**Keyboard Shortcuts**

| | |
|---|---|
| **P** | Select the Pen tool |
| **PP** | Select the Pen Delete tool |
| **Option-W** | Turn audio level overlays on and off in the Timeline |
| **Command-Option-W** | Turn waveforms on and off in the Timeline |
| **Option-0** | Open the Voice Over tool |
| **Option-6** | Open the Audio Mixer |
| **Control-. (period)** | Pan a selected clip's audio to the center |

# 11

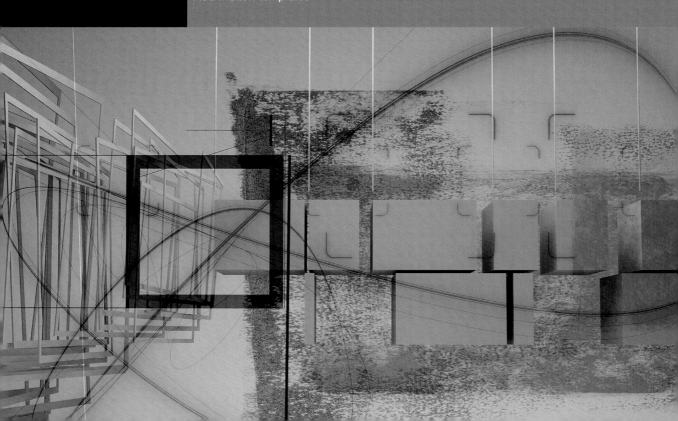

## Lesson 11
# Creating Titles

All projects, from the simplest to the most complex, will seem more complete when you add text, titles, and graphics. But in Final Cut Pro you don't need to capture or import text clips. Titles—along with items such as color mattes, color bars, and other effects—can be generated within Final Cut Pro and accessed whenever you need them.

In this lesson, you will add text to existing sequences using several methods, including some that generate preformatted text or animate the text automatically. You'll also create a sequence of still images and edit it into another sequence. In addition, you can apply a Motion template to your project to create a more sophisticated look.

Multilayered graphics file used as a lower third

## Preparing a Project for Titles

There are a few things you can do to streamline the process of adding text to a sequence. You can import a reference clip that contains a style you want to copy. You can place all the text clips onto one track so they can be turned off or on together. And, if your project will be broadcast, you can turn on an overlay to ensure that your titles fit within a "safety zone" so they can be seen on any television monitor.

**1** Open the Lesson 11 Project file, and close any other open projects.

In this lesson, you will work with a new set of footage from a documentary on street musicians, *Playing For Change: Peace Through Music.*

▶ **Playing For Change: Peace Through Music**

Director and creator Mark Johnson traveled around the world recording street musicians as they added their voices to a collective music track with other musicians. Cinematographer Kevin Krupitzer filmed and taped the performers as they laid down the tracks. From these recordings and performances, co-director and editor Jonathan Walls and the production team created a documentary. The footage was shot using DV, HDV, XDCAM, and 16 mm cameras. The DV footage was shot in anamorphic mode, so the image area appears in a 16:9 aspect ratio. Sometimes a matte was added to give the images a wide-screen look. The editorial process was challenging because footage from several countries and multiple formats was combined into one project and edited into one sequence that was used to create the *Playing For Change: Peace Through Music* DVD.

**2** Press Control-U to return to the default standard layout, and in the RT popup menu, make sure that Unlimited RT is selected. In the Timeline, play the *Playing For Change* sequence.

Several street performers contributed to the first two verses of "Don't Worry," written by Pierre Minetti of Nancy, France, who introduces the song. Although the sequence needs no editorial changes, it would be nice to identify the performers and their locations.

In the second verse of the song, after Pierre sings, the color of the clips changes with each new performer. These colors can help guide you in placing new titles.

**NOTE ▶** In the original *Playing For Change* Final Cut Pro sequence, color labels were used to identify a particular song ("Don't Worry" was green), and each performer had a dedicated track. The Razor Blade tool was used to segment the clips, and clips that were not used were disabled (and appeared darker). The purple text clips appear on V17 and V18, above the other tracks.

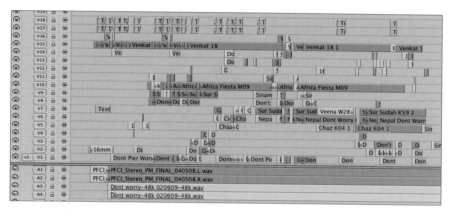

Timeline of "Don't Worry" from the original *Playing For Change* sequence.

3   In the Browser, open the **Don't Worry** clip and play it.

This QuickTime movie, taken from the *Playing For Change* documentary, is the full-length version of "Don't Worry." Notice the editing style and how text was used to introduce the segment and to identify the performers.

**4**    In the Viewer, move the playhead to the head of the clip, and press Shift-M (or Shift–Down Arrow), to move forward to the first marker. Press Shift-M again to move to the next marker, and the next. Notice that each credit shares the same font size and style.

Markers have been placed on frames containing titles that you will re-create in this lesson. The markers have also been given colors that match their corresponding sequence clips. You can use these markers as references for spelling names and reviewing text styles.

**5**    With the Viewer window active, choose View > Show Title Safe. Replay the first portion of this clip.

Two rectangular outlines appear as overlays in the Viewer. The inner box represents the title safe boundary, and the outer box represents the action safe boundary. The recorded frame size of broadcast video is actually larger than the viewable area of a television monitor. When text is positioned within the title safe boundary, you can be sure the text will be seen on any television monitor when the show is broadcast. Likewise, when an important action within a clip appears within the action safe boundary, you can be sure that action will be seen by the home viewer. You will work with the action safe boundary in the next lesson.

**NOTE** ▶ Because this footage was shot DV-NTSC anamorphic, black appears above and below the image, but the titles fit neatly within the title safe area.

There is another way to access the title safe boundary and other overlays.

6    In the Viewer, click the View pop-up menu button, and choose Show Title Safe. Choosing this command turns the overlay off or on.

This View pop-up menu contains several of the same items you find in the View menu, but in a more convenient location. The Canvas window also has a View pop-up menu button. Since you will be using the Canvas to edit new text clips, let's turn on the title safe boundary for that window.

7    In the Canvas, click the View pop-up menu button and choose Show Title Safe.

**TIP** ▶ If the Show Overlays command is not selected in the View pop-up menu, the title safe boundary will not appear. Make sure that both Show Overlays and Show Title Safe are selected.

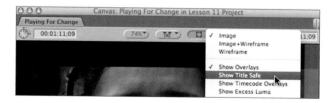

When you edit text clips, you use the Viewer window to enter text changes. When a text clip is loaded into the Viewer, you will lose your reference to the **Don't Worry** clip.

Let's open that clip in a separate Viewer window so you have access to it throughout the lesson.

**8**  In the Browser, Control-click the **Don't Worry** clip and choose Open in New Viewer from the shortcut menu. Reposition this new Viewer window over the Browser window, and move the playhead to the first marker in the clip.

Now you can continue editing and refer to the **Don't Worry** clip as necessary.

## Working with Video Generators

The clips you have used so far were captured from source material or imported from other files. But Final Cut Pro can internally create certain clips using *generators*. These generated items include color bars and tone, which are used as color references; slugs to fill a space with black; color mattes and gradients to create vivid backgrounds; and text. Some generated items stand alone, such as color bars at the head of a sequence; some items can be used in conjunction with other video clips.

When selected, most generated items appear in the Viewer with a length of 2 minutes and a marked 10-second default duration. All generated items are video-only except for color bars and tone. You can choose video generators from one of two places, in the Viewer or in the Browser Effects tab.

**1**  In the Timeline, position the playhead at the head of the sequence.

If someone else on the production team needs to review the sequence, you may want to add some elements before the actual scene begins, such as a slate that identifies the upcoming scene, or other *leader* material, such as a countdown. If the sequence is intended for broadcast, you may also want to include a color reference so that viewers can properly set up their monitors.

**2**  In the lower-right corner of the Viewer, click the Generator pop-up button and look at the different generator categories.

**3**    From the pop-up menu, choose Bars and Tone > Bars and Tone (NTSC). Play a few seconds of this clip.

The **Bars and Tone** clip includes video bars and two tracks of −12 dB tone. All generated items are given a default 10-second duration.

**4**    In the Viewer's Timecode Duration field, enter 5. (5 period), and press Return. Insert this clip at the head of the sequence.

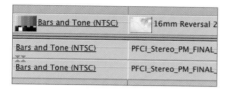

To identify your sequence, let's add a slate after the color bars. You can create a slate using the basic Text generator.

**5**    Click the Generator pop-up again, and choose Text > Text from the pop-up menu.

**TIP** ▶ You can also press Control-X to automatically load this Text clip into the Viewer.

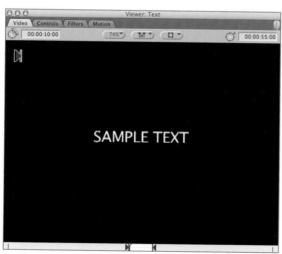

In the Viewer, the words *SAMPLE TEXT* appear over the image area. This is a default text line. To modify this text clip, and to see the changes at the same time, you will first edit the clip into the sequence.

**NOTE ▶** Editing a text clip to the Timeline is an important step in your workflow. Not only can you see the changes in the Canvas as you modify the text, but you preserve those changes as well. If you were to open a clip in the Viewer over a text clip before it was edited, you would lose any changes you may have made.

**6**  In the Viewer's Timecode Duration field, enter 5. (5 period), and press Return. Insert this clip after the **Bars and Tone** clip, and zoom in to the clip in the Timeline.

All generated text items appear in the Timeline as purple clips, with the specific type of text as the name of the clip—in this case, it's the basic "Text." To make changes to this clip, you open it as you would any other clip in a sequence.

**7**  In the Timeline, position the playhead over the new **Text** clip to see it in the Canvas, then double-click it to open it in the Viewer. Click the Controls tab.

**NOTE ▶** When you select a clip in the Timeline, a cyan outline appears around the edge of the clip in the Canvas. When the title safe boundary is visible, you see three rectangles. To hide the outer box, you can deselect the clip in the Timeline.

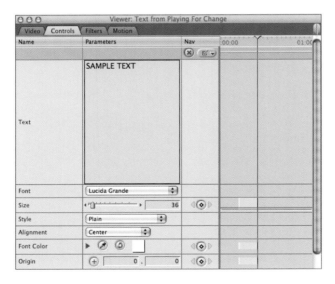

A Controls tab is present in the Viewer for most generated items. Note the attributes you can modify, such as font, size, style, and alignment. Scroll down to look at the other attributes, then scroll up to the Text parameter.

**NOTE ▶** To the right of the attributes are keyframe buttons and a keyframe graph area where you can set keyframes to animate text parameters. You will animate effect parameters in the next two lessons. You can also reset parameters to their default status by clicking the red Reset button (X) in the upper-right corner of the Controls tab.

8   Click in the Text field, and when *Sample Text* is highlighted, type *"Playing For Change"* and press Tab to see the new text in the Canvas window.

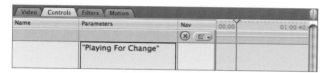

Slates may be very simple one-line introductions to a sequence, or they may include a variety of information such as show name, episode name or number, editor, director, or producer.

9   In the Viewer, click at the end of the text line, and press Return to move the cursor to the next line. Continue entering the slate information, and press Tab when finished to update the text in the Canvas. You can use the following figure as a guide:

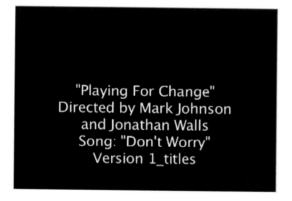

As you continue to add more lines of text, the text begins to move down in the Canvas. This is because the first line is positioned in the center of the image area, and the additional lines appear beneath it. Depending on the number of lines, the text could move out of the title safe area. There's usually plenty of room for the text in the Canvas image area; you just have to reposition the text higher.

**10** In the Viewer, scroll down to the Origin parameter, and click the point control (crosshair button). In the Canvas, drag the crosshair up to reposition the center of the text higher.

**11** To add more distance between the individual lines, change the Leading to 20.

Typically, you follow a slate with a few seconds of black or a countdown of some kind, signaling the start of the sequence. In Final Cut Pro, you can edit a generated item called a *slug* to create black video and two tracks of empty audio. Let's add a few seconds of black after this slate.

> **TIP** You can also use slugs to hold the place of a clip in a sequence, such as footage that hasn't been captured or a graphic that hasn't yet been completed.

**12** In the Viewer's Video tab, click the Generator pop-up menu and choose Slug.

**13** In the Viewer's Timecode Duration field, enter *2.* (2 period), and press Return. Insert this clip at the end of the **Text** clip, and play the first few clips of this sequence.

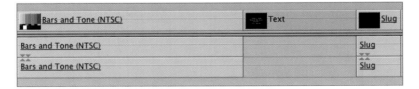

## Take 2

You're ready to start adding the performers' titles. But the new assistant director is taking his job a little too seriously. Before moving forward, he wants you to add a 5-second countdown leading into the sequence. He reminds you that you only need the numbers 5-4-3-2 and should leave black for the last second. You ask for some time to prepare it. In truth, you know that once you create the first number, you can Option-drag the number to create each of the following numbers. To make an even bigger impression, you could later add a sound effect to each number, similar to the countdown in the television series *24*.

**TIP** ▶ If you customize a countdown and want to use it in other shows, you can export that section of the Timeline as a QuickTime movie. You will learn to do this in Lesson 14.

## Adding a Lower Third

Final Cut Pro offers more than one kind of text, each with its own set of parameters. Some of the generated text items are preformatted for specific purposes—such as the *lower third*, which most often identifies a person, place, or thing. For example, when you watch a television news story, you know the reporter's name and location by the text in the lower third of the screen, which appears over the introductory shot. The Final Cut Pro **Lower 3rd** clip automatically creates two lines of text information within the title safe boundary in the lower left of the image area.

To keep the text clips organized in this sequence, you will edit them all to the V2 track. But rather than target the V2 track directly, you will use a different type of edit to *superimpose* the text over an existing clip in the Timeline.

1   In the **Don't Worry** clip, press Shift-M or Option-M to move the Viewer playhead to the first marker.

For this documentary, the lower third format was used to introduce each segment and to identify the performers and their countries. The titles in the documentary were centered beneath each performer, but you will explore other options by placing lower thirds in the left and right corners of the image.

2   In the Viewer, click the Generator pop-up menu and choose Text > Lower 3rd.

**NOTE** ▶ In the menu, text options that will play in real time are displayed in boldface.

In the Viewer, a new text clip appears with two default lines of sample text. As you did with the basic text clip, you will edit this clip into the Timeline and then open it up in the Viewer to see the changes as you make them.

Since you want this clip to appear over a specific clip on the V1 track, you can use a superimpose edit. With this type of edit, Final Cut Pro uses the Timeline playhead and the v1 Source control to identify a clip's track, duration, and position in the sequence. It then places the new clip on the track directly above the reference clip, matching its length and position.

3 In the Timeline, position the playhead anywhere over **Pierre W13**. Make sure the v1 Source control is targeting the V1 track clip.

**NOTE** ► These clips were originally named after the song and performer (for example, "Don't Worry Pierre"), so they would be grouped together by song in the Browser. Also, the letters on the clip names represent the shooters. Each shooter covered a different framing of an event, such as close-ups or wide shots, so this labeling system helped create an efficient editing workflow.

With the V1 track targeted, and the playhead over the sequence clip, Final Cut Pro knows to use this clip as a reference when editing the new text clip.

4 In the Viewer, drag the **Lower 3rd** clip to the Superimpose section of the Canvas Edit Overlay.

Final Cut Pro automatically superimposes the clip directly above the targeted track with the same length and location as the reference clip.

In the Canvas, you see that the two lines of lower third text fit neatly within the title safe area over the background clip.

Although you may sometimes want text to stand alone over black, such as with the slate, you will often want it to appear over an image. All text clips in Final Cut Pro contain an *alpha channel* that drops away, or makes transparent, the nontext portion of the text clip and allows you to superimpose just the text over any background image.

**5**   In the Timeline, double-click the **Lower 3rd** clip to open it in the Viewer, and click the Controls tab.

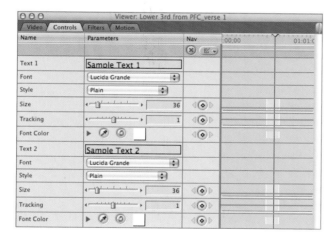

**TIP** Pressing and holding down the Command and Option keys *after* you've started dragging a generated item to the Canvas (or to the Timeline) will automatically open that clip in the Viewer with the Controls tab active.

In this clip, there are two separate areas where you can change each line of text.

**6**   Click in the Text 1 field, and enter *Pierre Minetti*. Make the font Helvetica, change Style to Bold/Italic, change Size to 30, and change Tracking to 4. In the Text 2 field, enter *Nancy, France*, and give it the same Font and Style, but change Size to 24 and Tracking to 2. Play the clip.

While superimposing this clip saved a few editing steps, you may not want the title to remain visible this long. You can easily change the clip length, and add a default cross dissolve to smooth out the edit point. Let's start this text clip 4 seconds later.

**7** In the Timeline, select the In point of the **Lower 3rd** clip, and type *4.* (4 period), and press Return. Then press Command-T to add a default cross dissolve.

With a transition added, and the clip length shortened, the title looks more professional and closer to the original.

The only thing missing from this title is a drop shadow. In Final Cut Pro, the drop shadow function appears in the Viewer on the Motion tab. Although not every clip is a text clip, every clip can have its own drop shadow.

**MORE INFO ▶** You will work more with Motion parameters in Lesson 12.

**8** Position the playhead over the Pierre lower third. In the Viewer, click the Motion tab, then select the Drop Shadow checkbox. Click the disclosure triangle to reveal its parameters.

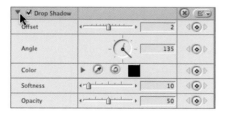

When you turn on Drop Shadow, the shadow appears behind the text in the Canvas. However, the default Drop Shadow attributes don't match those used in the documentary.

**TIP ▶** You can zoom in to the image area in the Viewer and Canvas to take a closer look at the drop shadow. Try pressing the Z key and dragging around the text to zoom in to that area. Don't forget to press A to return to the default Selection tool, and press Shift-Z in the Viewer and Canvas windows to return to the full-screen images.

**9**   In the Drop Shadow parameters, click in the Offset field and enter *1.5*. Change Softness to 0, and Opacity to 100.

The opacity of an image ranges from completely solid, or opaque (100%), to completely transparent, or invisible (0%). As a rule of thumb, the more opaque and crisp a shadow is, the closer the text seems to the background; the more transparent and soft the shadow, the farther the text seems from the background image.

**10**   To see the next title in the **Don't Worry** clip window, press Shift-M to move to the second (orange) marker, where you see drummer Junior Kissangwa Mbouta's credit.

Notice how this lower third credit follows the same general style as the previous lower third clip. Rather than edit a whole new text clip from scratch, you can open the first lower third clip and superimpose it over the Junior clip.

**11**   In the Timeline, double-click the **Lower 3rd** clip, and position the Timeline playhead over the orange **Junior M09** clip. In the Viewer, drag the **Lower 3rd** clip to the Canvas as a superimpose edit.

**12**   Move the playhead to the second **Lower 3rd** clip, and double-click it. Click the Controls tab, if necessary. Click the Text 1 field and enter *Junior Kissangwa Mbouta*. In the Text 2 field, enter *The Congo*. Press Tab.

**TIP** ▶ In the Lower 3rd controls, you can choose a background to help the text stand out against a lighter image. When you choose Solid from the Background parameter, you can change the color of the background and adjust its opacity.

## Applying a Boris Title

If you don't find the options you need in the Text generator, you can try another category of text generators—called Boris—in the Generator pop-up menu. Boris contains an advanced set of text generators that provide great flexibility and high-quality output. The Boris submenu lists four text generators. Unlike the text options previously covered in this lesson, these access a separate window, offering a wider variety of parameters, including 3D control of individual characters (Title 3D). The Boris text options, which are part of the Final Cut Pro installation, allow you to make a number of style choices as well.

1 In the Timeline, move the playhead to the middle of the first green clip, **Dinesh M45**. In the **Don't Worry** reference clip, press Shift-M to move to the green marker.

Since the performer is standing on the left of the frame, for this credit, you might consider placing the lower third on the right and identifying the instrument he's playing. Since the Lower 3rd text clips are preformatted to have only two lines and appear in the lower left of the frame, you have to use a different Text generator to create this credit. With the Boris Text generator, you can create right-margin justified text and add additional lines.

2   In the Viewer, click the Video tab, and then click the Generator pop-up menu and choose Boris > Title 3D. (Because there is no "Sample Text," the image is black.) Drag this clip to the Canvas as a superimpose edit.

3   In the Timeline, double-click the clip to open it in the Viewer, and then click the Controls tab. In the Text Entry and Style field, click the Title 3D (Click for options) box.

**TIP**   The Boris Title 3D window may take some time to open depending upon the number of fonts installed on your system.

In the Boris Title 3D options, you don't enter text information in the Controls tab; instead, you use a separate window.

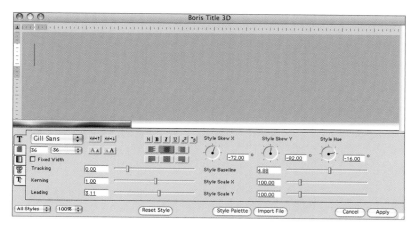

A large window opens with several small tabs running vertically down the left side of the window. The tabs are Text Style, Text Wrap, Text Fill, Edge Style, and Shadow Type. Next to some of the items are tiny checkboxes for turning them on and off.

**4** With the first tab selected, type *electric bass* as the first line of information, and then add the additional two lines as they appear in the **Don't Worry** clip. In the large gray text area, drag over the text to select it all, or press Command-A.

**NOTE ▶** The Boris window retains the most recently used font and size, so your text may not match the image below. You will change those in the next step.

The goal is to follow the same general style in this clip as in the other lower third clips, but it will appear in the lower-right area of the image. Some of the changes will be made to all of the text, and some to individual lines.

**5** Change the attributes of this clip as follows:

▶ Click the Right Justify button to justify the text on the right side of the image.

▶ Click B for Bold, and click I for Italic.

▶ Click the Font pop-up and choose Helvetica.

▶ Click in the Font Size field, and enter *24*.

▶ Deselect the text, and select just the second line.

▶ Enter 30 in the Font Size field.

> **TIP** ▶ In the Boris Title 3D window, you can even change individual letters. Just select the letters, words, or lines you want to change, and adjust their parameters. Only the selected text will be modified.

**6**   In the lower-right corner of the Boris Title 3D window, click Apply.

In the Canvas, the text style appears as it should, but it is not automatically placed in the corner of the title safe area as the Lower 3rd text clips are.

**7**   In the Controls tab, click the crosshair button in the Position X/Y parameter. In the Canvas, click in the center of the text (close to the current red center crosshair) and drag down and to the right to position the text just inside the title safe area.

Since you've already set the correct drop shadow parameters in an earlier text clip, you can simply copy that clip and paste the drop shadow attributes to this clip.

**8**   Select the first **Lower 3rd** clip and press Command-C to copy it. Control-click the **Title 3D** clip and choose Paste Attributes from the shortcut menu. In the Paste Attributes window, make sure Drop Shadow is selected, and click OK.

> **MORE INFO** ▸ The Boris Title 3D text window offers numerous ways to change text parameters, including several preset text styles. You can also add a drop shadow in the window. To learn more about these options, see the Final Cut Pro User Manual.

## Take 2

The director likes arranging the credits based on the performer's position within the image. He wants you to add credits for the remaining performers and use your own judgment about left or right placement. You might start by dragging a copy of the Title 3D clip you just created to the next colored clip. To show the director a polished sequence, don't forget you can shorten the length of the lower thirds, add transitions, and reposition a text clip anywhere over its background clip. If time allows, you can add Pierre's introduction at the beginning of the sequence. You can find it toward the beginning of the **Don't Worry** clip.

## Adding Mattes, Effects, and Still Images

There are many more video generators than text, including those for color mattes; shapes; and render items such as gradient, noise, and lens flare. You can use a color matte as a simple color background behind text or behind a clip or still image that has been resized or cropped. When you place a render effect on top of a color matte, you could have the perfect background for show credits, a show open, or a bumper to take you into and out of commercial breaks.

For this exercise, you will edit a matte and a render effect, then import and edit still images that were taken from the *Playing For Change* production shoot. While not all projects utilize still images, some projects require nothing but stills, perhaps edited to music or a narration track. In Final Cut Pro, still images are imported as graphics files.

Your final credit effect will consist of four layers: a color matte on V1, a render effect on V2, still images on V3, and the credits on V4. To build this four-layer effect, you will choose generated items from the Browser Effects tab and nest a group of clips (still photos) into its own sequence for greater control.

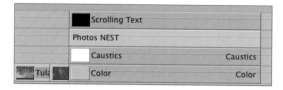

**NOTE ▶** You will prepare the effect in this lesson by editing the tracks and adjusting the text. In the next lesson, you will add the finishing touches when you learn how to change motion parameters.

1    In the Timeline, click the Out point of the **Don't Worry–48k.wav** clip. Type *23.* (23 period), and press Return. This is the duration of the musical interlude over which the credit effect will appear.

2    Position the playhead over the red marker, *matte color*. In step 4, you will choose a color from this image for the background matte.

**3**   In the **Don't Worry** Viewer window, click the close button. In the Browser, click the Effects tab, and click the disclosure triangle next to the Video Generators bin. Then click the disclosure triangle next to the Matte bin.

Like transitions, the video-generated items, represented by icons with a frame of color bars, are organized into bins. The Matte bin contains two types of color mattes. When you edit generated items from the Effects tab, you can drag them from the Browser directly to the Timeline, or open them in the Viewer.

**4**   Double-click the **Color** clip to open it in the Viewer, and click the Controls tab. In the Color controls, click the Select Color eyedropper, and in the Canvas, click a tan color in the church in the background.

You choose colors for color mattes just as you choose colors for transition effects. You can also use this method to pick a text color.

**5**   Click the Video tab. In the Viewer's Timecode Duration field, enter *23.* (23 period) and press Return. In the Timeline, move the playhead to the end of the V1 clips, and click the Overwrite button to edit this matte to the V1 track.

With the color matte on the V1 track, you can add an animated render effect on V2 that could liven up the static tan background. Let's look at a few render items.

6    In the Effects bin, from the Video Generators folder, open and play each of the following Render folder items in the Viewer: **Caustics**, **Clouds**, **Lens Flare**, **Membrane**, **Noise** (second one), and **Swirly**. Each of these items creates some pattern or movement that could be used in conjunction with a background image or color matte.

To match the length of the color matte, you will superimpose the render effect over the matte. Rather than first opening the effect into the Viewer, you can drag it directly from the Effects tab to the Canvas Edit Overlay.

7    In the Timeline, position the playhead over the **Color** clip. From the Browser Effects tab, drag the **Caustics** clip to the Superimpose section of the Canvas Edit Overlay. Play these clips in the Timeline.

As in text clips, this particular render effect has an alpha channel that drops out the black portion of the image when combined with other clips.

The next stage of building this effect is to edit photos to the V3 track above the color matte and the render effect. Before you edit the photos, however, you will use some interesting Final Cut Pro tricks to import and organize them. For example, the length of each measure in the music track is 2:26. Rather than import and mark each image manually, you can configure Final Cut Pro to create that duration as it imports the stills.

8    Choose Final Cut Pro > User Preferences, or press Option-Q. In the Editing tab, highlight the Still/Freeze Duration field and enter *2.26*. Press Return, and then click OK.

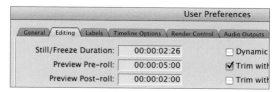

**9**   In the Browser, click the Lesson 11 Project tab. Choose File > Import > Folder. In the Choose a Folder dialog, navigate to FCP7 Book Files > Media > Playing For Change. Select the Still Images folder, then click Choose.

Final Cut Pro can import graphics files in many formats, such as TIFF, JPEG, and so on. You import, screen, and edit graphics just as you do other clips.

**10**   In the Browser, display the contents of the Photos bin. Notice that the still images are represented by graphic icons. If necessary, adjust the Browser columns so you can see the Duration column. Each clip is marked with a 2:26 duration.

**TIP** ▶ To more clearly read the names of these still images, you may want to delete the .JPG suffix.

In the next step, you will edit the entire folder of stills at one time. To make the images appear in a specific order in the sequence, you can use the storyboard editing approach, or as in this case, you can add a number to each image name to place it in the order you wish.

Before you edit these stills into the sequence, let's take a moment to think about the changes you might apply to them. You could reduce the photos' sizes to see the tan background and the render effect behind them. You could add a drop shadow or border to the stills, and give them a more uniform look by cropping the top and bottom of the effect to match the video clips. But rather than change each clip individually, you can group the stills into their own sequence and change that sequence.

This is one way the final effect might look.

**11** From the Sequences bin, open the *Photos NEST* sequence. From the Browser, drag the Still Images bin directly to the V1 track at the head of the sequence and release the bin (group of clips) as an overwrite edit.

**TIP** ▶ When you work with still images in Final Cut Pro, you may see a "Preparing video for display" message. If your entire project consists of still images, you can increase your system's capacity to cache stills by choosing Final Cut Pro > System Settings and clicking the Memory & Cache tab. Raise the Still Cache amount to 50% and click OK.

Now that you have all of the photos grouped into one sequence, you can edit, or *nest,* this sequence into the *Playing For Change* sequence.

**12** In the Timeline, click the *Playing For Change* sequence tab and place the playhead over the **Caustic** render clip. To superimpose the *Photos NEST* sequence above the V2 **Caustic** clip, target the V2 track.

**13** From the Browser Sequence bin, drag the *Photos NEST* sequence to the Superimpose section of the Canvas Edit Overlay. Play this section of the *Playing For Change* sequence.

**TIP** ▶ While not required, adding the word NEST to a nested sequence name can be a helpful reminder that this is not a typical clip.

When you nest one sequence into another, it allows you to treat a group of stills or clips as a single clip. When you make changes or add effects, you do it only once to the nested sequence. Whatever you do to the nest affects the individual clips within it.

**TIP** ▶ To make a change to an individual clip in the nest, such as replacing a photo or altering a duration, double-click the nest to open the original sequence. Changes made here will also appear in the parent sequence.

At the moment, the still images are not uniform in size, and one even needs to be rotated. You will make those changes in the next lesson. For now, you will continue to build the credit effect by adding the text layer to the V4 track.

## Take 2

The *Playing For Change* photographer just popped in to see how you liked the photos. You show him the effect you're building, one layer at a time, by turning off and on each Track Visibility control. He really likes the render effect and asks if you can make changes to it. You say, "Sure," because you know you can change a generated item's properties in the Controls tab. So turn off visibility for the V3 track, open the render effect, and tweak away. Turn on visibility to all tracks when you're done.

## Creating a Credit Roll

At the beginning of a film or television show, credits often reveal or display one name at a time. When you want to create the type of credit roll you often see at the end of a feature film, you will use the Final Cut Pro animated Scrolling Text generator. This text generator automatically rolls the text up from the bottom of the image and off at the top. In this exercise, you will edit the text clip on the V4 track as part of the credit effect you started in the previous exercise.

1   In the Timeline, Control-click the **Photos NEST** clip, and from the shortcut menu, choose Clip Enable to deselect it.

    **NOTE** ▶ Choosing Clip Enable performs the same function as clicking one of the Track Visibility controls, but it toggles visibility for just the selected clip or clips.

    By turning off visibility for **Photos NEST**, you can see the titles against the color matte and render effect, and you won't be slowed down by the still images.

**2**  Position the playhead in the middle of the **Photos NEST** clip. To superimpose a text clip over the still images, patch the v1 Source control to the V3 destination control.

Even though there is currently no V4 track, Final Cut Pro will create one automatically when you superimpose a clip above an existing track.

**3**  In the Viewer, click the Video tab, then from the Generator pop-up menu, choose Text > Scrolling Text. To superimpose this clip, press F12, the superimpose edit shortcut, or click the Superimpose button in the Canvas window.

**TIP** ▶ You can make any of the Canvas Edit Overlay sections appear as the third edit button in the Canvas. Click and hold down the arrow next to the blue Replace button, and select the purple Superimpose button to make it the default third edit button for this sequence.

**4**  In the Timeline, double-click the **Scrolling Text** clip to open it in the Viewer, and click the Controls tab.

Since the credits will roll up and off the screen, if the playhead is parked at the end or beginning of the clip, you won't see the text. With the playhead in the middle of the clip, you can see the text as you enter it.

**5**  In the Text field, enter the following information—including the asterisks between the credit and person's name—and press Return after each line. Press Tab after the last line to update the text in the Canvas:

*Directors\*Mark Johnson*
*\*Jonathan Walls*
*Cinematographer\*Kevin Krupitzer*
*Editor\*Jonathan Walls*

**TIP** ▶ When you want to list more than one name for a particular job title, press Return to move to the next line, type just the asterisk, and then type the name. Doing so will align the second name beneath the first.

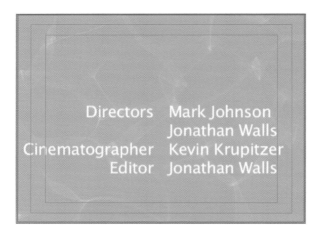

Final Cut Pro creates two columns separated by a gap where the asterisks were entered. As you can see, you will have to make additional changes to improve the text's appearance within the title safe area.

**NOTE** ▶ Although it may be intuitive to place a space before and after the asterisks, it is not necessary and will not create the desired effect.

6   Drag the scroller down to the lower Controls parameters. Change Size to 24 and change Leading to 120%. Adjust Gap Width to 4% to reduce the distance between the two columns. Play this clip in the Timeline.

The clip is programmed to animate the scroll for the full length of the clip. If you want the fade to move faster, you can shorten the clip.

7   Select the In point of the **Scrolling Text** clip, type *10.* (10 period), and press Return. Play this clip again.

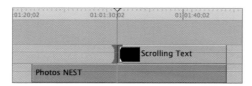

The shortened clip plays more quickly, and can be repositioned anywhere over the effect.

You can also set the Fade Size parameter to fade the credits in and out as they appear on and off the screen. And you can copy and paste a drop shadow as you did in a previous exercise.

8   In the Fade Size parameter, enter a Fade Size of *15%*. To add a drop shadow, copy the **Title 3D** clip. Control-click the **Scrolling Text** clip and choose Paste Attributes from the shortcut menu. In the Paste Attributes window, make sure Drop Shadow is selected, and click OK.

> **TIP** If the text clip isn't playing smoothly on your computer, you can select it and render it. Make sure the render status color is selected in the Sequences > Render Selection menu before rendering.

Opacity is another parameter that can be changed on any clip. It determines how transparent or opaque an image is. A clip can be completely transparent, completely solid, or any percentage in between. Opacity can be changed in any sequence clip by dragging an opacity overlay, which is similar to the audio level overlay on an audio clip. Looking at the current layers, you may find that the render effect distracts somewhat from the text. Changing that clip's opacity could help balance the overall effect.

9   In the Timeline, click the Clip Overlays control. In the **Caustics** clip, drag the opacity overlay down to 50%, and play the effect again. Turn off clip overlays.

The opacity parameter appears in the Motion tab just above Drop Shadow. If you double-click the **Caustics** clip and click the Motion tab, then click the Opacity disclosure triangle, you see that the percentage is 50% there as well.

> **TIP** Changing opacity on a clip that sits above another clip in the Timeline is a good way to create a *composite* effect that includes several images.

NOTE ▶ There are two other animated text generators you can experiment with on your own: Crawl and Typewriter. Crawl reveals text moving horizontally across the screen from the left or right. You may have seen weather warnings broadcast this way. The Typewriter text generator reveals one letter at a time until the full text is revealed, as if a typewriter were typing the text.

## Using Master Templates

Also included among the Final Cut Pro generated items is a set of master templates that were created in the Final Cut Studio Motion 4 application. The master templates contain 16 design concepts, each with its own set of animated templates that you can use for opens, lower thirds, backgrounds, bumpers, and so on. You edit these templates into a sequence as you would any other generated text item, and change the text of the template in the text fields of the Controls tab. You can even add an image to the template by dragging it into a drop zone.

To change or alter a template design, you can open the template in the Motion application, or send the clip to Motion and make the changes there. In Motion, you can change the primary color scheme or make other changes to the template design. When changed in Motion, those new attributes are also changed and updated in *all* uses of that template in the Final Cut Pro sequence.

1   In the Timeline, move the playhead to the end of the *Playing For Change* sequence.

2   In the Viewer Video tab, click the Generator pop-up and choose Master Templates > Sketch > Sketch – Lower Third.NTSC. Drag this clip directly to the Timeline, and *after* you've started to drag, press and hold down the Command and Option keys. Then release the clip on the V1 track as an overwrite edit.

    This animated graphics clip automatically opens in the Viewer with the Controls tab active. In the Controls tab you see a single line of text and a drop zone for an image of your choice.

3   In the Text Here field, enter *Playing For Change*, and set Text size to 20. In the Browser, from the Still Images bin, drag the **1_MJ headsets.JPG** clip to the Viewer Controls tab and onto the drop zone clip well. Play the clip in the Timeline.

**NOTE** ▶ If a "Report Dropped Frames on playback" dialog opens when you play this clip, selecting the "Don't warn again" checkbox will allow you to preview the effect.

You could continue to add this Motion template throughout the sequence for segues or bumpers to go in and out of sections. Some Motion templates are designed for opens, and some for lower thirds that you place over existing video clips in your sequence.

## Working with Graphics

As you complete the titles for your project, you may want to incorporate graphics that were created in other applications. Many types of single-layer graphics files may be imported to Final Cut Pro, as well as Adobe Photoshop multilayered graphics files. When a multilayered Photoshop file is imported, it appears in Final Cut Pro as a sequence. You can open the sequence and make changes or toggle Track Visibility off or on for each individual layer or track.

Before you edit a graphics file into your sequence, be aware that a video-based pixel aspect ratio could be different from a graphics file's ratio because computers and graphics programs display square pixels, whereas digital video uses nonsquare pixels. To be absolutely accurate, and to please those clients who use circles in their logos, make sure you choose settings in your graphics program that will match your sequence settings.

**MORE INFO** ▶ The Final Cut Pro User Manual contains a chart of additional graphics format conversions.

## Editor's Cut

Although you've worked with *Playing For Change* footage in this lesson, you haven't actually heard much about the documentary's story. In the Sequences > Editor's Cut bin in the Browser, you will find the *Director's Intro* sequence, in which director Mark Johnson tells the *Playing For Change* story and previews a few of the performers. To review what you've learned in this lesson, add titles to a few of the performers' clips, and nest the *Director's Intro* sequence at the head of the *Playing For Change* sequence after the leader material.

**TIP** ▶ To see how Final Cut Pro converts a multilayered graphics file to a sequence, double-click the *MJ Title* clip in the *Director's Intro* sequence. On import, the original multilayered Photoshop file was converted to this sequence. The sequence was then nested into the *Director's Intro* sequence.

## Lesson Review

1.  From what two places can you choose a generated item such as text?

2.  What tab in the Viewer do you select to make changes to text clips?

3.  When you superimpose an edit over a V1 clip, to what track should the Source control be patched for the superimposed clip to be placed on V2?

4.  What type of generated text identifies a person, place, or thing?

5.  In what menu can you find the Show Title Safe option?

6.  What generated item is used as a color and sound reference at the head of a sequence?

7.  Where can you find the Drop Shadow attribute?

8.  In what text generator does a separate window appear for making text changes?

9.  What automated text generator is often used for credit rolls?

10. How can you adjust a clip's opacity?

11. When you choose a color for a color matte, you can pick a color only from the Colors window. True or false?

12. What is it called when you edit one sequence inside another?

13. What category of generated items can you use to apply a Motion template?

*Answers*

1.  Choose from the Browser Effects tab or from the Generator pop-up menu in the Video tab in the Viewer.

2.  The Controls tab.

3.  The V1 track.

4.  A lower third.

5.  The View menu, and the View pop-up in the Viewer and Canvas.

6.  Bars and tone.

7.  In the Motion tab in the Viewer.

8.  The Boris text generator.

9.  The Scrolling Text generator.

10. Drag the opacity overlay on a video clip in the Timeline, or open a clip in the Viewer and change the Opacity parameter in the Motion tab.

11. False. You can use the Select Color eyedropper to pick a color from any clip in any open sequence.

12. Nesting.

13. Master templates.

## Keyboard Shortcuts

| | |
|---|---|
| **Control-X** | Open the Text generator into the Viewer |
| **Option-Control-X** | Open the Boris Text generator into the Viewer |
| **Hold Down Command and Option** | After beginning to drag a clip from the Viewer to the Canvas or Timeline, holding down these keys will automatically open the clip into the Viewer with the Controls tab active. |

# Adding Effects
and Finishing

# 12

# Lesson 12
# Changing Motion Properties

There's something quite satisfying about chiseling a precise sequence from a relatively rough chunk of media files; completing it by adding music, titles, and transitions; and then finishing and preparing the sequence for delivery to a client, the web, or the world.

The really fun part of that completion process is adding the refinements and embellishments that make a sequence sparkle and shine. In the next two lessons, you will explore two approaches to adding effects and finessing a sequence—changing the motion properties and adding filters. In the final lesson, you will learn to output and export a finished sequence.

A multi-frame image displays several clips at the same time.

In this lesson, you will learn how to change the motion properties of a clip. You'll change clip speed, create a freeze frame, and fit a clip of one length into the sequence space of a different length using the fit to fill edit. Then, you'll resize and reposition clips by stacking them on top of each other to create a split-screen or multi-frame effect, and use keyframes to animate motion properties over time.

## Evaluating a Project's Needs

Even when a sequence is complete, you may find it still has some additional needs or even unrealized potential. For example, does an action want to freeze at a climactic moment? Do multiple clips beg to share the screen at the same time? By changing the motion properties of a clip, you can alter its appearance and give it more style or visual appeal.

But you can also alter motion properties for more practical reasons: perhaps to remove a camera or microphone from a shot, or crop an image to focus on just one performer. You may even slow down a clip to make it long enough to cover a narration track.

Let's evaluate three before-and-after sequences—each with different needs—that you will work with in this lesson.

1   Open Lessons > Lesson 12 Project, and close any other open projects.

> **TIP** Make sure snapping is turned on for this lesson so you can easily snap to sequence markers.

2   In the Timeline, click the *Quest Motion_v2* sequence tab, and play the area under each marker. Then click the *Quest Motion* sequence tab, and move the playhead to each marker in that sequence.

To create a composite effect in which two or more images appear on the screen at the same time, the images must first be placed on top of each other in the Timeline such as they are in both sequences. In the *Quest Motion_v2* sequence, however, the motion properties—such as size, position, and opacity—have already been changed on the clips above the base V1 track, so all the clips can be seen.

By adjusting the motion parameters of the stacked clips in the *Quest Motion* sequence, you will create split screens similar to those in the *Quest Motion_v2* sequence.

**NOTE ▶** If a clip such as a title or render effect contains an alpha channel, that clip will appear over its background image without changing motion properties. You can also apply certain filters to create a composite effect.

3   In the Timeline, click the *Quest Motion_v2* sequence tab again, and play the clips under the "animate scale" marker.

Just as you animated volume on audio clips, you can also use keyframes to animate motion parameters. Here, the clip's size, or *scale*, was animated to start at full frame, or 100%, and to end at 0%.

**TIP** ► When working with several sequences at once consider matching the marker colors of a sequence to its color label. This unifies the color-coding and makes it easier to recognize and differentiate between open sequences.

4    Click the *Playing For Change_v2* sequence tab, and look at the image at the Tula marker. Then click the *Playing For Change* sequence tab and compare the same location.

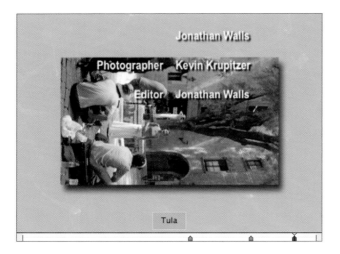

You have already added titles to this sequence, but you still have to resize the nest of still images and add a drop shadow. You'll see a few opportunities to create a split-screen effect between the performers to see them sing at the same time. To correct the photo of Tula, you will use the same set of motion parameters to rotate this image upright as you will to create the split-screen images.

**NOTE** ► In this sequence, each performer's clip has been placed on its own track, similar to the original *Playing For Change* workflow, to allow for the possibility of creating split screens.

5    Click the *Quest Speed_v2* tab, and play the sequence.

Notice that some clips play slower than usual, some play faster, and one freezes on an action.

**6**    When you've finished comparing these before-and-after sequences, close the three sequences that end in _v2. Your Timeline should resemble the following image:

> **TIP** ▶ In the Timeline, click the RT pop-up menu and choose Unlimited RT and Dynamic to see the highest number of speed changes in real time.

## Entering Speed Changes

Changing clip speed in Final Cut Pro is an easy task, and one that you can perform to address either a function or style issue. If your camera operator shot a zoom-out of someone's face, but you really want to see a zoom-in, you can play the clip in reverse. Or perhaps a *Quest* video shot falls short of covering a portion of the narrator's voiceover. Slowing down a clip lengthens it, making for an easy fix.

Changing speed can also add style to a sequence. In fact, many reality shows and dramas such as *Leverage* apply a speed change to a clip to transition from one scene to another, or to move the action forward.

There are several ways to change clip speed. You might enter a speed rate, or drag a clip using the Speed tool. In this exercise, you will change speed by entering information in the

Change Speed dialog. You also will use a *fit to fill edit* to automatically change the speed of a clip to fit into an existing space in the sequence. In the following exercise, you will focus on more manual, or *hands-on*, ways to change clip speed.

**1**  In the Timeline, click the orange *Quest Speed* sequence tab. At the end of the sequence, play the **sunset quest** clip under the "reverse" marker.

In dramatic material, zooming in to a clip often adds tension. In scenic material such as this, zooming out reveals more of the vista. To change the direction of a zoom, you can reverse the clip playback.

**2**  Select this clip, and choose Modify > Speed, or press Command-J.

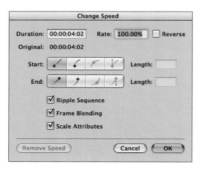

A Change Speed dialog opens with several attributes, including total clip duration, speed rate, and direction (reversed or not).

**3**  Select the Reverse checkbox, and note the color change in the Rate field. Click OK, and play this clip again. Then zoom in to the clip in the Timeline.

In the Change Speed dialog, when you select the Reverse checkbox, the number in the Rate field turns red to indicate that the clip will play in reverse.

In the Timeline, notice the *(–100%)* next to the clip name. The minus sign indicates that this clip is playing in reverse, and *100%* indicates that it's playing at 100 percent of its normal speed.

4   Move the playhead to the **my fall** clip, and play it. Notice the speed with which the whale emerges from the ocean.

5   Select the **my fall** clip and press Command-J. In the Change Speed dialog, enter *50* in the Rate field, and make sure the Ripple Sequence checkbox is selected. Click OK, and play this clip again.

Notice the *(50%)* reference next to the clip name to indicate the adjusted clip speed. Slowing this clip to 50 makes it twice as long and ripples the remaining video clips in the Timeline. Since this sequence is already the desired length, you don't want the speed change to ripple the sequence.

**TIP** ▶ When you are building a rough cut, or when sequence timing isn't already set, you may want to leave Ripple Sequence selected.

6   Press Command-Z to undo the last step. Select the **my fall** clip again, and press Command-J. In the Change Speed dialog, enter *50* in the Rate field, and deselect the Ripple Sequence checkbox. Click OK and play the clip.

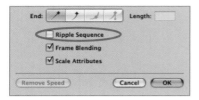

With Ripple Sequence deselected, the speed change is applied without rippling the other clips in the sequence, and the clip and sequence length remain unchanged.

**NOTE ▶** When playing a clip at a slower speed, you sometimes see a strobe or stuttering effect. Frame blending helps minimize this effect, which is why it's selected as a default option. When possible, it might be preferable to shoot the original footage in slow motion, making frame blending unnecessary.

**7** To access the Change Speed dialog a different way, Control-click the **fur** clip (under the 200% marker) and choose Change Speed. In the Change Speed dialog, enter *200* in the Speed percent field, and click OK. Play the clip.

This clip now plays at 200% from the first frame to the last. If you prefer to gradually ramp up to the speed change, creating a more subtle effect, you can use the Start and End buttons in the Change Speed dialog.

**8** Select the **fur** clip and press Command-J. In the Change Speed dialog, click the second Start button (Curve From Start). Then click the second End button (Curve to End). Click OK, and play the clip again.

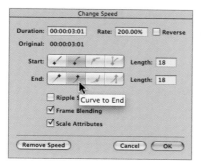

Clicking the Start and End Curve buttons provides a smooth transition into and out of the target speed. Curve From Start ramps up to the desired speed and Curve to End ramps down the speed just before the end of the clip.

**NOTE ▶** The default Start and End buttons—Linear From Start and Linear to End—indicate that no ramping has been applied.

Another way you can change clip speed is to edit a clip of one length into a sequence space of a different length. To do this, you use the fit to fill edit.

9    Move the playhead to the head of the **teachers** clip, and press X to mark this clip length. Play this clip, and then press F to load the master clip into the Viewer.

It would be nice to use the entire clip of the seal performing its fun activities, but without changing the length of the sequence. You can do this by making a fit to fill edit. The fit to fill edit changes the speed of the source content between its In and Out points to fit (or fill) the duration between the sequence's In and Out points.

**10** In the Viewer, press Option-X to remove the current In or Out points, and compare the Viewer duration with the Canvas duration.

The duration of this source clip is 17:18, whereas the duration of the clip in the Timeline is only 4:05. Using the fit to fill edit, Final Cut Pro will speed up the longer source clip to fit the entire 17:18 length into the 4:05 marked duration of the sequence.

**11** Drag the clip from the Viewer to the Fit to Fill section of the Canvas Edit Overlay. Play the new edit in the Timeline.

**TIP** To use fit to fill to cover several clips in a sequence, set an In and an Out point around the clips or area you want to fill, then mark and edit your source clip as a fit to fill edit.

## Using the Speed Tool

The Speed tool is another way to change the speed of a clip. It can be applied to an edit point between two adjacent clips. It can also be used to change the speed of a single clip on one side of an edit point.

Using the Speed tool is a much more hands-on approach to changing clip speed in that you don't enter a speed percentage or have Final Cut Pro automatically fit a clip to fill a space. Instead, you drag an edit point as though you were rolling it. You can also drag in a special area of the Timeline that creates speed keyframes.

**1**   Move the playhead to the "speed tool" marker and play the clips beneath it. Zoom in to this area of the Timeline.

The camera pan on the first clip is very slow, while the pan on the second clip is much faster. One way to use the Speed tool is to apply it to the edit point between two adjacent clips, as you would use the Roll tool. Dragging left or right makes one clip faster and the other clip slower.

**2**   In the Tool palette, hold the fifth tool (Slip) until the tool options appear beneath it, then click the third tool, or press SSS.

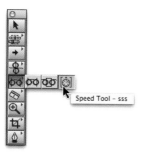

**3**   With the Speed tool, drag the edit point to the left until the information box displays "Time Delta: –01:00."

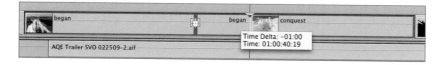

The Time Delta value is the amount you have rolled the edit point (1 second earlier), and the Time value is the new edit point location in the Timeline. When you release the edit point, the new speed percentages appear on the clips.

4   Play these clips again and notice the improved speed match.

With the Speed tool, you can also change the speed of a single clip in the sequence by pressing the Shift key while dragging.

5   In the Timeline, play the **wings** and **fins** clips. Zoom in to this area of the Timeline and notice that they are both playing at their normal speeds.

6   Position the Speed tool just to the right of the edit point, and Shift-drag the edit point to the left until the Time Delta is at about –20. Play the clips.

While the **fins** clip on the right changes speed, the adjacent **wings** clip on the left remains at its constant speed, but is shorter due to the rolling effect of the Speed tool.

7   To see a visual display of the speed changes, click the Clip Keyframes control in the Timeline, or press Option-T.

In the Timeline, a speed indicator area appears beneath the sequence clips. The tiny vertical bars are speed tick marks. When a clip is playing faster than normal speed, the tick marks are closer together. When the clip is playing slower, the tick marks are farther apart. When a clip is playing in reverse, the tick marks are red.

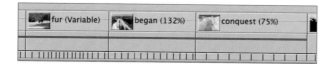

**NOTE ▶** When any motion parameter has been changed in a clip, a blue bar appears beneath the clip.

Notice the speed ticks beneath the **fur** clip. Choosing the Start and End options created a variable speed clip. You can also vary clip speed by dragging one of these tick marks with either the Speed tool or the Selection tool.

8  Press A to choose the Selection tool. Under the **survival** clip, move the pointer into the speed indicator area, snap the Pen tool to the "*speed ticks*" marker, and click.

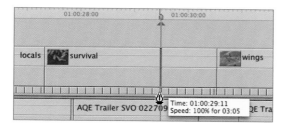

A keyframe appears among the tick marks where you clicked. Similar to the way the Speed tool adjusts clips at their combined edit points, the keyframe can be dragged left or right to change the speed on either side of the keyframe.

9  Move the pointer over the keyframe. When you see the point control (crosshair) appear, drag left until you see "Time: 01:00:28:00" in the information box, and play the clip again.

When you add speed keyframes to a clip, you create speed segments. You will work with speed segments in the next exercise.

**Take 2**

When the director screened the current *Quest Speed* sequence, he noticed that you made quite a few speed changes to the second half of the sequence, and none to the first half. He'd like to see more consistency throughout the sequence and asks you to make some changes. Try speeding up the boat in the **journey** clip and slowing down the **poets** clip. Then apply the Speed tool to the edit point between the first two clips.

## Creating a Freeze Frame

Another way to modify the speed of a clip is to stop the motion altogether and freeze a specific frame. This technique is applied frequently in television shows to freeze a shot before fading to black and going to commercial. While that's a style choice, freezing a shot can also help fix a problem by extending a too-short clip, for example, or keeping the audience from knowing that on the frame after the freeze, the camera fell off the tripod. Freeze frames can be created in the Timeline or in the Viewer and are given the default duration set in User Preferences. Since you changed that duration in the previous lesson when importing still images, let's begin by returning it to its default setting.

> **NOTE** ► In video, a freeze frame is actually created by repeating one frame over and over for a specific length of time. This process is handled automatically by Final Cut Pro.

1   In the Browser, in the Quest > Clips bin, open the **teachers** clip and move the playhead to the marker named "freeze frame." To create a freeze frame at this location, choose Modify > Make Freeze Frame, or press Shift-N.

A separate clip is created in the Viewer with a total length of 2 minutes and a marked duration. Notice the freeze frame name contains the timecode number where the freeze was created.

**TIP** ▶ If you wish to create several freeze frames of a specific duration, you can change the duration in the Still/Freeze area in the User Preferences > Editing tab, just as you did when importing still images.

You can now mark and edit this freeze frame into a sequence as you would any other clip; but be careful. When you create a freeze frame, it is held in the Viewer only until you open a different clip. If you want to save a freeze frame to edit later, you have to create a separate freeze frame clip by dragging the frame from the Viewer to the Browser.

2   In the Browser, Control-click the Quest > Clips bin, and from the shortcut menu, choose New Bin. Scroll to this bin, name it *Freeze Frames*, and click its disclosure triangle to see its contents.

3   Drag the **teachers 14:00:18:08** freeze frame image from the Viewer to the Freeze Frames bin you created in the Browser.

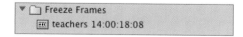

The freeze frame appears as a graphic icon, also used to represent other graphics files such as TIFF or JPEG images. This freeze frame is now its own master clip, which you can use throughout the editing process.

**TIP** ▶ To see the thumbnail images of these freeze frames, open the Freeze Frame bin and change it to icon view.

4   Repeat the process of creating a freeze and saving it (in steps 1 and 3) for the **poets** clip.

Oftentimes you think about creating a freeze frame only after a clip has been edited into the sequence. Sometimes you create a sequence freeze frame to stand alone, and other times you may want a clip to play and *then* to freeze action on a specific frame. You might call this a *run-and-freeze* effect.

Let's create a freeze frame of the whale and then create a run-and-freeze effect of the whale emerging from the ocean. As in the Viewer, you begin by positioning the play-head over the frame you want to freeze.

5   Drag the Timeline playhead to the "freeze frame" marker above the **my fall** clip. Choose Modify > Make Freeze Frame, or press Shift-N.

A 2-minute freeze frame appears in the Viewer with a marked duration, just as it did in the previous steps. In the Viewer title bar, the sequence name appears along with the sequence timecode of the frame. To save this freeze frame, you would drag it into the Freeze Frame bin as you did previously.

**NOTE** ▶ If the Auto Select control is turned off for the track you want to freeze, the command will not appear in the Modify menu.

To freeze the whale action in the sequence, you need to create a clip segment and then change the speed of that segment. Clip segments are created by setting speed keyframes in the clip.

**6**    In the speed indicator area, snap the pointer to the playhead, and when you see the Pen tool appear, click to add a keyframe at this location.

This additional keyframe creates a new clip segment that can be changed independently of any other segment or segments in this clip.

**7**    Control-click the clip segment to the right of the new keyframe, and choose Change Speed Segment.

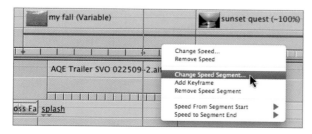

8   In the Change Speed Segment dialog, enter *0* in the Rate field, and click OK. Then play this clip.

When a clip is at 0 speed, no tick marks appear at that location.

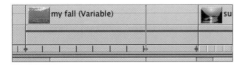

9   Click the Clip Keyframes control, or press Option-T, to hide the keyframe area.

## Changing Motion Parameters

In Final Cut Pro, every clip in your project has a set of default built-in motion parameters, such as size, position, crop, and rotate. All of these parameters can be changed and animated in the Motion tab in the Viewer. You might enlarge a clip and then reposition it to hide an unwanted element in the scene, such as a light or other piece of equipment. Or you might reduce the size of a clip so additional images can appear on the screen at the same time, creating a split-screen or multi-frame effect.

In this exercise, you will use the Motion tab and the Image+Wireframe mode to size, reposition, rotate, and crop images in two sequences you screened earlier in this lesson.

1   In the Timeline, click the *Playing For Change* sequence tab, and move the playhead to the Tula marker over the credit effect. Then double-click the **Photos NEST** clip to open it as its own sequence in the Timeline.

In the Timeline, you see the *Photos NEST* sequence with the individual photos. In the Canvas, you see the **6_Tula** image. Because the photo was shot as a vertical image, Final Cut Pro rotated it when it was imported. To use this clip in the credit effect, it has to be rotated, resized, and repositioned.

**2**    In the *Photos NEST* sequence, double-click the **6_Tula** image, and then click the Motion tab.

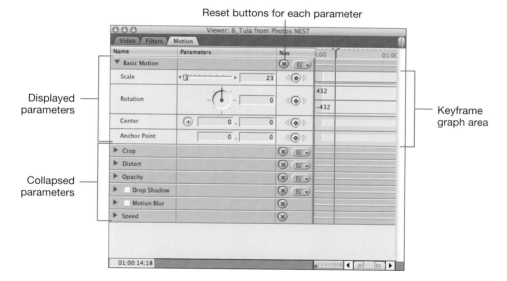

The Motion tab contains several motion attributes that can be accessed by clicking their disclosure triangles. Within the set of Basic Motion attributes are controls to resize (Scale) and reposition (Center) an image, rotate it, and change the pivot point around which the rotation occurs (Anchor Point).

**NOTE ▶** While most video clips are 100%, the current scale of this still image is 23%. When importing high-resolution still images, Final Cut Pro automatically resizes them to the sequence resolution.

**3**    Explore the Motion parameters by dragging the Rotation Angle control (the dial) to rotate the Tula image right side up. Adjust the Scale parameter to make the image fill the Canvas image area. Then click the Center point control (crosshair button) and reposition the image to reveal the production team in front of her.

> **TIP** ▶ An easy way to adjust a Motion wheel or slider is to position the pointer over it and drag the mouse ball or scroll wheel.

> **TIP** ▶ If you have several vertical images in your sequence, you can correct one, copy it, and use Paste Attributes to paste the entire set of Basic Motion parameters to the other clips.

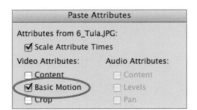

> **NOTE** ▶ To see the upright Tula image in the credit effect, in the Timeline, click the *Playing For Change* sequence tab. Changes made to the still image sequence are automatically updated in the parent sequence.

Rather than fix another image, let's use these and other motion parameters to create a split-screen effect. Split screens have been around since the early days of film, when two people were shown talking on the phone in the same frame. Today, you may see two, three, or even more images on the screen at the same time, and sometimes for the same reason, to cover a phone conversation.

However, sports shows might use the effect to compare athletes, while music videos could use it to show different performers playing at the same time. Some television action shows, such as  the Fox Network's *24*, use a multi-frame approach to show several actions occurring at the same time.

**4**    In the Timeline, click the *Quest Motion* sequence tab, and move the playhead to the first frame of the **teachers** clip beneath the "split screen" marker. Then double-click the **teachers** clip, and click the Motion tab.

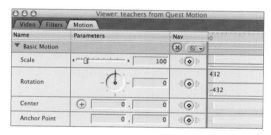

Notice the Scale of this clip is set to its default 100%, and the other Basic Motion parameters are at the default 0. This time, instead of changing the parameters in the Motion tab, you will use a manual approach and make changes directly to the image in the Canvas. To do this, you will access the Image+Wireframe mode.

**5**    In the Canvas, click the View pop-up menu and choose Image+Wireframe. You can also choose View > Image+Wireframe, or press W with the Timeline or the Canvas window active.

A large white X appears corner-to-corner over the image area, and a number appears at the center point, indicating the clip's track number.

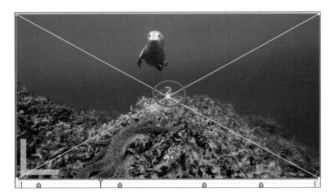

With the Image+Wireframe mode selected, and using just the default Selection tool, you can change several motion parameters in the Canvas by dragging specific areas of the wireframe image, called *handles*.

**6**   To explore changing motion parameters using the Image+Wireframe mode, try dragging different wireframe handles in the Canvas image:

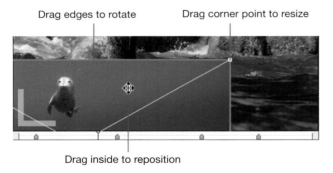

Drag edges to rotate          Drag corner point to resize

Drag inside to reposition

**NOTE** ▶ As you reposition or resize the upper V2 image, the V1 image beneath it becomes visible.

▶   Move the pointer into the Canvas image area, and when you see the Move pointer (Center handle), drag the image left, right, up, or down.

▶   Move the pointer over any one of the four corner points (Scale/Distort handles) of the wireframe. When the pointer changes to a crosshair, drag the handle inward or outward to change the clip's size.

▶ Move the pointer over the one of the vertical or horizontal edges (Rotational handles) of the image, and when you see the circular Rotate tool appear, drag the handle up or down to rotate the image.

**TIP** ▶ You can also zoom in to or out of an image in the Canvas (and Viewer) using the three-finger Multi-Touch gesture.

7 In the Viewer Motion tab, notice that the parameters reflect the changes you made to the Canvas image. Click the Reset button to return the clip to its default parameters.

**TIP** ▶ When resizing or repositioning an image, it may be helpful to see the image area along with the space around it. To zoom out, click the Canvas Zoom pop-up and choose a smaller percentage than the current percentage value. To return to the full screen image, press Shift-Z to select Fit to Window.

Zoom pop-up          Clip outline outside image area

8 Move the pointer into the Canvas image area, and Shift-drag the image to the left.

**TIP** ▶ Holding down Shift as you drag an image left, right, or up and down will confine the movement to a straight horizontal or vertical path.

As you move this clip to the left, you start to lose the seal, which is centered in the frame. To keep the seal in the frame, and allow room for the V1 clip on the right, you will have to crop the empty water on the right side of the image. You can crop the image in the Motion tab using sliders, or crop the image directly in the Canvas.

**9**   In the Tool palette, click the Crop tool (the eighth tool), or press C. In the Canvas, move the pointer over the right side of the image and drag the Crop handle left to hide this empty portion of water.

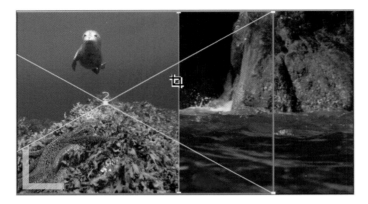

Now you're ready to apply similar changes to the V1 clip on the right. You can create a split screen in a number of ways, by overlapping the images or by allowing empty black space to show between them. Let's allow a little black space between the two images.

**10**   In the Timeline, click the **poets** clip, or click the image in the Canvas, to select it. Shift-drag right until you see the poet appear in the right side of the frame.

> **TIP** ▶ Remember to look for the track number in the center of the wireframe to make sure you're adjusting the correct image.

**11** With the Crop tool still selected, position it over the clip's left Crop handle and drag right to create some black space between the two images. Play the two images in the Timeline.

Building any type of effect requires finessing. But before you begin tweaking, there is a familiar aid you can access in the Canvas window to help you accurately position the images.

**12** In the Canvas window, click the View pop-up and choose Show Title Safe. Reposition each image so its action is contained within the action safe boundary. Doing this may require repositioning or even resizing an image.

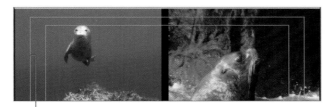

Action safe

**NOTE** ▸ If something in an image is important, such as a hand gesture or set decoration, make sure it's included inside the action safe boundary.

As you build these effects, you don't have to limit yourself to just two clips. You can literally fill the screen with smaller images to create a show open. Or you can arrange three or four clips on the screen to show what different characters—or animals—may be doing at the same time.

Another way to combine two images is to blend them by changing the opacity of the upper clip.

**13** In the Timeline, move the playhead to the "opacity" marker, and double-click the **going** clip. In the Motion tab, click the Opacity disclosure triangle, and drag the slider to 50.

As you play the clips in the Timeline, you see a blended image effect.

**TIP** ▶ You can also change clip opacity by turning on clip overlays in the Timeline and dragging the opacity overlay on a video clip.

Clip opacity can be changed in the Timeline or the Motion tab.

## Take 2

The director is very excited about creating split screens with the *Quest* footage but is hungry for more. In the *Quest Motion* sequence, change the motion parameters of the three clips under the "multi-frame effect" marker to combine them on the screen at the same time. You can refer to the *Quest Motion_v2* sequence to see one possible solution. And don't forget to add transitions to smooth a clip's entrance.

**NOTE ▶** It's very important not to increase the size of a video image too much. An adjustment under 20% is generally acceptable. When using low-resolution footage, or applying a greater increase in size, you may start to see pixilation in the image.

## Animating Motion Parameters

In addition to changing motion parameters, you can also set keyframes to animate motion parameters over time. One good use of this is to animate text to move on- and offscreen. Another use is to animate a clip to change size or position over time.

Animating a motion parameter requires at least two keyframes. You set one keyframe to identify the starting size or position of a clip. Then you move the playhead to a different timecode location and change that parameter. A new keyframe is automatically added.

**NOTE ▶** For this exercise, turn off Show Title Safe and Image+Wireframe (by choosing Image.) Press A to return to the default Selection tool, and make sure the Canvas zoom is set to Fit to Window.

1   In the Timeline, in the *Quest Motion* sequence, move the playhead to the "animate scale" marker, and double-click the **test skills** clip to open it in the Viewer.

**TIP** ▸ Whenever you open a clip from the Timeline in the following steps, click the Motion tab to access the clip's Motion parameters.

You will set keyframes in the **test skills** clip to zoom out or scale down from 100% to 0%, revealing the V1 clip beneath it. But first, let's expand the Viewer window to see the keyframe area.

2 To widen the Viewer window, drag the Viewer over the Browser, then snap the right boundary of the Viewer to the Canvas window.

Show/Hide keyframes pop-up menu

Keyframe navigation buttons

Keyframe graph area

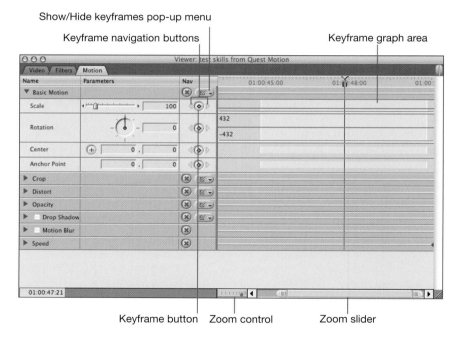

Keyframe button    Zoom control    Zoom slider

Each Basic Motion parameter has a keyframe button to set keyframes, and a keyframe graph where individual keyframes appear. The playhead moves in tandem with the Timeline playhead, and the Zoom control and Zoom slider help to focus on a specific area. The brighter portion of the graph represents the length of the sequence clip. You can zoom in to that area so it is prominent in the keyframe graph.

**NOTE** ▸ For this exercise, always keep the highlighted or brighter portion of the keyframe graph, which represents the clip length, in full view.

In the Canvas, you see the full-screen image. To set the starting keyframe, you need to position the playhead where you want the Scale parameter to start changing.

**3**  In the Scale parameter, click the Keyframe button.

A diamond-shaped keyframe is added to the green keyframe graph at this location, which sets the beginning scale for this clip. Now you're ready to set the second Scale parameter keyframe at the end of the clip.

**TIP** ▶ To enlarge the keyframe graph for a parameter, move the pointer over the bottom portion of the parameter boundary line and when the pointer turns into the Resize pointer, drag it down.

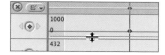

**4**  In the Timeline, move the playhead to the Out point of the **test skills** clip. In the Motion tab, drag the Scale slider to the left to 0 percent. Play the scale changes in the Timeline.

On the Scale keyframe graph, a new keyframe has been added automatically. When the playhead is directly over a keyframe, the diamond on the keyframe button is solid green. The arrows next to the keyframe button are keyframe navigation buttons, which become solid when there is a keyframe to which you can move forward or backward. You can also press Shift-K to move forward to a keyframe and Option-K to move backward to a keyframe.

**TIP** ▶ To delete a keyframe, move the playhead to that frame in the keyframe graph and click the keyframe button. The diamond on the keyframe button is no longer displayed as a solid green; it becomes hollow. You can also Control-click the keyframe and choose Clear from the shortcut menu.

Let's animate the V2 **Text** clip at the end of the sequence to move onto the screen. You will position the clip offscreen to set a starting keyframe, then move it onscreen to its final destination.

**TIP** ▶ For the following steps, turn on Image+Wireframe and change the Canvas zoom to see around the image area.

5   In the Timeline, play the **Text** clip at the end of the sequence. Move the playhead to the first frame of the clip, and double-click it to open the clip in the Viewer.

This text has a drop shadow added to it. As you learned in Lesson 11, the Drop Shadow parameter appears on the Motion tab.

6   In the Canvas, with Image+Wireframe selected, Shift-drag the text offscreen to the left until you no longer see the text letters.

Pressing Shift as you drag ensures that the text will move along a straight horizontal line.

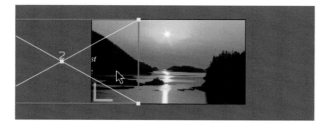

7   In the Motion tab, click the Center parameter Keyframe button to set a starting keyframe at this location.

In the Canvas, the center point becomes green, indicating that a keyframe is set at this location.

With the first keyframe set, you have a sort of tracking system in place. Whenever a parameter has a keyframe, a change to that parameter at any other location in the clip will automatically create another keyframe to indicate or track the change from the previous keyframe.

**TIP** ▸ Remember, keyframes mark an action at a specific timecode location, and the placement of the playhead determines that location.

8   In the Timeline, move the playhead forward 2 seconds to the final text destination. In the Canvas, Shift-drag the **Text** clip to the right until the full text appears centered in the frame. Or you can enter a 0 in the Center parameter fields in the Motion tab. Play the clip.

**NOTE** ▸ In the Center parameter, you will see a positive number if you move a clip horizontally to the right of center. If you move a clip to the left of center, you will see a negative number. The second field represents vertical movement: Upward movement shows as a negative number, and downward movement shows as a positive number.

As you drag, you see tick marks stretching from the first keyframe to the second. This is the *motion path* of this clip, which represents the clip's movement over time.

**TIP** ▸ To save a specific set of keyframes as a favorite, select the clip in the Timeline and choose Effects > Make Favorite Motion, or press Control-F. The motion will be saved in the Effects Favorites bin in the Browser. You can then drag this effect onto any clip in the Timeline.

**9** To display this text at an angle, drag the Rotation handle in the Canvas. If you want the clip to remain at this angle, there is no need to set keyframes for the Rotate parameter.

Depending on the computing power of your Mac, the clips in your sequence may become sluggish as you change the motion parameters and add additional effects. You can use a Final Cut Pro tool to preview effects or composite images in real time without rendering them.

**10** Choose Tools > QuickView, or press Option-8. In the QuickView window, adjust the Range slider to 4 seconds. Click the Play button.

QuickView will play slowly through the clips and cache the frames to your computer's RAM within the specified range. After caching the frames, it plays the clips in real time. You can also use this tool when you're zoomed in to an image to see how the final composition plays without changing the zoom level of the Canvas.

**TIP** If you want to animate text, It's very important that you change text size only in the Viewer Controls tab. When you adjust the Size parameter there, the text remains vector-based, and the quality remains high. When you enlarge text using the Scale slider in the Motion tab, the text becomes pixilated.

## Editor's Cut

In the *Playing For Change* sequence, there are several opportunities to create a split-screen effect with two performers. Remember, the clips must be stacked over each other in the Timeline to appear together on the screen. For these clips, you can create additional split-screen opportunities by extending some of the edit points to the left or right, over existing clips. If you want to create a split screen with only part of the clip, use the Razor Blade tool to divide the clip into segments. You can also try animating the clips on or off the screen.

If you would like to go further and create a composite of images like the image at the beginning of the chapter, open the **Photos NEST** clip, stack the clips on top of each other, then size and position your favorite stills around the screen. To practice speed changes, open the *Believe News* sequence and make changes to the video clips. You'll also find a few great opportunities to freeze a frame and to create a multi-frame effect.

## Lesson Review

1. In what menu do you choose Speed?

2. How can you tell if the speed of a sequence clip has been changed?

3. What type of edit can change clip speed automatically as you edit it into the Timeline?

4. Where does the Speed tool appear in the Tool palette?

5. When you create a freeze frame, does a new freeze frame clip appear in the Browser automatically?

6. How do you reveal the speed indicator area in the Timeline?

7. How can you create a speed segment in a clip?

8. Where do you access motion parameters?

9. How can you change motion parameters directly in the Canvas?

10. How can motion attributes be copied and pasted?

11. Where are motion keyframes set and adjusted?

12. What is a motion path?

13. What tool do you use to hide unnecessary portions of an image?

14. How is rotation measured in the Motion tab?

### *Answers*

1.  In the Modify menu.

2.  A speed percentage will appear next to the sequence clip name.

3.  A Fit to Fill edit.

4.  Under the Slip tool.

5.  No, but you can drag the freeze frame image from the Viewer to the Browser if you like.

6.  Click the Clip Keyframes control.

7.  Click in the speed indicator area with the Speed tool or the Selection tool to create a speed keyframe.

8.  In the Motion tab.

9.  Choose Image+Wireframe from the Canvas View pop-up menu.

10. Copy the clip and use the Paste Attributes window to paste specific attributes.

11. In the Motion tab keyframe graph area.

12. The path a clip moves along between two or more keyframes.

13. The Crop tool.

14. In degrees.

### Keyboard Shortcuts

| | |
|---|---|
| **C** | Select the Crop tool |
| **Command-J** | Open the Change Speed dialog |
| **Shift-K** | Move forward to next keyframe |
| **Option-K** | Move backward to previous keyframe |

## Keyboard Shortcuts

| | |
|---|---|
| **Shift-N** | Create freeze frame from playhead position |
| **SSS** | Select the Speed tool |
| **Option-T** | Toggle on clip keyframes |
| **W** | Toggle among Image, Image+Wireframe, and Wireframe modes |
| **Option-8** | Open the QuickView tab |
| **Control-F** | Save Motion effect to the Favorites bin in the Effects tab |

# 13

**Lesson Files**   FCP7 Book Files > Lessons > Lesson 13 Project

**Media**   FCP7 Book Files > Media > Quest; Playing For Change; Imports

**Time**   This lesson takes approximately 60 minutes to complete.

**Goals**   Apply audio and video filters

View and modify filters

Apply filters for image correction

Apply filters to multiple clips

Use tools to adjust filters

Animate filters using keyframes

# Applying Filters

In Final Cut Pro, effects are divided into two groups: transitions and filters. Unlike transitions, which are applied to the edit point between two clips, filters are applied to the content, or body, of a clip. Filters are like rose-colored glasses. When you put them on, you see things differently. Some filters create illusions, transforming images into a kaleidoscope of colors or a dizzying array of lights. Other filters conceal their effects—correcting the color of an image or changing the direction someone is facing—so that most viewers don't even know a filter was applied.

Like motion effects, filters serve both style and function. In this lesson, you will apply filters to create visual magic and to correct or improve some aspect of an image. You'll also share filters with other clips and animate them.

A filter converted the original colors into vector colors.

## Evaluating a Project for Effects

Typically, you'll add filters during the finishing stage of a project, sometimes to make images stand out visually, and other times to correct them. In the following exercises, filters are added to two completed sequences to refine their look and sound. Let's start by examining some before-and-after examples.

1   Open the FCP7 Book Files > Lessons > Lesson 13 Project file, and close any other open projects.

2   In the Timeline, click the *Quest Filters* sequence tab, and play the sequence.

This sequence contains several speed changes similar to those you created in the previous lesson. When finishing a project, you often work with motion properties and filters together to create the desired effect. You will use this sequence to apply filters and give each clip a different visual style.

**TIP** ▶ To play as many real-time effects as possible, click the RT pop-up menu in the Timeline and choose Unlimited RT and Dynamic.

3   Play the section under the "two filters" marker and notice that the narrator's audio level is low. You will apply audio filters to change this clip's volume and add an effect.

4   Play the *Quest Filters_v2* sequence.

The filters applied to the clips in this sequence are fanciful and bring some fun to the images. Adding a different filter to each clip in this situation is a good way to preview filter effects.

5   In the Timeline, click the *Playing For Change_v2* sequence tab, and play a portion of
the credit effect.

You've resized, repositioned, and added a drop shadow to this image nest. To put the
finishing touches on the effect, you will apply two filters: a border that encases the
images, and a widescreen matte that crops the top and bottom of the color matte so
that it conforms to the other clips in the sequence.

6   In the Timeline and Canvas windows, position the sequence tabs as they appear in the
following image. Since you won't be editing the *_v2* sequences, you can either close
them, or leave them open as a reference.

## Applying and Viewing Video Filters

If you're comfortable applying transitions, then you already know how to apply a filter.
You can drag a filter from the Video Filters bin in the Effects tab and apply it directly to
a clip in the Timeline. Or, you can select, or *target*, the clip in the Timeline and choose a
filter from the Effects menu. Filters are applied in the Viewer or the Timeline.

In this exercise, to acquaint you with some of the filters used to create style, you will apply
a variety of filters to clips in the *Quest Filters* sequence. Each of these filters can be modified, as you'll learn in the next exercise.

> **TIP** ▶ Additional filters from Apple's Motion application are accessible in the Effects
> menu and the Effects tab. To see only the Final Cut Pro filters you need for this lesson,
> choose Effects > Effect Availability > Only Recommended Effects.

**1** In the Timeline, click the *Quest Filters* sequence tab, and move the playhead to the
first clip, **pw sound**.

As when placing transitions, selecting a clip targets it, and parking the playhead on
the clip allows you to see in the Canvas how that clip is changed as you apply or
modify a filter.

**2** Choose Effects > Video Filters, and scroll through some of the categories in the
submenu.

Each filter has a submenu. From the names of the filter categories, you can anticipate
that some filters might add an interesting visual effect to a clip, whereas others might
be used to correct images. Let's apply a Viewfinder filter to the selected clip.

**3**   Choose Effects > Video Filters > Video > Viewfinder, and play the clip.

**NOTE** ► When you apply a filter in the Timeline, you are not changing the master clip in the Browser or the media file on your hard disk; you are changing only the sequence clip.

This filter creates the illusion that you are seeing the image through a video camera's viewfinder.

Look at the Timeline ruler. If an orange render bar appears above this clip, the clip will play in real time but may drop frames during playback. If the render bar is red, the clip must be rendered to play in real time. You can also press Option-P to preview the effect, but not in real time.

**NOTE** ► Clicking the Track Visibility controls to disable tracks in the Timeline will delete any render files for that track.

**4**   Move the playhead to the third clip, **journey**. Choose Effects > Video Filters > Blur > Radial Blur, and play the clip.

This filter creates a swirling vortex around the center of the image, as though the boat were swept up in the Bermuda Triangle. In the next lesson, you will change the center of the effect to be the boat itself.

Now let's add a filter by dragging it from the Effects tab.

**5**   Move the playhead to the second clip, **fishing**. In the Browser, click the Effects tab, display the contents of the Video Filters bin, and then display the Tiling bin contents.

**NOTE ▶** All filter icons look the same regardless of how a specific filter affects a clip.

**6**   Drag the Kaleidoscope filter to the **fishing** clip, but don't release the mouse button yet.

When you drag a filter to apply it, a brown boundary appears around the entire clip.

**7**   Release the mouse button, and play the clip. This filter turns the pink and gold colors of the fish into an interesting kaleidoscopic image, which could even be used as the background for a title.

8   In the Effects tab, close the Tiling bin, and display the Stylize filters. Notice the different Stylize filter names. Drag the Replicate filter to the fourth clip in the sequence, **teachers**, and play the clip.

The Stylize filters provide a number of ways you can change a clip's look or style. You can create a noisy looking image, make it look like bad TV, convert the image to line art, or alter the colors to create a solarized effect. The default Replicate filter creates two images across and two down.

9   In the Effects tab, from the Stylize bin, drag the Vignette filter to the fifth clip, **poets**. While this filter is initially subtle, you can change its parameters to create a cameo of the subject.

Filters can be copied and pasted from one clip to another, and applied to a group of clips at one time. Since the **wings**, **fins**, and **fur** clips are grouped together around the narration, let's apply the same filter to all three clips.

**10** Beneath the "wings" marker, select the **wings**, **fins**, and **fur** clips. In the Effects tab, close the Stylize bin, and display the Perspective filters. Drag the Mirror filter to any one of the selected clips in the sequence.

**11** Deselect these clips, and play them.

Now all three clips have the same visual style, or treatment.

**12** Select the **began** clip beneath the "two filters" marker. Choose Effects > Video Filters > Perspective > Basic 3D. (You won't see any change until you adjust this filter's parameters.) To apply a second filter, choose Effects > Video Filters > Border > Bevel.

Sometimes, a filter won't change the look of a clip until the filter parameters are altered from their default settings. In the next exercise, you will make changes to this Basic 3D filter and modify its effect on the Bevel filter.

**NOTE** ▶ Any number of filters can be added to any type of clip, including text, audio, and graphics. It might take several filters to create a desired effect. Or you might try multiple filters to preview or compare one filter with another.

## Take 2

The *Quest* director just stepped out of the edit bay. Little does she know you've been moonlighting as an editor for *Playing For Change*. Since you've just added a Bevel border to the *Quest Filters* sequence, take a moment to apply the same filter to the image nest in the *Playing For Change* sequence in the Timeline. Applying this filter to the nest—rather than to each individual image—should make you appreciate nesting even more.

**TIP** ▶ To apply the most recently used filter, choose Last–[effect name] from the top of the Effects menu. You can also create a Last Effect button in one of the button bars.

## Viewing and Modifying Filter Parameters

Every filter has a set of parameters you can modify to fine-tune its effect. These parameters appear in the Viewer within the Filters tab. Here you can modify parameters, delete the filter, turn it off or on (to compare the clip with and without the effect), or save it as a favorite.

You can also specify the priority of filters, which can change the overall look of the clip. But before you can make any of these changes, you need to open the clip into the Viewer from the Timeline.

1   In the *Quest Filters* sequence, position the playhead over the **teachers** clip. To replicate more seagoing teachers in the image, double-click the clip to open it in the Viewer, and click the Filters tab.

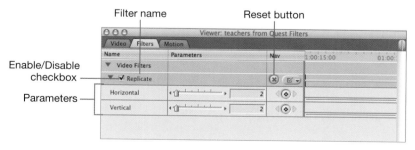

All filter parameters have default settings. You modify filter parameter settings as you modify motion effects settings: using sliders, dial controls, and numerical fields. In addition, some filters use color pickers for color selection.

**2**  In the Horizontal field, enter *4*, and in the Vertical field, enter *3*. Press Tab or Return, and play the clip again. Now you see an even dozen smart seals.

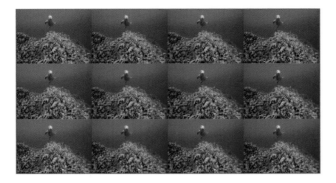

**NOTE** ▶ With the Filters tab active in the Viewer, you can double-click another clip, and that clip will open with the Filters tab active.

**3**  Move the playhead to the **poets** clip, and double-click it to open it in the Viewer. Explore this Vignette filter by changing the Size to 1, Blur Amount to 8, and Darken to 0.5. Experiment with the Fallout parameter to see how it highlights the poet seal.

**TIP** ▶ To change a filter parameter using a scroll mouse, position your pointer over a slider or dial control and rotate the mouse wheel or ball up and down. When entering a value in a parameter field, don't forget to press Tab or Return to see the result of your entry in the Canvas window.

**4**  To see this clip without the filter, deselect the Vignette filter checkbox to turn off the filter. Then turn it back on.

Turning a filter off and on does not delete it from the clip. It simply allows you to view the clip before and after the filter is applied.

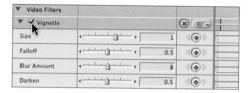

After you've modified a filter, you can save it as a favorite and apply its specific attributes to other clips in any open project.

**5**   In the Viewer, choose Effects > Make Favorite Effect, or press Option-F. In the Browser Effects tab, reveal the contents of the Favorites bin. Change the name of this favorite filter to *poet vignette*.

**NOTE ▸** You can also make a favorite effect from the Timeline by selecting a sequence clip, and choosing Effects > Make Favorite Effect, or pressing Option-F.

**TIP ▸** You can apply a favorite by dragging it to the Timeline or choosing it from the Effects menu. You can also access favorites by using keyboard shortcuts, which are based on the order each effect appears in the Favorites bin.

**6**   Move the playhead to the **journey** clip, and double-click it. If necessary, click the Filters tab. To position the radial blur directly over the boat, click the Center point control. In the Canvas, click the boat.

You might modify a filter's parameters differently for one project than you would for another project. Sometimes, just experimenting with a filter's parameters is a good way to become familiar with how you might use it elsewhere.

**7** Move the playhead to the first clip, **pw sound**, and open it in the Viewer. Explore this filter by changing the mode, font, size, and color of the text. If you want to revert to the default settings, click the red Reset button.

In the previous exercise, you applied two filters to one clip to create a special effect. Let's explore how these filters will affect the image when you change the parameter settings and the order in which they are applied.

**8** In the Timeline, move the playhead to the "two filters" marker, and double-click the **began** clip. To first focus on the Basic 3D filter changes, deselect the Bevel filter check-box, and click the disclosure triangle to hide its parameters.

**TIP** A good way to sample or "shop" for the best filter is to apply several filters to a clip, then enable them one at a time and see how each looks in the Canvas.

**9** In the Basic 3D parameters, change the X axis Rotation to –35, the Y axis Rotation to 50, and the Scale to 85. Then center the clip in the frame.

The first filter that you apply always appears at the top of the filter list, followed by the other filters in the order in which they are applied. When you add one filter after another, there is a cumulative effect in which the most recent filter affects not only the clip but also any other filters added before it.

**10** Select the Bevel filter checkbox.

Because the Bevel filter was applied *after* the Basic 3D filter, it was not altered when you changed the Basic 3D parameters. To include the Bevel filter in the 3D changes, you must reposition the filter order on the clip.

**11** Drag the Bevel filter name above the Basic 3D filter. When a dark bar appears above the Basic 3D filter, release the mouse button.

When the Bevel filter is positioned above the Basic 3D filter, the 3D changes are applied to the original image *and* the bevel border.

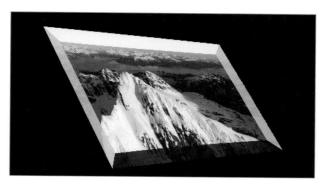

Once you modify one or more filters, you may want to copy and paste them to another clip, such as the scenery shot that follows.

**12** Select the **began** clip and press Command-C to copy it. Control-click the **conquest** clip, and from the shortcut menu, choose Paste Attributes. In the Paste Attributes dialog, select the Filters checkbox, and click OK. Play these two clips.

**TIP** ▶ To preview filter changes on the fly, you can use the QuickView tab. As you preview the effect, you can enable and disable individual filters in the Viewer Filters tab to see which filters suit your clip and which do not. You can even make changes to filter parameters as QuickView plays the clip. This is a helpful way to preview filters that may require rendering or that don't play every frame in real time.

Now that you're comfortable applying filters, take a moment to try the different ways to delete one or more filters. You can press Command-Z to restore a deleted filter.

To delete a single filter, do one of the following:

▶ Click its name in the Filters tab and press Delete.

▶ Control-click the filter name and choose Cut from the shortcut menu.

To remove all video filters from a clip:

▶ Click Video Filters to select them, and press Delete.

## Take 2

The director has been having fun sampling filter effects with you. But when she receives a call that the producer wants to see the finished effects right away, she dashes off a quick to-do list and leaves the room so you can work.

Apply the filters to the clips below and modify them as needed. If the director hasn't returned by the time you've finished the *Quest* filters, move on to *Playing For Change* to complete the credit effect.

*Quest Filters* sequence:

▶ **locals**—Distort > Ripple

▶ **test skills**—Stylize > Find Edges, and Perspective > Flop

▶ **my fall**—Stylize > Relief

▶ **sunset quest**—Stylize > Vectorize Color

**NOTE** ▶ You can change a camera zoom to perform a pull-out instead of a push-in by reversing the clip's playback direction. You can also correct camera framing by applying the Flop filter to change the direction a subject is facing.

*Playing For Change* sequence:

▶ **Color**—Matte > Widescreen (Type = 1.70:1)

**TIP** ▶ You change filter parameters for a nest in the Viewer as you would change parameters for clips. However, to open a nest into the Viewer, hold down Option and double-click the nest.

## Applying Audio Filters

Once the audio tracks of your sequence are mixed together, they often go unnoticed until the final output. But there will be times when you need to improve or correct a clip's sound or add an audio effect before putting the project to bed.

In this exercise, you will apply two filters to one clip. One filter will improve the clip's volume level, and another will create the illusion of someone speaking in a stadium.

You will also combine a few basic Final Cut Pro functions to make previewing an effect more efficient. Audio filters are applied just like video filters, by dragging them from the Effects tab or choosing them from the Effects menu.

1   In the *Quest Filters* sequence, play the area beneath the "two filters" marker and focus on the volume of the narration clip, **AQE Trailer VO 4**. Then position the playhead on the "two filters" marker, and deselect any selected clips in the Timeline.

> **TIP** ▶ If a red audio render line appears in the Timeline ruler above these audio tracks, open User Preferences, and in the General tab, change Real-time Audio Mixing to 12 tracks. If the red line is still present, raise that number, or render the clip.

The volume of this clip seems lower than the other narration clips and doesn't pop above the music and sound effects. Let's start by raising the volume of this clip in the Timeline.

2   To display the clip overlays, press Option-W. Drag the audio level overlay for this clip to its highest level (12 dB). Turn off the clip overlays and play the clip again.

When raising the level of a clip still doesn't give you the volume you want, you can apply a Gain filter to boost the volume even more. But you have to be careful you don't add the filter to all the clips beneath the playhead.

3   Choose Effects > Audio Filters > Final Cut Pro > Gain. Double-click the **AQE Trailer VO 4** clip to open it in the Viewer, and click the Filters tab to see the Gain filter. In the Timeline, double-click the **wind** sound effect clip (beneath the narration clip). Notice it too has a Gain filter.

When clips are stacked on multiple tracks in the Timeline, the audio or video filter will be placed on all clips beneath the playhead unless either the target clip is selected or the Auto Select controls are turned off for the other tracks. You can turn off all audio or video Auto Select controls at one time by using the Option key.

4    Press Command-Z to undo the previous step and deselect the Timeline clips. In the Timeline patch panel, Option-click the A1 Auto Select control to turn off the other audio tracks, and deselect the clips in the Timeline.

5    Choose Effects > Last – Gain. Double-click the narration clip to open it in the Viewer, and click the Filters tab.

In an earlier lesson, you modified a clip by choosing Apply Normalization Gain in the Modify > Audio menu. When you choose this command, Final Cut Pro automatically adds a Gain filter with an adjusted gain level. In this step, you are manually applying this filter and will manually make any adjustments.

Before you begin changing the Gain level, there are a few Final Cut Pro functions you can engage to make this process more efficient.

6    In the Timeline, turn off the V1 Auto Select control. With the playhead over the **AQE Trailer VO 4** clip, press X to mark the length of this audio clip.

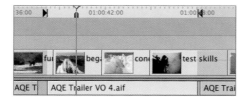

With the Auto Select control turned off for the V1 track—which is the priority track—Final Cut Pro looks to the A1 clip and marks the length of that clip. With this clip marked, you can loop the playback between the In and Out points, giving you more preview time to adjust the level.

**7**    Choose View > Loop Playback, or press Control-L. Press Shift-\ (backslash) to play the clip. Move your pointer into the Viewer and over the Gain (dB) level slider. You can drag the slider or use a mouse scroll wheel or scroll ball to adjust the volume on the fly.

Combining these two functions allows you to focus on getting the correct volume rather than pressing Shift-\ (backslash) over and over again.

As with video filters, you can also drag an audio filter from the Effects tab in the Browser. When you apply a filter by manually dragging it to a clip, the Auto Select controls have no effect.

**8**    In the Browser, click the Effects tab, and display the contents of the Audio Filters bin, then display the contents of the Final Cut Pro audio filters. The audio filter icon looks like a speaker with a filter overlay.

When the clip you want to apply a filter to is open in the Viewer, you can drag a filter from the Effects tab directly to the Viewer.

**9**    Drag the Reverberation filter to the Viewer Filters tab. When you see the black outline appear, release the mouse button. Press Shift-\ (backslash) to play from the In to the Out.

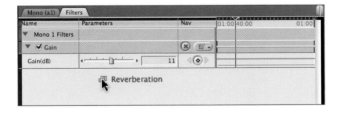

**NOTE** ▸ Once a clip is selected or opened in the Viewer, you can apply a filter from the Effects menu without applying it to the other clips in the Timeline stack.

The narrator now sounds as though he's showing the *Quest* trailer to a large crowd. Final Cut Pro has an assortment of audio filters that allow you to improve a clip's sound or, in this case, change it altogether.

The Reverberation filter has four parameters and several types of reverb effects. Let's apply a different type of reverberation.

**10** As the narration clip is playing, from the Type pop-up menu, choose a different reverb type. You can continue to choose reverb types as the clip is playing to audition the effect of each. When you've selected a type, adjust the other Reverberation parameters as the clip plays.

As you adjust one filter or another, it may be distracting to hear the background music and sound effects. With the narration clip selected in the Timeline, a simple shortcut will solo that clip.

**11** Make the Timeline window active. With the narration clip selected, press Control-S to solo that clip. Any clip that overlaps that clip is now muted. Press Shift-\ (backslash) again and make any necessary adjustments to the Gain or Reverberation filters.

**NOTE ▶** You can save an adjusted audio filter as a favorite just as you would save a video filter. When more than one filter is applied to a clip, however, all the audio or video filters are saved together as a set, placed in a bin, and given the sequence name. You can drag this bin to any clip or group of clips if you want to apply the entire set of filters.

After changing settings for a particular purpose, it's always a good idea to return to your default configuration. For now, let's turn off some of the functions you used in this exercise.

**12** To turn off looped playback, press Control-L. In the Timeline, remove the edit points, turn on the Auto Select controls for all tracks, and press Control-S to turn Solo off on the selected narration clip. Press Option-W to turn off the clip overlays.

**TIP** You can also Option-click deselected Auto Select controls to select them.

## Take 2

You know the director likes to have fun while editing, but you're not quite sure she'll go for the narration sounding as if it was recorded in a tunnel. Choose Reverberation settings you think the director will like, and copy that filter to the other narration clips in the sequence.

## Using a Color Correction Filter

While some productions may have the time to set and adjust lights, which will ensure a high-quality video image, others must shoot on the fly with very little, if any, camera setup or lighting support. In these situations, you often have to capture the existing footage and later worry about improving the video quality or, as they say, "fix it in post."

There are several video filters available that can correct a clip's color or otherwise improve its look. These filters can change the color balance of an image, adjust the luminance and black levels, add more color, or remove color entirely. Before you make color adjustments to a clip, let's review a few basic color principles.

### Understanding Color Basics

Video is an additive color system, meaning that all colors added together will create white. So your reference to white is very important. For example, if you white-balance your camera for indoor lighting, and then shoot outdoors, the outdoor footage won't be color balanced because the camera's indoor reference to white will not match the white in the outdoor scene. If your white balance is off, the overall balance of colors in the image will be off as well.

Another aspect of color correction is the *hue* of the image. Hue is the color itself, sometimes represented by a name but most often represented by a number on a 360-degree color wheel. Each color appears at a different location around the wheel. For instance, the three primary colors in video are red, green, and blue, and they fall at 0 degrees, 120 degrees, and 240 degrees, respectively.

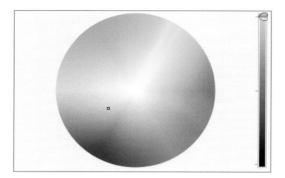

Some color wheels display more than just the hue. They also reflect the *saturation* of a color. Saturation is the amount of color, or *chroma,* in an image. For all colors, 0 percent saturation shows the color as white. If red is fully saturated at 100 percent, decrease the saturation to 50 percent and you will get rose. Decrease it to 25 percent and you will get pink. Each of these colors is part of the red family in that they share the same hue but not the same level of saturation.

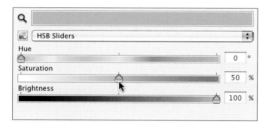

The brightness, or *luminance,* of an image is the amount of lightness or darkness present. A 100 percent value is the highest or brightest level, whereas a 0 percent value is black, regardless of the hue or saturation.

### Using the Color Corrector 3-Way Filter

Final Cut Pro includes several filters that you can apply to correct or adjust the color in an image. Each offers a different approach to achieve similar results. For example, you could choose the Image Control > Proc Amp filter, which has parameters similar to the controls on a professional videotape recorder (VTR). Or from the Image Control category, you could choose Brightness and Contrast, or Levels, to adjust those aspects of your clip.

However, Final Cut Pro includes a general all-purpose filter to color-correct an image, and it is a real-time effect: the Color Corrector 3-way filter. In these exercises, to understand how to apply a color-correcting filter, you will perform a basic white-balance correction by changing the bluish tint in one of the *Quest* clips.

> **NOTE ▶** Color-correcting a video image is a comprehensive subject. For high-level professional color correction, you can send a clip or sequence to Apple's Color application, which is part of Final Cut Studio.

1  In the *Quest Filters* sequence, move the playhead to the "color correct" marker. Double-click the **fins** clip to open it into the Viewer. Click the Filters tab.

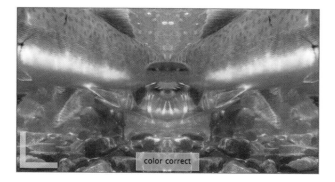

The source clip has a bluish tint because in some situations, such as shooting underwater, the lighting can be difficult or even impossible to control.

2  Choose Effects > Video Filters > Color Correction > Color Corrector 3-way.

The Color Corrector 3-way filter appears in the Filters tab, but the parameter details are not in view. Instead, you see a button named Visual and a separate tab called Color Corrector 3-way.

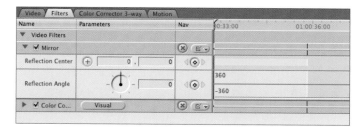

**3**   Click the disclosure triangle next to the Color Corrector 3-way checkbox, and drag the vertical scroller down to see all the parameters. Then click the disclosure triangle again to hide those parameters.

These parameters control the color of an image, but there is a much easier approach—a more *visual* approach—to adjusting this filter.

**4**   Click the Visual button next to the Color Corrector 3-way name, or click the Color Corrector 3-way tab.

Although this filter is very complex and has lots of parameters, it also has a streamlined visual interface. Working within the visual interface lets you focus on the look of the image without getting distracted by the numeric interface.

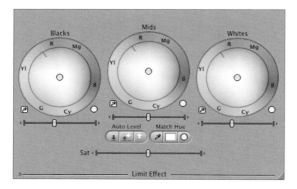

In the visual display, the Color Corrector 3-way filter has three color balance controls—Blacks, Mids, and Whites—which modify the color balance in those ranges. The sliders beneath the balance controls set the brightness levels in the image pixels within each range. The Sat (saturation) slider beneath the balance controls increases or decreases the amount of color in the image.

One way to improve the color of the **fins** clip is to reset (or redefine) what true white is in the clip's image.

**5**   Under the Whites balance control, click the small Auto-Balance eyedropper.

With the eyedropper, you can select a new white reference from the image in the Canvas. The belly of the fish in the clip will make a good reference to true white.

**6**  In the Canvas, click in a white area of the fish belly.

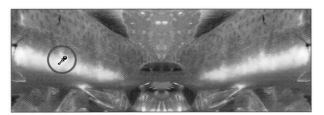

All the colors are rebalanced and the image looks as though the white you clicked was true white. Look at the Whites balance control. The indicator in the center of the wheel has moved away from blue and toward yellow and red to represent the new color balance of the image.

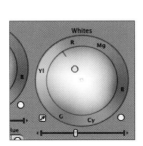 

**TIP** ▶ When adjusting color balance controls, Command-drag to more quickly move the balance control indicator. To reset a color balance control to its default setting, click the Reset button at the lower right of the wheel.

**7**  Select and deselect the Enable/Disable checkbox so that you can see the image with and without the Color Corrector 3-way filter applied. Leave the filter enabled.

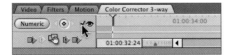

**TIP** ▶ Adjusting the Mids slider is a good way to bring out more detail in an image that is too dark or underexposed, or to remove the washed-out effect of an over-exposed image.

Just changing the white balance for this image has improved it considerably. Sometimes, when you're adjusting a clip's color, you may simultaneously want to compare the image with and without the filter applied. You can use the Frame Viewer to do so.

8   Choose Tools > Frame Viewer, or press Option-7. When the tool opens in the Tool Bench window, reposition the window over the Browser.

**NOTE** ▶ The Tool Bench window is placed over the Viewer or at the last position it was used in the interface. You may not see the same frame as in the preceding figure.

The Frame Viewer displays a clip in a split-screen before-and-after configuration. You can choose what you want to see on each side of the frame and easily compare one clip with another or compare one clip with and without its applied filters.

9   In the lower left of the window, click the Frame Viewer pop-up menu, and choose Current Frame, if it's not already selected. From the pop-up menu to the right, choose Current w/o Filters.

In this view, you see the color-corrected fish image on the left and the original, uncorrected image on the right.

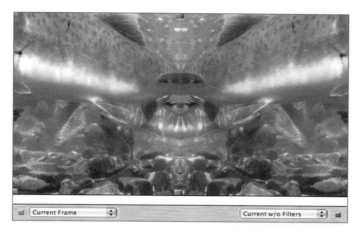

**NOTE** ▶ You can click the V-Split (Vertical), Swap, or H-Split (Horizontal) split-screen buttons to divide the frame differently or to swap the image locations. You can also choose Tools > Video Scopes, or press Option-9, to see the image displayed on a video scope.

**MORE INFO** ▶ In Lesson 14, you will use video scopes to measure the video signal.

Since the color filter change was so effective on this clip, you can save the filter as a favorite to apply to other bluish underwater clips in this project.

**10** Close the Tool Bench window. In the Viewer, drag the Drag Filter icon to the Favorites bin in the Effects tab. Rename this filter *blue fish correction*.

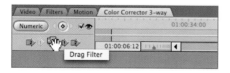

**TIP** ▶ You can apply the Color Corrector 3-way filter with these settings to a different clip in this or another sequence. To use this filter, drag the Drag Filter icon to the target clip.

## Animating Filters

If you want to change a filter parameter over time, you can animate that parameter by adding keyframes, just as you did when animating motion parameters. Sometimes animating filters supports a visual style you're creating, and sometimes it provides dynamic correction that a shot needs.

For example, you may have a clip that doesn't require color correction throughout the entire clip, but does require correction at the end or beginning. You can animate the color correction to start in one location and stop or change at another location.

In the *Quest Filters* sequence, you will add filters and animate some of the filter parameters to begin a clip in black-and-white and gradually fade to its normal color. Television programs often use this style when going in or out of commercial breaks.

> **NOTE** ▶ If you've applied all the filters throughout this lesson, you can continue working with the *Quest Filters* sequence. If not, open the *Quest Filters_v2* sequence to perform the next exercise. To review the results of this exercise, open and play the *Quest Filters_v3* sequence.

1   In the Timeline, double-click the **pw sound** clip to open it in the Viewer. Choose Effects > Video Filters > Image Control > Desaturate. If necessary, click the Filters tab.

In the Canvas, you see a black-and-white image. The Desaturate filter can remove some or all of a clip's color. At 100%, which is this filter's default, the clip is completely desaturated, or 100% without color. At 0%, no desaturation is present, and the clip appears with its original saturation levels.

You also see a black-and-white viewfinder because the Desaturate filter was added after that filter. It would be nice if the color came back to the image after a few seconds, and if the viewfinder were not desaturated.

2   In the Viewer Filters tab, drag the Desaturate filter above the Viewfinder filter. In the Timeline, move the playhead to the head of the clip.

This is where you will begin to return the color to the image, and where you will place your first keyframe. Notice the cyan marker in the Viewer Filters tab. Both clip and Timeline markers appear here as references. You will use the cyan marker as the target for your second keyframe.

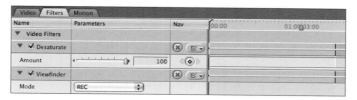

**TIP** ▶ When adding keyframes in the Viewer, you can expand the window to see more of the keyframe graph area, as you did when setting motion keyframes. You can also zoom in to the area and increase the height of an individual parameter graph.

3   Click the Amount parameter's Keyframe button. Move the playhead to the "animate" marker, and drag the Amount slider to its center position, 0, and play the clip.

Since you have a starting keyframe, changing the value at a different timecode location automatically adds a new keyframe. Now the clip's color saturation changes over time.

In the keyframe graph of the Filters tab, notice the blue keyframe references on the Desaturate line. These blue keyframes provide an additional reference should you need to add keyframes to other filters at the same locations. Let's add a blur to this image and use the blue keyframes as a reference to place additional keyframes.

> **TIP** ▶ When several filters are placed on a clip, it's helpful to hide the parameters of those filters you've already changed.

**4**  Click the disclosure triangles on the Desaturate and Viewfinder filters. Choose Effects > Video Filters > Blur > Gaussian Blur. Change the Radius amount to 30, and play the clip. To keep from blurring the viewfinder, drag the Blur filter above the Viewfinder filter.

**5**  In the Filters tab, move the playhead to the first blue keyframe, if necessary, and click the Keyframe button for the Gaussian Blur Radius parameter. Then reposition the playhead to the second blue keyframe, and change the Radius to 0. Play the new opening.

Now you can see the combined visual effect of the image gradually coming into focus and color at the same time. The viewfinder, however, is in color and focus throughout the effect because you positioned it as the last filter.

Some filters have a Mix parameter, where you can set what percentage of the original image you want to mix with the filter. When you animate this parameter, it allows you to *dissolve* the filter into the image to create a different-looking effect.

**6**  In the Timeline, move the playhead to the first frame of the third clip, **journey**, and double-click to open it in the Viewer. In the Filters tab, click the Keyframe button for the Mix parameter, and change the parameter to 0.

When the Mix parameter is at 0, you will see 0 percent of the applied filter. When the Mix parameter is at 100, you see 100 percent of the filter.

7    In the Timeline, move the playhead to the last frame of the **journey** clip. In the Viewer Filters tab, change the Mix parameter to 100. The second keyframe is automatically added. Play the clip.

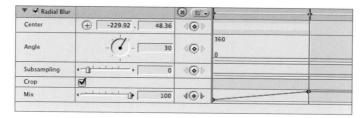

As with audio keyframes, you can reposition filter keyframes by dragging them left or right. If you drag up or down, you will change the amount of the filter or parameter.

8    In the Filters tab, drag the second Mix keyframe to the left about 1 second, and replay the clip. Now the filter is mixed into the image 100% 1 second before the clip ends.

**TIP**▶ You can also animate a filter using the Razor Blade tool. After you divide a clip, you can apply a filter to one of the clip segments, and apply a transition to dissolve between the segments.

## Editor's Cut

You've applied filters and changed motion properties to flop an image or change the direction of a camera zoom, as well as to create a style. But there's no need to stop there. Artist Tereza Djurkovic (www.telenova.us) applies Final Cut Pro filters and speed changes to create serene and naturally soothing video art.

*Continues on next page*

**Editor's Cut** (continued)

In the Browser, in the Sequences > Editor's Cut bin, open the *Filter Art* sequence, and begin by applying the changes below to the two clips. You can model your art after the French impressionist Monet or a 1970s lava lamp. Once you have a look you like, try animating a few of the parameters.

▶ **willow pond**—Stylize > Diffuse (Radius = 4, Repeat Edges on); Motion > 30% speed (Ripple Sequence selected)

▶ **yucca blades**—Distort > Whirlpool (Amount = 50, Repeat Edges on), Color Correction > Color Corrector 3-way (raise the mids); Motion > 30% speed, 50% scale, reposition to left side; duplicate image onto V2, reposition to right; add Flop filter to V2 clip (Perspective bin).

To see the finished versions the artist created, open and play the *Filter Art Gallery* sequence.

## Lesson Review

1. Describe two ways to apply a video or audio filter.
2. How do you view, modify the priority of, and disable filters applied to sequence clips?
3. How do you delete one or all filters in the Filters tab?
4. What real-time filter can you use to change the hue, saturation, and brightness of an image?
5. What tool provides a split-screen before-and-after comparison of a filter?
6. Where do you modify filter parameters?
7. How do you apply a filter from one clip to another clip? to several clips?
8. How do you save an adjusted filter as a favorite effect?
9. How do you add filter keyframes in the Viewer?
10. If a filter appears first in the Filters tab, does it affect all the filters below it?

*Answers*

1. Drag a filter from the Effects tab to the clip in the Timeline, or select the clip (or move the playhead over it) and choose a filter from the Effects menu.

2. To view the filter's effect, position the playhead over the clip in the Timeline. Open the clip in the Viewer, and click the Filters tab. To change the priority of a filter, drag the filter name above or below another filter. To disable the filter, click the Enable/Disable checkbox to deselect it.

3. Click the filter name, and press Delete. To delete all video filters, click Video Filters, and press Delete.

4. The Color Corrector 3-way filter.

5. The Frame Viewer.

6. In the Filters tab.

7. Drag the filter name from the Filters tab to another clip in the Timeline. To copy a filter to several clips at once, select those clips before dragging the filter. You can also use the Paste Attributes command.

8. Drag the filter name from the Viewer window to the Favorites bin, press Option-F, or choose Effects > Make Favorite Effect.

9. Position the playhead where you want to start or end a filter change, and click a parameter Keyframe button. Reposition the playhead, and change that parameter.

10. No, filters that appear last in the Filters tab affect all the filters above it.

## Keyboard Shortcuts

| | |
|---|---|
| **Option-F** | Save modified filter in Favorites bin |
| **Control-L** | Toggle looped playback |
| **Option-P** | Preview an effect |
| **Option-7** | Open the Frame Viewer tab |
| **Option-8** | Open the QuickView tab |
| **Option-9** | Open the Video Scopes tab |

# 14

**Lesson Files**    FCP7 Book Files > Lessons > Lesson 14 Project

**Media**    FCP7 Book Files > Media> Leverage; Quest; Playing For Change; SeaWorld

**Time**    This lesson takes approximately 60 minutes to complete.

**Goals**    Detect audio peaks

Adjust video levels for broadcast

Share clips and sequences

Export a QuickTime movie

Export using QuickTime conversion

Export a still image

Output a sequence to tape

Create a timecode window burn

Back up a project

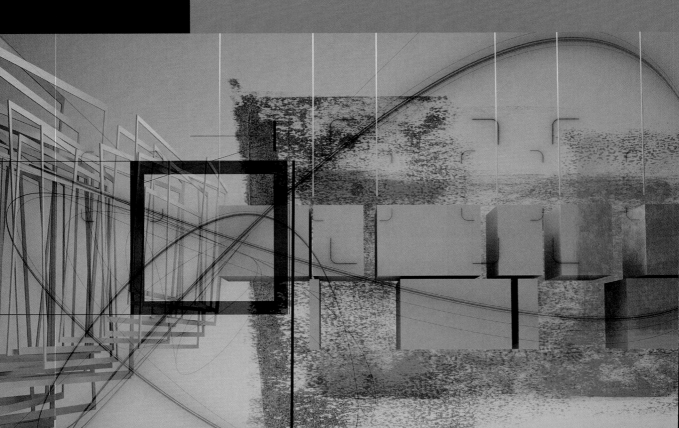

# Lesson 14
# Finishing and Outputting

After making all your creative and editorial decisions, and completing and finessing your sequence, you're finally ready to send your masterpiece out into the world. There are two ways you might do this. One way is to export the sequence as a digital file that you can use on the web, in DVDs, or with devices such as iPhone, iPod, or Apple TV.

The other way to deliver your sequence is to output it to tape for broadcast or screening, or just to archive it for posterity. You might also want to export a file for use by other departments, such as a still frame for graphics, or to export only the audio tracks for an audio postproduction company.

The Range Check function reads the luma and chroma levels of a sequence clip.

Even if your project will only be viewed on a computer or an in-house system, you should make sure that the audio and video conform to specific industry or broadcast standards. Once you've created the output tapes or files, you will also want to back up or archive the elements so you can retrieve or re-create them if the need should ever arise.

## Preparing the Project for Finishing

Since this lesson is about fixing and outputting a completed sequence, you will work with sequences you've completed in earlier lessons.

1    Open the FCP7 Book Files > Lessons > Lesson 14 Project file, and close any other open projects.

These four completed sequences represent the work you've done throughout these lessons. Although your reasons for outputting the sequences may vary, you still apply the same standards and prepare them the same way.

> **TIP** ▶ Take a moment to reposition the sequence tabs in the order you will use them: Believe, Leverage, Quest, Playing For Change.

In some cases, you may find you want to use source clips to change your finished sequence, perhaps to rework an edit or swap music tracks to improve the sound mix. Although it may seem backward from importing clips and then editing, Final Cut Pro knows where the media files are that link to the sequence clips and can bring them into the project.

2    In the Browser, select the *Believe* sequence, and choose Tools > Create Master Clips. Click the disclosure triangle for this new bin.

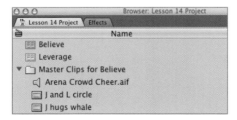

3    Double-click the **J and L circle** clip to open it in the Viewer. Then double-click some of the other clips in this bin.

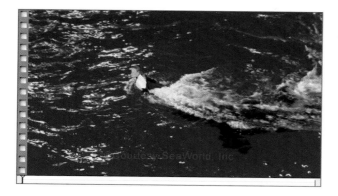

All the audio and video clips used in this *Believe* sequence appear as master clips and are available for you to use in the project.

4   In the Timeline, play the first four video clips of the *Believe* sequence.

While the sequence may sound and look good, it's impossible to know whether it satisfies broadcast standards simply by listening and looking. To verify that the audio in this sequence is not peaking anywhere—and thereby *clipping* the audio—and that the video is within FCC regulations, you will rely on two tools: the Audio Mixer and Video Scopes.

Instead of opening a new window and finding a place for the tools in the interface, let's use a preset window layout.

5   Choose Window > Arrange > Audio Mixing. Then choose Tools > Video Scopes to add the scopes to the Tool Bench. Click the Audio Mixer tab to make it active.

6   To maximize the Timeline window, locate the boundary between the Browser and Timeline and drag it to the left. With the Timeline window active, press Shift-Z to see the entire sequence.

You're now ready to make final corrections to this sequence. Let's start by correcting the audio.

## Detecting Audio Peaks

For any given project, you may have corralled tracks from a variety of audio sources, such as narration recorded in a studio, ambient sound recorded in the field, sound on tape, and music tracks from iTunes or CDs. You could have mixed those tracks to your liking, but you still need to do a final sweep of the sequence to see if there are any audio levels that need correction.

As discussed previously, audio levels that peak too high can become distorted. The one absolute rule is never to allow the audio to peak over 0 dB and cause clipping. Final Cut Pro can help you pinpoint exactly where the audio may be peaking over 0 dB in your sequence by placing a marker in the Timeline at each peak.

1   In the Timeline, play the first half of the *Believe* sequence again. In the Audio Mixer, watch the clipping indicators in the Master audio meters to see if any peaks occur in these clips.

While you can use the standard audio meters to monitor audio, the Master audio meters in the Audio Mixer extend above 0 dB, which shows you the amount you may need to reduce your volume.

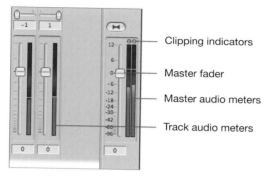

Clipping indicators

Master fader

Master audio meters

Track audio meters

When audio peaks over 0 dB in the Timeline, a red clipping indicator lights up on one or both audio meters, depending on which track peaked. The indicator remains lit until you stop playing the sequence.

**NOTE ▶** After a sequence is mixed, there may be times when the volume of a clip is readjusted, or when an additional sound effect is added at the last minute. While these changes may be minor, they can impact the overall sound level of that group of clips.

Although these indicators tell you there was an audio peak, they don't pinpoint exactly where it occurred in the sequence. Final Cut Pro can detect the peak for you.

2    In the Timeline, press Command-Shift-A to make sure no clips are selected. Then choose Mark > Audio Peaks > Mark. A progress bar appears while Final Cut Pro examines the sequence.

When the detection is complete, markers are placed in the Timeline ruler wherever audio peaks occur in the sequence. If the peak is sustained for more than an instant, a long marker—or a marker with a duration—appears over the clip to indicate the length of the peaking audio.

**3**   Move the playhead to the first audio peak marker. Then zoom in to get a better view.

Each audio peak marker is given the name *Audio Peak*, along with a sequential number that identifies the specific peak or peak area. When the playhead is over an audio
peak marker, its name is displayed in the Canvas.

**4**   Press Shift-M a few times to move the playhead to the next area of audio peak markers over the **_DF_ambassadors** clip.

Audio meters reflect the levels of the combined audio tracks in the sequence. You have
to identify which individual tracks are causing the peaking. Since the first set of markers is isolated above the **_SA_favorite behavior** clip, and the second set is isolated above
the **_DF_ambassadors** clip, let's start by modifying those two clips.

**TIP** ▶ If you have the master clips in the Browser, you can open a questionable clip
to double-check its original volume level.

**5**   Select the **_SA_favorite behavior** clip and Command-click the **_DF_ ambassadors** clip
to add it to the selection.

**6**   To see the audio level overlays on the clips, press Option-W. Then choose Modify >
Levels, or press Command-Option-L.

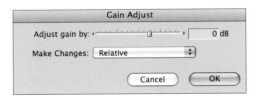

**7**  In the Gain Adjust dialog, in the "Adjust gain by" field, enter *–4* to reduce the gain by 3 dB, and leave the Make Changes pop-up menu set to Relative. Click OK. Watch the audio meters as you play through these two clips. These clips no longer cause the audio to peak above 0 dB.

**8**  To clear the audio peak markers from the Timeline, deselect the sequence clips, and choose Mark > Audio Peaks > Clear. To double-check your results, choose Mark > Audio Peaks > Mark again.

Now that you've corrected the audio peaks, you can take another look at the overall volume level of the sequence. If you're trying to stay within a particular output level, such as –12 dB, you can adjust that level using the Master fader. The Master fader controls the output level of your entire mix while you're playing the sequence, outputting it to tape, or exporting it as a movie file. It does not affect the audio levels of individual clips.

NOTE ▶ If you are delivering your project to a sound company for additional work, make sure you identify and implement any additional requirements for audio levels or other standards that company may have. Audio requirements can vary among facilities.

Currently, the sequence plays at a little over –6 dB. Broadcast television has a limited audio dynamic range and cannot exceed –6 dB for most standards. Since there are peaks in this sequence beyond that level, let's lower the volume of all the tracks down to a safe –12 dB.

**9**  Drag the Master fader down to about –12 dB. You can also enter *–12* in the audio level field beneath the meters, and press Tab. Play the sequence again and look at the audio meters.

By finding and correcting audio peaks in this sequence, and changing the overall audio level to an optimum level, you've successfully prepared the audio portion of this sequence for output.

NOTE ▶ The Track Visibility controls in the Timeline turn tracks on and off in the computer processor. Tracks turned off using this method will not be included on output. Solo and Mute buttons affect audio only during playback and will not exclude tracks during output.

## Take 2

Everyone on the production team is thrilled with how easily you can find peaking audio in a sequence. Instead of having you finish the current sequence, they want you to test for audio peaks in each of the other sequences and make any necessary changes … while they watch!

Remember, although some sequences may not have audio peaks, their overall audio output levels may still need adjustment. So keep an eye on the Audio Mixer's Master fader.

## Adjusting Video Levels for Broadcast

Like the audio tracks in a project, the video you captured may also have come from multiple sources. Some footage may have been shot indoors, some outside at night, and some outside in bright sunlight.

Just as you monitor audio for peaks, so you must do the same for video. One of the most common problems with video levels is that the whites, or *luminance* levels, are sometimes too bright. The FCC mandates that no video to be broadcast can have a luminance level over 100 IRE, which is considered to be *broadcast safe*.

NOTE ▶ *IRE* is a unit of measurement in video named for the organization that created it—the Institute of Radio Engineers.

If video luminance does go over 100 IRE, the video level is clipped during broadcast. This can cause audio interference or noise in the signal. Some networks or facilities may reject the tape and choose not to air it at all.

Final Cut Pro has range-checking tools that will measure both the *luminance* (brightness) and *chrominance* (color saturation) values of a clip to determine whether they are within a broadcast safe range. When you find clips that are not within broadcast specifications, you can apply the Broadcast Safe filter to correct them.

NOTE ► Luminance and chrominance are often abbreviated as *luma* and *chroma*.

1   In the Timeline, in the *Believe* sequence, move the playhead to the middle of the first clip, **uw_rotations**.

2   In the Tool Bench, click the Video Scopes tab, then click the Layout pop-up menu and choose Waveform.

The Waveform Monitor enables you to see the luminance values of the current frame. Broadcast standards specify a maximum luminance level for any video. This is represented in the Waveform Monitor as 100%.

3   Move the pointer up and down over the Waveform Monitor.

A yellow horizontal line follows the movement of the pointer, and a number in the upper-right corner displays the luma percentage of the current pointer location in the scope.

4   To check the luma level of the current clip, make the Timeline active and choose View > Range Check > Excess Luma, or press Control-Z.

When you turn on range checking, each clip in the sequence will appear with one of three symbols that indicate whether the luminance level of that clip is within the legal range for broadcast use.

For the current clip, a green circle and a checkmark appear in the Canvas, indicating that the luminance levels for that frame are below 90 percent and are broadcast safe.

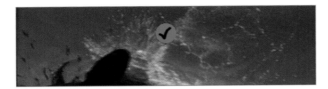

**5**  Move the playhead to the middle of the second clip in the sequence, the **_DS_show concept** clip.

An in-range icon appears with a checkmark and an upward arrow, indicating that some luma levels are between 90 and 100 percent. The affected areas are indicated by green zebra stripes. Although it's reaching the upper limit of the broadcast safe range, this is still acceptable video.

**6**  Move the playhead to the middle of the **_SA_favorite behavior** clip.

A yellow warning icon appears, indicating that some luminance levels are above 100 percent. Red zebra stripes show the areas of the image that are above 100 percent. The Waveform Monitor shows by how much those luminance values exceed 100 percent.

You can see that this frame needs correcting, but what about the frames of this clip that follow?

**7**  Play this clip for a few seconds, then stop and press Option-P to see the range check warning appear on every frame of the clip.

**TIP** ▶ The range check symbol appears only when the clip is not playing unless you access the Play Every Frame option by pressing Option-P, or by choosing Mark > Play > Every Frame. With that option selected, the range check display remains on the screen and updates each frame. This is a good way to double-check individual frames in suspect clips throughout the sequence.

Final Cut Pro has numerous correction filters you can apply to improve a clip. One filter has a specific job: to reduce the luminance level of a clip so that it is broadcast safe.

8   In the Timeline, select the **_SA_favorite behavior** clip, and choose Effects > Video Filters > Color Correction > Broadcast Safe. Double-click the clip to open it in the Viewer, and click the Filters tab to see the filter parameters.

**NOTE** ▶ If you have already applied a Color Corrector 3-way filter to a clip, and the luminance levels are out of range, you can try reducing the white level to bring the levels back into range.

With the Broadcast Safe filter applied to this clip, the red zebra stripes in the Canvas turn to green, and the Waveform Monitor shows that the luminance levels have been limited to 100 percent.

**TIP** ▶ If you have an entire sequence with problem luminance levels, you could apply the Broadcast Safe filter to all of the clips; but rather than apply it to each clip individually, you can nest the sequence clips and apply a Broadcast Safe filter to the nest.

9   To continue checking for out-of-range clips, move the playhead to each clip in the sequence, and apply the Broadcast Safe filter when necessary. When you've finished, choose View > Range Check > Off, and press Control-U to return to the default standard window layout.

**Take 2**

The thrill of prepping sequences for output is starting to fade for the production team and they're wandering away from your edit bay. That's OK, because you have work to do. While they're gone, spot-check the video levels in the other sequences.

**TIP** ▶ Like audio waveforms and clip overlays, range checking is turned off and on for each individual sequence.

## Exporting and Sharing Files

When you think about exporting your sequence, you should first ask how and where the output file will be used. For example, if you were creating a file to post on the Internet, you would need to use a different file format or codec than if you were creating a DVD.

Final Cut Pro uses QuickTime as its standard media format to view, create, import, and export media files. As a multiplatform, multimedia file format, QuickTime can handle many kinds of media, including video, sound, animation, graphics, text, and music.

Depending on which type of file you wish to create, you can choose from several export options. Final Cut Pro's Share option can provide an easy solution for converting a clip or sequence to a file for a specific platform or device, such as the Internet, a cell phone, Apple TV, Blu-ray Disc, and so on.

But you may also need to export using the same settings as the current sequence's without changing or converting the file type. And for more advanced export requirements, you can custom-design your own export options. In this section, you will explore three ways to export a portion of a sequence.

**NOTE** ▶ Preparing media for digital distribution is a constant compromise between quality and performance—higher data rates produce higher quality but place more demands on your computer's processing power. While trial and error can create a balance between the two, you can save time by choosing preset options designed for a specific distribution medium and audience.

## Sharing Clips and Sequences

In today's postproduction world, editors can take advantage of creative ways to share their projects with clients, friends, and audiences. In Lesson 3, you shared a rough cut from Final Cut Pro using iChat. But let's say you've finished the sequence and you need final approval from a group of people you need to reach in different ways. Perhaps you need to screen a DVD with the producer, post it on YouTube for the world to see, watch it on Apple TV with your friends, or review it on an iPod while you're on the go. To perform well in these destinations, the sequence has to be compressed and transcoded into a different format for each purpose.

Instead of choosing one delivery file format and exporting it, then choosing another and exporting that, you can use the Share command in Final Cut Pro to create *and* deliver output media files without advanced knowledge of transcoding or opening any other applications.

You can export a sequence or a clip from the Viewer or the Timeline. You can also export from the Browser, as long as you first select the item or group of items you want to export. Let's export a portion of the *Leverage* sequence

> **NOTE** ▸ To export an entire sequence, make sure there are no marks in the Timeline. To export a portion of a sequence, mark In and Out points around the segment (or clip) you want to export.

1   In the *Leverage* sequence, move the playhead to the "In point" marker. To set In and Out points using this and the following marker, choose Modify > Mark to Markers, or press Control-A.

This is the portion of the sequence you will export for this exercise.

**NOTE ▶** Sometimes the production team needs to sign off on the beginning or ending of a sequence, or may simply need to approve a particular shot.

**2**   Choose File > Share.

 Consider placing the Share button in the Timeline button bar for easy access.

**3**   In the Share window, click the Choose button next to the Destination Folder pop-up, and navigate to the FCP7 Book Files > Media folder. Select the Exports folder as the destination for the new media files.

**TIP ▶** If you've previously selected an export destination, you can click the Destinations Folder pop-up menu and choose that destination.

**4**   From the Output Type pop-up menu, choose Apple TV.

Rather than specify a compression codec, such as MPEG or H.264, you simply choose the destination device, or how you would like to use the exported file. Final Cut Pro will export the file using the appropriate codec.

In the main Share window, to the right of the sequence name, you see Apple TV. This information will be added to your file to identify its file type and intended use.

**NOTE** ▶ *Codec* is a term created from two words, *compression* and *decompression*. It identifies the way in which a file is compressed or decompressed on export and playback.

5    Select the Add to iTunes Library checkbox.

When you select this checkbox, an action drawer appears in which you can also choose a particular iTunes playlist. After the file is exported, Final Cut Pro will automatically deliver this file to iTunes for easy access and viewing, as well as syncing to Apple TV.

**TIP** ▶ If you will be using the Share function to export your sequences, you may want to create a Movies Exports playlist in iTunes to manage these files.

6    To create another export option for the marked portion of the sequence, click the Add Output (+) button to the right of the output.

In the Share window, you can choose several different ways to export a single sequence at the same time. You can also choose to burn a DVD or a Blu-ray Disc. If you don't have a Blu-ray Disc recorder or a blank DVD on hand, you can create a disk image (.img) file on your hard drive and burn a disc or DVD from it at a later time.

7    From the Output Type pop-up menu, choose Blu-ray. Under the pop-up menu, select the "Create Blu-ray disc" checkbox. In the action drawer, notice that you can choose an output device, a template, and several other options. Click the Output Device pop-up menu and choose Hard Drive (Blu-ray).

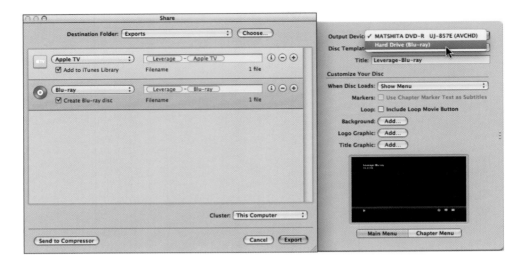

**NOTE ▶** When you choose a DVD or disc recorder as your output device, you will, of course, need to put a blank disc into your computer or device in order for Final Cut Pro to start burning.

▶ **Exporting to Blu-ray Disc**

When exporting to Blu-ray, you have three options. If you have a Blu-ray Disc burner, you can use that to burn an H.264 Blu-ray Disc. If you don't have one connected to your Mac, that option will not appear in the Output Device pop-up menu in the Blu-ray action drawer. Instead, you will see two other options: the internal Mac DVD burner and your hard drive.

Burning a Blu-ray Disc on your Mac DVD burner produces a Blu-ray-compliant disc that will play on a Blu-ray player, but the disc will not play on your Mac. Also, this disc won't hold as much content as a true Blu-ray Disc. (Make sure the Blu-ray player you use supports AVCHD Blu-ray Discs.) The third option, burning to your hard drive, will produce a disk image (.img) file that you can burn at another time or on another computer station.

Each of the export destinations, such as Blu-ray, DVD, iPod, and Apple TV, has an action that helps complete the delivery of your export.

**8**  To add a third export option, click the Add Output button to the right of the Blu-ray output line. From the Output Type pop-up menu, choose iPod, and select the Add to iTunes Library checkbox.

**9**  Click the Add Output button once more. This time, choose YouTube in the Output Type pop-up menu. Select the Publish to YouTube checkbox to see the options in the side window. You won't be publishing this movie to YouTube, so click the Remove Output (−) button to remove this option.

**NOTE ▶** The footage in this book is intended for use with these exercises and no permissions have been granted to publish this material to the web or in any other way outside of this book.

**10**  In the lower right of the Share window, click the Export button. A progress bar appears indicating that Final Cut Pro is exporting the files.

**NOTE ▶** Before you export a file and add it to your iTunes Library, make sure you have previously opened the app and agreed to the licensing.

The beauty of using the Share command is that the exporting and transcoding continues in the background, allowing you to get back to your editing.

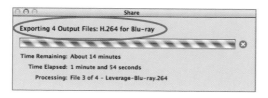

**NOTE ▶** When one of your export destinations is DVD or Blu-ray Disc, you will see a higher file count because the audio and video are recorded as separate files. A Blu-ray burner creates a H.264 video file and a Dolby Digital Professional (.ac3) audio file.

When the exporting is complete, if any of the action boxes were checked, such as Add to iTunes Library, Final Cut Pro will initiate those actions. Let's take a look at what you created.

**11** Press Command-H to hide Final Cut Pro. In a column view Finder window, navigate to the FCP7 Book Files > Media > Exports folder. Notice the suffixes that Final Cut Pro added to each file to identify the file type. Notice also the Blu-ray .img file.

**TIP** You can export more than one sequence at a time. To do this, in the Browser select the group of sequences you want to export, then choose File > Share and follow the prompts.

▶ **Share Delivery Actions**

For every format in the Share window, Final Cut Pro can perform an additional action to deliver the exported file(s) to the final destination.

▶ Apple TV, iPhone, iPod—add the output media file to an iTunes playlist.

▶ Blu-ray Disc—automatically burn the program to an attached Blu-ray recorder or a hard drive, or to an AVCHD Blu-ray Disc using your Mac's DVD burner.

▶ DVD—automatically burn the program to standard DVD media or a hard drive.

▶ YouTube—automatically upload the output media file to a YouTube account.

▶ MobileMe—automatically upload the output media file to a MobileMe Gallery.

▶ Apple ProRes 422 and QuickTime H.264—create a QuickTime movie and automatically open the file with QuickTime Player or other specified application.

▶ Other—access more than 100 Apple (preset) settings as well as custom settings you create.

## Exporting a QuickTime Movie

You've gotten final approval on your sequence. Now it's time to archive it, pass it on, combine it with other segments of the project, or import it to another application using its current settings.

At this stage, you want to maintain the highest media quality, and you don't want to recompress the sequence or media file. To do this, you use Final Cut Pro's QuickTime Movie export option, which creates a QuickTime file with the same settings and quality as your current clips and sequences. No additional media compression is performed. This allows FCP to export your clips quickly with virtually no loss in quality.

> **TIP** When a project is an hour or more in length, you can export each act or segment and import it as a separate clip into a new sequence that is intended just for output. To do this, you would use the QuickTime Movie export option to retain the current clip and sequence settings.

**1**   To export from a different sequence, in the Timeline window, click the *Quest* sequence tab, and mark an In and Out at the two markers above the mirrored clips.

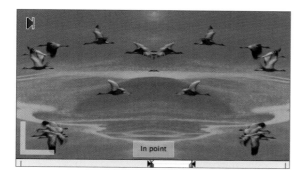

You may choose to use this segment of the sequence in a different version of the show, or in a different project altogether. Exporting this segment as a QuickTime movie will convert the segment clips to a single media file.

**2**   Choose File > Export > QuickTime Movie. In the Save As field, add *mirror* to the name of the sequence to identify the segment.

**3**   If the Exports folder is not the current destination, navigate to the FCP7 Book Files > Media folder, and select the Exports folder as the destination for the new file.

**4**   Make sure the Setting pop-up menu is set to Current Settings, the Include pop-up menu is set to Audio and Video, and the Markers pop-up menu is set to None.

When you choose Current Settings, you are using the current settings of the clip or sequence to create the new file.

**NOTE ▶** In the Markers pop-up menu, you can select markers that may have been created for a DVD or Soundtrack Pro audio project.

**5**   Make sure the Recompress All Frames box is deselected.

When selected, this option recompresses all the frames in the selected export item. This can introduce compression artifacts into the file and increase the export time. If Final Cut Pro ever has trouble processing certain frames in your clips, exporting them with this option selected may be a good troubleshooting technique.

**6**   Make sure the Make Movie Self-Contained checkbox is selected.

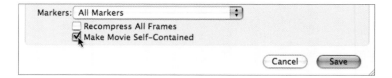

There are two types of QuickTime movies:

▶   **Self-contained**—A self-contained QuickTime movie can play on any computer because it contains all of the media (not just the clip links) that are in the clip or sequence. A self-contained movie will have a larger file size because the media files are contained within the movie.

▶   **Not self-contained**—You can play these movies on your computer and even use them to create a DVD. However, you can't play them on another computer unless that system has all of the source media files on its hard disk.

**7**   Click Save. A dialog appears showing the exporting progress.

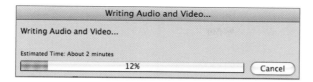

**NOTE** ► When audio files are exported, the process can be so quick that no dialog appears.

With the Share command, files can be delivered to iTunes for instant access and viewing. To view an exported QuickTime movie file, you can locate it in a Finder window on your desktop, or import the file back into Final Cut Pro.

8   Press Command-H to hide Final Cut Pro. In a column view Finder window, navigate to the FCP7 Book Files > Media > Exports folder, and select the **Quest mirror** clip. Click the Quick Look button to screen the clip.

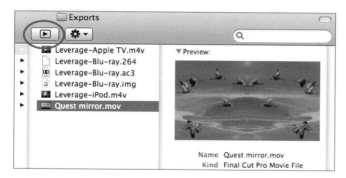

9   In the Finder window, double-click the **Quest mirror** clip.

Because you created this clip with Final Cut Pro settings, it opens in a separate clip window within the application.

**TIP** ▸ To open a Final Cut Pro movie file in QuickTime Player, Control-click the clip in the Finder. In the shortcut menu, choose Open With > QuickTime Player.

10  In the **Quest mirror** clip window, click the Stereo tab, and play the clip.

Although this segment was originally a portion of a sequence, it's now a single clip, and the multiple tracks of audio have been combined into one stereo pair.

**11**  Close the **Quest mirror** clip window.

Even though you viewed the clip in Final Cut Pro, you haven't imported it into the project, so it doesn't appear as a clip in the Browser. Once you do import the clip, you can edit it as you would any other clip.

**NOTE ▸** As with the Share command, you can export a sequence or a clip from the Viewer or the Timeline. You can also export from the Browser, if you first select the item you want to export.

## Using Other Export Options

If you have a more demanding project, you may need to use a different export option. Final Cut Studio includes a program called Compressor that is dedicated to efficiently compressing and exporting your files. You can choose from numerous presets, or you can customize your own export options.

Although a full exploration of Compressor is outside the scope of this book, you can access many of its presets, and the application itself, via the Share window.

**TIP ▸** You can export a sequence to use as a video reference in Soundtrack Pro or LiveType. In these applications, you can create a music score for the sequence, clean up audio noise, and add 32-bit animated titles. Choose these export options from the File menu.

**1**  Click the Timeline window, and choose File > Share. The Share window appears with the same options you chose previously.

**2**   Click the Remove Output (–) button on all but the first export line so that only one
line remains.

**3**   From the Output Type pop-up menu, scroll to the very bottom of the menu and
choose Other.

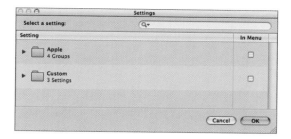

A Settings table appears with two options: Apple and Custom. When you create or customize an export option in Compressor, it appears as a preset in this Custom folder.

**4**   To explore some of the Apple presets, double-click the Apple folder or bin, or click
its disclosure triangle. Then double-click a category, such as the DVD bin, to see the
DVD options available. You can also double-click a bin to close it.

> **TIP** ▶ When creating a DVD using these presets, you can choose between quality
> and performance. A better-quality DVD will take longer to encode, whereas a faster
> encoding will produce lower quality.

To choose an option, you must select one of the presets *inside* the bin. Notice that you
can also select the In Menu checkbox to add an item to the Share Output Type pop-
up menu.

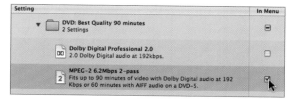

**5**   Click Cancel to close the Settings table. In the lower left of the Share window, notice the Send to Compressor button. Clicking this button sends the current file or sequence to the Compressor application for additional export options. For now, click Cancel to close the Share window.

**NOTE ▶** The H.264 codec is often used in QuickTime to create high-quality content with a relatively small file size. However, it's not a good choice for creating clips to edit because the compression scheme used in this codec creates only one full frame for about every 15 frames.

## Exporting a Still Image

Sometimes your exporting needs are more specific. The audio mixing house needs just the sequence audio, or the graphics department may want stills from the sequence clips to create a publicity poster. Or production needs the sequence exported as an AVI file. The QuickTime Conversion export option within Final Cut Pro allows you to export media as a specific file type, such as an AIFF audio file or an Adobe Photoshop image file.

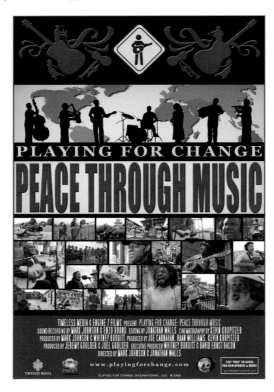

Playing For Change poster created with exported stills from Final Cut Pro

NOTE ▶ When you export using the QuickTime Conversion method, you cannot perform any other Final Cut Pro activities during the exporting process as you can when
exporting via Share.

1   In the Timeline, click the *Playing For Change* sequence tab. Move the playhead to one
    of the markers labeled "Export Still," or choose your own favorite frame of a perform-
    ing musician. Then choose File > Export > Using QuickTime Conversion.

    As you did in previous steps, you can name the file and choose the Exports folder as
    the destination.

2   Click the Format pop-up menu and look at the export options. Choose Still Image.

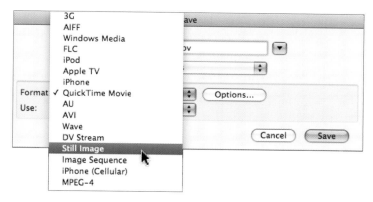

    Each format type—AIFF, AVI, Still Image—has options that can further define how
    you export your file.

3   Click the Options button. In the Export Image Sequence Settings dialog, click the
    Format pop-up menu, and choose Photoshop as the file type. Click OK, and click
    Save in the Save dialog to export this file.

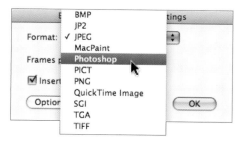

**TIP ▶** If you want to export a still image or freeze frame from interlaced video, you can add a De-Interlace filter to reduce any flickering or shaking in the image. This filter is also useful when outputting a QuickTime movie for computer playback because computer screens display lines progressively.

**MORE INFO ▶** You can also send a clip or sequence to a different Final Cut Studio application to make changes to it, and then import it back into Final Cut Pro to continue editing. This is referred to as "round-tripping," and it's covered in the Apple Pro Training Series book *Final Cut Pro 7 Advanced Editing,* from Peachpit Press.

## Take 2

The *Playing For Change* publicity department just called and needs three more stills to complete the poster. Find three unmarked still images of different performing musicians and export them as TIFF files.

## Outputting to Tape

Some television programs and films are produced using a tapeless workflow in which all of their needs are served by working with digital media files. Their cameras record files on media cards; editors edit with those files and then export and deliver the final sequence as a file. Still, many production companies require you to deliver your project on good old videotape.

Through a FireWire connection, Final Cut Pro can output to DV, DVCPRO, HDV, and DVCPRO HD. With additional hardware, it can output to other tape formats from VHS to DigiBeta. You will usually record a master copy of your sequence to the same tape format you started with or to the required delivery format; but you may also want to make a viewing copy in another tape format, such as DV.

When you output a sequence to tape, you generally want to lead the sequence with color bars and tone, a slate of what's to come, and possibly a countdown to indicate when the sequence will begin to play. This is collectively called *leader material*, which you added to a sequence in an earlier lesson.

**NOTE ▶** Before you begin outputting, make sure your recording device is properly connected to your computer and turned on.

As with exporting files, you can output the entire sequence or just a section of the sequence as defined by In and Out points in the Timeline.

There are three ways to output your sequence to tape:

▶   Manually recording the sequence

▶   Using the Print to Video command

▶   Using the Edit to Tape command

The first two methods, manual recording and Print to Video, are available when you use any FireWire recording device. The third method, Edit to Tape, is available only when you use devices that Final Cut Pro can control remotely.

## Recording Manually

The easiest way to output to tape is simply to start the connected recording device—camera or deck—and play the sequence while the device records. This is referred to as *manual recording*. You use this option when you want to make a quick dub to tape.

Though this output method is the simplest, it is also the least precise. It is very much a "what you see is what you get" proposition. To record manually, you should edit any pre-program or leader material—bars and tone, slate, black slug—into your sequence in the Timeline, as you did in Lesson 11. And you should also mix down your audio and render any unrendered video.

1   In the Timeline, click the *Playing For Change* sequence tab. Notice the leader material before the sequence and the **Slug** clip at the tail of the sequence.

When you output a sequence manually, the frame on which the playhead is parked as the tape begins recording will appear as a freeze frame until you start playing the sequence. When the playhead reaches the last frame of the sequence, it will freeze on that final frame. Having a slug of black or other leader material before your sequence begins and after it ends will ensure that no frame of the sequence is used as the starting or ending freeze frame.

Next, you want to make sure the sequence is playing back the highest-quality images.

**2**   In the Timeline, click the RT pop-up menu, and make sure you see a checkmark next to these settings: Safe RT, High (under Playback Video Quality), and Full (under Playback Frame Rate). You may have to click the RT pop-up menu to choose each option.

**3**   If red, yellow, or orange render bars are displayed in the Timeline ruler, choose Sequence > Render All, and make sure the same render level colors that appear in the Timeline ruler are selected in the Sequence > Render All menu. Press Option-R to render everything in the Timeline.

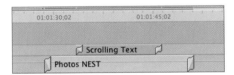

**4**   Cue up your recording device, and begin recording.

**5**   After at least 5 seconds, play the sequence.

> **NOTE ▶** If you want the sequence to repeat, choose Loop Playback in the View menu. The amount of black you want to play between the looped sequences is determined by the slug edit at the tail and head of each sequence.

**6**   When the sequence has finished playing, continue recording a few seconds, and then stop the recording device.

## Printing to Video

The second output option combines the convenience of manual recording with some automation. Rather than edit the leader material at the head of your sequence, you can choose it from a checklist before outputting to tape.

During the output process, Final Cut Pro will automatically generate these items as though they were clips in your sequence. This is a good method to use when you want to save time and take advantage of the automatic leader options but don't have a device that can be controlled remotely using timecode.

Also, you don't have to render your sequence. The Print to Video command automatically renders and plays your sequence at high quality even if the Timeline playback settings are set to Low Quality or Dynamic.

> **NOTE ▶** To output HDV material to tape, you would use the Print to Video option.

1   Click the *Quest* sequence tab, or open a sequence you want to output. If you are outputting the entire sequence, press Option-X to remove the In and Out points.

2   Choose File > Print to Video, or press Control-M.

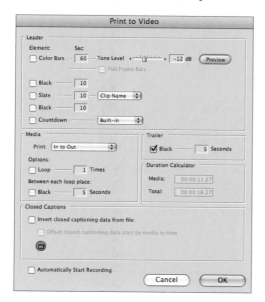

There are five areas in this dialog: Leader, Media, Trailer, Duration Calculator, and Closed Captions. In each area, select a checkbox to include that option in the output or choose an option from the pop-up menus. You can also enter a specific amount of time for some items.

**3**   In the Leader area, select the Color Bars checkbox, and change the duration to 10 seconds.

**NOTE** ▶ Generally, you record from 10 to 60 seconds of color bars, depending on the sequence's intended use and delivery requirements.

**4**   Select all the checkboxes in the Leader area. For a sample output, shorten the Black durations to 2 and Slate to 5.

**5**   From the Slate pop-up menu, choose Text. In the field that appears to the right, type *Quest Final.* You can add additional slate information here as well.

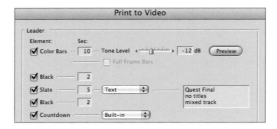

**TIP** ▶ You can also create your own slate or countdown with graphics and a company logo. To include these personalized files, choose the File option from the Slate or Countdown pop-up menus and navigate to the file.

**6**   In the upper-right corner of the Print to Video dialog, click the Preview button to test the audio level going into your recording device. If the level is not high enough, adjust it using the dB slider. When you're finished adjusting the tone, click Stop.

The tone level you set here should represent the audio level of your sequence. If you used −12 dB as the audio level reference during the editing process, the output tone should be set to −12 dB here.

**7**   In the Media area, from the Print pop-up menu, choose Entire Media to output the entire Timeline contents.

> **TIP** ▶ If your sequence is short, such as a promo, commercial, or music video, use the Loop option to loop it several times so that you won't have to rewind the tape to see it again.

8  In the Trailer area, select Black, and change the duration to 10 seconds.

9  Look at the Duration Calculator to see how long the total output will be, and make sure the tape you have selected is long enough.

> **MORE INFO** ▶ To add closed captioning data to the output video, select the "Insert closed captioning data from file" checkbox, then click the Bin button and navigate to the closed caption data file. For more information about working with closed captions, see *Final Cut Studio Workflows*, available at http://documentation.apple.com/en/finalcutstudio/workflows.

10  Click OK.

A progress bar appears as Final Cut Pro renders files and mixes down audio to prepare the sequence for output.

> **TIP** ▶ Keep in mind that this mixdown is temporary and available for only one printing. If you decide to print the sequence again to make another copy, Final Cut Pro has to do another mixdown. To create a render file of the mixdown to use for additional outputs, choose Sequence > Render Only > Mixdown.

When Final Cut Pro is ready to play the sequence and any additional elements, a message will appear telling you to begin recording.

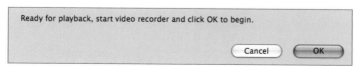

11  Start recording on your recording device, and after about 5 seconds, click OK to start the playback of your sequence and elements.

## Editing to Tape

The third way you can output your sequence to tape is the Edit to Tape method.

It is similar to Print to Video in that the same leader and other options are available for you to select and include with the output. The primary difference is that the Edit to Tape window also has transport buttons for controlling the deck, and you can set an In point where you want to begin recording your sequence. Depending on the recording device you're using, you can also set an Out point if you want to stop recording at a certain location on the tape. You can also choose to output just audio or video.

1   With the Timeline active, choose File > Edit to Tape.

   If you do not have a controllable device connected, an alert will appear.

   If the device is properly connected, the Edit to Tape window opens.

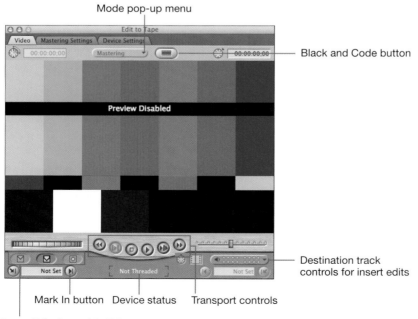

2   If you know the exact location where you want to begin recording, enter it in the
    Mark In field. If not, play the tape, and click the Mark In button (or press I) to mark
    where you want to begin recording.

3   Click the Mastering Settings tab, and select your settings just as you did in the Print
    to Video exercise.

4   Click the Device Settings tab and make sure they are set to control your recording
    device.

5   Click the Video tab. From the Browser, drag the *Believe* sequence to the Preview area
    of the Edit to Tape window and into the Assemble section, then release the mouse
    button.

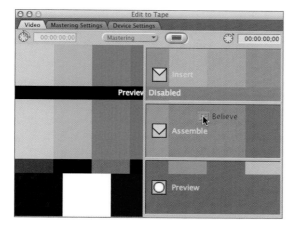

6   When the Ready for Playback dialog appears, click OK to start the recording process.

    The tape is cued up automatically, and the first elements of the output are recorded,
    starting at the In point you have set. As with the Print to Video option, you don't
    need to render anything in your sequence. Final Cut Pro automatically renders the
    video at full quality before outputting it.

7   Close the Edit to Tape window.

## Making a Timecode Window Burn

Often during the output process, someone will request a screening tape of the current sequence with a visible timecode superimposed on the image. This timecode display is sometimes called a *timecode burn-in* or *window burn*.

A window burn is helpful when others need to screen your sequence and provide feedback referencing precise locations. In an earlier lesson, you worked with the Timecode Viewer, which displayed the clip or sequence timecode in a floating window. But that display is not exported or recorded into the image during output. To output the sequence timecode as part of the image, you apply the Timecode Reader filter.

1   In the Timeline, click the *Quest* sequence tab and move the playhead over the third clip, **journey**. Select this clip.

2   Choose Effects > Video Filters > Video > Timecode Reader. Then double-click the **journey** clip to open it in the Viewer. Compare the window burn in the Canvas image with the Canvas's Current Timecode field, and then with the Viewer's Current Timecode field.

The Timecode Reader filter reflects the source timecode as seen in the Viewer's Current Timecode field.

When you apply this filter to a clip in the Timeline, the timecode that appears is that of the source clip, not the sequence. Since the objective is to have a display of the sequence timecode, you have to nest the sequence clips, then apply the filter to the clips as a nested group.

3   Press Command-Z to undo the last step. Press T to select the Select Track Forward tool, and click the first clip in the *Quest* sequence. All the V1 clips become selected.

4   Choose Sequence > Nest Items. In the Name field, add the word *NEST* to the end of the sequence name, and click OK.

All the clips on the V1 track are nested into a single clip. In the Browser, a new sequence appears, *Quest NEST*.

**NOTE ▶** To return to the individual clips in the sequence, you can double-click the icon in the Browser, or double-click the V1 nest in the Timeline.

5   In the Timeline, move the playhead forward once again to the middle of the **journey** clip (around 1:00:12:00). Choose Effects > Video Filters > Video > Timecode Reader.

Now, the Timecode Reader filter is applied to the nest of clips, and you see the sequence timecode in the Canvas.

6    Click a few different places in the Timeline ruler and make sure the timecode display in the Canvas image matches the timecode number in the Current Timecode field in the Canvas and Timeline.

Depending on your media, you may want to change the timecode display to make it smaller or more opaque, or to position it in a different part of the screen. To open the nest in the Viewer, you have to use a different approach from the one used to open a normal sequence clip.

7    Option–double-click the nested sequence in the Timeline to load it into the Viewer, and click the Filters tab. You can also select the nest in the Timeline and press Return.

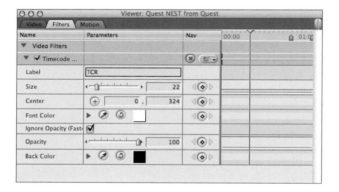

8    Adjust the size, color, opacity, and position of the timecode display so that it is easily seen over the video in the sequence, yet not too distracting. If necessary, from the View pop-up menu, turn on the Title Safe overlay.

9    Output the sequence to tape using any one of the output methods described earlier in this lesson. Or export it as a QuickTime movie.

TIP ▶ To export a media file of the nested sequence with burned-in timecode, create the nest and apply the filter. Then follow the exporting steps in the previous exercises.

# Backing Up Projects

After you've fine-tuned and output your sequence, you may want to think about backing up your project. Each project may require a different backup strategy, not only when you are finished with a project, but also throughout the editing process.

If Autosave Vault is active, Final Cut Pro will automatically save a backup of your project at set time intervals as you work. In addition to this automatic backup system, here are a few other general strategies to keep in mind:

▶   Store your project files on a drive separate from your Autosave Vault drive. That way, if one drive goes down, you will always have your project on the other drive.

▶   Save a few versions of your project throughout the life of the project. This reduces the chance of file corruption by ensuring that you don't work on the same physical file for an extended period of time.

▶   Every few days, back up your project to a flash drive, an iPod, a FireWire device, or a server. The idea is to protect the project and yourself in case your computer or drive goes down.

  **TIP** ▶ An easy way to remember how to save your project is to think locally, globally, and remotely. Locally is on your own computer; globally is on a server or backup drive; and remotely is on a flash drive or a drive you can take with you.

Some editors like to print or retain a list of all the clips in their projects, including the information they entered in the Browser columns. You can do this by using the Batch List function. However, you will need the help of a spreadsheet program such as Apple's Numbers, Microsoft's Excel, or a program that can interpret the tab delineations created in the batch list.

Follow these steps to create a list of clips contained in your project:

1   In the Browser, select the Master Clips for Believe bin.

2   Choose File > Export > Batch List. Name the list *Believe Batch List*, and choose Exports as the target destination. Make sure that Tabbed Text is chosen as the Format option, and click Save. If a warning appears about clip reel numbers, click OK

3   In Final Cut Pro, choose File > Open. Navigate to the Exports folder, select Believe Batch List, and click Choose.

A window appears with your clip information. At the moment, it doesn't look helpful. But it will shortly.

**4**   Press Command-A to select all the information in this window, and press Command-C to copy it.

**5**   Open your spreadsheet program, and press Command-V to paste this information into the first cell. Adjust the column widths to allow the information to be read easily.

| Name | Duration | In | Out | Media Start | Media End |
|------|----------|----|----|-------------|-----------|
| * Master Clips for Believe | | | | | |
| Arena Crowd Cheer.aif | 00:00:14;05 | | | 00:00:00;00 | 00:00:14;04 |
| J and L circle | 0:1:22:10 | | | 0:13:54:19 | 0:15:16:28 |
| J hugs whale | 00:00:54;14 | | | 00:00:00;00 | 00:00:54;13 |
| J rotations | 0:0:18:04 | | | 0:12:07:04 | 0:12:25:07 |
| narration_2 | 00:00:18;18 | | | 00:35:13;00 | 00:35:31;17 |
| performance_S spray jump | 0:0:10:29 | | | 6:19:46:11 | 6:19:57:09 |
| Scuba Breathing.aif | 00:00:54;15 | | | 00:00:00;00 | 00:00:54;14 |
| Track 8_guitar.aif | 00:01:26;09 | | | 00:00:00;00 | 00:01:26;08 |
| um_propel jump | 00:00:16;28 | | | 00:06:09;08 | 00:06:26;05 |
| um_push two trainers | 0:0:11:16 | | | 0:1:28:15 | 0:1:40:00 |
| um_rotations | 00:00:09;19 | | | 00:03:37;16 | 00:03:47;04 |
| Water Lake 1.aif | 00:01:02;16 | | | 00:00:00;00 | 00:01:02;15 |
| _DF_ambassadors | 0:0:32:00 | | | 2:1:45:02 | 2:2:17:01 |
| _DS_show concept | 0:0:23:13 | | | 0:0:54:17 | 0:1:17:29 |
| _SA_favorite behavior | 0:0:30:29 | | | 1:3:00:20 | 1:3:31:18 |

Because the batch list is in a tab-delimited format, the information is placed into separate cells in the spreadsheet. You can now print the batch list as part of your backup process.

**TIP** ▸ Sometimes, the markers in a project contain valuable information that you might want to keep in the project archives. To export a list of markers, choose File > Export > Markers List as Text.

**MORE INFO** ▶ When you need to organize, copy, convert, or remove media files from your hard disk, you can access the Media Manager tool in the File menu. This is covered in the Apple Pro Training Series book *Final Cut Pro 7 Advanced Editing* from Peachpit Press, and also in the Final Cut Pro User Manual.

## Editor's Cut

Choose your favorite sequence in this project and take it through a top-to-bottom finishing and exporting process.

If you've already checked the audio and video output levels, determine whether or not you want to export files with timecode burned into the image. If so, nest the clips and apply the Timecode Reader filter. Then, use the Share function to export the sequence for a number of destinations: website, iPod, DVD.

Connect your camera, output the sequence to tape, and back up the project. The more familiar you are with the steps in the finishing process, the more likely you are to include them as part of your own personal workflow. Happy editing!

## Lesson Review

1. What is the most efficient way to find the audio peaks in a sequence?
2. How are audio peaks indicated in the Timeline?
3. What can you do to determine whether an image falls within the broadcast safe range?
4. How can you correct an out-of-range clip so that its range is acceptable for broadcast?
5. What two tools can you use to help prepare the audio and video of your sequence for output?
6. What export function can you use to quickly post your sequence on YouTube?
7. What is a self-contained QuickTime movie?
8. When might you use QuickTime Conversion?
9. What are the three ways you can output a sequence to tape?
10. What Export command do you choose to create a list of clip information?

*Answers*

1.  Using the Audio Peaks > Mark command, located in the Mark menu.

2.  By markers in the Timeline ruler where each audio peak occurs.

3.  Choose View > Range Check > Luma, and move through the sequence to see where the out-of-range clips are.

4.  Apply the Broadcast Safe filter to the clip.

5.  The Audio Mixer and Video Scopes.

6.  From the File menu, use the Share command.

7.  A movie that uses Final Cut Pro sequence presets and that can be played on any computer without having the original media files present.

8.  When you want to export a still image, an audio file in a particular format, an AVI file, and so on.

9.  Recording manually, or using the Print to Video or Edit to Tape options.

10. Batch List

## Keyboard Shortcuts

| | |
|---|---|
| **Command-Option-L** | Open the audio Gain Adjust dialog |
| **Control-Z** | Turn on and off range checking for excess luma |

# Glossary

**16-bit** A standard bit depth for digital audio recording and playback.

**16 x 9** The standard display aspect ratio of a high definition television set.

**32-bit** A four-channel image with each channel 8 bits deep. Typically, a CGI image with red, green, blue, and alpha channels.

**4 x 3** The standard display aspect ratio of a standard video home television set.

**8-bit** For video, a bit depth at which color is sampled. 8-bit color is common with DV and other standard definition digital formats. Some high definition acquisition formats can also record in 8-bit, but usually record in 10-bit.

**#**

**action safe** The area inside a border that is 5 percent smaller than the overall size of the video frame. Most of the time, anything in your video image that's outside this border will not be displayed on a video screen.

**A**

**A/D converter box** Equipment that changes an analog signal into a digital signal.

**add edit** Working like the Razor Blade tool, adds an edit point to all clips in the Timeline at the current position of the playhead.

**AIFF (Audio Interchange File Format)** Apple's native uncompressed audio file format created for the Macintosh computer, commonly used for the storage and transmission of digitally sampled sound.

**affiliate clip** A copy of a clip that shares properties with the original, or master, clip.

**alpha channel** An image channel in addition to the R, G, and B color channels that is used to store transparency information for compositing. In Final Cut Pro, black represents 100 percent transparent, and white represents 100 percent opaque.

**anamorphic** An image shot in a widescreen format and then squeezed into 4 x 3 frame size. When played back in Final Cut Pro, the image is played wide screen.

**anchor point** In the Motion tab, the point that is used to center changes to a clip when using motion effects. A clip's anchor point does not have to be at its center.

**animation** The process of changing any number of variables such as color, audio levels, or other effects over time using keyframes.

**aspect ratio** The ratio of the width of an image to its height on any viewing screen. Standard TV has an aspect ratio of 4:3; HDTV's is 16:9.

**attributes** All of the unique settings that have been applied to either audio or video clips.

**audio meters** A graphic display of the audio level (loudness) of a clip or sequence. Used to set incoming and outgoing audio levels and to check for audio distortion and signal strength.

**audio mixing** The process of adjusting the volume levels of all audio clips in an edited sequence, including the production audio, music, sound effects, voice-overs, and additional background ambience, to turn all of these sounds into a harmonious whole.

**audio peaks** The highest audio levels in a track. Peaks that exceed 0 dB will be clipped, or distorted.

**audio sample rate** The rate or frequency at which a sound is sampled to digitize it. 48 kHz is the standard sampling rate for digital audio; CD audio is sampled at 44.1 kHz.

**audio waveform** A graphical representation of the amplitude (loudness) of a sound over a period of time.

**Autosave Vault** A function that automatically saves backup copies of all your FCP open projects at regular intervals. It must be turned on, and you can specify the intervals.

**AVI** A PC-compatible standard for digital video no longer officially supported by Microsoft but still frequently used. Some AVI codecs will not play in QuickTime and will be inaccessible in Final Cut Pro without prior format conversion.

**axis** An imaginary straight line (horizontal, vertical, 3D diagonal) along which an object can move or rotate in space.

**B**

**backtiming** Using In and Out points in the Viewer and only an Out point in the Timeline. The two Out points will align, and the rest of the clip will appear before (to the left) of this point.

**bars and tone** A series of vertical bars of specific colors and an audio tone used to calibrate the audio and video signals coming from a videotape or camera to ensure consistent appearance and sound on different TV monitors.

**batch capture** Capturing multiple clips and or sequences with a single command.

**batch export** The process of exporting multiple clips and or sequences with a single command by stacking them up in a queue. It is particularly useful when exporting will take a lot of time.

**batch list** A list of all the clips in a project, including all the information entered into Browser columns.

**Bezier handle** The "control handles" attached to a Bezier curve on a motion path that allow you to change the shape of the curve.

**bin** A file folder in the Browser window used to keep media clips grouped and organized. Derived from film editing where strips of film were hung over a cloth bin for sorting during the editing process.

**black level** The measurement of the black portion of the video signal. In analog television, this should not go below 7.5 IRE units. In digital television, black may be 0 units.

**blanking** The black border around the edges of a raw video image, created by the video camera CCDs. These black pixels should be cropped out of your image if you plan to composite over other footage.

**blue screen** A solid blue background placed behind a subject and photographed so that later the subject can be extracted and composited onto another image.

**broadcast safe** The range of color that can be broadcast free of distortion, according to the NTSC standards, with maximum allowable video at 100 IRE units and digital black at 0 IRE, or analog black at 7.5 IRE units.

**B-roll** A term used to describe alternate footage that intercuts with the primary sound-track used in a program to help tell the story, or to cover flaws. B-roll is usually referred to as *cutaway* shots.

**Browser** An interface window that is a central storage area where you organize and access all of the source material used in your project.

**cache** An area of a computer's random access memory (RAM) dedicated to storing still images and digital movies in preparation for real-time playback.

**Canvas** The window in which you can view your edited sequence.

**capture** The process of digitizing media in the computer.

**capture card** Hardware added to a computer (often an internal circuit board) to enhance video-acquisition options, such as enabling the capture of analog video formats.

**center point** Defines a clip's location in the x-y coordinate space in the Motion tab of the Canvas.

**chroma** The color information contained in a video signal consisting of hue (the color itself) and saturation (intensity).

**clip** Media files that may consist of video, audio, graphics, or any similar content that can be imported into Final Cut Pro.

**clipping** Distortion during the playback or recording of digital audio due to an overly loud level.

**codec** Short for compression/decompression. A program used to compress and decompress data such as audio and video files.

**color balance** Refers to the overall mix of red, green, and blue for the highlights (brightest),midtones, and shadow (darkest) areas in a clip. The color balance of these three areas can be adjusted using the Color Corrector 3-way filter.

**color correction** A process in which the color of clips used in an edited program is evened out so that all shots in a given scene match.

**color depth** The possible range of colors that can be used in a movie or image. In computer graphics, there are usually four choices: grayscale, 8-bit, 16-bit, and 24-bit. Higher color depths provide a wider range of colors but also require more disk space for a given image size. Broadcast video is generally 24-bit, with 8 bits of color information per channel.

**color matte** A clip containing solid color created as a generated item.

**Composite Mode** An option in the Modify menu that offers many methods of combining two or more images.

**compositing**  The process of combining two or more video or electronic images into a single frame. This term can also describe the process of creating various video effects.

**compression**  The process by which video, graphics, and audio files are reduced in size. The reduction in the size of a video file through the removal of redundant image data is referred to as a *lossy* compression scheme. A *lossless* compression scheme uses a mathematical process and reduces the file size by consolidating the redundant information without discarding it. See also *codec*

**compression marker**  A marker placed in a Final Cut movie that will flag DVD Studio Pro to stop so that an I-frame (intra-frame) can be changed.

**contrast**  The difference between the lightest and darkest values in an image. High-contrast images have a large range of values from the darkest shadow to the lightest highlight. Low-contrast images have a more narrow range of values, resulting in a "flatter" look.

**cross fade**  A transition between two audio clips where one sound is faded out while the other is faded in. Used to make the transition between two audio cuts less noticeable.

**cut**  The simplest type of edit where one clip ends and the next begins without any transition.

**cutaway**  A shot that is related to the current subject and occurs in the same time frame; for instance, an interviewer's reaction to what is being said in an interview or a shot to cover a technically bad moment.

**D**

**data rate**  The speed at which data can be transferred, often described in megabytes per second (MB/sec). The higher a video file's data rate, the higher quality it will be, but it will require more system resources (processor speed, hard disk space, and performance). Some codecs allow you to specify a maximum data rate for a movie during capture.

**decibel (dB)**  A unit of measure for the loudness of audio.

**decompression**  The process of restoring a video or audio file for playback from a compressed video, graphics, or audio file. Compare with *compression*

**De-Interlace filter**  Used to convert video frames composed of two interlaced fields into a single unified frame: for example, a still image of an object moving at high speed.

**desaturate**  To remove color from a clip. 100 percent desaturation results in a grayscale image.

**digitize**  To convert an analog video signal into a digital video format. A method of capturing video. See also *capture*

**dissolve**  A transition between two video clips where the first one fades down at the same time the second one fades up.

**drop frame timecode**  A type of timecode that skips ahead in time by two frame numbers each minute, except for minutes ending in *0*, so that the end timecode total agrees with the actual elapsed clock time. Although timecode numbers are skipped, actual video frames are not skipped. Drop frame timecode is a reference to real time.

**drop shadow**  An effect that creates an artificial shadow behind an image or text.

**DV**  A standard for a specific digital video format created by a consortium of camcorder vendors, which uses Motion JPEG video at a 720 x 480 resolution at 29.97 frames per second (NTSC) or 720 x 546 resolution at 25 fps (PAL), stored at a bit rate of 25 MB per second at a compression of 4:1:1.

**DVD marker** A location indicator that can be seen in DVD Studio Pro used to mark a chapter.

**dynamic range** The difference, in decibels, between the loudest and softest parts of a recording.

**Easy Setup** Preset audio/video settings, including capture, sequence, device control, and output settings.

**E**

**edit point** (1) Defines what part of a clip you want to use in an edited sequence. Edit points include In points, which specify the beginning of a section of a clip or sequence, and Out points, which specify the end of a section of a clip or sequence. (2) The point in the Timeline of an edited sequence where the Out point of one clip meets the In point of the next clip.

**Edit to Tape** The command that lets you perform frame-accurate insert and assemble edits to tape.

**EDL (Edit Decision List)** A text file that uses the source timecode of clips to sequentially list all of the edits that make up a sequence. EDLs are used to move a project from one editing application to another, or to coordinate the assembly of a program in a tape-based online editing facility.

**effects** A general term used to describe all of Final Cut Pro's capabilities that go beyond cuts-only editing. See *filters*, *generators*, and *transition*.

**extend edit** An edit in which the edit point is moved to the position of the playhead in the Timeline.

**fade** An effect in which the picture gradually transitions to black.

**F**

**faders** In the Audio Mixer, vertical sliders used to adjust the audio levels of clips at the position of the playhead.

**favorite** A frequently used customized effect. You can create favorites from most of the effects in Final Cut Pro.

**field** Half of an interlaced video frame consisting of the odd or the even scan lines.

**field dominance** The choice of whether field 1 or field 2 will be displayed on the monitor first.

**filters** Effects you can apply to video and audio clips or group of clips that change some aspect of the clip content.

**finishing** The process of fine-tuning the sequence audio and video levels and preparing the sequence for output to tape or other destination, such as the web or DVD. Finishing may also involve recapturing offline clips at an uncompressed resolution.

**FireWire** Apple's trademark name for the IEEE 1394 standard used to connect external hard drives and cameras to computers. It provides a fast interface to move large video and audio files to the computer's hard drive.

**fit to fill edit** An edit in which a clip is inserted and re-timed into a sequence such that its duration matches a predetermined amount of specified track space.

**frame** A single still image from either video or film. For video, each frame is made up of two interlaced fields (see *interlaced video*).

**frame blending** A process of inserting blended frames in place of frames that have been duplicated in clips with slow motion, to make them play back more smoothly.

**Frame Viewer** A tab in the Tool Bench in which you can compare adjacent clips in a sequence or, by splitting the screen, a clip with and without filter effects applied.

**frequency** The number of times a sound or signal vibrates each second, measured in cycles per second, or hertz.

**G**

**gain** In video, the level of white in a video picture; in audio, the loudness of an audio signal.

**gamma** A curve that describes how the middle tones of an image appear. Gamma is a nonlinear function often confused with "brightness" or "contrast." Changing the value of the gamma affects middle tones while leaving the whites and blacks of the image unaltered. Gamma adjustment is often used to compensate for differences between Macintosh and Windows video cards and displays.

**gap** Locations in a sequence where there is no media on any track. When output to video, gaps in an edited sequence appear as black sections.

**generators** Clips that are synthesized by Final Cut Pro. Generators can be used as different kinds of backgrounds, titles, and elements for visual design.

**gradient** A generated image that changes smoothly from one color to another across the image. The change can occur in several ways: horizontally, vertically, radially, and so on.

**green screen** A solid green background placed behind a subject and photographed so that later the subject can be extracted and composited into another image.

**H**

**handles** Extra frames of unused video or audio that are on either side of the In and Out points in an edit.

**head** The beginning of a clip.

**histogram** A window that displays the relative strength of all luminance values in a video frame, from black to super-white. It is useful for comparing two clips in order to match their brightness values more closely.

**hue** A specific color or pigment, such as red.

**I**

**I-frame** In compressed video, a frame that contains all of the information needed to display that frame. Also called a *keyframe*.

**incoming clip** The clip that is on the right-hand side, or B-side, of a transition or cut point.

**In point** The edit point entered either in the Viewer, Canvas, or Timeline that determines where an edit will begin.

**insert edit** To insert a clip into an existing sequence into the Timeline, which automatically moves the other clips (or remaining frames of a clip) to the right to make room for it. An insert edit does not replace existing material.

**interlaced video** A video scanning method that first scans the odd picture lines (field 1) and then scans the even picture lines (field 2), which merges them into one single frame of video. Used in standard definition video.

**IRE** A unit of measurement for luminance in an analog signal established by the Institute of Radio Engineers (IRE).

**jog** To move forward or backward through your video one frame at a time.

**JPEG (Joint Photographic Experts Group)** A popular image file format that lets you create highly compressed graphics files. The amount of compression can vary. Less compression results in a higher-quality image.

**jump cut** A cut in which an abrupt change occurs between two shots.

**J**

**keyframe** In Final Cut Pro, a point at which a filter, motion effect, or audio level changes value. There must be at least two keyframes representing two different values to show a change. See also *I-frame*.

**K**

**keying** The process of dropping out a specific area of an image, such as its background, so that the image can be composited with another. You can key out information in a clip based on brightness and darkness, or color.

**kilohertz** A measure of audio frequency equal to 1000 hertz (cycles per second). Abbreviated kHz.

**labels** Terms that appear in the Label column of the Browser, such as "Best Take" and "Interview." Labels can also be assigned to clips and media to help distinguish and sort them. Each label has an associated color that is also applied to clips.

**L**

**letterbox** A method of displaying widescreen video to fit within a standard 4:3 monitor, resulting in a black bar at the top and bottom of the picture.

**lift edit** An edit function that leaves a gap when material is lifted from the Timeline.

**link** (1) To connect audio and video clips in the Timeline so that when one item is selected, moved, or trimmed, all the items linked to it are affected. (2) The connection between a clip and its associated source media file on disk. If you move source media files, change their names, or put them in the Trash, the links break and associated clips in your Final Cut Pro project become *offline clips*.

**linked selection** An option in the Timeline that, when enabled, maintains connections between linked clips.When linked selection is turned off, linked items behave as if they are not connected.

**locked track** A track whose contents cannot be moved or changed. Crosshatched lines distinguish a locked track on the Timeline. You can lock or unlock tracks at any time by clicking the Lock Track control on the Timeline.

**log and capture** The process of playing clips from a device and logging and capturing the clips you want to use in editing.

**Log bin** A specific bin where all the logged or captured clips go when using the Log and Capture window.

**logging** The process of entering detailed information, including the In and Out points from your source material, log notes, and so on, in preparation for a clip to be captured.

**lower third** Lines of text used to identify a person, place, or thing in a clip typically appearing in the "lower third" of the frame.

**luma** Short for luminance. A value describing the brightness part of the video signal without color (chroma).

**luma key** A filter used to key out a luminance value, creating a matte based on the brightest or darkest area of an image. See *keying* and *matte*.

**M**

**markers** Location indicators that can be placed on a clip or in a sequence to help you find a specific place while you edit. Can be used to sync action between two clips, identify beats of music, mark a reference word from a narrator, and so on.

**Mark In** The process of indicating with a mark in the Viewer, Canvas, or Timeline the first frame of a clip to be used.

**Mark in Sync** A command in the Modify menu that marks a selected audio clip as being in sync with a selected video clip.

**Mark Out** The process of indicating with a mark in the Viewer, Canvas, or Timeline the last frame of a clip to be used.

**Marquee** The rectangular lasso of dashed lines that the pointer generates as it is dragged in the Browser or Timeline to select items.

**mask** An image or clip used to define areas of transparency in another clip. Similar to an *alpha channel*.

**master clip** The status given to a clip the first time that clip is used in a project. It is the clip from which other affiliate clips, such as sequence clips and subclips, are created.

**Mastering mode** A mode in the Edit to Tape window that lets you output additional elements such as color bars and tone, a slate, and a countdown when you output your program to tape.

**master shot** A single long shot or wide shot of some dramatic action. It is often used to establish a new scene and is sometimes referred to as an establishing shot.

**Match Frame** A command that looks at the clip in the Timeline at the playhead and puts that clip's master into the Viewer. The position of the playhead in the Viewer matches that of the playhead in the Canvas, so both the Canvas and the Viewer will display the same frame. The In and Out points of the clip in the Viewer will match those of the sequence clip.

**matte** An effect, such as a widescreen matte or a garbage matte, that hides or reveals a part of a clip.

**media file** A generic term for captured or acquired elements such as QuickTime movies, sounds, and pictures.

**Media Manager** A tool that helps you manage your projects, media files, and available disk space quickly and easily in Final Cut Pro.

**midtones** The middle brightness range of an image. Not the very brightest part, nor the very darkest part.

**mono audio** A single track of audio.

**motion blur** An effect that blurs any clip with keyframed motion applied to it, similar to blurred motion recorded by a camera.

**motion path** A path that appears in the Canvas when Image+Wireframe mode is selected and a clip has center *keyframes* applied to it.

**MPEG (Moving Picture Experts Group)** A group of compression standards for video and audio.

**multicam editing** This feature lets you simultaneously play back and view shots from multiple cameras and cut between them in real time.

**multiclip** A clip that allows you to group together multiple sources as separate angles and cut between them. Up to 128 angles can be synced, of which 16 can be played back at a time.

**N**

**natural sound** The ambient sound used from a source videotape.

**nest** To place an edited sequence within another sequence.

**non-drop frame timecode** A type of timecode in which frames are numbered sequentially and run at 30 fps. NTSC's frame rate, however, is actually 29.97 fps; therefore, non–drop frame timecode is off by 3 seconds and 18 frames per hour in comparison to actual elapsed time.

**noninterlaced video** The standard representation of images on a computer, also referred to as "progressive scan." The monitor displays the image by drawing each line, continuously one after the other, from top to bottom.

**nonlinear editing (NLE)** A video editing process that uses computer hard disks to randomly access the media. It allows the editor to reorganize clips very quickly or make changes to sections without having to re-create the entire program.

**nonsquare pixel** A pixel whose height is different from its width. An NTSC pixel is taller than it is wide, and a PAL pixel is wider than it is tall.

**NTSC (National Television Systems Committee)** Standard of color TV broadcasting used mainly in North America,Mexico, and Japan, consisting of 525 lines per frame, 29.97 frames per second, and 720 x 486 pixels per frame (720 x 480 for DV).

**O**

**offline clip** Clips that appear in the Browser with a red slash through them. Clips may be offline because they haven't been captured yet, or because the media file has been moved to another location. To view these clips properly in your project, you must recapture them or reconnect them to their corresponding source files at their new locations on disk.

**offline editing** The process of editing a program at a lower resolution to save on equipment costs or to conserve hard disk space. When the edit is finished, the material can be recaptured at a higher quality, or an *EDL* can be generated for re-creating the edit on another system.

**OMF (Open Media Framework)** OMF is an edit data interchange format.

**opacity** The degree to which an image is transparent, allowing images behind to show through.

**outgoing clip** The clip on the left-hand side of the cut point or the A-side of the transition.

**Out of sync** Said of the audio of a track when it has been shifted horizontally in the Timeline, causing it to no longer match the video track.

**Out point** The edit point entered in the Viewer, Canvas, or Timeline where an edit will end.

**overlays** Icons, lines, or text displayed over the video in the Viewer and Canvas windows while the playhead is parked on a frame, in order to provide information about that frame.

**overwrite edit** An edit where the clip being edited into a sequence replaces an existing clip. The duration of the sequence remains unchanged.

**P**

**PAL (Phase Alternating Line)** The European color TV broadcasting standard consisting of 625 lines per frame, running at 25 frames per second, and 720 x 546 pixels per frame.

**pan** To rotate a camera left or right without changing its position.

**Parade scope** A modified Waveform Monitor that breaks out the red, green, and blue components of the image, showing them as three separate waveforms. Useful for comparing the relative levels of reds, greens, and blues between two clips, especially in a graphics situation.

**patch panel** The section of the Timeline containing the Audio, Source, Destination, Track Visibility, Lock Track, and Auto Select controls.

**peak** Short, loud bursts of sound that last a fraction of a second and can be viewed on a digital audiometer that displays the absolute volume of an audio signal as it plays.

**phase** An attribute of color perception, also known as hue.

**PICT** The native still-image file format for Macintosh developed by Apple.

**pixel** Short for "picture element," one dot in a video or still image.

**pixel aspect ratio** The width-to-height ratio for the pixels that compose an image. Pixels on computer screens and in high definition video signals are square (1:1 ratio). Pixels in standard definition video signals are nonsquare.

**playhead** A navigational element that shows the current frame in the Timeline, Canvas, or Viewer.

**post-production** The phase of film, video, and audio editing that begins after all the footage is shot.

**post-roll** The amount of time that a tape machine continues to roll after the Out point of an edit, typically between 2 and 5 seconds.

**poster frame** The representative still frame of a clip that is the Thumbnail image.

**pre-roll** A specified amount of time, usually 5 seconds, given to tape machines so they can synchronize themselves to the editing computer before previewing or performing an edit.

**preview** To play an edit to see how it will look without actually performing the edit itself.

**Print to Video** A command in Final Cut Pro that lets you render your sequence and output it to videotape.

**proc amp (processing amplifier)** A piece of equipment that allows you to adjust video levels on output.

**project** In Final Cut Pro, the top-level file that stores the editing information associated with a program, including sequences and clips of various kinds.

**QuickTime**   Apple's cross-platform multimedia technology. Widely used for editing, compositing, CD-ROM, web video, and more.

**QuickTime streaming**   Apple's streaming media addition to the QuickTime architecture. Used for viewing QuickTime content in real time on the web.

**Q**

**RAID (Redundant Array of Independent Disks) drive**   A method of formatting a group of hard disks to act as a single large storage volume with built-in redundancy for data protection.

**R**

**Range Check**   A View submenu with options that enable zebra striping to immediately warn you of areas of a clip's image that may stray outside the broadcast legal range.

**real-time effects**   Effects that can be applied to clips in an edited sequence and played back in real time, without requiring rendering first. Real-time effects can be played back using any qualified computer.

**record monitor**   A monitor that plays the previewed and finished versions of a project when it is printed to tape. A record monitor corresponds to the Canvas in Final Cut Pro.

**render**   To process video and audio with any applied effects, such as transitions or filters. Effects that aren't real time must be rendered in order to be played back properly. Once rendered, your sequence can be played in real time.

**render file**   The file produced by rendering a clip to disk. FCP places it in a separate hidden folder so it does not show up in the Browser but is referenced and played in the Timeline.

**render status bars**   Two slim horizontal bars, in the Timeline ruler area, that indicate which parts of the sequence have been rendered at the current render quality. The top bar is for video, and the bottom for audio. Different colored bars indicate the real-time playback status of a given section of the Timeline.

**replace edit**   Allows you to replace an existing shot in a sequence with a different shot of the same length.

**RGB**   An abbreviation for red, green, and blue, which are the three primary colors that make up a color image.

**ripple edit**   An edit that trims the In or Out point of a sequence clip, and repositions (or "ripples") subsequent clips, while lengthening or shortening the entire sequence.

**roll edit**   An edit that affects two clips that share an edit point. The Out point of the outgoing clip and the In point of the incoming clip both change, but the overall duration of the sequence stays the same.

**RT Extreme**   Real-time effects processing that scales with your system.

**sampling**   The process during which analog audio is converted into digital information. The sampling rate of an audio stream specifies how many samples are captured. Higher sample rates yield higher-quality audio. Examples are 44.1 kHz and 48 kHz.

**S**

**saturation**   The purity of color. As saturation is decreased, the color moves toward pastel, then toward white.

**scale**   In the Motion tab of the Viewer, an adjustable value that changes the overall size of a clip. The proportion of the image may or may not be maintained.

**scratch disk** The hard disk designated to hold your captured media, rendered clips, and cache files.

**scrub** To move through a clip or sequence by dragging the playhead. Scrubbing is used to find a particular point or frame or to hear the audio.

**scrubber bar** A bar below the Viewer and the Canvas that allows you to manually drag the playhead in either direction.

**SECAM (Séquentiel Couleur à Mémoire)** The French television standard for playback. Similar to PAL, the playback rate is 25 fps and the frame size is 720 x 546.

**sequence** An edited assembly of video, audio, or graphics clips. A sequence can contain your entire edited program or be limited to a single scene.

**sequence clip** A clip that has been edited into a sequence.

**shuttle control** The slider located at the bottom of the Viewer and the Canvas. This control is useful for continuous playback at different speeds, in fast and slow motion. It also shifts the pitch of audio as it plays at varying speeds.

**slate** A small clapboard, placed in front of all cameras at the beginning of a scene, which gives basic production information such as the take, date, and name of scene. A slate or clapper provides an audio/visual cue for synchronization of dual-system recordings.

**slide edit** An edit in which an entire clip is moved, along with the edit points on its left and right. The duration of the clip being moved stays the same, but the clips to the left and to the right of it change in length to accommodate the new positioning of the clip. The overall duration of the sequence and of these three clips remains the same.

**slip edit** An edit in which the location of both In and Out points of a clip are trimmed at the same time, without changing the location or duration of the marked media.

**slug** A solid black video frame that can be used to represent a video clip that has not yet been placed in the Timeline.

**SMPTE (Society of Motion Picture and Television Engineers)** The organization responsible for establishing various broadcast video standards like the SMPTE standard timecode for video playback.

**snapping** A setting in the Timeline that affects the movement of objects such as the playhead, clips, and markers. With snapping enabled, when dragging these objects close together, they "snap," or move directly, to each other to ensure frame accuracy.

**solo** An audio monitoring feature in which one audio track from a group may be isolated for listening without having to be removed from the group.

**SOT** Acronym for sound on tape.

**sound bite** A short excerpt taken from an interview clip.

**split edit** An edit in which the video track or the audio track of a synchronized clip ends up being longer than the other; for example, the sound may be longer than the video at the head of the clip, so it is heard before the video appears. Also referred to as an L-cut.

**spread** An audio control that allows you to adjust the amount of separation of stereo channels.

**square pixel** A pixel that has the same height as width.

**static region**  An area in a sequence in the Timeline that you lock so that it is visible even when you scroll to see other tracks. The static area can contain audio tracks, video tracks, or both.

**stereo audio**  Sound that is separated into two channels, one carrying the sounds for the right ear and one for the left ear. Stereo pairs are linked and are always edited together. Audio level changes are automatically made to both channels at the same time. A pair of audio items may have their stereo pairing enabled or disabled at any time.

**storyboard**  A series of pictures that summarizes the content, action, and flow of a proposed project. When the Browser is displayed in icon view, clips can be arranged visually, like a storyboard. When dragged as a group into the Timeline, the clips will be edited together in the order in which they appear in the Timeline, from left to right, and from the top line down to the bottom.

**straight cut**  An edit in which both the video and audio tracks are cut together to the Timeline.

**streaming**  The delivery of media over an intranet or over the Internet.

**subclip**  A clip created to represent a section of a master clip. Subclips are saved as separate items within a bin in the Browser, but do not generate any additional media on the hard disk.

**superimpose edit**  An edit in which an incoming clip is placed on top of a clip that's already in the Timeline at the position of the playhead. If no In or Out points are set in the Timeline and Canvas, the previously edited clip's In and Out points are used to define the duration of the incoming clip. Superimposed edits are used to overlay titles and text onto video, as well as to create other compositing effects.

**super-black**  Black that is darker than the levels allowed by the CCIR 601 engineering standard for video. The CCIR 601 standard for black is 7.5 IRE in the United States, and 0 IRE for PAL and for NTSC in Japan.

**super-white**  A value or degree of white that is brighter than the accepted normal value of 100 IRE allowed by the CCIR 601.

**sweetening**  The process of creating a high-quality sound mix by polishing sound levels, rerecording bad sections of dialogue, and recording and adding narration, music, and sound effects.

**sync**  The relationship between the image of a sound being made in a video clip (for example, a person talking) and the corresponding sound in an audio clip. Maintaining sync is critical when editing dialogue.

**tail**  The end frames of a clip.

**T**

**three-point editing**  The process of creating an edit by setting three edit points that determine source content, duration, and placement in the sequence. With three edit points selected, Final Cut Pro calculates the fourth.

**thumbnail**  The frame of a clip, shown as a tiny picture for reference. In Final Cut Pro, the thumbnail is, by default, the first frame of a clip. You can change the frame used as that clip's thumbnail by using the Scrub Video tool.

**TIFF (Tagged Image File Format)**  A widely used bitmapped graphics file format that handles monochrome, grayscale, and 8- and 24-bit color.

**tilt**  To pivot the camera up and down, which causes the image to move up or down in the frame.

**timecode**  A numbering system of electronic signals laid onto each frame of videotape that is used to identify specific frames of video. Each frame of video is labeled with hours, minutes, seconds, and frames (01:00:00:00). Timecode can be drop frame, non-drop frame, or time of day (TOD) timecode, or EBU (European Broadcast Union) for PAL projects.

**timecode gap**  An area of tape with no timecode at all. Timecode gaps usually signify the end of all recorded material on a tape, but timecode gaps may occur due to the starting and stopping of the camera during recording.

**Timeline**  A window in Final Cut Pro that displays a chronological view of an open *sequence*. Each sequence has its own tab in the Timeline. You can use the Timeline to edit and arrange a sequence. The order of the tracks in the Timeline determines the layering order when you combine multiple tracks of video. Changes you make to a sequence in the Timeline are seen when you play back that sequence in the Canvas.

**time remapping**  The process of changing the speed of playback of a clip over time. The equivalent of varying the crank of a film camera.

**title safe**  Part of the video image that is guaranteed to be visible on televisions. The title safe area is the inner 80 percent of the screen. To prevent text in your video from being hidden by the edge of a TV set, you should restrict any titles or text to the title safe area.

**Tool Bench**  A window that contains interface elements that supplement information displayed in the Viewer and Canvas. The Tool Bench can contain up to three tabs—QuickView, Video Scopes, and Voice Over.

**Tool palette**  A window in Final Cut Pro that contains tools for editing, zooming, cropping, and distorting items in the Timeline. All tools in the Tool palette can also be selected using keyboard shortcuts.

**tracks**  Layers in the Timeline that contain the audio or video clips in a sequence. Also refers to the separate audio and video tracks on tape. Final Cut Pro allows up to 99 video and 99 audio tracks to be used in a single sequence.

**transition**  A visual or audio effect applied between two edit points, such as a video cross dissolve or an audio cross fade.

**Transition Editor**  A specialized editor that appears in the Viewer when you double-click a transition in the Timeline; it is used to make detailed changes to a transition's timing and effects parameters.

**Trim Edit window**  A window in Final Cut Pro that displays both sides of an edit: the Out point of the outgoing clip on the left and the In point of the incoming clip on the right. You can use this window to adjust the edit point between two clips very precisely, frame by frame.

**trimming**  To precisely add or subtract frames from the In or Out point of a clip. Trimming is used to fine-tune an edited sequence by carefully adjusting many edits in small ways.

**two-up display**  A display in the Canvas that appears when using some type of trim or adjustment mode, such as Roll, Ripple, Slip, or Slide. Two individual frames appear to display either the frames being adjusted or the border frames.

**U**  **undo**  A feature that allows you to cancel the last change made.

**variable speed** Speed that varies dynamically within a clip among a range of speeds, in forward or reverse motion.

**Vectorscope** A window in Final Cut Pro that graphically displays the color components of a video signal, precisely showing the range of colors and measuring their intensity and hue.

**video level** The measurement of the level (amplitude) of a video signal. It is measured using the Waveform Monitor in FCP.

**video scopes** Tools you can use to evaluate the color and brightness values of video clips in the Viewer, Canvas, or Timeline. Video scopes display an analysis of the video frame located at the current playhead position.

**Video Scopes tab** A tab in the Tool Bench that contains the four Final Cut Pro video scopes: Waveform Monitor, Vectorscope, Parade scope, and Histogram.

**Viewer** A window in Final Cut Pro that acts as a source monitor. You can use the Viewer to watch individual source clips and mark In and Out points in preparation for editing them into your sequence. You can also customize transitions, modify filters, and view and edit various effects. Clips from the current sequence in the Timeline can be opened in the Viewer to refine edits, effects, and audio volume.

**Voice Over tool** Allows you to record audio in Final Cut Pro while simultaneously playing back a specified section of a sequence from the Timeline.

**VTR / VCR** Videotape recorder/videocassette recorder. A tape machine used for recording pictures and sound on videotape.

**VU meter (Volume Unit meter)** An analog meter for monitoring audio levels.

**W**

**Waveform Monitor** A window in Final Cut Pro that displays the relative levels of brightness and saturation in the clip currently being examined. Spikes or drops in the displayed waveforms make it easy to see where the brightest or darkest areas are in your picture.

**white balance** The reference to the shade of white that is made during recording. This reference can be changed within FCP, correcting or improving it in order to display true white.

**white level** An analog video signal's amplitude for the lightest white in a picture, represented by *IRE* units.

**wide-screen** An aspect ratio such as 16:9 or 2.35:1 that allows for a wider image, suitable for widescreen television or film projection.

**wide-screen matte filter** A mask that blacks out the top and bottom of a 4 x 3 image, which creates a wide-screen image, such as 16:9.

**window burn** Visual timecode and keycode information superimposed onto video frames. It usually appears on a strip at the bottom or top of the frame, providing code information to the editor without obscuring any of the picture.

**wipe** A type of transition that uses a moving edge to progressively erase the current clip to reveal the next clip.

**wireframe** A visual substitute for a clip that simply represents the outline of the clip's video frame. Clips in the Viewer and Canvas can be viewed in Wireframe mode.

**X**

**x axis** Refers to the x coordinate in Cartesian geometry. The x coordinate describes horizontal placement in motion effects.

**Y**

**y axis** Refers to the y coordinate in Cartesian geometry. The y coordinate describes vertical placement in motion effects.

**YCrCb** The color space in which digital video formats store data. Three components are stored for each pixel—one for luminance (Y) and two for color information, Cr for the red portion of the color difference signal and Cb for the blue color difference signal.

**YUV** The three-channel PAL video signal with one luminance (Y) and two chrominance color difference signals (UV). It is often misapplied to refer to NTSC video, which is YIQ.

**Z**

**z axis** Refers to the z coordinate in Cartesian geometry. The z coordinate describes perpendicular placement in motion effects, which includes zooming toward or away from the viewer, or rotating an image in space.

**zebra stripes** Animated diagonal "marching lines" that are superimposed over illegal areas or areas very near the broadcast legal limits in an image. Zebra stripes are enabled when you use Final Cut Pro's range-checking options.

**zoom** To change the magnification of your image or Timeline.

# Index

## Symbols and Numbers

# Apple Certification
## Fuel your mind.
## Reach your potential.

Stand out from the crowd. Differentiate yourself and gain recognition for your expertise by earning Apple Certified Pro status to validate your Final Cut Pro 7 skills.

This book prepares you to earn Apple Certified Pro—Final Cut Pro 7 Level One. Level One certification attests to essential operational knowledge of the application. Level Two certification demonstrates mastery of advanced features and a deeper understanding of the application. Take it one step further and earn Master Pro certification in Final Cut Studio.

### Three Steps to Certification

1   Choose your certification path.
More info: training.apple.com/certification.

2   Select a location:

**Apple Authorized Training Centers** (AATCs) offer all exams (Mac OS X, Pro Apps, iLife, iWork, and Xsan). AATC locations: training.apple.com/locations

**Prometric Testing Centers** (1-888-275-3926) offer all Mac OS X exams, and the Final Cut Pro Level One exam. Prometric centers: www.prometric.com/apple

3   Register for and take your exam(s).

> "Now when I go out to do corporate videos and I let them know that I'm certified, I get job after job after job."
>
> —Chip McAllister, Final Cut Pro Editor and Winner of The Amazing Race 2004

### Reasons to Become an Apple Certified Pro

- **Raise your earning potential.** Studies show that certified professionals can earn more than their non-certified peers.

- **Distinguish yourself from others in your industry.** Proven mastery of an application helps you stand out from the crowd.

- **Display your Apple Certification logo.** Each certification provides a logo to display on business cards, resumes and websites.

- **Publicize your Certifications.** Publish your certifications on the Apple Certified Professionals Registry to connect with schools, clients and employers.

### Training Options

Apple's comprehensive curriculum addresses your needs, whether you're an IT or creative professional, educator, or service technician. Hands-on training is available through a worldwide network of Apple Authorized Training Centers (AATCs) or in a self-paced format through the Apple Training Series and Apple Pro Training Series. Learn more about Apple's curriculum and find an AATC near you at training.apple.com.

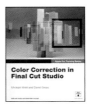

# Making memories for today and tomorrow!

## SeaWorld
### ADVENTURE PARK
*San Antonio*

THE ART OF THE CON.

THE BRAINS

THE HITTER     THE HACKER

THE GRIFTER     THE THIEF

LEVERAGE

STARRING ACADEMY AWARD® WINNER TIMOTHY HUTTON
Visit **tnt.tv** for full episodes, games and exclusive video.

TNT

WE KNOW DRAMA

# PLAYING FOR CHANGE

*is proud to present*

## PEACE THROUGH MUSIC

A feature length documentary film
connecting the world through music.

## Join the movement at
## www.playingforchange.com

# WATCH READ CREATE

## Meet Creative Edge.

A new resource of unlimited books, videos, and tutorials from the world's leading experts.

Creative Edge is your key to staying at the top of your game—bringing you the inspiration and training you need so you can focus on what you do best—being creative.

Access any day, any time you need it. Only $24.99 per month.

**creativeedge.com**